17.84

ORGANIZATION
BEHAVIOUR
AND GENDER

ORGANIZATIONAL BEHAVIOUR AND GENDER

Fiona M. Wilson

Lecturer in Organisational Behaviour
University of St Andrews

The McGraw-Hill Companies

London · New York · St Louis · San Francisco · Auckland
Bogotá · Caracas · Lisbon · Madrid · Mexico
Milan · Montreal · New Delhi · Panama · Paris · San Juan
São Paulo · Singapore · Sydney · Tokyo · Toronto

Published by
McGraw-Hill Publishing Company
Shoppenhangers Road, Maidenhead, Berkshire, SL6 2QL, England
Telephone 01628 23432
Fax 01628 770224

British Library Cataloguing in Publication Data

UCSM

Wilson, Fiona M.
  Organizational Behaviour and Gender
  I. Title
  302.35083

  ISBN 0–07–707615–X

Library of Congress Cataloguing-in-Publication Data

Wilson, Fiona.
  Organizational behaviour and gender / Fiona M. Wilson.
  p.   cm.
  Includes bibliographical references and index.   305.4 WIL
  ISBN 0–07–707615–X
  1. Organizational behavior. 2. Women—Employment. 3. Sex role in the work
  environment. 4. Sexism. 5. Psychology, Industrial.
I. Title.
HD58.7.W549   1995
305.4'2–dc20   94–29854
                                                                    CIP

McGraw-Hill

A Division of The McGraw-Hill Companies

2345   CUP   9876

Typeset by Computape (Pickering) Ltd, Pickering, North Yorkshire
and printed and bound in Great Britain at the University Press, Cambridge

Printed on permanent paper in compliance with ISO Standard 9706

Contents

Foreword

'... autobiography and biography should *not replace* the received patriarchal voice; rather it should *juxtapose* it. ... The resultant third voice, retaining the personal power of the first and the intersubjectivity of the second, might thereby open a window on as yet unimagined, ungendered possibilities of speaking, knowing and living.' Muriel Dimen

This page, like the book it prefaces, is unconventional. It has not proved easy to write for I am middle-aged and male. Yet, I have enjoyed the experience of penning it.

I am father to three daughters: Clare, Anna and Katy. I want them to have happy, fulfilled lives. I want them to enjoy going to a place of work. I want them to understand the forces operating upon them. I want them to succeed in overcoming these forces. I want them to think that the discipline their father professes is worth something.

Organizational Behaviour and Gender is part of an answer to these specific but deep-seated problems. Clare and Anna are new to Social Science and know nothing, indeed desire to know nothing of Organizational Behaviour (OB). How does one convince them that OB can illuminate their lives and help them negotiate their confrontation with a world of employment? Well, Fiona Wilson has produced a book that will impact in a host of constructive ways upon all those third- or second-year undergraduate students in management, the sociology of work and organizational psychology who read it. Using statistical data, cartoons, pertinent questions to arrest the reader on mid-page, cases and detailed reading lists, she constructs a picture of organizational life which young students will find, in turn, revelatory and depressing. Clare and Anna both read an earlier version of the text in draft form and it engendered in them this range of responses. Now (and this is a considerable achievement) they think OB has something to offer. On the other hand, Katy, a virtual chemist, refused to spend time reading the book. Paternalistic authoritarianism cuts no ice on this or any other occasion.

Yet Dr Wilson's book would be ideal for the likes of Katy. She will enter a world of industrial chemists, work for a large multinational which liquefies the air, travel widely, commission high-technology plant—and at every step confront the gendered nature of work. Were Katy to read Fiona's book it would instantly appeal to her for it is written 'from a female perspective'. This stands in opposition to the 'mainly male vision' which permeates OB and is so evident in its myopia to issues of gender. Systematically, the book addresses the weaknesses in most OB 'manuals' which, in adopting versions of a phallogecentric perspective, trivialize and marginalize the everyday work lives awaiting the likes of Clare, Anna and Katy. There may not be *one* 'female perspective' for the three of them but that's for them to decide.

But hang on a minute. How come, you ask, is a man writing this Foreword? One moment's reflexivity will be enough to suggest that we all have gender. It is not only a women's issue. *Organizational Behaviour and Gender* encourages the reader to reflect on the public world of work within organizations. It is also directly relevant to thinking about how we organize our lives privately. Fiona Wilson encourages us on almost every page to stop, reflect on what is being said and on what is being done and then to proceed with caution. This signalling to the reader works for both men and women. As you can see from the beginning of this Foreword, it spoke to me very directly.

Much more importantly, it has the capacity to speak to Clare, Anna and Katy of past, present and future experiences. It might not change lives, Katy, but it explains them. You really should read it. But, you're not listening to me—and why—after all—should you?

Gibson Burrell
Professor of Organizational Behaviour
Warwick Business School
University of Warwick

Acknowledgements

This book was begun with the encouragement and support of two then St Andrews undergraduate students, Linda Murray and Heli Lahtinen; they persuaded me that a book like this should be written and Linda helped gather some initial material and most of the press cuttings. Another ex-St Andrews student, who wishes to remain anonymous, wrote the first draft of the case on sexual harassment as a result of her experiences and I am very grateful to her too.

Many thanks are due to the reviewers—Joanna Liddle, Gibson Burrell, Albert Mills, Derek Pugh, David Wilson, Nina Colwill, Beverly Alimo-Metcalfe, Sandra Nutley, Valerie Fournier and one anonymous reviewer. I would not have made much headway without Interlibrary loans, University of St Andrews who acquired 195 articles and books for me in just one 18-month period while I was working sporadically on the book. Any flaws, errors, or omissions I claim as my own.

The work is dedicated both to those optimists who wish to argue that men and women have now, or will soon achieve equality of opportunity and to those pessimists (like me) who can see very little change.

Introduction

Most of us believe in the autonomy of the individual and his or her rights to equality, freedom of choice, and personal self-fulfilment. We live in what we call a democracy and would like to believe our organizations treat the individuals who live and work in them with fairness and respect. But those who work in organizations are not all equal or enlightened and there are formidable barriers preventing the advancement of women, minority ethnic groups, and the disabled. Behaviour in organizations which mitigates against women and minorities is viewed as normal and therefore, in some way, acceptable. If it were not, why are these barriers there, why would we feel obliged to laugh at the misogynist remarks, ignore the sexist and racist comments, allow gender-driven power manoeuvres to sway decision making, and allow issues important to women and minorities to be trivialized and marginalized?

Organizational behaviour, as a discipline has done little to address these questions. Organizational behaviour has been presented as evaluatively neutral and apolitical. But it has chiefly represented the work of men. The assumption is that it is chiefly men who work, who are the breadwinners, and therefore men who should be studied. Half the population of organizations has been ignored, left at the edge or just tagged onto organizational behaviour texts.

Organization studies have been pursued from male-oriented perspectives which, at best, treat aspects of organizational behaviour as typifying men and women alike (e.g. the Hawthorne studies) and at worst treat women as peripheral to organizational life (Mills, 1988a). When the Hawthorne studies and Crozier's work on French bureaucracies were re-examined by Acker and Van Houton (1992), it was found that there had originally been questionable or incomplete interpretations resulting from failure to consider adequately the sex dimensions of organizational processes.

The Hawthorne studies involved the study of a group of females in the 'test room' and a group of men in the 'bank wiring room'. The men were observed under normal working conditions while the female group was pressured, by male supervisors, into an experimental situation. Despite the fact that output was increased by the women and restricted by the men, the overall findings were

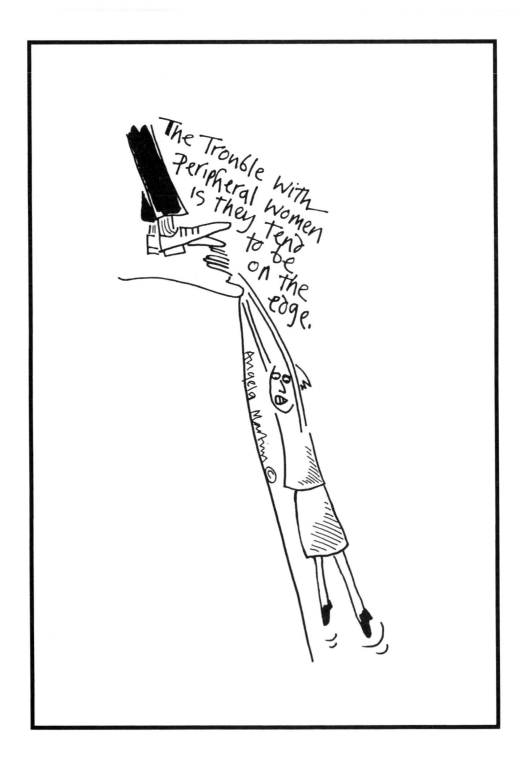

presented as an explanation of the behaviour of employees *per se*. Similar problems can be found in a reinterpretation of the work of Coch and French (Mills, 1992: 96) in their work on resistance to change.

Virtually all theories of effective management have been based on observations of male managers (Powell, 1988). They have made judgements about effective management, not recognizing that the majority of managers are men and judge on their adherence to the masculine gender stereotype. It is not surprising, then, that masculinity remains prevalent in the ranks of management. The fact that managers tend to be masculine does not necessarily mean that better managers are masculine.

Women and issues about their work have been considered by many as less important than that of men. If not ignored altogether in organizational theory, women as employees are regarded as indistinguishable from men in any respect relevant to their attitudes and actions at work, or as giving rise to special problems. Women's perspectives and ideas have often been absent, buried, or set to one side and marginalized. When women and issues of concern to women are studied, the research questions are too often framed through the eyes of men (Unger and Crawford, 1992).

Even when gender is acknowledged in books, the male-as-norm syndrome appears. For example, a textbook on communication in small groups has a distinct index entry for 'women in groups' (Bormann, 1990: 303). There is no entry for men in groups, which suggests that a group is normal only if it consists of males. If women are in groups, this is not the norm and therefore deserves research. In a male-dominated organizational world the expectation is that women's experiences can be adequately understood through the filter of the dominant gender culture, and thus the reality of gender in not addressed (Sheppard, 1992: 152).

If men are the norm, then women are 'the other'. There is now a literature on women in management but it is considered as something separate. 'Prior to the entrance of women there is (apparently) no "gender" in management' (Calas and Smircich, 1990). Furthermore it appears that it is only women who are 'gendered'; the implicit formula underlying the literature is gender = sex = women = problem.

The perception of female otherness occurs in every field—science, law, medicine, history, economics, literature, and art. In art there are works of general excellence and, separately, works by women artists, generally regarded as different and lesser (Tavris, 1992).

We accept the idea of male as norm implicitly. In a university setting a course, on female writers of the twentieth century would be a specialized course, yet if the lecturer were to call their course 'White Male Writers' it would be considered odd as the works of white male writers are regarded as literature itself.

The ideas and interests of racial minorities (Nkomo, 1992), lesbians, homosexuals, the non-Christian, and the disabled are also largely ignored by

---

Discussion Point

This view of women that sees women as other and lesser is to be found in all aspects of life, even in fairytales. Imagine a fairytale where Cinderella and her sisters are successful business women, where Cinderella does not want to go to the ball but goes anyway and finds the king in financial ruin. Cinderella helps the king plan a turnaround in palace finances and becomes chief executive of Palace Enterprises. She is disinterested in the prince who is besotted by her; she tells the prince not to be so crass and to examine his assumption that every woman should want to marry him because he is a prince but asks him to help her in the campaign to ban dangerous glass slippers.

Think of other fairytales you know and how women are presented as different and lesser.

Source: Maeve Binchy (1992) 'Cinderella Re-examined' in *Ride on Rapunzel: Fairytales for Feminists*, Attic Press, Dublin.

organizational behaviour. Women, minorities, non-Christians, and the disabled are rendered invisible or relatively unimportant in all but the most obvious areas of study, e.g. when equal opportunities are considered. The language of organizations, particularly the use of metaphor, derives from the language of the Christian faith (Ray, 1986; Wilson, 1992). When it comes to the disabled most UK companies ignore the existing toothless law on employing a 3 per cent quota of disabled staff but a few are trying to give the disabled a fair deal (*Personnel Today*, 23 November 1993: 25) The same is true of lesbians and homosexuals; they too are rendered invisible. Yet one in six homosexuals has suffered discrimination in the workplace and 5 per cent of those complain of physical violence (*Personnel Today*, 23 November 1993: 4). This too is important organizational behaviour yet there is a dearth of research material on which to draw.

Organizational behaviour has also tended to produce a sanitized view of what work and jobs are about. The studies in sociology that have covered deviant or 'dirty' work rarely appear in organizational behaviour texts. There is little said about the work done in nurseries, mortuaries, among prostitutes, prison guards, or sewage workers. Perhaps, like Hughes (1958), we should be encouraging our students to look at these kinds of jobs, not only because they are interesting in their own right but because they may help highlight experiences that we may take for granted in looking at more conventional work.

This book is specifically concerned with the interests of women in relation to behaviour in organizations. Almost all behaviour in organizations is gender specific. If you consider the aims of the book deviant, reflect on the question why.

Men have power in organizations that women often lack. Male power is a structural dimension of society as well as organizations and is a feature of all interpersonal encounters between men and women in organizations yet is rarely acknowledged in many 'male-stream' texts. Sexual harassment occurs in organizations but is a subject rarely found in textbooks on organizational behaviour. The gendered nature of organizations and their management has not been a dominant theme. Questions concerning how women are perceived, how they are motivated, what provides job satisfaction for them—these are all ignored in mainstream texts.

Another example of how the organizational focus is implicitly gendered can be found in the techniques for selection and assessment in organizations. Psychology in general adheres 'to the dominant liberal mode of equal opportunity that assumes that individuals compete in a free market for jobs with fixed characteristics' (Webb, 1987: 4; 1991) But the processes of assessment have to be understood in terms of the power relations that underlie gender. Power relations are usually ignored (Hollway, 1991).

Organizational theory is gender-blind, the gendered nature of organizational life is generally ignored, and there is no recognition that women's work experience may be different to that of men's as a result of power relations that differentiate society at large (Burrell and Hearn, 1989). Women face a series of barriers to their progress in organizations (Kelly, 1991). The first set are internal barriers such as gender role socialization, a passive self-concept, and role prejudice. A second set are support availability barriers such as limited financial resources, education and training, collegial networks, role models and mentors, and domestic restraints. A third, and final, category are structural barriers such as employer biases, sex-segregated jobs, sexual harassment, and pay inequities. Men and women help maintain these barriers to women's progress.

If you are unconvinced about male power, just look at the organizations of which you are a member. Institutions of higher education are male institutions with very limited and rigid career patterns. Although women are to be found in equal numbers, in the main, in student bodies, they are segregated into traditional female roles, notably service roles—cleaning, catering, and clerical work—and are rare in the higher reaches of administration or teaching. There are general structural mechanisms in higher education which reproduce a patriarchal order and see academic women as actual or potential threats to that order. Ramazanoglu (1987) has argued that these specific mechanisms for keeping women in their place need to be understood as forms of violence. Insults, leers, sneers, jokes, patronage, bullying, vocal violence, and sexual harassment are the sanctions imposed on women to 'keep them in their place'. We live in a culture that, in general, condones male entitlement and privilege (Van Nostrand, 1993). The male excludes, discounts, devalues; the female endures and withdraws.

The 'founding fathers' of organizational theory, according to Hearn *et al.*

(1989), have done little to bring the nature of gendered relations at work to prominence. We have been left a legacy of male terms such as 'organization man' (Whyte, 1956), 'corporate man' (Jay, 1972), and 'bureaucratic man' (Kohn, 1971). Until relatively recently, few women, other than Follet and Woodward, have been acknowledged as leading exponents in the field. Those women involved were usually researchers and collectors of data (Sheriff and Campbell, 1981). Organizational sociology and organizational theory, like general sociology, have suffered from a neglect of gender issues (Hearn and Parkin, 1992).

There has been a real growth in the production of research and theory of women in various disciplines. With a few published exceptions (e.g. Calas and Smircich, 1989; Hearn *et al.* 1989; Marshall, 1984, 1989; Martin, 1990; Mills 1992) much of the discussion has been going on outside the borders of organization theory (Calas and Smircich, 1990). There is little that can be said that is new, but this research and theory has not been located in the context of organizational behaviour and theory and now needs to be firmly placed within the discipline.

The book is designed to take a fresh look at why inequality of opportunity, and inequity of outcome has come about by exploring traditional topics of concern to organizational behaviourists, but with a different focus. The contention is that, to date, organizational behaviour has produced a mainly male vision. The material is drawn mainly from the psychology and sociology of work, but also from the related fields of cultural studies, anthropology, education, counselling, and psychotherapy. The literature from which the book could have drawn has a very broad range and I cannot claim that it has been comprehensively reviewed here. Although enriched by the breadth of perspectives, the focus has been mainly a psychological and sociological one, reflecting the disciplines I know best. The work also, for the same reason, has a British focus, having been written in Scotland.

This book is written for men and women. It is self-defeating for men not to be interested in these issues. Women are already the majority population and are almost numerically equal to men in the workforce. Both men and women need to understand how our organizations work and how fundamental distinctions between men and women affect our behaviour and our relations with one another in organizations.

There is a danger that this book will be seen as an 'addendum' to existing organizational behaviour texts, simply supplementing established organizational behaviour, focusing on what has been left out or overlooked and therefore acting as a gap-filling exercise. But reading the book should help in 'seeing reality differently' (Stanley and Wise, 1979), to help reformulate how organizational behaviour can be viewed. The male-oriented values to be found in organizational behaviour need to be dug up to be seen, the invisible needs to be visible, women should be brought out from under the twin spheres of social reality and cultural belief systems (Oakley, 1974).

A gendered analysis is adopted, using research on gender to help re-examine organizational behaviour. The questions which originally guided the research for this book were: Why have we accepted the male-as-norm model of management for so long? Why do the current views of organizational behaviour appear, at first sight, to be so eminently logical and non-sexist? If we were to examine studies of how women are perceived, how women are motivated and achieve job satisfaction, women and leadership, and so on, what would be found? Would there be different material available to use, differing perspectives to gain? There appears to be no shortage. There is an alternative view of behaviour in organizations which does not accept the male model of management and behaviour as the only view. The book takes a female perspective in that women are central to the research for the book, not just an addition or there to provide a comparative viewpoint. The implication of making women's experience central is not to focus exclusively on women but to utilize the female perspective to foster the development of a more genuinely human view, to deepen our understanding of the whole human experience, both male and female (Wilkinson, 1986). The aim is not just to make organizational behaviour more comprehensive but to begin to pose new questions and render suspect our pre-existing knowledge on the subject.

The book acts, in part, as a source book so readers can be introduced to the topics but follow through with their own research. The book does not pretend to have dealt with any of the topics at length or with complete thoroughness. Review questions at the end of each chapter are designed as project, essay, or dissertation topics to help lead the reader into further exploration, research, and knowledge. The book also acts as an initial challenge to the conventional thinking on organizational behaviour.

Reading this book ought to be relatively easy for undergraduate students, with minimum work experience, to understand as the issue of gender affects us all everyday in our lives. Everyone has experience of being male or female in an organization. The book is also designed for a postgraduate audience to help them re-evaluate the behaviour they have observed in organizations. Writing and re-searching this book was an education to me so I hope there will be ideas here which will challenge every reader's current thinking about organizational behaviour. To begin, let us look in more detail at the facts about women and work, what we know about how the social identity of women in organizations is constituted, and how their place at home and work is seen.

REFERENCES

ACKER, J. and VAN HOUTON, D. R. (1992) 'Differential Recruitment and Control: The Sex Structuring of Organisations', Chapter 1 in A. J. Mills and P. Tancred (eds), *Gendering Organizational Analysis*, Sage, London.

BINCHY, M. (1992) 'Cinderella Re-examined', in *Ride on Rapunzel: Fairytales for Feminists*, Attic Press, Dublin.

BORMANN, E. G. (1990) *Small Group Communication: Theory and Practice*, 3rd edn, Harper & Row, New York.

BURRELL, G. and HEARN, J. (1989) 'The Sexuality of Organization', in J. Hearn, D. L. Sheppard, P. Tancred-Sherif and G. Burrell (eds), *The Sexuality of Organizations*, Sage, London.

CALAS, M. B. and SMIRCICH, L. (1989) 'Using the F Word: Feminist Perspectives and the Social Consequences of Organizational Research', Academy of Management, Best Papers Proceedings, Washington, DC , pp. 355–359.

CALAS, M. B. and SMIRCICH, L. (1990) 'Re-writing Gender into Organizational Theorizing: Directions from Feminist Perspectives', Chapter 12 in M. I. Reed and M. D. Hughes (eds), *Rethinking Organization: New Directions in Organizational Research and Analysis*, Sage, London.

HEARN, J. and PARKIN, P. W. (1992) 'Gender and Organizations: A Selective Review and a Critique of a Neglected Area', Chapter 3 in A. J. Mills and P. Tancred (eds), *Gendering Organizational Analysis*, Sage, London.

HEARN, J., SHEPPARD, D. L., TANCRED-SHERIFF, P. and BURRELL, G. (eds) (1989) *The Sexuality of Organization*, Sage, London.

HOLLWAY, W. (1991) *Work Psychology and Organizational Behaviour: Managing the Individual at Work*, Sage, London.

HUGHES, E. C. (1958) *Men and their Work*, Free Press, New York.

JAY, A. (1972) *Corporate Man*, Cape, London.

KELLY, R. M. (1991) *The Gendered Economy: Work, Careers and Success*, Sage, London.

KOHN, M. M. (1971) 'Bureaucratic Man: A Portrait and an Interpretation', *American Sociological Review*, **36**(3), 461–474.

MARSHALL, J. (1984) *Women Managers: Travellers in a Male World*, Wiley, Chichester.

MARSHALL, J. (1989) 'Re-visioning Career Concepts: A Feminist Invitation', in M. B. Arthus, D. T. Hall and B. S. Lawrence (eds), *Handbook of Career Theory*, pp. 275–291, Cambridge University Press, Cambridge.

MARTIN, J. (1990) 'Deconstructing Organizational Taboos: The Suppression of Gender Conflict in Organizations', Organizational Science, **1**, 1–21.

MILLS, A. J. (1988a) 'Organization, Gender and Culture', *Organizational Studies*, **9**(3), 351–370.

MILLS, A. J. (1992) 'Organization, Gender and Culture', Chapter 5 in A. J. Mills and P. Tancred (eds), *Gendering Organizational Analysis*, Sage, London.

NKOMO, S. M. (1992) 'The Emperor Has No Clothes: Rewriting Race in Organizations', *Academy of Management Review*, **17**(3), 487–513.

OAKLEY, A. (1974) *The Sociology of Housework*, Martin Robertson, Oxford.

POWELL, G. N. (1988) *Women and Men in Management*, Sage, Newbury Park, Calif.

RAMAZANOGLU, C. (1987) 'Sex and Violence in Academic Life or You Can Keep a Good Women Down', Chapter 5 in J. Hanmer and M. Maynard (eds), *Women, Violence and Social Control*, Macmillan Press, Basingstoke.

RAY, C. A. (1986) 'Corporate Culture and the Last Frontier of Control', *Journal of Management Studies*, **23**(3), 287–297.

SHEPPARD, D. (1992) 'Women Manager's Perceptions of Gender and Organizational Life', Chapter 8 in A. J. Mills and P. Tancred (eds), *Gendering Organizational Analysis*, Sage, London.

SHERIFF, P. and CAMBELL, E. J. (1981) La place des femmes: un dossier sur la sociologie des organizations, *Sociologie et sociétés*, **13**, 113–130.

STANLEY, L. and WISE, S. (1979) *Breaking Out: Feminist Consciousness and Feminist Research*, Routledge & Kegan Paul, London.

TAVRIS, C. (1992) *The Mismeasure of Woman*, Simon & Schuster, New York.

UNGER, R. and CRAWFORD, M. (1992) *Women and Gender: A Feminist Psychology*, McGraw-Hill, New York.

VAN NOSTRAND, C. H. (1993) *Gender Responsible Leadership*, Sage, Newbury Park, Calif.

WEBB, J. (1987) 'Gendering Selection Psychology', *Occupational Psychologist*, **3**, December: special issue on gender issues in occupational psychology.

WEBB, J. (1991) 'The Gender Relations of Assessment', in J. Firth-Cozens and M. West (eds), *Women at Work: Psychological and Organizational Perspectives*, Open University Press, Milton Keynes.

WILKINSON, S. (1986) *Feminist Social Psychology: Developing Theory and Practice*, Open University Press, Milton Keynes.

WILSON, F. M. (1992) 'Language, Technology, Gender and Power', *Human Relations*, **45**(9), 883–904.

WHYTE, W. M. (1956) *The Organization Man*, Simon & Schuster, New York.

1. *Women's Place at Work and Home*

'THE MASTER RULES'

Our views of work take, as their starting point, the male-as-norm. It is easy to think of work as an activity which takes place on a daily basis, that you 'go out to', is paid employment, is full time, lasts a lifetime, and is an uninterrupted commitment, usually based in manufacturing industry. But this model of work would describe a male model of work. The male-as-norm model and the ensuing attitudes constitute significant occupational and employment barriers for women. Views of masculinity and femininity are bound up with the dichotomy between 'the home' and 'the world'. Since work and home are contrasted, housework is typified as non-work, women's paid work is regarded as marginal and temporary and working wives and mothers are 'problems' (Allen and Barker, 1976). Where attitudes like 'men go out to work while women stay at home' are generally accepted common attitudes, they are subtle but highly effective barriers. No one questions the desirability of holding these views and few challenge the implicit discrimination.

A model which might adequately describe women's work is different to the male model of work. It would need to take account of both home work and paid work. 'Women's paid employment does not exist in isolation. It is inextricably linked to women's unpaid work in the household and community' (Huggett *et al.* 1985: 200). Women all over the world have primary responsibilities for the non-material well-being of their families. Any employment for women entails a trade-off which involves implicit and explicit costs, particularly for married women and women with children. How can women's work be described?

SOME FACTS ABOUT WOMEN AND WORK

To begin, let us look at women's place at work and home, drawing from employment statistics and sociological studies so that we have an informed perspective of women's position in employment and home. Not all women's work is paid and outside the home; there is housework and voluntary work. The importance of women's work, whether paid or unpaid, is encapsulated in the fact that women do two-thirds of the world's work, receive 10 per cent of the world's

income and own 1 per cent of the world's resources (Scott, 1985; Spender, 1985). It is impossible to estimate women's activities in the 'informal' economy (women's work in informal paid work, voluntary work, and in the domestic field), but women's participation in the formal economy has steadily increased during the last hundred years.

Between 1950 and 1985 female economic activity rates (work which contributed directly to the formal economy) in the advanced industrial nations increased from 38.2 to 55.9 per cent while the male economic activity rates declined from 87.4 to 84.3 per cent (Bakker, 1988: 19). Within the European Community the proportion of women in the workforce grew in every state. Denmark and the UK have the highest female work activity rates. These rates are predicted to continue increasing.

Women employees outnumber men in nine counties in England and Wales and in two Scottish regions. During the last 20 years there has been a 2.8 million fall in the number of men in work in Britain, and a 2 million rise in the number of women (Incomes Data Services Report, May 1993). It is estimated that by 1995 women will fill 80 per cent of new jobs and comprise 90 per cent of the increase of 1 million people in the labour force (Women and Training, 1991). As the number of women working has increased, the male-as-norm model has become less relevant.

You might think that as more women entered the labour force, women would gain more positions of power. A surprising statistic is that the proportion of women in positions of power in Britain declined between 1911 and 1971 (Hakim, 1981). There are enormous differences in the types of jobs women and men do, the pay they receive, the hours they work, the skills they acquire, and their patterns of employment (Dex, 1985; Marnani, 1992).

WOMEN AND PART-TIME WORKING

Many women in Britain work on a part-time basis (42 per cent) and do temporary work. Part-time work is attractive to both married women employees and to employers for the flexibility it gives. It gives employers flexibility in scheduling work. Many working activities experience peaks and troughs throughout the day and week—at check-outs in supermarkets, for example, or in transport. Part-time working has expanded with skill shortages and demographic changes. The recessions of the early 1980s and the early 1990s accelerated the shift towards part-time employment patterns. Analysts predict that much of the upturn in employment during the recovery will be in part-time jobs for women.

Women do not necessarily prefer part-time work; for many it is a matter of compelled circumstance, not a matter of preference. As long as women remain largely responsible for work involved with the maintenance of the family and home life, there will be a limit on how much work they can do outside the home. Of all the women who held part-time jobs in Canada in 1986, 12.5 per cent did so because for 'personal or family responsibilities' (other than children), 20.3 per cent were 'going to school', 27.4 per cent 'could only find part-time work' and 38.5 per cent did not want full-time work. It is relevant that 86 per cent of those who did not want full-time work were married which means they had domestic responsibilities. This is not the profile of a population that 'prefers' part-time working (Peitchinis, 1989: 35).

The largest concentrations of women working part-time are in the service industries (education, retail, hotels and catering, medical and other health services). In several of these industries the expansion of part-time employment occurred while full-time employment contracted. In education, in Britain, for example, between 1981 and 1985, 60 000 women's full-time jobs and 1800 men's jobs were lost. At the same time 69 700 new women's part-time jobs were created. (Beechey and Perkins, 1987: 39).

Part-timers are clustered in low-pay, low-skill categories of work. The average hourly earnings of part-timers are not much more than half those of the average male full-timer. Frequently the part-time working woman works too few hours to qualify to pay the British National Insurance stamp. She therefore misses out on contributory benefits such as sick pay and maternity pay. She is normally excluded from any occupational pension scheme. She has fewer employment rights and can be laid off more easily than the full-time worker (Cockburn, 1991: 80).

Due to the unavailability of full-time work at hours she can manage, she sometimes does two part-time jobs, often an early morning and a twilight shift (Beechey and Perkins, 1987; Robinson, 1988). The number of women in the European Community with second jobs doubled between 1983 and 1988, suggesting that women want, or need, more work hours (Hammond and Holton, 1991).

The rationale for the expansion of part-time work for women was to enable them to combine paid employment with domestic responsibilities. But it is possible to increase women's economic activity without increasing the number of part-time jobs—as Australia, Canada, Belgium, Finland, Spain, Sweden, Britain, and the USA have shown. Provision of better childcare facilities and maternity benefit may help; women in France enjoy more of these benefits than British women (Beechey and Perkins, 1987). In the UK the average maternity leave pay is about half of the salary and fewer than 50 per cent of children aged between 3 and 5 years have access to childcare provision. Benefits are better in other EC countries. Portugal and the Netherlands offer full maternity leave pay, and over 90 per cent of French children between 3 and 5 enjoy childcare facilities (Davidson and Cooper, 1993: 2). In Scotland, from where this book is being written, about only 34 per cent of 3 and 4 year old children are in nursery education (Cohen and Strachan, 1993).

One way to look at the fact and fiction surrounding women and how we see them as workers is to look at the myths and realities of women's work. Before we start to look at the facts and realities, let us look at your views and the facts you already know.

Which of these statements do you think are true?

1. Women do not work as many years as their male counterparts.
2. Training for women is costly and, for the most part, wasted.
3. Women are absent from work more often than men.
4. Labour turnover is higher among women employees.
5. Women already have equal opportunities.

What evidence can you find to substantiate any of the above statements?

We are now going to look at three commonly held myths about women workers and see what evidence there is to counteract the myths.

MYTH 1: WOMEN HAVE EQUAL OPPORTUNITIES

Despite more than 15 years of equal opportunities legislation in Britain and activities by organizations to improve equal opportunities, it is very evident that women are still clustered in certain sectors of the economy and at the base of organizational hierarchies. Additionally, in spite the adoption of equal opportunities policies in many organizations, little progress seems to have been made. For example a British survey of 20 different companies on how equal opportunities policies were working for them reveals that women are still not achieving equal access to the highest management levels. Women report that a range of obstacles impede their progress that include childcare arrangements, lack of flexible working, and access to training (Women and Work, 1993). Occupational segregation is probably the largest barrier women face. Examples of segregation exist in almost every industrial and service sector within the economy.

Segregation in employment is by ethnicity as well as gender, with complex patterns as these intersect (Walby, 1988: 3). Black women are subject to greater restrictions in their access to good employment conditions and pay than any other groups. Phizacklea (1988) shows how the employment niches available to black women are usually in the most vulnerable parts of the economy, e.g. in homeworking. Homeworkers of all races are extremely badly paid. A survey carried out in Leeds, England, found that the average wage of homeworkers was £1.16 per hour. It was estimated that there were about 5 000–10 000 homeworkers in Leeds alone (see Leppington, 1993).

Many women from ethnic minorities work in family firms—the corner shop, the Cypriot café and the Chinese takeaway (Westwood and Bhachu, 1988). Some came as 'family women' or on the promise of a job in a relative's business; this women's labour power is the mainstay of cheap labour costs and low wages in the ethnic economy. Let us look at occupational segregation for all women in some detail.

Occupational segregation exists where women are disproportionately repre-sented in certain jobs relative to their overall proportion in the workforce, and there are varying degrees of segregation. It refers to the division of the labour market into predominantly male and female occupations and occurs along two dimensions, horizontal and vertical.

Horizontal occupational segregation occurs where men and women are most commonly working in different types of occupation, for example where women predominate in occupations such as data preparation clerks and chambermaids, and men in occupations such as computer operators and kitchen porters. Horizontal segregation is maintained by the recruitment of men and women to different jobs. Jobs become sex typed into masculine or feminine jobs. It is usually the case that male jobs are usually ranked higher than female jobs.

Vertical segregation describes another structuring, where men are most commonly working in higher grade occupations and women in lower grades. This happens even in so-called women's occupations: in nursing, for example, where 9 per cent of nurses are men but they hold 45 per cent of the top nursing jobs (Stamp and Robarts, 1986). White collar work can be seen to be vertically segregated along gender lines with, for example, women performing the bulk of clerical and secretarial work, and men managerial and higher professional work. (The number of women in senior management roles is currently 1–2 per cent.) Women are much more likely to be found in the semi-professions (teacher, nurse, librarian) than professions (doctor, lawyer, chartered accountant), are in routine office work and shop work, but are less likely to be found in skilled manual work than men (Abbott and Payne, 1990: 17).

In manual employment, women are under-represented among the ranks of the skilled, but increasingly segregated into semi-skilled and unskilled work like packing and light assembly. Women recruited as assemblers in the mass production light industries are confined to this work and excluded from jobs as chargehands and supervisors (Glucksmann, 1986; Pollert, 1981). In *Women on the Line*, Ruth Cavendish (1982) showed how there was an almost absolute separation between jobs allocated to women and to men. She says that the qualification you needed for a better job was to be a man. Similarly Game and Pringle (1983) showed segregation in computing job markets where women are hired as data entry key-punchers and men predominated as operators, salesmen, systems analysts, and managers.

Once established, the pattern of occupational segregation by gender becomes fixed. Jobs are constructed either as masculine or as feminine in a manner which becomes accepted as normal by both men and women (Glucksmann, 1990: 4). All round the world women work alongside men, growing food, rendering services, making goods. Yet the work women do is habitually viewed as less important. Men and women perform different types of work. This sex typing of jobs, the allocation of specific tasks to men and women, can even be found when men and women are working side by side; men will be scything while women gather, women will be filing record cards when men do the accounts, and so on (Bradley, 1989). Women are the assistants to men's work. Which tasks and occupations are defined as men's and women's will vary according to time and place. Some tasks, even those that seem typically masculine to us, such as mining and forestry, have been performed by women.

Men's and women's work is also valued differently, with men's work consistently more highly valued than women's and regarded as requiring a level of skill which most women's work does not. We find, then, that women workers think men would be able to do women's work but would not want to, where as men simply think women are incapable of doing men's work (Martin and Roberts, 1984).

Vertical segregation is maintained by either differential recruitment or the confining of women to lower grades within internal labour markets. Well-documented examples of vertical segregation are to be found in the large white collar bureaucracies such as banks and insurance companies (Heritage, 1983; Crompton and Jones, 1984; Crompton, 1989). Women do not progress through the career hierarchies because of their lack of formal qualifications, broken employment patterns, and because they have been excluded by male managers from gaining access to the internal job hierarchy (Crompton and Sanderson, 1990).

Where men and women work in the same industry sexual demarcations are rigidly maintained. Women sew what men cut out, women serve what men cook, women run machines which men service, and so on. There are clear distinctions between men's and women's work; women's work is almost always lower paid, lacking in craft tradition, has weaker union organization, and is of unskilled status. The work is often deemed inferior simply because women do it. Skill is often an ideological category imposed on certain types of work by virtue of the sex and power of the workers who perform it (Philips and Taylor, 1980).

In Britain in 1987 women were concentrated in only seven industrial sectors. Women are more likely to be found in the service industries and form the majority of the footwear and clothing sector workers (74 per cent). Eighty per cent of those working in medical and other services are women and 71 per cent in personal services (e.g. cleaning and hairdressing). Examples of horizontal segregation abound.

In the spring of 1991, 78 per cent of all women of working age in employment are found concentrated in nine groups: clerical (18 per cent); personal service (13 per cent); sales assistants/check-out operators (9 per cent); other sales/ service occupations, e.g catering assistants, shelf fillers (9 per cent); secretarial (9 per

---

Discussion point

Headline: 'Women's deprecatory descriptions of their jobs undercut both status and pay'

The South Australian Department of Labour set up 'What's in a Word' (WIAW) to ask female clerical workers to describe their jobs while project workers audited their skills. It was found that the majority of the women 'invisiblised' their work by describing it in the broadest terms, like 'word processing operator', implying that the machine did the real job. But the word processing and copy-typing often involve converting a dictated text from spoken into written form as well as selecting fonts, lay-outs and producing graphics.

Women also regularly represented their skills in personality terms, as in 'you have to be a friendly person'. Bank tellers, for example, are forever chatting with customers and remembering personal details. Since there is now little to choose between most major banks, the bank's human face may be crucial in attracting or repelling custom. But if it is just part of the inherited package of femininity and not a form of labour, why should it be rewarded?

Thirdly, says WIAW, both women and the workplace undervalue female jobs, because people in charge of money are rated more highly than those attending to human beings.

The report says that women learn to devalue their skills from the workplace and wider culture. Do you agree? Have you seen examples of this?

Source: extracted from a report in *Guardian*, 15 June 1993, p. 9. © *The Guardian*, 1993.

---

cent); corporate managers and administrators (6 per cent); teaching professionals (5 per cent); health associate professionals, e.g. nurses, midwives (5 per cent); and managers and proprietors in service industries (4 per cent); (*Employment Gazette*, September 1992: 440).

What about women in management positions? A high labour force participation is no assurance of women's representation in management. For example, in Denmark where women are 47 per cent of the salaried labour force, they are only 14 per cent of the administrators/managers and 5 per cent of top management (Antal and Izraeli, 1993). This pattern is typical for all countries for which data were obtained.

For those who would like to argue that the situation for women managers is improving with time, there is little support. The data for Britain show a drop of 3.5 per cent in the proportion of women in senior management from 1975 to 1984,

---

Discussion point

You are attending a meeting of an Equal Opportunities Working Party in a university and discussing how to change segregation, and where the greatest impact can be achieved. Someone suggests that the best way is to encourage men to apply for secretarial and clerical posts. Knowing what you do about job segregation, would you oppose this suggestion? Give your reasons.

Here is another issue. A member of a board of directors of a company informs you that the board had appointed 2 women (in succession) to a senior post in the company. Both women had become pregnant, taken paid maternity leave, and then decided to leave the company. He believes that the board will be reluctant to appoint another woman to the post after this experience. What do you say?

---

although an increase of similar proportions was registered at the middle and lower management levels (Hammond, 1986) A similar decline in the proportion of women among senior managers occurred the the US between 1960 and 1980. (For an excellent review of these statistics see Antal and Izraeli, 1993.)

There are no UK statistics on the percentage of non-white female managers. In the USA in 1986 less than 9 per cent of all managers were ethnic minorities, including Blacks, Hispanics, and Asians.* From 1974 to 1984 the percentage of black women officials and managers grew to 1.7 per cent (Morrison and von Glinow, 1990). Not one black woman was among the top 25 black managers in 'Corporate America' in a survey conducted in 1988 by Black Enterprise (Harrison, et al., 1988). Reports (in Jones, 1986) indicated that there were no Asian American or Latina women in the senior ranks among the executives they surveyed. US research confirms that ethnic minority women managers are doubly disadvantaged (Nkomo, 1991). The issue for ethnic minority women has been described as one of breaking the concrete ceiling that restricts entry even into middle management (Ray and Davis, 1988). A similar situation exists in Canada (Mighty, 1991).

Equality of opportunity involves ensuring that women have no doors closed to them that are open to men. If, however, women's history and segregation prevent them from taking up opportunities, competing on equal terms for jobs, or finding comparisons for equal pay, then equality of results will never be achieved. Positive, or affirmative action, special action in terms of training or leave, are required if women are to make progress towards equality. But despite signing a

---

* The terms 'black' and 'ethnic minority' are used to refer to people who belong to racial minority groups living in the UK. For the most part this refers to people whose ethnic origins are in a continent other than Europe. The word 'black' predominates because it is a term which the majority of people so described prefer to identify with.

UN convention in 1979 ratifying the controversial Article 4 calling for positive discrimination in favour of women, UK law forbids all positive discrimination except where expressly permitted. The extent of the permitted positive discrimination is extremely small, amounting to little more than providing sex-specific training for a particular occupation or workplace in which one sex can be show to be under-represented. The provision applies to men as well as women (Cockburn, 1991). Sex segregation has, in some respects, increased in the late 1970s and early 1980s (Hakim, 1981).

Segregation exists, in part, because of the restrictive choices people make. Occupational choices from school leavers show gender preferences. Career choices made by women continue to reflect traditional stereotyping. A survey showed that girls fantasized about becoming airline stewardesses, kennel maids, nursery nurses, fashion models, and top secretaries, while boys produced a list of about 100 occupations including spaceman, millionaire, football player, artist, and politician (Swords-Isherwood, 1985). Figures for Scottish school leavers reveal girls choices to be narrower than boys. Seventy-five per cent of girls chose jobs in three groupings—clerical, nursing, and sales. The same proportion of boys had jobs in seven groupings.

However, women in Scotland enter higher education in greater numbers than in the rest of Britain and emerge to a greater extent with the kind of degrees thought to bring success in the business world. For example, in 1987 in Scotland, females formed 15 per cent of entrants to university undergraduate computer courses; in England the equivalent figure was 8 per cent (McKinlay, 1989). Educationally successful women are mainly the product of single-sex schools. They show levels of qualification which are well above average and a trend towards acquiring management qualifications (White et al., 1992).

Girls in Scotland are more highly qualified than boys when leaving school—there are more girls than boys with five or more Highers (Regional Trends, 1989). They have almost equal levels of participation in university (45 per cent in 1988/9) and the labour force (45.6 per cent in 1989) in Scotland. The same is true for British women; while women leave full-time education with qualifications comparable to, if not better than, those of men, they are failing, by comparison with men, to obtain the specific occupational and professional qualifications needed for progress within an internal labour market (Dale, 1988).

In the UK in general there has been a gradual increase in female entry into higher education. Women constituted 44 per cent of university undergraduates in 1989 and 37 per cent of postgraduates, compared with 41 per cent and 32 per cent respectively in 1983. While the majority of women study education or arts subjects (including languages), 26 per cent of science undergraduates are female (Davidson and Cooper, 1992). An increasing number of women are studying social administration and business degrees (45 per cent compared with 10 per cent in 1973). Nevertheless women are still finding it very difficult to reach upper middle and

Maybe the segregation starts in schools?

Find out, from your class if there were different choices made by males and females in school subjects. Do these choices now limit future choices in any way?

senior management positions. Hirsh and Jackson (1989) estimate there are around 3 million managers in Britain but only about one-fifth are women. Of the million or so middle and senior managers, at most 4 per cent are women. Women graduates underachieve in the labour market compared with men. Women graduates, in one longitudinal survey of 4000 graduates, were found to have lower status jobs, more limited promotion prospects, and earn significantly less than men. Women are less successful than men irrespective of the type of course followed (Chapman, 1989).

We should not be surprised to hear that female postgraduates also underachieve compared with their male counterparts. A recent study by Cox and Harquail (1990), following the career paths and career success of male and female graduates in the US, found that women experience lower levels of salary progression, fewer management promotions, and achieve lower management positions than comparable male managers even when controlling for career path variables.

The segregation then continues into work. Vertical segregation in the educational sector is illustrated by data from Loughborough University of Technology (Aitkenhead, 1991) where it was found that 90 per cent of academic staff were men; 70 per cent of clerical staff were women. Female academic staff occupied lower positions in the hierarchy: 14 per cent of male and 0 per cent of female academics were professors; 31 per cent of males and 18 per cent of females were senior lecturers. In administration, 34 per cent of male and 15 per cent of female were to be found in the top two grades. Women were primarily in the bottom grades: 68 per cent versus 32 per cent of males. The segregation had repercussions for the composition of decision-making structures within the university. Of the 765 committee places available, only 5 per cent were occupied by women; over half the committees had no female representation at all.

In 1988 four women lecturers at Newcastle Polytechnic took their employer to court claiming sex discrimination because the college had not appointed or short-listed them for promotion. They lost their case. The number of cases being brought under the Sex Discrimination Act in Britain rose from 1577 in 1990 to 3112 in 1991 but only 365 reached court. Only a quarter of those were won by the applicant. Sex discrimination is hard to prove as a woman is unlikely to be told she will be unable to do the job due to her gender. Instead she will be told that, for example, her management style is unsuitable for the job. The burden of proof is on the woman

(*Independent on Sunday*, 26 July 1992, p. 20). Legal enactments are, to a large extent, a reflection of dominant or widespread social values. In any event sexist understandings of the role of women permeate the legal system itself (Kahn and Mills, 1990; Wolf, 1990).

The total percentage of women in university academic posts in 1989 was 14 per cent; an 1993 Association of University Teachers (AUT) survey of professorial and senior staff in 11 institutions showed that less than 5 per cent of the UK's top academics were women. Scotland has the lowest proportion of female academics at 10.7 per cent (Halsey, 1990). The percentage of female managers in 1987 was 27 per cent, having risen from 24 per cent in 1983; in Scotland 24.2 per cent of managers were women in 1987 (SIACE, 1990). It is accepted wisdom that 'Women require more qualifications than men to reach the same levels in management' (SIACE, 1990). Overall, however, in the past women have not received the same levels of education and training as men in Scotland (Nelson, 1988) or in the UK as a whole (Acker and Piper, 1984; Byrne, 1978; Wickham, 1986).

With lack of jobs comes lack of power. Within the professions, women are failing to reach the professions' ruling élites. Women make up about 17 per cent of the main professions—architects, barristers, chartered accountants, doctors, and so on. Comparison of these professional groups shows great diversity: from 0.5 per cent of engineers who are women to 40 per cent of pharmacists. Numbers of women are small on ruling bodies where, on average, they make up only 9 per cent of members (Inter-Professional Group Working Party Report, reported in the *Times*, 29 June 1990).

A British Institute of Management (BIM) survey (1989) found that only 8 per cent of executive positions were held by women. A Hansard Society survey found that of 144 companies in their survey, less than 1 per cent of main board executive directors were women. The Society of Telecom Executives published a survey of 1000 female managers which revealed that while women constitute 30 per cent of the company's workforce, only 15 per cent of management grades were occupied by women. They held only 2 per cent of senior management grades, and only a handful have penetrated the very highest level. A study of more than 1000 women managers in local government in England and Wales (Young and Spencer, 1990) remarks on the near absence of women from top management positions in local government. Moreover there was little evidence of impending change as there was an overwhelming preponderance of men at middle and lower levels.

Women managers have been found, in general, to possess higher educational levels, with 61 per cent working in the private sector holding a first degree, compared with only 44 per cent of men. In the public sector the percentages were 73 and 65 respectively (Alban-Metcalfe and West, 1991: 155). In a British survey by Scase and Goffee (1990) 37 per cent of women managers had degree-level qualifications compared to 22 per cent of men. Women, then, seem to need better qualifications than men in order to achieve positions of similar status.

The problems that women face entering management and being in management over the last 20 years have been well documented (see, for example, Leavitt, 1982; Davidson and Cooper, 1984; Alban-Metcalfe, 1985; Adler and Izraeli, 1988; Kanter, 1989). Hearn (1992) argues that it is men and managements who need to change. Women are confronted by a 'glass ceiling' when it comes to entering positions of power in organizational senior executive levels as well as government—'a ceiling often requiring a sledge-hammer to shatter! This glass ceiling is invisible but women experience it as a real barrier when they vie for promotion to top jobs' (Davidson and Cooper, 1992).

An Institute of Directors (*Personnel Today*, 1992: 4) survey found that one in three female directors blamed male attitudes for poor opportunities for women in business. The survey showed that women want positive action, e.g. providing workplace nurseries not positive discrimination. Male attitudes towards women at work have been negative. Another early UK survey showed that, in that sample, the majority of men responsible for recruitment and hiring of employees held the view that a woman is likely to be inferior to a man as an employee (Hunt, 1975). Only 43.9 per cent thought it would be a good thing to have more women in senior positions.

The traditional anti-female bias is particularly tenacious in Scotland. (Top Women Survey, *Scottish Business Insider*, May and June 1993) Only some 20 per cent of managerial posts in Scotland are held by women, compared with 26 per cent in Britain as a whole. Of 1206 directorships of the Top 200 Scottish companies, only 33 are held by women. Male chauvinism is the main obstacle, Scottish business women believe, but low self-esteem and lack of confidence are also strong contributing factors to slow female advancement.

What can women do to have their achievements recognized, to be seen as successful managers? Some 68 per cent of the British Telecom women believed they have to perform better than men to get the same promotion. This view is strongly supported by Anne Morrison, a director of the Centre for Creative Leadership in North Carolina, who discovered, in a 1987 survey of the progress of 76 top female executives in America's biggest companies, that women's progress is slowed because their companies force them to perform to higher standards than men. This is often because businesses believe it is risky to promote women to senior positions. More women than men fail to get to the top because of a poor image or because they were too ambitious or not ambitious enough. 'Women are expected to have more strengths and fewer faults than their male counterparts', says Morrison.

The women senior executives who had 'made it' and broken to glass ceiling shared six prominent characteristics or attributes (Morrison *et al.*, 1990):

- *Help*—each had had help from above through sponsors or mentors.
- *Achievement*—each had a proven track record.

- *Desire*—most were characterized by a passion to succeed, worked long hours, made personal sacrifices, and demonstrated willingness to get the job done.
- *Management*—most demonstrated competence in managing subordinates.
- *Risk taking*—they had taken risks in career moves to broaden business experience.
- *Tough, decisive, and demanding*—they had to demonstrate their ability to be aggressive, make hard decisions, and say what was on their minds.

'The key to success is for the executive woman to demonstrate that she can pick and choose from sex stereotypical behavior patterns to adopt male behaviors (without being too macho) and retain female behaviors (without being too feminine)' (Morrison *et al.*, 1990). Those who had failed had an inability to adapt, wanted too much, and had performance problems. (Women looking for recipes for success may also like to read, for example, Loden, 1985, and Mitchell and Burdick, 1985.)

There are heavy penalties for those companies who breach equal opportunity law. An Opportunity 2000 signatory, British Gas, was recently forced to pay compensation for sex discrimination. A tribunal ordered the company to reinstate one of its senior managers to the £45 000-a-year job from which she was demoted after a major restructure. Her post was given to a male colleague. The woman claimed she was the only manager in her division not to be given her job back at the same level after privatization. The tribunal said the woman had been the victim of institutionalized discrimination and ordered British Gas to pay her £8 000 (*Personnel Today*, 1992: 3).

There is certainly no equality when it comes to *income*. Statistics show that, in general, women are less highly rewarded. In the last decade the average weekly age for a man has been £233.50; for a women £135.50. The British Annual New Earnings Survey shows that the average wage of female manual and white collar workers remains at its 1975 level of two-thirds that of an equivalent male.

Examples of inequality in pay can be found in universities. Despite the fact that women make up nearly one-third of all academic staff employed in US universities, only 14 per cent of full professors are women and their average wage is 89 per cent of their male colleagues (AUT Update, 22 October 1992). In Canada a 1991 survey indicated that of female academics in universities in English-speaking Canada, only 6.86 per cent were full professors while the great majority (52.4 per cent) were employed at lecturer level (Mills and Simmons, 1994). A 1993 UK survey revealed that university women are on average paid £1500 less than their male colleagues (AUT Update, 7 June 1993). The same is true of Australia and most OECD countries. In 1989, for example, women in Australia earned only 65 per cent of male total weekly earnings. Although part of this differential stemmed from women's concentration in part-time employment, women in full-time employment in Australia still earn only about 78 per cent of their male counterparts (Baxter, 1992).

This inequality in pay is also found among management executives. The BIM survey found that female executives earned between 76 and 96 per cent of male executive earnings, even when doing jobs classed broadly at the same level. According to the Department of Employment, however, in the year to April 1992, women's earnings increased more than men's, going up by 8.4 per cent average, compared with 6.6 per cent for men. But a woman only earns, on average, 70 per cent of a man's wage.

This point is emphasized by a report published by Equity, the union of the acting profession, in 1992 (*Guardian*, 3 March 1992: 2) showing that the annual average earnings for men in television are £26 466 and for women £13 178. Work in television commercials shows an even wider gap—an average of £18 031 for men and £6 650 for women. Women have shorter careers and find it harder to get work once past 30, while men carry on without effect.

Despite the Equal Pay Regulations of 1984, little has changed. It has been difficult to enforce the principle of equal value in the Equal Pay Regulations, either through collective bargaining or the courts. Tribunals have proved ungenerous in their interpretation of the law. Cases won have often been overturned at a higher level on appeal and women who have brought such cases have reported a punishing experience (Cockburn, 1991: 33). Those who have won cases found the cash compensation mean (Leonard, 1987). Gains in compensation for women ceased around 1977 and little more has been achieved since (Department of Employment, 1987). Employers introduced yet clearer distinctions between men and women's work so the two could not be considered comparable (Snell *et al.*, 1981).

One way that women can earn wages comparable to a man is to integrate into non-traditional work, defined as jobs where 75 per cent of employees are males (Lenikan, 1983). But research shows high labour turnover among women who have entered skill crafts, e.g. carpentry and electrical work. The reason is the obstacles to achieving work tenure in the all-male domain of non-traditional work (Walshok, 1981). Blue collar jobs may be more difficult for women to enter and keep than is the case with professional occupations (Gerson, 1982).

As a result of increases largely in part-time and low-paid jobs, only a minority of women earn enough to enjoy full economic independence (EOC report quoted in *Personnel Today*, 2–15 June 1992: 48). Many women do not earn sufficient wages to keep their families above the poverty level (Shortridge, 1986). No wonder, then, that it is thought that women only work for 'pin money'.

Why women hit the ceiling

A recent study by Hilary Homans of 193 males and females then employed in clinical chemistry laboratories in a regional health authority, and a further 191 who had left the same authority's employment, highlights some attitudes towards equal opportunities. Women are clearly underrepresented in senior positions and overrepresented in lower grades (for details see Homans, 1984, 1987). A senior male scientist said 'I do not think that opportunities for women are lacking. I think it is the women who are lacking themselves. I don't think anything can be done to improve the situation because I think it is genetic—I do seriously.'

A male biochemist commented: 'All the laws on equal opportunities fail if you have someone who basically feels that women should stay at home and look after the baby. And that is quite common in our profession.'

What are your views?

MYTH 2: WOMEN ONLY WORK FOR PIN MONEY

Women are often thought of as supplementary family workers. Their earnings help supplement the family income which is implicitly presumed to be adequate. However, many of the women who work (39 per cent) are single mothers; one in seven families are headed by single parents. Many women are, then, totally dependent on their own earning power. Two-thirds of women who work are self-supporting and more than one-third are the sole wage earners (Chusmir, 1982). The Royal Commission on the Distribution of Income and Wealth found that without the wife's earnings three times as many families would be below the poverty line (cited in Carter 1988: 105). Finance has always been the biggest factor in women's choice to return to work (Dex, 1984). Unfortunately women are often expected to take a job of a lower status and salary on their return to work. The experience of downward occupational mobility is common for women, particularly for women returning to part-time work after having children (Dex, 1987). Childbirth can cause a major disruption to a woman's career. In addition, Joshi and Newell (1987) have shown that women incur substantial losses in lifetime earnings as a result of breaks for childbirth.

Many feel that they cannot afford any loss of earnings. Couples can be dependent on dual incomes. Nearly half of all women managers earn more than their husbands and so are the prime earners (BIM Survey 1989). For double-income families a relocation, if it comes with a subsequent loss of one income, can have a devastating effect on their lifestyle. Most people who turn down expatriate assignments do so because they are concerned about losing a partner's income.

Four out of five companies offer no financial compensation for loss of a spouse's income (*Personnel Today*, 4 May 1993: 48).

Relocation can also have negative psychological effects as it is a major break in life, ranking only below a death in the family or divorce in terms of stress. Working women, and their partners, are increasingly resisting company moves as these disrupt careers and family income. Almost half the 130 firms in a CBI study (*Daily Telegraph*, 22 January 1990) said employees were opposing moves because of damage to a spouse's career. Almost one in ten of the companies in the survey were offering a 'spouse employment assistance' package. There are signs, then, that the increasing numbers of women working are having an impact on employment practices. But the extent of these changes is very limited.

MYTH 3: WOMEN'S WORK COMMITMENT IS LESS THAN THAT OF MEN

The sense of commitment that the individual brings to work is important to the organization. The assumption often is that the individual should be prepared to work longer hours when the need arises, to relocate when the organization wishes, and place a greater emphasis on the interests of the organization than on personal interests if the two are in conflict. Men are perceived as having more of this type of commitment to work, yet excessive commitment may lead to over-zealous or unethical behaviour.

It can be argued that the male model of a career pattern is founded on continuity and commitment. Total commitment is demanded in the fulfilment of day-to-day working obligations. The career is made masculine with little accommodation for the women who work in it. Women are expected to conform to the norm in pursuit of their careers, but as many women have 'broken' career patterns—to allow for the bearing and raising of children, or looking after elderly relatives—this norm is obviously disadvantageous to them.

The disadvantage women experience due to this male model of a career pattern is closely coupled with the 'cultural mandate', the assumed primacy of the commitment of women to the home and family; all of this is highly significant in terms of their marginalization. What evidence is there to support or refute this cultural mandate? We can answer this question by looking at findings on the effect of dependents on the work patterns of those who care for them, the effect of marriage and family on women, and absenteeism and labour turnover among women employees. First let us look at what happens when women become carers, with dependent relatives to look after.

WHEN WOMEN ARE CARERS

A study by the Policy Institute reveals that only a small proportion of carers give up work to care for their dependents, but as many as one in four have to change their working pattern in some way (*Personnel Today*, 4 May, 1993: 33) It is not only women, though, who are carers (see Gibeau and Anastas, 1989). The majority of carers of severely disabled elderly people are women, but over one-third of co-resident carers are men (Arber and Gilbert, 1989). But the assumed primacy of women's domestic commitments leads to prejudice against them, detracting from the notion that women can be committed professionals and this damages their prospects for promotion (Spencer and Podmore, 1987).

Pause for thought

ICL found that only 8.6 per cent of women who left between 1982 and 1988 were pregnant. How many managers who assume that women are less reliable as employees have used data on labour turnover among men *and* women in their organization to inform their view?

WOMEN AND CHILDREN

An additional factor contributing to lack of equality of opportunity may be that men are just prejudiced against women who could become, or are, mothers. A survey commissioned by CPM Field Marketing (reported in *Personnel Today*, 28 July 1992: 2) says that 47 per cent of men believe mothers should not work. If women do chose a career in management, they have to make a total, long-term commitment in which other family responsibilities must be subordinated. As Kreps (1983) puts it so bluntly, no one can expect an employer to 'compensate at rates equal to men, a woman who thinks she deserves eight years of maternity leave'. Nor can a career woman expect to step out of a career into home and then back again with no guilt, loss of identity, or slipping on the career ladder (1983: 1–2).

Discussion point

How would you produce an argument to counteract an employer who said that he would not employ women because they could not make a total commitment to the organization?

It is still assumed that women management trainees are a poor investment as they leave the organization sooner than men, and before they have 'paid off' the money invested in their training. But this is not true. Women leave to have babies after 5–7 years; men switch employers after 5–7 years. Gold and Pringle's (1989) study of women managers indicates that work was central to their lives and that any interruptions to paid work were mostly of short duration. Would you rather lose an employee temporarily to have children, or to one of your competitors?

There is a 'myth of pregnancy' in the minds of employers (Homans, 1987). The myth is that all women will leave to have babies and that wastage due to pregnancy is greater than for any other reason. The pervasiveness of this, and other myths, was shown by the way in which they influenced practices at selection in the NHS where, for example, only women were asked questions about marital status and dependent children (Homans, 1987). They also influenced notions of who could become a manager; women who are at risk of pregnancy should not be promoted. The reasoning for asking questions at interview about marital status and dependent children was that women with children may require extra time off for school holidays and children's illnesses, and that responsibility for childcare is a mother's problem and not a parental one. Further, it is in the 'best social interests' of the country that women who are mothers should not work.

Homans (1987) found that pregnancy did not emerge as the largest cause of wastage in the NHS. The most common reason was 'promotion and sideways move to another department' followed by 'change of career'. (Twice as many men as women left for promotion. The group of leavers with the shortest length of service were those who left for promotion or sideways moves; men were more likely to be early leavers than women.) Pregnancy was the next most common reason, although as Siltanen (1981) has suggested, data giving pregnancy as a cause of leaving work may be overrepresented and mask other reasons for leaving, e.g. intolerable working conditions or low pay. The leavers who were pregnant had spent the longest periods of time in the NHS before leaving.

The myths managers hold, however, remain. When it comes to women in management we should not be surprised to hear the results of a Management Centre Europe Survey in 1982 (quoted in Alban-Metcalfe, 1990) that found that fewer than half of managers (49 per cent) had ever employed a female manager. Of the remaining 51 per cent, 15 per cent stated that they would never promote a woman into management.

Yet working mothers value their jobs as much as fathers. Men and women are equally likely to want to carry on working when their children are born even if they do not need the money, a Mintel survey shows (*Personnel Today*, 10 August 1993: 4). Mothers are not less committed to their work and careers than fathers.

What about executive women: do the same assumptions hold? The common assumption does seem to be that married women executives with children will not have time to be committed to a job as well as a family. Yet of the 76 top women executives interviewed for the Morrison *et al.* (1987) study, only one in four was *unmarried* and over half had at least one child: 'The willingness to be mobile and to devote themselves to their company, despite cultural obligations to marry, have children, run a household, and so on, were applauded and noted as a factor in the success of a number of executive women' (p. 64).

Perhaps some women have given up the idea of having husbands and families in order to be successful. In the Alban-Metcalfe and West (1991) sample of women managers, a far greater proportion of women were single or divorced (29 and 10 per cent respectively versus 3 and 3 per cent for men). Of those female managers who were, or who had been married, nearly half of them were without children compared with just over one-tenth of the corresponding male sample. Family size of the female sample was significantly smaller that that of the males. Scase and Goffee (1990) also found that far fewer women managers were married than their male counterparts: 55 per cent compared with 93 per cent of the men. Of these women only four in ten had children. Powell (1988: 197) also notes that female managers are more likely to be single, separated, or divorced, and are less likely to have children than male managers.

It would appear that natural assumptions about women and their commitment to work are challenged by the research. If a woman is childless then it might be assumed that she would be more committed than a working mother. However, two decades ago it was found that working women without children were less committed to work than those with children (Fogarty *et al.*, 1971). As early as 1971 a majority of married women saw themselves as committed to work (Fuchs, 1971). There is a strong tie between high work commitment and family structure (the extent to which husbands and wives share household and family roles, with particular emphasis on how strong a part the father plays in the household). The longer women are married, the more committed to work they are (Haller and Rosenmayr, 1971). Despite the dependence of capitalism on married women as a permanent and essential part of the workforce, employers are still apt to behave as if they were doing women a favour by employing them. They still act as if women should somehow be grateful for the chance to be exploited (Rowbotham, 1973: 83–4).

We cannot think of men and women's career patterns in the same way. Powell and Mainiero (1992) argue that women's careers or work lives cannot be understood fully without simultaneous examination of their non-work lives. Women are influenced by cultural expectations, employment opportunities, marital demands, childbirth, and family concerns. At any one time women may place primary emphasis on careers and personal achievements at work, or on family and personal relationships outside work, or try to strike some kind of balance between the two (Goldsmith, 1989). What seems to matter most to women (and men) is whether they see themselves as successful on their own terms.

It might be argued that women are less committed to their careers and organizations because they have other responsibilities, but research also shows that females are more committed to their organizations than men (Angle and Perry, 1981). The explanation given is that women enjoy less inter-organizational mobility than men and therefore tend to become restricted.

Powell *et al.* (1985) also showed women managers to be more committed to their careers, as opposed to their family or home lives, than male managers with equivalent ages, salaries, education, and managerial levels. Women's work habits were more in line with organizational preferences—for example, they were significantly more likely to give up attending a home function which conflicted with an important job-related function and significantly less likely to turn down a promotion due to its effects on their lifestyles or doubts about their ability to handle the job. In other words, women tended to place more emphasis on success in their jobs even when it meant a sacrifice in their personal lives than did men.

The myth of lack of commitment may well come about because men do not want to accept women in management posts. In terms of job involvement, a survey of managers in Northern Ireland has shown that there are no differences in the job involvement of men and women at the same job level; but men are less predisposed to accept women as managers than are women (Cromie, 1981).

Women's roles are difficult despite the fact that many succeed in challenging careers. A review of the literature also shows that women's level of job commitment is strongly and negatively affected by sex-role conflict (Chusmir, 1982). Society in general, and family in particular, saddle the working woman with conflicting expectations and roles. The pressures dominate to such an extent that many women have had to give up work and sacrifice promising professional careers for family duties (Terborg, 1977). This same conflict is not to be found among working men. Hopfl (1992) argues that in terms of social regulation of organization, women are seen to constitute a threat because their commitment is problematic: they have difficulty in presenting themselves as full organizational members because they have a primary commitment to domestic life outside the organization.

When attitudes towards women working are not always favourable and women have a heavier burden of domestic duties, one might expect absenteeism levels to be higher. Scott and McClellan (1990) have shown that women were not found to exhibit significantly higher occurrences of absenteeism than men but did have more days off. Women averaged 3.92 occurrences compared to 3.29 for men. However, the duration of each of these was significantly higher for women. The mean number of days taken off by women is 6.92 in contrast to 4.83. This figure for women is related to the number of dependents they have. Women were more satisfied with their work and their job in general than men in the sample. Fifteen years ago, studies showed women in general (Biles and Pryatel, 1978) and women executives (Corporate Woman, 1979) to have lower job turnover rates than their male counterparts. A steadily diminishing number of women leave the workforce for marriage and children; even when they do leave, a majority return when their children reach school age.

British statistics show that more than 90 per cent of women whose first child was born in the late 1950s–early 1960s returned to work (Sparrow, 1990). Women are choosing to have a career and a family. In 1986 a survey by the UK magazine *Working Woman* showed that the majority of women questioned regarded a job as a lifetime career, and nearly half (40 per cent) saw job and career success as being a priority in life. A survey of UK managers found that 'there appears to be little foundation for the popular myth that women are less ambitious and career-oriented than men'.

A recent study of women pharmacists found that 95 per cent of women planning to take time out of work to have a child intended to return (Women in Management Association, 1989). A further study of the same occupation (Bevan *et al.*, 1990) found, however, that older women pharmacists who had taken career breaks showed a strong interest in career progression but that their ambition was not fully appreciated by their managers.

WOMEN, LABOUR TURNOVER, AND ABSENTEEISM

It is often assumed that due to family responisibilites women take more time off work and leave jobs more frequently than men. But absenteeism and turnover rates are seen by some as a function of a person's occupational level or other situational characteristics and have nothing to do with gender (Chusmir, 1982). It is the situation that causes the behaviour and so, given the same situation, men and women are likely to exhibit the same degree of turnover, absenteeism, and/or job commitment. But, as we have seen, women hold more lower level positions, and turnover and absenteeism rates tend to be higher in lower level jobs.

Where higher rates of turnover have been found among, for example, women accountants, the major cause of the turnover has been the perception of limited chances for promotion and advancement (Barcelona *et al.*, 1975a; Jancura, 1974; Knapp, 1980) and discrimination in favour of men (Barcelona *et al.*, 1975b). Research has also shown how female accountancy students anticipate promotional discrimination (Lambert and Lambert, 1974).

WOMEN AND RETIREMENT

Most accept that the retirement age for men is 65 while for women it is 60. However, this does not always suit women. The Sex Discrimination Act allows for the equal treatment of women in this respect. A case arose where 16 women working for British Gas were all retired at the age of 60 in 1986 while the men were allowed to stay on to 65. The women took their case to court and won more than £800 000 in compensation (*Personnel Today*, 25 January, 1994: 2). The age of retirement is, then, yet another issue of equality of opportunity that companies need to take seriously.

WHAT CAN BE CONCLUDED ABOUT WOMEN'S COMMITMENT TO WORK?

Women managers achieve equivalent status to men 'by being better qualified, more ambitious and more mobile' (Alban-Metcalfe and Nicholson, 1984: 41). Scase and Goffee (1990) report that while male managers in their survey assessed themselves as less ambitious in their jobs, female managers rated themselves as more ambitious. While only 18 per cent of male managers ranked career achievements as the most important source of satisfaction in their lives, this was the case for no fewer than 30 per cent of women. Female managers thus appear, if anything, to be more ambitious and committed to their careers than many men (Alban-Metcalfe, 1989).

Combining family life with a career provides a set of hurdles over which women have to jump. Women managers may be better able to afford the cost of childcare but are still affected by the lack of adequate childcare in the UK, the problems of covering long and erratic hours of work, and the perception that they have stepped off the career ladder if they take a significant career break. Some may choose a management career once they have raised their children but management careers are not at present open to such late entrants (Hirsh and Jackson, 1989).

Provision of childcare facilities in the workplace seems to be important. This is born out from examples from both Russia and America where nursery provision in one case and tax concessions on childcare expenses on the other have made a significant difference in helping women maintain career jobs (see Dex and Shaw, 1986). Dex and Shaw reported that 57 per cent of women in the United States were returning to work soon after childbirth as opposed to 30 per cent of British mothers. This British trend is now improving, however, so that nearly half (45 per cent) of women return to work within eight or nine months of having a baby and nearly two-thirds are economically active (McRae, 1991). What, then, can be done to help women overcome the barriers created by the myths?

Having looked at some of the myths which prevent women's progress at work, let us now look at one way in which women can be helped over the hurdles placed in their way.

MENTORING

We noted earlier how a mentor or sponsor can help lead to success in a career. Mentoring implies a relationship between a younger adult and an older, more experienced adult who supports, guides, and counsels the younger person as she or he becomes integrated into the world of work. Mentoring can either be part of the formal policy of the organization or be informal, a private arrangement between two people. Mentoring can happen, for example, in an educational context, as a one-to-one learning relationship. In the last 15 years dozens of colleges and universities in America have implemented mentoring programmes for undergraduates. It is thought that mentoring can improve students' levels of academic achievement, assist students at risk of dropping out to graduate, feed the pipeline to graduate schools and the professoriate, and humanize large and impersonal institutions. But Jacobi (1991) argues that the concept of mentoring remains unclear and imprecise and the effectiveness of mentoring in promoting academic success is assumed rather than demonstrated.

In a work context, a mentor could provide information, advice, and support. American research has shown that mentorship is related to career progress, organizational influence, and advancement in organizations (Burke, 1984; Fagenson, 1989; Scandura, 1992). Burke (1984) reports that, generally, the mentoring experience is a positive one and may well have a place in the successful implementation of affirmative action programmes.

In the UK the pace of growth of mentoring increased in the mid to late 1980s. A late 1989 survey (reported in Clutterbuck, 1991: 8) showed that of 145 organizations, 44 had mentoring programmes. Not all UK programmes were a success but mentoring can hold considerable benefits for both the mentor and the protégé. Mentoring can help protégés find their feet more quickly and establish a clear sense of career direction and purpose. It often rejuvenates the mentor and may advance their career too.

In the US Zey (1984) looked at how a mentor could affect people's careers, their chances of success, and could enhance the quality of their work life by interviewing managers in large and small corporations over a two-year period. A mentor can increase the protégé's exposure to lines of power, through teaching, personal support, intervention, and promotional activities; all this can affect the protégé's career.

Fagenson's (1988) study of power found that those individuals with mentors had more power than those without. A British study by Arnold and Davidson (1990) confirms this: the majority of male and female managers in this in-depth study found that their mentors were important for introducing them to the formal network of power relations in the organization in which they worked. Fagenson (1989) found people who were mentored reported higher levels of satisfaction, career mobility, and a higher rate of promotion than those not mentored, regardless of their sex or level. British research on mentoring also includes Clutterbuck and Devine (1987).

Dreher and Ash (1990) found business school graduates with extensive mentorship relations reported more promotions, higher income and benefits satisfaction than their counterparts with less extensive experience with mentors. Kaufmann (1986) has found that having a mentor tends to equalize the earning power of men and women. Finally Whitley *et al.* (1991) found career mentoring practices to be significantly related to financial compensation and number of promotions.

Kram (1983) identified two mentor functions from in-depth interviews with

15 managers: career-related and psychosocial functions. Career-related functions included providing sponsorship, exposure, visibility, coaching, protection, and challenging assignments—all of which can help career advancement. Psychosocial functions included providing role modelling, acceptance, confirmation, counselling, and friendship which influence the individual's self-image and competence.

Discussion point

How many mentoring relationships have you witnessed. What results did you see? Could you set up a research project to look at mentoring? If you could, what problems might you anticipate?

Male or female mentors can buffer women from discrimination and help them advance. A female mentor can help women's identification with female models and give a positive incentive through illustrative success. But other research contends that women face more barriers to obtaining a mentor than men (Kram, 1985; Ragins, 1989; Ragins and Cotton, 1991) and so do not receive as much mentoring as men. There is a paucity of women in positions of power to serve as mentors. One example of this can be found in the case of professional psychologists (Bogat and Redner, 1985).

Women may be reluctant to initiate a relationship with a man as a mentor for fear that the mentor or others will, for example, misconstrue such an approach as a sexual advance (Bowen, 1985). Clutterbuck (1991) notes how male/female mentoring poses special problems of gossip and personal behaviour. Men may perceive mentoring women as complicated. Role expectations encourage men to take aggressive roles; women are passive in initiating relationships, and may therefore fear doing this. Also women have fewer informal and formal opportunities than men for developing mentoring relationships with men. An example of the informal is that they do not go to men's clubs or participate in sport with male groups.

Some research shows that a woman having a mentor can be a disadvantage. Dependency, fear of not meeting the mentor's expectations, and ending the mentoring relationship are all problems more commonly encountered by female than male managers (Arnold and Davidson, 1990). Baum (1992) warns of the unconscious fantastic meanings that can be brought to the relationship and the potentially subversive nature of the relationship. The manager is advised to allow protégé and mentor the time and space to initiate and work through a passionate relationship that may develop and interfere with work.

Further, the women protégé runs the risk of being seen as needing assistance, as requiring help. Male mentors describe their male protégés as having a long-term commitment to their careers. They describe their female protégés as needing help to get on (Paludi, 1987). Some women in White *et al.*'s (1992) study of successful women managers felt that having a mentor was a sign of weakness as the relationship was inherently one of dependency on the part of the protégé.

Similar results are reported by LaFrance (1987). As women get the mentoring they need, they will be seen as needing that mentoring. Bronstein *et al.* (1986) found that male mentors, in their letters of recommendations of female protégés for faculty positions, described the woman's family responsibilities as a burden. For men a family life was presented as an asset. None of the female protégés mentioned families in their CV; male mentors mentioned it. Women just do not win! What other attitudes exist which mitigate against equal opportunities?

MEN AND WOMEN AT HOME

Women's sexuality is always significant for men. The way women do or do not fit into the schema of paid employment and organizational life is linked to their marital status and whether or not they have children. 'This is what women are to most men (and to most women): people who have domestic ties. Even if the woman in question is celibate or childless she is seen and represented as one of the maternal sex' (Cockburn, 1991: 76). The practice of having women raise children, keep house, and have less economic independence of their husbands is of great advantage to men. A woman's domestic identity constitutes her as a disadvantaged worker, while being a low earner and subject to male authority at work diminishes her standing in the family.

Some men may want to have women at home and not working. There are great advantages to be reaped if men can have women at home. The average man, due to women's work at home, has more leisure time; most men have wives, mothers, or daughters who cook, clean, and look after their clothing for them. Men might have an interest in keeping women at home, but if the wife works and maintains her domestic commitment, then he can witness the best of both worlds.

The proportion of men who state that if they had a choice, they would prefer their spouses to have paid work, has gradually increased. In 1975 in the nine EC countries 33 per cent of married or cohabiting men surveyed said they would prefer their spouses to have paid work. By 1983 the proportion had risen to 39 per cent and by 1987 to 47 per cent. The younger the men, the more educated, and higher the family income, the more likely the men were to favour their wives working. However, the men with working wives are not universally positive about the situation. In the 1987 survey only 70 per cent of the men with working wives were in favour of the situation (*Employment Gazette*, October 1982: 494).

The notion of 'the family' consisting of a husband, wife, and children, where the wife and children are financially dependent on the husband, has taken on almost mythical status. Charles (1993: 67) argues that the reality is that most households do not conform to this ideal type of family and have never done so.

Within British society only 29 per cent of households actually contain a man, a dependent woman, and dependent children (Henwood *et al.*, 1987). If households do conform to this ideal type, it is usually only for a few years when children are very young (Charles and Kerr, 1988).

How do men and women view roles of homemaker and breadwinner? In 1987 a survey of 12 European countries asked men and women to state which of the following three arrangements corresponded most closely to their idea of a family:

■ A family in which both husband and wife have equally absorbing work, and in which the household tasks and looking after the children are shared equally between husband and wife (*egalitarian option*).

■ A family in which the wife's work is less absorbing that the husband's, and in which she takes on more of the household tasks and looking after the children (*middle option*).

■ A family in which the husband only works and the wife runs the home (*homemaker and breadwinner option*).

Support for the traditional roles of homemaker and breadwinner was least: only 25 per cent of respondents stated that this arrangement corresponded most closely to their idea of a family. Forty-one per cent supported an egalitarian division of labour and 29 per cent supported the middle option. (The remainder supported no option or did not answer the question.) The difference in the proportion of men and women favouring the egalitarian model was small: 39 per cent of men as compared with 42 per cent of women. The younger the men or women, the more likely they were to prefer this model (*Employment Gazette*, October 1992: 495). Denmark was top of the league in supporting the egalitarian model.

Is there a relationship between espoused attitudes and preferences and actual behaviour? Is behaviour in the domestic domain becoming more equal? A 1990 Eurobarometer survey asked 'Who usually took care of the following tasks during your first child's pre-school years, you or your partner?' Across all the countries among men living with a woman in a couple the tasks that men were more likely to take responsibility for were shopping (61 per cent), washing up (41 per cent), and taking children to and from nursery school or childminder (31 per cent). The least popular activities were dressing children (26 per cent), cooking (25 per cent), and cleaning (25 per cent). But the picture is bleaker than it appears. These quantities refer to men who actually did at least one of these activities, but only 40 per cent of men took care of any one of these tasks. Dutch and Danish men were most likely to be involved (1 in 2) and Spanish men least likely (1 in 5) (*Employment Gazette*, October 1992: 497).

The Danish are the most egalitarian and yet in families with dependent children it was found that men were mostly taking responsibility for traditional tasks such as indoor repair jobs. Women in about half the families were solely responsible for cooking and cleaning the house, and in only a third of families did husbands and wives share tasks. Yet this is a society where the great majority of women are economically active.

If men and women are working full time one might anticipate that household tasks would be shared. But in a British survey women were responsible for general domestic duties in 72 per cent of households; in only 22 per cent were they shared. Where neither worked, in 76 per cent women were mainly responsible and in 15 per cent domestic duties were shared equally (Witherspoon, British Social Attitudes Survey, SCPR, 1988).

All available evidence, from Australia, the United States and Britain, shows that women's movement into paid employment does not lead to a reorganization of domestic responsibilities (Berk, 1980; Harper and Richards, 1986; Sharpe, 1984). In North America, for example, men whose wives work, spend about ten minutes more a day on housework than men whose wives stay at home (Cowan, 1989: 200). Consequently women who undertake both paid work and unpaid domestic work are likely to have less time available for overtime, further education, retraining programmes, or other activities that might improve their position and lead to promotion.

Women in the household are largely responsible for cooking, cleaning, shopping, washing, and ironing, while men's domestic tasks consist of repairs (Henwood et al., 1987). Most women seem happy with this state of affairs (Martin and Roberts, 1984) as only 20 per cent of women in a British survey thought their partners should do more around the house. Men, on becoming unemployed, do not take on more housework (Pahl, 1984).

The unwillingness of men to be seen to be doing 'women's work', in this case housework, has its amusing angle. Here is a quote from a woman interviewee who had asked her husband to 'get the vac out and run it round the floor' while she washed dishes.

> So I was in the kitchen and I dashed in and he was on his knees, pushing the vacuum cleaner round himself, and I said, 'What are you doing?' He said, 'I'm doing it so nobody sees me through the window ... ' He was actually on his knees turning round in circles. ... And something else, he won't go out and get washing off the clothes line—it's really funny—in case somebody saw him doing it! (Sharpe, 1984: 181–2)

Women also have a disproportional share of childcare. An in-depth survey by Newell (1992) of mothers with young children shows that not only did the

---

How much do you know about women in public life?

1. The number of women Members of Parliament virtually doubled in the 1987 general election and increased again after the election in 1992. What percentage of MPs are women now?

        9 per cent   15 per cent   23 per cent   41 per cent

2. By the beginning of 1994 there were 176 appointees made to the House of Commons Select Committees. How many were women?

        87   40   22

3. Among the top levels of the police force in December 1991 there were 105 Deputy Chief Constables and Chief Constables. How many were women?

        0   10   37   89

4. In England and Wales women constitute just under four-fifths of full-time nursery and primary school teachers and just under half of all secondary school teachers. What percentage of women teachers are head teachers in secondary schools?

        20   45   60

The answer is the smallest figure each time.

Source: *Women and Men in Britain*, Equal Opportunities Commission, Manchester, 1993.

majority of women undertake a greater proportion of childcare than their partner, irrespective of whether they worked full time, part time or not, but a majority felt that the partners should have more responsibility. The deep-seated traditional attitudes about a woman's mothering role are still pervasive. It is not too surprising, then, that in a 1990 Eurobarometer survey about 8 out of 10 women and 4 out of 10 men said they would prefer not to work full time when their children were under school age.

    In Sweden new fathers are entitled to parental leave but only one in five fathers uses this leave and those who do take, on average, only 41 days to care for their baby (Svenska Institutet, 1987). In Norway men reduced their working week by five hours, but increased their household work by only 12 minutes a day: the rest became increased leisure time (Lingsom and Ellingsaeter, 1983).

    What we have here is not just a shapeless heap of data but a description of a social structure, an organized field of human practice and social relations (Connell, 1987). Men and women's personal lives and collective social arrangements are linked in a fundamental and constitutive way. The practice of work does not float free but must respond to and is constrained by the circumstances which those structures constitute. The myths will prevail despite the counter-evidence. One of the consequences of the myths is that there is a lack of confidence in women being able to do the same job as men.

CONFIDENCE IN WOMEN?

If you were on an aeroplane and nervous of flying, how would you feel if you heard the captain speak to the passengers and realize the captain was a woman? People to do not have the same confidence in men and women to carry out their roles in some occupations. A European survey enquired about the confidence placed in men and women carrying out a number of jobs. The results show that the UK has a less egalitarian attitude than a number of other EC countries, but other countries produce even lower averages. Italy and Ireland are 'the sexists of Europe' (*Independent*, 8 October 1992).

Confidence in both sexes for jobs

	Bus or train driver	Surgeon	Barrister	MP	
Denmark	86	85	82	86	84
Netherlands	75	83	75	79	78
France	77	70	70	68	70
UK	61	70	66	75	68
Italy	54	56	55	59	56
Ireland	43	51	50	61	51

Figures are percentages; average of four jobs.

Source: *Men and Women in Europe, 1987 Women of Europe*, Supplement No. 2, Commission of the European Communities, 1989. Adapted from 'Irish and Italians are the Sexists of Europe', *Independent*, 8 October 1992.

These kinds of negative attitudes can lead to staff wastage. The Royal Society of Chemistry, concerned that women may be leaving the profession early, surveyed 1405 women and 1211 men and found that one-third of female chemists had experienced sex discrimination at work. One-quarter had encountered sexual harassment.

Many women managers feel that their male colleagues create stress for them and seem to be threatened by them (Davidson and Cooper, 1992: 105). There is a 'masculine consciousness' (Larwood and Wood, 1979) which feels threatened

The fire brigade as a male preserve

In 1993 there were 39,412 firefighters in Britain but only 116 of them were women.* Eight out of ten women are presently excluded from the fire service as they are not 5 ft 6 in tall. But sexual harassment may be dissuading women from applying for jobs. An investigation by the Home Office revealed incidents in which women were subjected to abuse including being referred to as 'firetarts', forced to look at pornography and having their hair forcibly cut by male colleagues. In one case a bucket of urine was thrown over a woman officer. The women also suffered unwanted attentions of men on night watches. Lone women fire officers frequently have to share a station with up to 50 male colleagues, often with no private sleeping area or washing facilities.

*Source: Annual Report of the Equal Opportunities Joint Committee of the Central Fire Brigades Advisory Councils, London, September 1993.

and so men often exclude women from their social interactions. Some men feel particularly threatened because they see their organizations increasingly promoting a few women as 'tokens' (Powell, 1988). They are particularly distressed about a 'less competent' woman achieving success over them (Davidson, 1985).

You might assume that as the proportion of women increases in an organization, the sex bias and 'threatened male colleague syndrome' decreases. But Harlan and Weiss (1980) have shown that while there is a high resistance by male managers to the first women in the company and a rapid decrease in resistance as the proportion of women managers rises by about 10–15 per cent, there is a rapid

Personal experience

Debbie has been a London cabbie for two years. Sometimes she is told to go home and do her old man's dishes. When that happens she takes out her make-up bag, tilts forward the rear view mirror of her black cab and starts applying her lipstick. She faces hostility from male drivers who call her 'a dyke' for daring to enter their territory. 'They find it hard to accept women. It's been a man's world for a long time.' Fewer than 1 per cent of London's 20 000 drivers are women. In Birmingham there are two women in a city of 13 000 black cab drivers.

Source: adapted from a story in *The Guardian*, 29 August 1991. © *The Guardian*, 1991.

increase again in resistance when this proportion becomes large enough to become powerful and threatening. Davidson suggests that it may be the more ambitious or achievement-orientated male executives who feel the most threatened by women due to affirmative action (in the United States) or equal opportunities legislation and company policy. What explanations can be put forward to say why this situation exists?

THE EXPLANATIONS OF INEQUALITY

One explanation might be that equality of opportunity goes unnoticed by decision makers, or is not an issue of concern, and is therefore not acted upon. Douglas (1987) argues persuasively that thinking is socially ordered. Organizations constrain our thinking because in the structural and procedural fabric they weave it simply becomes easier to remember some things and forget (or never think about) other things. Certain thoughts and the conceptualizations necessary to sustain them are well integrated into organizational tasks, procedures and values; others are not. People do not notice or act upon inequality as it remains hidden from their thoughts.

We saw earlier how women do not progress in banking and insurance industries because they lack formal qualifications and have broken employment patterns. There are less subtle ways in which women can be dissuaded from progressing in an organization. Crompton and Jones (1984: 145) reported having researched careers among staff at a major clearing bank, that 'young women were actively discouraged from taking bank examinations—which ... were regarded as virtually automatic for young male recruits'. Of the women interviewed, 46 per cent said they had been actively dissuaded from taking the Institute of Bankers exams. Men were encouraged to progress and women were not.

The possibility of career progress from junior to senior jobs for the male career was premised on the fact that large amounts of routine work were carried out by women who were not eligible for promotion, so allowing the prospects of these men in routine jobs to be enhanced (Crompton, 1986; Crompton and Jones, 1984). Most organizations operate a strictly gendered grading system in which women and men are recruited into different grades of employment with different salary scales and promotion prospects. Women who are recruited into the lower levels within occupational categories are likely to stay there.

A set of rules within an organization's bureaucracy control the recruitment, appraisal and promotion of staff. The rationality of bureaucracies is presented by Max Weber as gender neutral. Weber's ideal type of bureaucracy stressed the need for expertise, hierarchical structure, interchangeability of personnel, records, job security and organizational rationality. Some argue, however, that bureaucracies have a male orientation and bias (Ferguson, 1984). It is men who dominate and make the rules. As Barbara Reskin (1988: 73–74) says: 'Like other dominant groups, men make rules that preserve their privileges.' Pringle agrees (1989: 161), saying that there is in fact a new patriarchal structure where 'The apparent neutrality of rules and goals disguises the class and gender interests served by men.' The rules work similarly for primary school teachers who cannot easily become secondary school teachers, physiotherapists who cannot be quickly transformed into orthopaedic surgeons.

A good example of how the rules work in the favour of men can be seen in the way in which skill is divided along lines of gender. Men are classed as skilled as tradesmen—joiners, bricklayers, electricians—and are much more likely than women to have received training (Martin and Roberts, 1984). Women's work is more likely to be labelled unskilled. Moreover men have been able to protect their skill status and ensure their skills are recognised and rewarded (Cockburn, 1985). The two sets of women's skills utilized frequently in employment are caring—used in nursing, nursery work, childminding, and so on—and dexterity needed, for example, in electrical assembly work. These are seen as innate and natural to women, are not labelled skills and so are not recognised or rewarded.

The 'rules' of organizations mitigate against women. Females adapt and react in the context of male-oriented organizational value-systems (Clegg, 1981; Morgan, 1986). Organizations reflect 'extra-organizational rules' about the social worth of women (and of non-whites and the disabled) in ways that reproduce and maintain those values. As a result organizations often segment opportunity structures and job markets in ways which enable men to achieve positions of power and prestige more easily than women, and the subsequent reality is maintained on a day-to-day basis. 'The way organizational realities come to be structured and maintained also has profound implications for the way we come to view ourselves, for our identity, for our sense of self' (Mills and Murgatroyd, 1991). The sense of self is mediated through a set of master rules (Mills, 1988) that differs not just individually but according to what class of person you have been designated. Any consideration of organizational life must, then, centrally come to terms with the dynamics of gender (Clegg, 1981; Leonard, 1984; Mills, 1988).

Stereotyping of men and women is one of the social processes taking place of which we seem to have little awareness. Women are seen as different and are often evaluated less favourably than men. As we have so little awareness of the extent to which sex stereotypes influence our evaluations of others, we have little opportunity to disconfirm these beliefs because they are both unrecognized and universally shared. (Stereotyping is discussed in Chapter 2).

These sex biases can even influence comprehension and memory (Hamilton and Henley, 1982). In a study by Crawford and English (1984) women's recall of essays 48 hours later was worse when the essays were written with masculine generics (using, for example, 'he' to mean 'he/she') than when written with unbiased grammatical forms. This effect was stronger for good learners than for poor ones and occurred despite the fact that participants did not notice which pronouns had been used. If we allow this invisibility of gender to continue, the stereotyping will continue with the accompanying inequality.

To make equality visible and an integral part of the fabric of the organization requires a change in the perception and awareness of individuals in these issues, a fundamental change in the values, attitudes and procedures. There also needs to be a monitoring of employment practices. In the case of implementing equality of opportunity in an organization, this would mean that information would be required on what the present situation was, what information should be monitored, what could be done to implement change and ensuring change happened. This rarely happens as those with the power to change the visibility of the issue have no interest in doing so. As a result fewer than half of women employees in the SCIACE (1990) survey believed there were equal opportunities.

The case of Lloyds Bank

Lloyds Bank employs about 50 000 people in the United Kingdom. Sixty-two per cent of these are women. The proportion of women in management has been steadily rising since 1986, so that by the end of 1991 19 per cent of assistant managers were female and 7.5 per cent of managers. Fifty per cent of graduate intake is female.

To help men and women combine family commitments with work Lloyds has introduced flexible working arrangements which include career breaks. The Careerbreak scheme is open to men and women with five years' service and 'good performance'. This allows staff to stop work for up to five years then return to a job in the same grade.

Reduced hours working is also available to parents. In 1988 Lloyds were the first bank to introduce reduced hours workers to the pension fund. Mortgages and pro rata benefits followed. The bank also have term-time only working and job sharing (*Lloyds Bank News*, May 1992: 8,9).

These have been the efforts of one organization. What do you think the problems might be? What else could Lloyds do?

There is a large amount of underachievement in women's early choices of employment as related to their academic achievement (Dex, 1987). Professional women deter themselves from seeking out senior positions. Women do not always apply for senior posts for which their ability and experience would qualify them. In one survey it was found that there was, on average, one female applicant for every 68 male applicants for posts as head teachers in secondary schools, but the success rates of female candidates was higher (Brown, 1990). When Kettering Health Authority advertised for a general manger recently there were 80 applicants but none of them were women. No women had applied for managerial posts in West Midlands, Yorkshire, or Northern Regions, yet women represent 79 per cent of the NHS workforce (*British Medical Journal*, 1992). What deters women from applying for senior posts in the NHS?

Alban-Metcalfe (*Guardian*, 1992), having studied the assessment of 1600 NHS managers, found that although women appeared to be as capable, they were perceived by their male assessors as less efficient because their methods were different. Instead of relying on rewards or punishments, women succeeded by motivating staff. However, of 170 general managers, 27 per cent were on a top performance-related pay scale but only 13 per cent of women managers. Only 1 per cent of consultant general surgeons are women. There are two reasons for this, according to Allen (1988). The first is that surgery is thought to need a full-time commitment, which women either cannot or do not want to give. The second is that male surgeons are prejudiced against female doctors.

Negative attitudes deter women. There are restrictive attitudes towards women striving for senior positions (Burnhill and McPherson, 1984; SIACE, 1990). Remarks are made to demean ambitious women and to foster guilt.

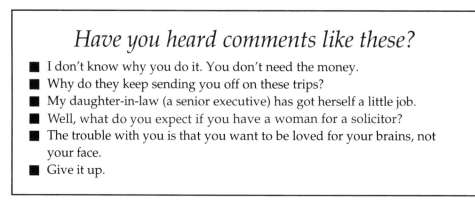

Have you heard comments like these?

- I don't know why you do it. You don't need the money.
- Why do they keep sending you off on these trips?
- My daughter-in-law (a senior executive) has got herself a little job.
- Well, what do you expect if you have a woman for a solicitor?
- The trouble with you is that you want to be loved for your brains, not your face.
- Give it up.

Source: from Brown (1990).

A study looking at the career goals and employment experiences of young doctors recently trained in general practice (Osler, 1991) found that female doctors, particularly the married women with children, were significantly less likely than their male contemporaries to be doing the job they had hoped for. Men were more likely to have obtained posts as principals. The difference in results could not be attributed to lack of commitment as few (only 6 per cent) of the women had stopped work even temporarily either because of marriage or to care for young children. One explanation is that married women accepted jobs more readily than their contemporaries; many women had been tied geographically by their husband's jobs.

We have looked at the experiences of the employee but what of the attitudes and practices of employers. Can they be shown to be discriminatory? A study focusing on the north-east of England, on recruitment to fill 101 job vacancies in retail sales and clerical work, showed that the 'personal qualities' (e.g. common sense, confidence, liveliness) of the candidate were the most important factors (Curran, 1988). 'Personal qualities' are not amenable to precise measurement and are entirely dependent of the subjective judgement of the interviewer.

Almost half of the employers in the survey indicated that gender was a significant element in their requirements and preferences. Fourteen per cent wanted to appoint men, while 33 per cent wanted to appoint women. About half of those who wanted to appoint women identified the job as a 'woman's job' as the job was of low status, unworthy of a man, and therefore suitable for a women. A number of respondents regarded women as having particular aptitudes for meticulous (and probably boring) clerical work and as having 'feminine skills' of gentle persuasion, physical attractiveness or in fostering a co-operative and non-threatening atmosphere.

In a study of promotional discrimination among 625 women and 512 men in a large Australian bureaucracy, Snizek and Neil (1992) found that a greater proportion of men than women adhered to gender stereotypes; these stereotypes were found to be centred around domestic roles, and not abilities. Further, when women work primarily with other women, or when women have men reporting to them, day-to-day discrimination is minimal. By contrast, women who occupy jobs and job ladders where power and money are at stake often find themselves the target of promotional discrimination by men.

Some might also argue that individuals have a social identity which maintains the status quo of inequality. Salaman (1986) details the effects of organizational structure on behaviour attributions and social identity. People occupy particular places in organizations and interactions with others are con-strained. There are ingroups and outgroups; people exhibit strong ingroup prefer-ences as a strategy for maintaining a strong group identity. He argues that there is a degree of consciousness in interest groups, a consciousness of separate and opposed interests, but not associated with a preparedness to act.

Examples of how professional groups, as interest groups, can protect their male dominance and male orientation can be found in medicine (Elston, 1980; Lawrence, 1987; Lorber, 1975; Witz, 1986), management (Legge, 1987; Kanter, 1975), the civil service (Walters, 1987), insurance (Collinson and Knights, 1986), television (Coyle, 1988), teaching (Al-Khalifa, 1988), and law (Podmore and Spencer, 1986).

If law is that which parliament and the courts say is law, then the membership of these decision-making bodies is crucial. Women are significantly underrepresented in both the judiciary and parliament. Women constitute 3.8 per cent of judges on the court of appeal, 4.8 per cent of judges in the high court and 4.9 per cent of circuit judges (Martin, 1993).

In law women are pushed to the margins of the profession; the marginalization is accomplished by a more or less conscious and explicit set of assumptions held by the dominant male sector of the profession about the nature of the profession and what women are like. The profession is seen as 'a man's game' (Spencer and Podmore, 1987) where the rules are man-made. It is, for example, perceived by men to be aggressive, objective, logical and pragmatic, and women do not have the right qualities for this; the men accept prejudice against women in the profession as a fact of life and a women's problem, not men's. Women too can assign negative values to the traits of female lawyers (see Marshall and Wetherall, 1989). For example women lawyers thought they would have to overcome feminine traits to become successful lawyers. Women solicitors have a high drop-out rate with over one-third having ceased practising after 10 years compared to only 12 per cent of men, despite the fact that in the late 1980s more women than men passed the final solicitors' exams and received higher-class degrees than men (Hansard Society, 1990).

Cockburn's (1983) study of the changes in printing chapels showed how these served to organize and maintain male power. Similarly Baron (1987) showed how gender and skill were constructed in the US print industry. Walby (1984) showed how sexual segregation in the cotton textiles, engineering industries, and in clerical work came about through patriarchal workplace organization and union strategies.

Through detailed case-study evidence from 45 private-sector organizations, concerning recruitment and promotion practices, Collinson et al. (1990) showed how a substantial number of employers are still 'managing to discriminate' on the grounds of sex though a variety of recruitment practices. One example of how this occurred was through manager's preconceptions about the domestic responsibilities of both sexes. Men's domestic responsibilities, whether real or imagined, were elevated as indicating stability, flexibility, compatibility, and motivation, while for women they were often viewed negatively as confirmation of unreliability and a short-term investment in work. Earlier Collinson (1987) had shown how selection and promotion decision disadvantaged women in the early stages of their careers. Examples raised included the allocation of jobs, closed promotion systems where jobs are not advertised internally, and, as we saw above, assumptions being made by personnel and line managers about women's career intentions and mobility.

Morgan and Knights (1991) have shown the rationale male managers use in the insurance industry to demonstrate why women do not make good sales representatives. The reasons included the fact that representatives have to travel by themselves at night to visit prospective clients; the job is lonely and there are 'bad patches' where women will be less resilient to the pressure; there is an *esprit de corps*, based on a shared male gender identity, which women would disrupt; women would be too sympathetic to the client and be inclined to settle for lower premiums. There was, then, no real position in which a woman could fit comfortably within the ethos and culture of the sales force.

Where there is an infiltration of people perceived as atypical into jobs, strong resistance will occur. Resistance can take the form of stories, gossip, rumour, anecdote, explanation, the construction of facts, theories, and moralities. Since gender is so prevalent both horizontally and vertically, subgroup formation will occur along gender lines. The concept of social identity is therefore very useful in helping us understand why formal attempts to improve opportunities fail. Perhaps we should do as Morgan (1988: 1) suggested and stop explaining the phenomenon of what women lack to be equal to men and try instead to understand how men have resisted the idea of sharing their privileges.

Witz (1986) has described two strategies of how the process of women's subordination in professions occurs—through the patriarchal strategies of closure and of demarcation. Closure strategies are primarily concerned with control over the group's own labour, while demarcation strategies relate to aspects of control that extend beyond the sphere of control of its own labour and touch upon related labour or occupations. She illustrates how, prior to the professionalization of medicine, the arts of healing were practised throughout history mainly by women. The emergence of professional control over medical practice between the 16th and 19th centuries brought about the demise of female medical practice. The witch hunts were one of the means whereby the female monopoly over healing was broken. The 1858 Medical Act effectively placed the exclusive right to legitimate medical practice in the hands of men as it legitimated only one route to medical knowledge, namely formal university education: women were excluded from university medical schools. One branch of medicine that did not achieve professional closure was midwifery, but later midwifery was fragmented so that certain aspects were incorporated into obstetrics and medical assistance was needed for abnormal labour; the midwife's sphere of competence was narrowed and strictly bounded.

Professions such as medicine maintain and develop patriachy. The semi-professions in medicine, such as radiography and midwifery, have a much more limited area of interest and act as 'handmaidens' to the profession in performing specific duties (Hearn, 1982). Women have not, however, acquiesced in the face of patriarchal practices but contested them, engaging in professional projects, attempting to be mistresses of their own fates rather than handmaidens to male professions (Witz, 1990).

It is in the interests of some groups to exclude the possibility of equal opportunity. Jobs can be segmented into two sorts: primary and secondary. Primary jobs are secure, well paid with pleasant conditions. Secondary jobs are poorly paid, done under arduous conditions and are insecure, often casual or part time. This segmentation may divide the workforce and create differences of attitudes and consciousness. This effect will be enormously enhanced if added to divisions which already exist, created by differences in gender, age, or ethnicity.

The demarcations can benefit those incumbents of primary sector jobs who are able to secure and retain advantage. As we have seen and Rubery (1978) has noted, workers will organize to control entry into an occupation, firm, or industry. Such control must be to the detriment of groups excluded from the organized sector as it reduces their mobility and could increase competition in the external labour market. Defence is, then, very important. It is easy, under these circumstances to argue that unequal distributions of power are due to lack of ability, motivation, or experience of people in the underrepresented groups. Alternatively it might be argued that equal opportunities already exist and therefore nothing needs to be done and if they hold the power, it is most unlikely that anything will be done. Women themselves might belong to these groups. People who disagree will be labelled trouble-makers, malcontents, extremists.

Should women 'by some relentless and wholly undesirable process come to dominate a field of employment, a profession or an occupation, the patriarchal relations of the external world come into play. The whole field is rapidly devalued relative to male fields' (Cockburn, 1991). When women have power within an occupation you can bet it is because that occupation has yet to attain power or (as is the case with personnel management) is losing ground within the organization or in the eyes of society (Legge , 1987).

Labour cannot be taken, then, as a genderless category. Male and female labour have had differing power and access to occupations. Female labour is both viewed differently and used differently by employers and managers. Different control strategies are deemed appropriate for use with male and female labour, different patterns of hierarchical and authority relations are developed, skills have a male monopoly, and technology is deployed differently (Bradley, 1986).

It is not just in employment that women seem to experience unequal treatment. It happens within the system of justice too. 'If prisons are places for dealing with serious and violent crimes', noted Helena Kennedy (*Independent*, 11 October 1992), ' . . . then most women in British prisons should not be there. Yet the overwhelming majority of women in prison are serving short "teach her a lesson" sentences for crimes of dishonesty.' Of the total prison population of 44 865 just 1607 are women. Of these only 21 per cent have been sentenced for violence, sex and drug offences. Dishonesty (such as shoplifting and cheque card frauds), criminal damage and non-payment of fines account for the rest. Women whose children are in care, who are divorced or separated, who do not fulfil expectations of women as wives, daughters, and mothers, encounter unmatched prejudice.

Women's work experience is very different to that of men but their orientations to work have much in common with men. When women and men are compared in similar situations what is notable is the similarity of response (Dex,

1988). The differences are probably explainable in terms of differing circumstances. If some men were put in the position of being segregated into secondary jobs, made responsible for childcare, then their attitudes might also vary from those of other men.

If we stop taking the male-as-norm view and look at the world of employment from the point of view of women workers, it is clear that the whole pattern of employment needs to be fundamentally reconsidered. Women's work is quite different to men's. Brown (1976) reviewed textbooks on the sociology of industry and found that in only one was there an adequate recognition and discussion of the distinctive characteristics of the situation of women as employees. Occupations studied were often wholly 'woman-free', or employees were treated as if their gender was irrelevant. Alternatively women employees were treated as problems. There was a need for an explicit consideration of when and how latent social identities of employees are of consequence in the industrial situation. We need to understand latent social identities—i.e. identities which are not culturally prescribed as relevant to or within rational organizations—and how they intrude upon and influence organizational behaviour. The relationship between structure and consciousness is a key issue and crucial for the understanding of the position of women as employees.

Women still have primary responsibility for children. Being a conscientious worker and conscientious parent should not be viewed as competing options from which people should chose; it ought to be possible to be both. For this to happen there needs to be a much greater degree of flexibility in patterns of work and the pejorative attitude to part-time work and part-time workers must change (Epstein *et al.*, 1986).

It would be difficult to argue that men and women exercise free choice in jobs when jobs are so sex-typed. Free choice is not really free when it is made in an environment in which tradition dictates the employments that are 'appropriate' for women and men, or in an employment environment where jobs are gender labelled, or in a training and working environment which is solely male or female (Peitchinis, 1989: 73).

As long as women are perceived as having different capabilities than men, and the perceived differences are not challenged with demonstrated evidence, women will remain typecast and disadvantaged in the labour market. Let us look now at how women are perceived in organizations, and then at how men and women are socialized and how they have learned to be different.

Review Questions

Compare and contrast part-time working with full-time, and part-time workers with full-time workers.

What are the working relations that characterize the lives of black and minority women in Britain? (See Westwood and Bhachu, 1988.)

If division of labour by sex was completely eliminated who would have the most to gain?

Women won't win when it comes to pay. Discuss.

Do you think 'women are lacking'? Could you produce two equally balanced arguments to say that they are and they are not and reach your own conclusions?

Taking law or medicine, or another professional group and using the sources cited here, describe the processes by which women have been excluded. You might like to look at women in accountancy; if so see, for example, Roberts and Coutts (1992), Welsh (1992), Bebbington et al. (1994).

Who is responsible for occupational segregation–the managers, the unions, ideology, families, women? Use the sources here and others (e.g. Beechey, 1987; Milkman, 1987; Walby, 1986; Phillips and Taylor, 1980; Cockburn, 1983, 1985) and work out who is to blame.

Is there a 'logic' to the segregation of jobs? Take some of the examples and cases to be found in these sources (e.g. Bradley, 1989; Witz, 1986) and explain what the 'logic' is.

Skim read any one (or all three) of Cynthia Cockburn's books cited here and review how men keep women out of jobs. If you wanted to disagree with her approach, how would you do it; what evidence would you cite?

What is the feminist case against bureaucracy? (See Ferguson, 1984.)

How do those involved with recruitment and promotion 'manage to discriminate'? (See Collinson, Knights, and Collinson, 1990.)

How can women's work commitment be described?

Do mentors matter? What advantages and disadvantages are there in the mentoring relationship? (See sources cited here and sections on mentoring in Sekaran and Leong, 1992.)

Research the employment conditions of homeworkers in your area.

REFERENCES

ABBOTT, P. and PAYNE, G. (1990) 'Women's Social Mobility: The Conventional Wisdom Reconsidered', Chapter 2 in G. Payne and P. Abbott (eds), *The Social Mobility of Women: Beyond Male Mobility Models*, Falmer Press, London.

ACKER, S. and PIPER, D. (1984) *Is Higher Education Fair to Women?*, SRHE and NFER-Nelson, Guildford.

ADLER, N. and IZRAELI, D. N. (eds), (1988) *Women in Management Worldwide*, Sharpe, New York.

AITKENHEAD, M. (1991) 'Understandings of Equal Opportunities: Social Constructions and Policy Development', paper given at GAPP Conference on the Anthropology of Organizations, University College of Swansea.

ALBAN-METCALFE, B. (1985) 'The Effects of Socialisation on Women's Management Careers', *Management Bibliographies and Reviews*, **11**, 3.

ALBAN-METCALFE, B. (1989) 'What Motivates Managers: An Investigation by Gender and Sector of Employment', *Public Administration*, **67**, 95–108.

ALBAN-METCALFE, B. (1990) 'Gender, Leadership and Assessment', adapted from a paper presented to the 3rd European Congress on the Assessment Centre Method, Geneval-Les-Eaux, Belgium.

ALBAN-METCALFE, B. and NICHOLSON, N. (1984) *The Career Development of British Managers*, British Institute of Management, London.

ALBAN-METCALFE, B. and WEST, M. (1991) 'Women Managers', Chapter 12 in J. F. Cozens and M. West (eds), *Women at Work*, Open University Press, Milton Keynes.

AL-KHALIFA, E. (1988) 'Pin Money Professionals? Women in Teaching', Chapter 4 in A. Coyle and J. Skinner (eds), *Women and Work: Positive Action for Change*, Macmillan Education, Basingstoke.

ALLEN, I. (1988) *Doctors and their Careers*, Policy Studies Institute, Blackmore Press, London.

ALLEN, S. and BARKER, D. L. (1976) 'Introduction: The Interdependence of Work and Marriage', in D. L. Barker and S. Allen, *Dependence and Exploitation in Work and Marriage*, Longman, London.

ANTAL, A. B. and IZRAELI, D. N. (1993) 'A Global Comparison of Women in Management', Chapter 3 in E. Fagenson (ed.), *Women in Management: Trends, Issues and Challenges in Managerial Diversity*, Sage, Newbury Park, Calif.

ANGLE, A. B. and PERRY, J. L. (1981) 'An Empirical Assessment of Organizational Commitment and Organizational Effectiveness', *Administrative Science Quarterly*, **26**, 1–14.

ARBER, S. and GILBERT, N. (1989) 'Men: The Forgotten Carers', *Sociology*, **23**(1), 111–118.

ARNOLD V. and DAVIDSON, M. J. (1990) 'Adopt a Mentor—The New Way Ahead for Women Managers? *Women in Management Review and Abstracts*, **5**(1), 10–18.

BAKKER, I. (1988) 'Women's Employment in Comparative Perspective', in J. Jenson, E. Hagen and G. Reddy (eds), *Feminisation of the Labour Force: Paradoxes and Promises*, Polity Press, Oxford, pp. 17–44.

BARCELONA, C. T., LELIEVRE, C. C. and LELIEVRE, T. W. (1975a) 'The Profession's Under-utilized Resource: The Woman CPA', *Journal of Accountancy*, **140**, 58–64.

BARCELONA, C. T., LELIEVRE, C. C. and LELIEVRE, T. W. (1975b) 'Women in Accounting: Eddies and Midstream Currents', *The Woman CPA*, **35**, 3–5.

BARON, A. (1987) 'Technology and the Crisis of Masculinity: The Social Construction of Gender and Skill in the US Printing Industry, 1850–1920'. paper presented at the 5th UMIST-ASTON Organisation and Control of the Labour Process Conference, Manchester, April, cited in Collinson *et al.* (1990)

BAUM, H. S. (1992) 'Mentoring: Narcissistic Fantasies and Oedipal Realities', *Human Relations*, **45**(3), 223–245.

BAXTER, J. (1992) 'Domestic Labour and Income Inequality', *Work, Employment and Society*, **6**(2), 229–249.

BEBBINGTON, J., THOMSON, I. and WALL, D. (1994) 'Accountancy Students and Constructed Gender: An Exploration of Gender in the Context of Accounting Degree Choices at Two Scottish Universities', working paper available from Jan Bebbington, Department of Accountancy and Business Finance, University of Dundee.

BEECHEY, V. (1987) *Unequal Work*, Verso, London.

BEECHEY, V. and PERKINS, T. (1987) *A Matter of Hours: Women, Part-time Work and the Labour Market*, Polity Press, Oxford.

BERK, S. (1980) *Women and Household Labor*, Sage, Beverly Hills, Calif.

BEVAN, S., BUCHAN, J. and HAYDAY, S. (1990) 'Women in Hospital Pharmacy', IMS Report no. 182, Institute of Manpower Studies, University of Sussex.

BILES, G. and PRYATEL, H. A. (1978) 'Myths, Management and Women', *Personnel Journal*, 57, 572–577.

BOGAT, G. A. and REDNER, R. L. (1985) 'How Mentoring Affects Professional Development of Women in Psychology', *Professional Psychology Research and Practice*, 16(6), 851–859.

BOWEN, D. D. (1985) 'Were Men Meant to Mentor Women?', *Training and Development Journal*, 39(2), 31–34.

BRADLEY, H. (1986) 'Technological Change, Management Strategies, and the Development of Gender-based Job Segregation in the Labour Process', Chapter 3 in D. Knights and H. Wilmott (eds), *Gender and the Labour Process*, Gower, Aldershot.

BRADLEY, H. (1989) *Men's Work, Women's Work: A Sociological History of the Sexual Division of Labour in Employment*, Polity Press, Cambridge.

BRITISH INSTITUTE OF MANAGEMENT (1989) Survey of Women Managers, Interim Report, September, Corby, Northants.

British Medical Journal, News and Political Review, vol. 304, 15 February, p. 399.

BRITISH SOCIAL ATTITUDES (1988) Report 1988–89, R. Jowell *et al.* (eds), Gower, Aldershot.

BRONSTEIN, P., BLACK, L., PFENNIG, J. and WHITE, A. (1986) 'Getting Academic Jobs: Are Women Equally Qualified and Equally Successful?', *American Psychologist*, 41, 318–322.

BROWN, R. (1976) 'Women as Employees: Some comments on Research in Industrial Sociology, Chapter 2 in D. Leonard Barker and S. Allen (eds), *Dependence and Exploitation in Work and Marriage*, Longman, London.

BROWN, S. (1990) 'Management of Education and Social Welfare in Scotland: The Places of Women', *Scottish Journal of Adult Education*, 9(3), 3–13.

BURKE, R. J. (1984) 'Mentors in Organizations', *Group and Organization Studies*, 9, 353–372.

BURNHILL, P. and MCPHERSON, A. (1984) 'Careers and Gender: The Experience of Able Scottish School Leavers in 1971 and 1981', in Acker and Piper (1984).

BYRNE, E. (1978) *Women and Education*, Tavistock, London.

CARTER, A. (1988) *The Politics of Women's Rights*, Longman, London.

CAVENDISH, R. (1982) *Women on the Line*, Routledge & Kegan Paul, London.

CHAPMAN, T. (1989) 'Women Graduates in Management and the Professions', *Women in Management Review and Abstracts*, 4, 10–14.

CHARLES, N. (1993) *Gender Divisions and Social Change*, Harvester Wheatsheaf, Hemel Hempstead.

CHARLES, N. and KERR, M. (1988) *Women, Food and Families*, Manchester University Press, Manchester.

CHUSMIR, L. (1982) 'Job Commitment and the Organizational Woman', *Academy of Management Review*, 7(4), 595–602.

CLEGG, S. (1981) 'Organization and Control', *Administrative Science Quarterly*, 26, 532–545.

CLUTTERBUCK, D. (1991) *Everyone Needs a Mentor: Fostering Talent at Work*, 2nd edn, Institute of Personnel Management, London.

CLUTTERBUCK, D. and DEVINE, M. (eds) (1987) *Business Women—Present and Future*, Macmillan, London.

COCKBURN, C. (1983) *Brothers: Male Dominance and Technological Change*, Pluto Press, London.

COCKBURN, C. (1985) *Machinery of Dominance: Women, Men and Technical Know-how*, Pluto Press, London.

COCKBURN, C. (1991) *In the Way of Women*, Macmillan Education, Basingstoke.

COHEN, B. and STRACHAN, Y. (1993) 'Reconciling Employment with the Care of Children', Chapter 4 in *A Woman's Place . . . ? Women and Work*, E. Templeton (ed.) St Andrew Press, Edinburgh.

COLLINSON, D. L. (1987) 'Banking on Women: Selection Practices in the Finance Sector', *Personnel Review*, **16**, 12–20.

COLLINSON, D. L and KNIGHTS, D. (1986) 'Men Only: Theories and Practices of Job Segregation in Insurance', Chapter 7 in D. Knights and H. Wilmott (eds), *Gender and the Labour Process*, Gower, Aldershot.

COLLINSON, D. L., KNIGHTS, D. and COLLINSON, M. (1990) *Managing to Discriminate*, Routledge, London.

COMMISSION OF THE EUROPEAN COMMUNITIES (1990) *Employment in Europe 1990*, Luxembourg.

CONNELL, R. W. (1987) *Gender and Power: Society, the Person and Sexual Politics*, Polity Press, Basil Blackwell, Oxford.

CORPORATE WOMAN (1979) 'Exploding a Myth of Executive Job Hopping', *Business Week*, 11 June 127 and 131.

COWAN, R. S. (1989) *More Work for Mother*, Free Association Books, London.

COX, T. and HARQUAIL, C. V. (1990) 'Career Paths and Career Success in the Early Career Stages of Male and Female MBAs', paper presented at the Academy of Management Conference, San Francisco, cited in B. Alimo-Metcalfe, 'Women in Management: Organizational Socialization and Assessment Practices that Prevent Career Advancement', *International Journal of Selection and Assessment*, **1**(2), 68–83.

COYLE, A. (1988) 'Behind the Scenes: Women in Television', Chapter 3 in A. Coyle and J. Skinner (eds), *Women and Work: Positive Action for Change*, Macmillan Education, Basingstoke.

CRAWFORD, M. and ENGLISH, L. (1984) 'Generic Versus Specific Inclusion of Women in Language: Effects on Recall', *Journal of Psycholinguistic Research*, **13**, 373–381.

CROMIE, S. (1981) 'Women as Managers in Northern Ireland', *Journal of Occupational Psychology*, **54**, 87–91.

CROMPTON, R. (1986) 'Women in the Service Class', in R. Crompton and M. Mann (eds), *Gender and Stratification*, Polity Press, Cambridge.

CROMPTON, R. (1989) 'Women in Banking', *Work, Employment and Society*, **3**(2), 141–156.

CROMPTON, R. and JONES, G. (1984) *A White-collar Proletariat? De-skilling and Gender in Clerical Work*, Macmillan, Basingstoke.

CROMPTON, R. and SANDERSON, K. (1990) *Gendered Jobs and Social Change*, Hyman, London.

CURRAN, M. M. (1988) 'Gender and Recruitment: People and Places in the Labour Market', *Work, Employment and Society*, **2**(3), 335–351.

DALE, A. (1988) 'Occupational Inequality, Gender and Life Cycle', *Work, Employment and Society*, **1**(3), 326–351.

DAVIDSON, M. J. (1985) *Reach for the Top—A Women's Guide to Success in Business and Management*, Piatkus, London.

DAVIDSON, M. J. and COOPER, C. C. (1984) 'She Needs a Wife: Problems of Women Managers', *Leadership and Organizational Development Journal*, **5**, 3.

DAVIDSON, M. J. and COOPER, C. (1992) *Shattering the Glass Ceiling: The Woman Manager*, Paul Chapman, London.

DAVIDSON, M. J. and COOPER, C. (1993) *European Women in Business and Management*, Paul Chapman, London.

DEPARTMENT OF EMPLOYMENT (1987) *New Earnings Survey 1980–1987*, Part A, tables 10 and 11, HMSO, London.

DEX, S. (1984) 'Women's Work Histories: An Analysis of the Women and Employment Survey', Research Paper no. 46, Department of Employment.

DEX, S. (1985) *The Sexual Division of Work: Conceptual Revolutions in the Social Sciences*, Harvester Wheatsheaf, Hemel Hempstead.

DEX, S. (1987) 'Women's Occupational Mobility: A Lifetime Perspective, Macmillan Press, London.

DEX, S. (1988) *Women's Attitudes Towards Work*, Macmillan Press, Basingstoke.

DEX, S. and SHAW, L. (1986) *British and American Women at Work*, Macmillan, London.

DOUGLAS, M. (1987) *How Institutions Think*, Routledge and Kegan Paul, London.

DREHER, G. F. and ASH, R. A. (1990) 'A Comparative Study of Mentoring Among Men and Women in Managerial, Professional and Technical Positions', *Journal of Applied Psychology*, **75**, 539–546.

ELSTON, M. A. (1980) 'Medicine', in R. Silverstone and M. Ward (eds), *Careers of Professional Women*, pp. 99–139, Croom Helm, London.

EPSTEIN, T. S., CREHAN, K., GERZER, A. and SASS, J. (eds) (1986) *Women, Work and Family in Britain and Germany*, Croom Helm, London.

FAGENSON, E. A. (1988) 'The Power of a Mentor', *Groups and Organization Studies*, **13**, 182–194.

FAGENSON, E. A. (1989) 'The Mentor Advantage: Perceived Career Experiences of Protégé vs. Nonprotégés', *Journal of Organizational Behaviour*, **10**, 309–320.

FERGUSON, K. (1984) *The Feminist Case Against Bureaucracy*, Temple University Press, Philadelphia.

FOGARTY, M. P., RAPOPORT, R. and RAPOPORT, R. N. (1971) *Career, Sex and Family*, Allen & Unwin, London.

FUCHS, R. (1971) 'Different Meanings of Employment for Women', *Human Relations*, **24**, 495–499.

GAME, A. and PRINGLE, R. (1983) *Gender at Work*, George Allen and Unwin, Sydney.

GERSON, K. (1982) 'Changing Family Structure and the Position of Women: A Review of the Trends', *American Planning Association Journal*, **49**, 138–148.

GIBEAU, J. L. and ANASTAS, M. S. (1989) 'Breadwinners and Caregivers: Interviews with Working Women', *Journal of Gerontological Social Work*, **14**, 19–40.

GLUCKSMANN, M. (1986) 'In a Class of their Own? Women Workers in the New Industries in Inter-war Britain', *Feminist Review*, **244**, 7–39.

GLUCKSMANN, M. (1990) *Women Assemble: Women Workers and the New Industries in Inter-war Britain*, Routledge, London.

GOLD, U. and PRINGLE, J. (1989) 'Management Promotions: Gender-specific Factors', *Women in Management Review and Abstracts*, **4**(3), 5–10 (published in association with the Equal Opportunities Commission, MCB University Press, Bradford).

GOLDSMITH, E. B. (ed.) (1989) *Work and Family: Theory, Research and Applications*, Sage, Newbury Park, Calif.

Guardian (1992) 'Women "Will Take the Lead in Business" ', *Guardian*, 8 January.

Guardian (1993) 'Women's deprecatory descriptions of their jobs undercut both status and pay', *Guardian*, 15 June

HAKIM, C. (1981) 'Job Segregation: Trends in the 1970s', *Employment Gazette*, December.

HALLER, M. and ROSENMAYR, O. (1971) 'The Pluridimensionality of Work Commitment', *Human Relations*, **24**, 501–518.

HALSEY, A. H. (1990) 'Long, Open Road to Equality', *The Times Higher Education Supplement*, 9 February, 17.

HAMILTON, M. C. and HENLEY, N. M. (1982) 'Detrimental Consequences of Generic Masculine Usage: Effects on the Reader/Hearer's Cognitions', paper presented at the meeting of the Western Psychological Association, Sacramento, Calif.

HAMMOND, V. (1986) 'Working Women Abroad: Great Britain', *Equal Opportunities International*, **5**(1), 8–16.

HAMMOND, V. and HOLTON, V. (1991) 'A Balanced Workforce—Achieving Cultural Change for Women', Ashridge Management College, Ashridge.

HANSARD SOCIETY COMMISSION (1990) *Women at the Top*, Hansard Society, London.

HARRISON, S., KING, S. and GREGG, E. (1988) 'Special Report: Black Women in Corporate America', *Black Enterprise*, **9**, 45–49.

HARLAN, A. and WEISS, C. (1980) 'Moving Up: Women in Managerial Careers: Third Progress Report', Wellesley Centre for Research on Women, Wellesley, Mass.

HARPER, J. and RICHARDS, L. (1986) *Mothers and Working Mothers*, 2nd ed, Penguin, Melbourne.

HEARN, J. (1982) 'Notes on Patriarchy, Professionalization and the Semi-professions, *Sociology*, **16**(2), 184–202.

HEARN, J. (1992) 'Changing Men and Changing Managements: A Review of Issues and Actions', *Women in Management Review*, **7**(1), 3–7.

HENWOOD, M., RIMMER, L. and WICKS, M. (1987) 'Inside the Family: Changing Roles of Men and Women', Family Policy Studies Centre, London, Occasional Paper 6, quoted in Charles (1993).

HERITAGE, J. (1983) 'Feminisation and Unionisation: A Case-study from Banking in E. Gamarnikow, D. Morgan, J. Purvis and D. Taylorson (eds), *Gender, Class and Work*, Heinemann, London.

HIRSH, W. and JACKSON, C. (1989) 'Women into Management—Issues Influencing the Entry of Women into Managerial Jobs', paper no. 158, Institute of Manpower Studies, University of Sussex.

HOMANS, H. (1984) 'Career Opportunities for Women in Clinical Chemistry Laboratories', report submitted to the Equal Opportunities Commission, Manchester EOC.

HOMANS, H. (1987) 'Man-made Myths: The Reality of Being a Woman Scientist in the NHS', Chapter 5 in A. Spencer and D. Podmore (eds), *In a Man's World*, Tavistock, London.

HOPFL, H. (1992) 'Commitments and Conflicts: Corporate Seduction and Ambivalence in Women Managers', *Women in Management Review*, **7**(1), 9-17.

HUGGETT, C., AMROCZEK, C., HENWOOD, F. and ARNOLD, E. (1985) 'Microelectronics and the Jobs Women Do', in W. Faulkener and E. Arnold (eds), *Smothered by Invention—Technology in Women's Lives*, Pluto Press, London.

HUNT, A. (1975) *OPCS: Survey of Management Attitudes and Practices Towards Women at Work*, HMSO, London.

INCOMES DATA SERVICES (1993) A Changing Workforce: Labour Market Analysis, IDS report no. 640.

JACOBI, M. (1991) 'Mentoring and Undergraduate Academic Success: A Literature Review', *Review of Educational Research*, **61**(4), 505–532.

JANCURA, E. G. (1974) 'The Woman CPA: A Professional Profile', *Woman CPA*, **36**, 2–13.

JONES, E. W. (1986) 'Black Managers: The Dream Deferred', *Harvard Business Review*, **64**, 84–93.

JOSHI, H. and NEWELL, M. L. (1987) 'Family Responsibilities and Pay Differentials: Evidence from Men and Women born in 1946', CEPR Discussion Paper no. 157, cited in McRae (1991).

KAHN, A. N. and MILLS, A. J. (1990) 'Sexual Harassment', *Solicitors Journal*, **134**(3), 67–69.

KANTER, R. M. (1975) 'Women and the Structure of Organizations: Explorations in Theory and Behaviour', in M. Millman and R. M. Kanter (eds) *Another Voice*, pp. 37–74, Anchor Books, Garden City, NY.

KANTER, R. M. (1989) *Men and Women of the Corporation*, Basic Books, New York.

KAUFMANN, F. A. (1986) 'The Nature, Role and Influence of Mentors in the Lives of Gifted Adults', *Journal of Counseling and Development*, **64**(9), 576–578.

KNAPP, M. C. (1980) 'Leaving Public Accounting: The Decision Process', *Woman CPA*, **42**, 7–12.

KRAM, K. E. (1983) 'Phases of Mentor Relationship', *Academy of Management Journal*, **26**, 608–625.

KRAM, K. E. (1985) *Mentoring at Work*, Scott, Foresman, Glenview, Ill.

KREPS, J. M. (1983) 'Women in a Changing Economy', in J. Farley (ed.), *Women in Management: Career and Family Issues*, ILR Press, Cornell University, Ithaca, NY.

LAFRANCE, M. (1987) 'The Paradox of Mentoring', paper presented at the International Interdisciplinary Congress on Women, Dublin and reported in Paludi (1987).

LAMBERT, I. D. and LAMBERT, S. J. (1974) 'Attitudes and Expectations of Women Accounting Managers Toward Employment in Accounting', *Nebraska CPA*, **9**, 13–15.

LARWOOD, L. and WOOD, M. M. (1979) *Women in Management*, Lexington Books, London.

LAWRENCE, B. (1987) 'The Fifth Dimension—Gender and General Practice', Chapter 7 in A. Spencer and D. Podmore (eds), *In a Man's World: Essays on Women in Male-dominated Professions*, Tavistock, London.

LEAVITT, J. A. (1982) *Women in Management: An Annotated Bibliography*, Oryz, Phoenix, Ariz.

LEGGE, K. (1987) 'Women in Personnel Management: Uphill Climb or Downhill Slide?', in A. Spencer and D. Podmore (eds), *In a Man's World: Essays on Women in Male-dominated Professions*, pp. 33–60, Tavistock, London.

LENIKAN, J. P. (1983) 'Women in Male Dominated Professions: Distinguishing Personality and Background Characteristics', *Psychology of Women Quarterly*, **8**, 144–165.

LEONARD, A. (1987) *Judging Inequality: The Effectiveness of the Industrial Tribunal System in Sex Discrimination and Equal Pay Cases*, National Council for Civil Liberties, London.

LEONARD, P. (1984) *Personality and Ideology—Towards a Material Understanding of the Individual*, Methuen, London.

LEPPINGTON, D. (1993) 'Home Truths about Homeworking', Chapter 13 in *A Woman's Place...? Women and Work*, Templeton, E. (ed.) St Andrew Press, Edinburgh.

LINGSOM, S. and ELLINGSAETER, A. L. (1983) *Arbeid, Fritid og Samvaer*, Central Bureau of Statistics, SA 49, Oslo.

LODEN, M. (1985) 'Feminine Leadership: Or How to Succeed in Business Without Being One of the Boys', New York Times Books, New York. Chapter with same author and title in J. L. Pierce and J. W. Newstrom (eds), *The Manager's Bookshelf*, 2nd edn, Harper & Row, New York.

LORBER, J. (1975) 'Women and Medical Sociology: Invisible Professionals and Ubiquitous Patients', in M. Millaman and R. M. Kanter (eds), *Another Voice*, pp. 75–105, Anchor Books, Garden City, NY.

MCKINLAY, A. (1989) 'Women in Computing in Scottish Higher Education', Scottish Institute of Adult and Continuing Education, Edinburgh.

MCRAE, S. (1991) 'Occupational Change Over Childbirth', *Sociology*, **25**(4), 589–605.

MARNANI, M. (1992) 'The Position of Women in the Labour Market: Trends and Development in the 12 Member States of the European Community, 1983–1990', Women of Europe Supplements, 36, Commission of the European Communities, March.

MARSHALL, H. and WETHERALL, M. (1989) 'Talking about Career and Gender Identities: A Discourse Analysis Perspective', Chapter 6 in S. Skevington and D. Baker (eds), *The Social Identity of Women*, Sage, London.

MARTIN, R. (1993) Women and the Law: Are They Compatible? *AUT Woman*, **30** (Autumn), 2.

MARTIN, J. and ROBERTS, C. (1984) *Women and Employment: A Lifetime Perspective*, Department of Employment, London.

MIGHTY, E. J. (1991) 'Valuing Workforce Diversity: A Model of Organizational Change', *Canadian Journal of Administrative Sciences*, **8**, 64–70.

MILKMAN, R. (1987) *Gender at Work: The Dynamics of Job Segregation by Sex During World War II*, University of Illinois Press, Urbana, Ill.

MILLS, A. J. (1988) 'Organizational Acculturation and Gender Discrimination', in K. Kresl (ed.), *Women and the Workplace*, Association of Canadian Studies, Ottowa.

MILLS, A. J. and MURGATROYD, S. J. (1991) *Organizational Rules: A Framework for Understanding Organizational Action*, Open University Press, Milton Keynes.

MILLS, A. J. and SIMMONS, T. (1994) *Reading Organizational Theory: A Critical Approach*, Garamond Press, Toronto.

MITCHELL, C. and BURDICK, T. (1985) *The Right Moves: Succeeding in a Man's World without a Harvard MBA*, Macmillan, New York.

MORGAN, G. (1986) *Images of Organization*, Sage, Beverly Hills, Calif.

MORGAN, G. and KNIGHTS, D. (1991) 'Gendering Jobs: Corporate Strategy, Managerial Control and the Dynamics of Job Segregation', *Work, Employment and Society*, **5**(2), 181–200.

MORGAN, N. (1988) 'The Equality Game: Women in the Federal Public Service (1908–1987)', Canadian Advisory Council on the Status of Women, Ottowa.

MORRISON, A. M. and VON GLINOW, M. A. (1990) 'Women and Minorities in Management', *American Psychologist*, Feb. **45**(2), 200–208.

MORRISON, A. M., WHITE, R. P. and VAN VESLOR, E. (1987) *Breaking the Glass Ceiling: Can Women Reach the Top of America's Largest Corporations?*, Addison-Wesley, Reading, Mass.

MORRISON, A. M., WHITE, R. P. and VAN VESLOR, E. (1990) *Breaking the Glass Ceiling: Can Women Reach the Top of America's Largest Corporations?*, in J. L. Pierce and J. W. Newstrom (eds), *The Manager's Bookshelf*, 2nd edn, Harper & Row, New York.

NELSON, S. (1988) Jobs for the Boys in the Scottish Office, *Observer Scotland*, 9 October, 13.

NEWELL, S. (1992) 'The Myth and Destructiveness of Equal Opportunities: The Continued Dominance of the Mothering Role', Working Paper, Aston Business School, Aston University.

NKOMO, S. M. (1991) 'Race and Sex: The Forgotten Case of the Black Female Manager', in S. Rose and L. Larwood (eds), *Women's Careers: Pathways and Pitfalls*, Praeger, New York.

OSLER, K. (1991) 'Employment Experiences of Vocationally Trained Doctors', *British Medical Journal*, **303**, 762–764.

PAHL, R. E. (1984) *Divisions of Labour*, Basil Blackwell, Oxford.

PALUDI, M. A. (ed.) (1987) *Ivory Power: Sexual Harassment on Campus*, State University of New York Press, Albany NY.

PEITCHINIS, S. G. (1989) *Women at Work: Discrimination and Response*, McClelland & Stewart, Toronto, Canada.

Personnel Today (1992) 'Pregnant Woman Wins Case', 24 March–6 April, p. 3 and 'Women at Top Hit Out at Men', p. 4.

PHILLIPS, A. and TAYLOR, B. (1980) 'Sex and Skill: Notes Towards a Feminist Economics', *Feminist Review*, **6**, 79–88.

PHIZACKLEA, A. (1988) 'Gender, Racism and Occupational Segregation', in S. Walby (ed.), *Gender Segregation at Work*, Open University Press, Milton Keynes.

PODMORE, D. and SPENCER, A. (1986) 'Gender in the Labour Process—The Case of Men and Women Lawyers', Chapter 2 in D. Knights and H. Wilmott (eds), *Gender and the Labour Process*, Gower, Aldershot.

POLLERT, A. (1981) *Girls, Wives, Factory Lives*, Macmillan, Basingstoke.

POWELL, G. N. (1988) *Women and Men in Management*, Sage, Newbury Park, Calif.

POWELL, G. N., POSNER, B. Z. and SCHMIDT, W. H. (1985) 'Women: The More Committed Managers?', *Management Review*, **74**(6), 43–45.

POWELL, G. and MAINIERO, L. A. (1992) 'Cross-currents in the River of Time: Conceptualizing the Complexities of Women's Careers', *Journal of Management*, **18**(2), 215–237.

PRINGLE, R. (1989) 'Bureaucracy, Rationality and Sexuality: The Case of Secretaries', in J. Hearn, D. L. Sheppard, P. Tancred-Sheriff and G. Burrell (eds), *The Sexuality of Organization*, Sage, London.

RAGINS, B. R. (1989) 'Barriers to Mentoring: The Female Managers' Dilemma', *Human Relations*, **42**, 1–22.

RAGINS, B. R. and COTTON, J. L. (1991) 'Easier Said Than Done: Gender Differences in Perceived Barriers to Gaining a Mentor', *Academy of Management Journal*, **34**(4), 939–951.

RAY, E. and DAVIS, A. (1988) 'Black Female Executives Speak Out On: The Concrete Ceiling', *Executive Female*, **6**, 34–38.

Regional Trends (1989) HMSO, London.

RESKIN, B. F. (1988) 'Bringing the Men Back In: Sex Differentiation and the Devaluation of Women's Work', *Gender and Society*, **2**, 58–81.

ROBERTS, J. and COUTTS, J. A. (1992) 'Feminization and Professionalization: A Review of an Emerging Literature on the Development of Accounting in the United Kingdom', *Accounting, Organizations and Society*, **17**(3/4), 379–395.

ROBINSON, O. (1988) 'The Changing Labour Market: Growth of Part-time Employment and

Labour Market Segmentation in Britain', in S. Walby (ed.), *Gender Segregation at Work*, Open University Press, Milton Keynes.

ROWBOTHAM, S. (1973) *Woman's Consciousness, Man's World*, Penguin, Harmondsworth.

RUBERY, J. (1978) 'Structured Labour Markets, Worker Organization and Low Pay', *Cambridge Journal of Economics*, **2**(1), 17–36.

SALAMAN, G. (1986) *Working*, Penguin, Harmondsworth.

SCANDURA, T. (1992) 'Mentorship and Career Mobility: An Empirical Investigation', *Journal of Organizational Behaviour*, **13**, 169–174.

SCASE, R. and GOFFEE, R. (1990) 'Women in Management: Towards a Research Agenda', *International Journal of Human Resource Management*, **1**(1), 107–125.

SCOTT, H. (1985) *Working your Way to the Bottom: The Feminisation of Poverty*, Pandora, London.

SCOTT, K. D. and MCCLELLAN, E. L. (1990) 'Gender Differences in Absenteeism', *Public Personnel Management*, **19**(2), 229–253.

SEKARAN, U. and LEONG, F. T. (1992) *Womanpower: Managing in Times of Demographic Turbulence*, Sage, Newbury Park, Calif.

SHARPE, S. (1984) *Double Identity: The Lives of Working Mothers*, Penguin, Harmondsworth.

SHORTRIDGE, K. (1986) 'Poverty is a Woman's Problem', in J. Freeman (ed.), *Women: A Feminist Perspective*, Mayfield, Palo Alto, Calif.

SIACE (1990) 'Efficiency and Equality: Training for Women for Management', Scottish Institute of Adult and Continuing Education, Edinburgh.

SILTANEN, J. (1981) 'A Commentary on Theories of Female Wage Labour', in Cambridge Women's Studies Group (ed.), *Women in Society: Interdisciplinary Essays*, pp. 25–40, Virago, London.

SNELL, M., GLUKLICH, P. and POVALL, M. (1981) 'Equal Pay and Opportunities: A Study of the Implications and Effects of the Equal Pay and Sex Discrimination Acts in 26 Organizations', Research Paper no. 20, Department of Employment, London.

SNIZEK, W. E. and NEIL, C. C. (1992) 'Job Characteristics, Gender Stereotypes and Perceived Gender Discrimination in the Workplace', *Organization Studies*, **13**(3), 403–427.

SPARROW, E. (1990) Report in *Women into Business*, **13**, May.

SPENCER, A. and PODMORE, D. (eds) (1987) *In a Man's World: Essays on Women in Male-dominated Professions*, Tavistock, London.

SPENCER, A. and PODMORE. D. (1987) 'Women Lawyers—Marginal Members of a Male-dominated Profession', Chapter 6 in A. Spencer, and D. Podmore (eds), *In a Man's World: Essays on Women in Male-dominated Professions*, Tavistock, London.

SPENDER, D. (1985) *Man Made Language*, 2nd edn, Routledge & Kegan Paul, London.

STAMP, P. and ROBARTS, S. (1986) *Positive Action: Changing the Workplace for Women*, National Council for Civil Liberties, London.

SVENSKA INSTITUTET (1987) Fact Sheet on Sweden, Stockholm.

SWORDS-ISHERWOOD, N. (1985) 'Women in British Engineering', in W. Faulkener and E. Arnold (eds), *Smothered by Invention—Technology in Women's Lives*, pp. 80–81, Pluto Press, London.

TERBORG, J. R. (1977) 'Women in Management: A Research Review', *Journal of Applied Psychology*, **62**, 647–664.

WALBY, S. (1984) 'Gender and Unemployment. Patriachal and Capitalist Relations in the Restructuring of Gender Relations in Employment and Unemployment', unpublished Ph.D. thesis, University of Essex.

WALBY, S. (ed.) (1986) *Patriarchy at Work*, Polity Press, Cambridge.

WALBY, S. (1988) *Gender Segregation at Work*, Open University Press, Milton Keynes.

WALSHOK, M. Z. (1981) *Blue-collar Women: Fioneer of the Male Frontier*, Anchor Books, New York.

WALTERS, P. A. (1987) 'Servants of the Crown', in A. Spencer and D. Podmore (eds), *In a Man's World: Essays on Women in Male-dominated Professions*, pp. 12–32, Sage, London.

WELSH, M. J. (1992) 'The Construction of Gender: Some Insights from Feminist Psychology', *Accounting, Auditing and Accountability Journal*, **5**(3), 120–132.

WESTWOOD, S. and BHACHU, P. (eds) (1988) *Enterprising Women: Ethnicity, Economy and Gender Relations*, Routledge, London.

WHITE, B., COX, C. and COOPER, C. (1992) *Women's Career Development: A Study of High Flyers*, Blackwell, Oxford.

WHITELY, W., DOUGHERTY, T. W. and DREHER, G. F. (1991) 'Relationship of Career Mentoring and Socioeconomic Origin to Managers' and Professionals' Early Career Progress', *Academy of Management Journal*, **34**, 331–351.

WICKHAM, A. (1986) *Women and Training*, Open University Press, Milton Keynes.

WITZ, A. (1986) 'Patriarchy and Labour Market: Occupational Control Strategies and the Medical Division of Labour', Chapter 1 in D. Knights and H. Wilmott (eds), *Gender and the Labour Process*, Gower, Aldershot.

WITZ, A. (1990) 'Patriarchy and Professions: The Gendered Politics of Occupational Closure', *Sociology*, **24**(4), 675–690.

WOLF, N. (1990) *The Beauty Myth*, Chatto & Windus, London.

WOMEN AND TRAINING GROUP (1991) 'Women and Training', Gloucester.

WOMEN AND WORK (1993) Report available from Riley Research, Riley House, 4, Red Lion Court, London EC4A.

WOMEN IN MANAGEMENT ASSOCIATION AND VICTORIA HOLTON (1989) 'The Female Resource: An Overview', Ashridge Management Research Group, Herts.

YOUNG, K. and SPENCER, E. (1990) *Women Managers in Local Government: Removing the Barriers*, INLOGOV, Birmingham.

ZEY, M. G. (1984) *The Mentor Connection*, Dow Jones Irwin, Homewood, Ill.

2 Perceiving Women in Organizations

A standard textbook on organizational behaviour might approach the subject of perception by looking at stimulus, perceptual organization, and interpretation, then the perceptual errors that can be made, e.g. assumed similarity, the halo effect, stereotyping. This approach is perfectly acceptable but often assumes a gender neutrality and tells us little about how women are perceived in organizations. It is a way of seeing that is not seeing, or not emphasizing, the particular social processes which affect women. In this chapter we are going to concentrate on looking at how women are perceived in organizations, to give insight into the perceptual process but questioning conventional approaches.

Looking at your own attributes

How do you see yourself? What attributes do you think you have. List 10 attributes that you see in yourself. Find a partner, preferably of the opposite sex, and ask them to list 10 attributes which apply to you, without showing them your list. Do the same for them. How do the four lists differ—the two you and the two they wrote? Show each other your lists. Are there different attributes for men and women?

Many studies of how men and women are perceived shows them to be opposites. Women and men are at opposite ends of bipolar scales. In a study of gender stereotypes, for example, in 25 nations, Williams and Best (1990) found that women were seen as sentimental, submissive, and superstitious in all countries; men were seen as adventurous, forceful and independent. In countries where there was a high proportion of Catholics, women were viewed more favourably and seen as nurturing parents and sources of order; in Muslim countries, stereotypes of women were less favourable. The acquisition of gender stereotypes usually begins

before the age of five, accelerates during the early school years, and is complete by adolescence.

Does negative stereotyping of women in organizations come about because of negative stereotyping in the culture, the differing characteristics men and women are seen to possess from birth and the socialization process? Or does this happen because of men and women's hierarchichal positions, with different positions leading to different character traits being used? Or is there another explanation?

Women may perceive themselves less favourably than they would perceive men. Research on pay equity supports the view that women see themselves differently and not as positively as men: women evaluate their contribution less favourably, or are more modest than men. In laboratory studies, women will pay themselves less for the same work and work longer for the same pay than will men (Major *et al.*, 1984a,b). In a typical situation a group of workers performs a task and one job incumbent is asked to allocate rewards among group members, either including or excluding themselves. When asked to include themselves, female incumbents take less reward for themselves than do similarly performing male incumbents (Lane and Messe, 1971; Leventhal and Anderson, 1970). But when allocating rewards only to others, men and women do not differ in their reward allocation strategies (Major and Deaux, 1982; Reis and Jackson, 1981). Women may, then, be contributing towards their own lack of equality of opportunity—but this is blaming the victim.

We saw in the previous chapter how women are seen as less committed to work and as potentially poorer employees. Judi Marshall (1984) has tried to rebut the various arguments about women as poorer employees. She proposes a revision of female attributes, developing a broad composite of female cultural traits, all defined in positive terms, instead of failing for not being like men. Women are seen as 'skilled at listening, artistic, sensitive, integrated, deep, inter subjective, empathetic, associative, affective, open, personalised, aesthetic, receptive, nurturing etc.' These, she concludes, are positive qualities which may make women different and potentially better managers than men. The problem with this argument, and all arguments which polarize male and female characteristics, is that they form the basis of arguments for legitimate social inequality.

It would appear that few have questioned the polarization of attributes assigned to men and women. The idea that such attributes are discrete and form mutually exclusive categories is both false and unproductive. These artificial divisions are the product of a particular kind of social reality and of the particular distribution of power which characterizes this (Spender, 1978). This approach identifies the sex differences that are believed to exist and attempts to explain the emergence of such differences. Bearing this point in mind, let us look at how this is done. Let us look at the negative evaluation of women in some more detail.

A personal view

ICC Financial Surveys Ltd have my name on their mailing list as I recently purchased a report from them. Each letter is addressed to 'Mr Fiona Wilson'. The NHS Training Directorate also have my name on their mailing list and include my full name and address at the top of their letters to me. But the address on the first line is 'Dear Sir'. A student, needing help with an appeal, made the same error. A hotel bill was made out for Mr Fiona Wilson. Does this just tell you that simple processing errors are taking place or does it say more about the place of women, what they are expected to do and not to do?

WOMEN ARE EVALUATED LESS FAVOURABLY THAN MEN

Negative stereotypical assessment of women can only hinder their development. Research by Dipboye *et al.* (1975, 1977), Fidell (1970), Goldberg (1968), Gutek and Stevens (1979), Haefner (1977), Rosen and Jerdee (1974), Schein (1975), Shaw (1972), and Terborg and Ilgen (1975) reinforces the belief that men and women are stereotyped and evaluated differently. Females are often evaluated less favourably than males. Haefner (1977), following a study of 588 employees (64 per cent of whom were male and 71.6 per cent white), found that the employees would prefer not to work with black people, women, older individuals or barely competent persons. In a choice between highly competent males and females, they indicated a strong preference for highly competent males. However, the females in the sample indicated a preference for other females as fellow employees.

If you are a female student could you be evaluated more negatively than a male student because of your sex? Sex differences in the evaluation of students have been observed but have usually been attributed to inherent differences between men and women students rather than to differential marking by examiners. Bradley (1984) found a clearly recognized pattern of sex bias in the marking of student projects. The implications of sex bias are disturbing as women students may be receiving lower second class degrees while men students, with comparable abilities, are awarded upper seconds. This is one good reason why students and staff should insist on anonymous marking. Belsey (1988) in a quasi-experimental study at the University of Wales College of Cardiff, following the introduction of blind marking, found that there was a dramatic increase in the number of 'good' degrees obtained by females. However, this increase was not sustained over a longer period (Perry-Langdon, 1990). More recently Newstead and Dennis (1993) have argued that there are inconclusive results concerning sex bias among markers.

Are female teachers evaluated differently? College students of both genders have been shown to rate male teachers (not their own) in a generally more favourable way than women (Denmark, 1979), evaluate men teachers as more intelligent and motivating than equally presented women teachers (Bernard *et al.*, 1981), rate male teachers as more powerful and effective (Kaschak, 1981), and prefer to take a course from a man (Lombardo and Tocci, 1979). Macke *et al.* (1980) discovered that when students judged professors, generating more class discussion was taken as a sign of incompetence—but only if the professor was female.

When chair*men* of 147 psychology departments rated credentials of potential faculty members with male and female names randomly assigned, what do you think they found? The mean faculty rank that the chairmen recommended offering was significantly lower for females as compared to males with identical credentials (Fidell, 1970).

A sample of chair*men* of graduate departments in the physical sciences preferred an average male to an average female applicant (with identical credentials) for a faculty position, and consistently gave men higher ratings on educational background and hiring possibilities (Lewin and Duchan, 1971). Kathleen Archibald (1970) in an experiment in the public service, asked ratees to grade five candidates for executive positions. The résumés were drafted so that two candidates, A and B, had a good chance of being rated first and second, respectively. C, D, and E were always shown as male. Half the raters received résumés in which candidate A was female, and C and B male, while the other half received résumés in which A was male and B was female. It was found that when male A competed against female B he was at the top of the eligibility list 86 per cent of the time, but when female A competed against male B she was at the top of the list only 58 per cent of the time. Or looking at it another way, male B had a 42 per cent chance of coming out in first place or tying for the top rank when in competition with female A, while female B had only a 14 per cent chance in competition with male A. Little has changed in the 1980s. Bronstein *et al.* (1986) found that women in their academic sample were at least as well qualified as the men but tended to obtain jobs with lower status at institutions of lower prestige.

Research by Rosen and Jerdee (1974) demonstrated clear bias against women in personnel decisions related to promotion, development, and supervision. Using an in-basket exercise with 95 bank supervisors, the design consisted of four separate experiments (in-basket items) in which an employee's sex and other situational attributes were manipulated. The results support allegations regarding discrimination against women in organizational settings.

Both men and women perceived the latter as having feminine characteristics. Women are reported as being more feminine than men (Fagenson, 1990). They are warm, kind, emotional, gentle, understanding, aware of other's feelings, and helpful to others (Feather, 1984; Putnam and Heinen, 1976: Schein, 1972). These studies show how men are seen as aggressive, forceful, strong, rational, self-confident, competitive, and independent. Schein says that female traits are less valued, and women are denied developmental tasks which then hinders promotion, and are therefore excluded from the organizational power network.

Inge Broverman and her colleagues asked a group of college students to list characteristics, attitudes, and behaviours in which they believed men and women differ. A second group examined the 122 items that appeared on the initial list and rated the extent to which they agreed the items were typical of an adult man or women. This yielded 41 items, some of which are shown in the following box.

Characteristics of masculine and feminine stereotypes

Feminine stereotype

Incompetence
Not at all aggressive
Not at all independent
Very emotional
Does not hide emotions at all
Very subjective
Very easily influenced
Very submissive
Warmth/expressiveness
Does not use harsh language at all
Very talkative
Very tactful
Very gentle
Very aware of feelings of others

Masculine stereotype

Competence
Very aggressive
Very independent
Not at all emotional
Almost always hides emotions
Very objective
Not at all easily influenced
Very dominant
Distant/inexpressiveness
Uses harsh language
Not at all talkative
Very blunt
Very rough
Not at all aware of feelings of others

Source: Extracted from Broverman *et al.* (1972).

Broverman *et al.* (1972, 1975) were led to the following conclusions. There is a strong consensus about the differing characteristics of men and women. The characteristics ascribed to men are more positively valued more often than characteristics ascribed to women. The positively valued masculine traits concern competence, rationality, and assertion. The positively valued feminine traits reflect warmth and expressiveness. These definitions are accepted to the extent that they are incorporated into self-concepts of men and women. Moreover, these differences are considered desirable by university students, healthy by mental health professionals, and even ideal by both men and women. Are men and women's characteristics to be equally valued as Marshall (1984) suggests? It would appear not.

Broverman's studies produced a great deal of discussion and criticism. They were criticized for their methodology, one of the reasons being that she and her colleagues had forced respondents to choose between adjectives in describing a normal male, normal female, and themselves. They had asked respondents to indicate the extent to which 122 pairs of adjectives (that were antonyms—each member of the pair was opposite in meaning from the other, e.g sneaky/direct, submissive/dominant), commonly used to describe people's personality traits, described the male, female, and themselves. It may be that people only stereotype when they are forced to and in doing so fall back on traditional cultural stereotypes they do not believe.

An alternative way of going about this research was created by Deaux and Lewis (1984) who asked students to list all the characteristics they thought were pertinent to males and females. They found that people used role behaviours (financial provider, meal preparer), physical characteristics (sturdy, graceful), and occupations (construction worker, telephone operator) as well as personality traits. Perceptions of these were closely associated with each other for a given sex. Stereotypes of females and males appear to be comprised of a tight network of associations that extends to virtually all aspects of human beings.

It is possible to conclude from further work, by Deaux and her associates, that men are seen to be like each other and not like women, that perceptions about the sexes appear to be conceived in terms of opposites, and that men and women are seen to have contrasting qualities even when respondent's choices are not constrained (Unger and Crawford, 1992). Beliefs about sex differences appear to have remained essentially the same since the late 1960s despite the increased attention given to gender stereotypes in the popular media since then (Ruble and Ruble, 1982). Women and men appear to be remarkably similar in the terms of the extent to which they see men and women as different. Few significant differences between men and women have been found in most studies of perception about the sexes (Wallston and O'Leary, 1981). We seem to have little awareness of the extent to which sex stereotypes influence our evaluations of others.

A more recent study of sexual stereotyping has been undertaken by Kirchler (1992) who conducted a content analysis on obituaries of senior managers appearing in four German and Austrian newspapers. Obituaries from three years (1974, 1980, 1986) were examined. The results showed that there were differences between the descriptions of male and female managers at all three points in time. The descriptions of male managers remained similar at all times: they were intelligent, knowledgeable, and experienced, outstanding instructors and unselfish opinion leaders with an entrepreneurial spirit. In contrast the women in 1974 and 1980 were described as adorable and likeable. In 1986 they were described as more courageous and highly committed than their male counterparts. But male managers were still perceived as more knowledgeable and expert in their field than female managers. Due to stereotyping, women's chances of success are, then, likely to be still less than those of men.

How would you feel about having a female boss?

The questions below focus on how you feel about female superiors. For each item circle the number that best represents your feelings concerning women superiors. Be completely honest.

	Strongly disagree	Strongly agree
1. I would like to see more women in positions of authority.	1 2 3 4 5	
2. There is no reason why a woman would not be as good a boss as a man.	1 2 3 4 5	
3. Positive discrimination in favour of women has led to to them being in positions of authority.	1 2 3 4 5	
4. Women are too emotional to be given positions of authority.	1 2 3 4 5	
5. A female boss will be distracted from work by family responsibilities.	1 2 3 4 5	
6. Women have the same staying power as men in top jobs.	1 2 3 4 5	
7. Women would have less problems supervising men than vice versa.	1 2 3 4 5	
8. I would prefer to work for a female manager than a male.	1 2 3 4 5	

Are these the 'right' questions to measure attitudes towards women as bosses? What questions would you include to look at attitudes towards this issue?

It is interesting to note that there is no research asking the parallel question of how people feel about having a male boss (Harriman, 1985).

As a result of the sex stereotyping influence, women are often evaluated as less acceptable candidates for stimulating, challenging jobs (Taylor and Ilgen, 1981)and not perceived as having the necessary attributes for success in high-status positions within their organizations (Heilman (1984). When judged by the standard set by men, women frequently fail to measure up (Forrest, 1989). Sex role stereotyping continues to have a substantial impact on human resource management decisions (Heilman, 1980, 1984; Heilman and Saruwatri, 1979; Terborg and Ilgen, 1975). The Terborg and Ilgen study found that students asked to allocate starting and second-year salaries to males or females with the same qualifications

and performance record recommended a significantly higher level of compensation to males than females.

Investigations of the evaluation of male and female performance in equivalent situations have frequently found that males tended to be rated more favourably than females when the presented evidence is identical. Thus when presented with information on the performance of a male or female painter (Pheterson et al., 1971) or applicants for an overseas study programme (Deaux and Taynor, 1973), male performance is rated more favourably than female. Deaux and Emswiller (1974) asked males and females to evaluate the performance of either a male or a female who had performed in an above-average manner on either a male or female related task. They found that performance on a masculine task was more attributed to skill, whereas an equivalent performance by a female on the same task was seen to be more influenced by luck. For an excellent review of the literature on the devaluation of women's competence see Lott (1992).

If women are being evaluated less favourably than men, then it is no wonder that there are so few women being selected for middle and senior management posts. The selection interview is open to personal bias. This is a good argument, then, for using more 'objective' assessment techniques that would identify specific, operationally defined criteria, such as those used in assessment centres. Assessment centres tend to be used for the assessment of 'élite' employees such as graduates or individuals within an organization being identified for fast-track senior management programmes. But Alimo-Metcalfe (1993) argues that assessment centres may be disturbingly more insidious and make discrimination more difficult to detect. The individuals who form the sample from whom the criteria for the centre will be identified are existing senior managers. Most senior managers, as we know, are male. If the qualities that women bring to management, or the styles that they adopt are different to men, then we have a bias within the sampling frame.

The activities of assessment and selection are 'irreducibly social and subjective' (Webb, 1991: 13). Research by the Civil Service of the scores of candidates revealed an uneven distribution between age groups and men and women. A larger percentage of men were passing the test and 20–28 year olds performed better than the younger or older groups. In the early 1980s further detailed examination of these unequal results, combined with the lack of evidence of actual differences in job performance of men and women executive officers of different ages, led to the decision to correct test scores for the effects of age and sex. Webb makes the point that

'... careful adjustments have been made to the test structures and interpretation of the scores to create equitable treatment for women and men of differing age groups. The 'objectivity' of testing is thus a socially constructed objectivity: carefully managed and manipulated to produce the desired results. This would seem to undermine any claims to the 'neutrality' of test *per se* and provide good evidence that test construction and test norms can be devised to produce any desired range of results, according to the dimensions of interest.'

Are men better drivers than women?

The Driving Standards Agency in Nottingham collects data on the percentages of men and women passing their driving tests around Britain. These are the results of percentages of men and women passing their driving test in 1989–92:

	men	women
April 1989–1990	56.96	47.32
April 1990–1991	57.79	47.48
April 1991–1992	56.79	46.08

Here are more recent data from Scotland for 1991–1993:

	Pass	Fail
1991–1992		
Men	41 697	28 358
Women	44 262	47 121
1992–1993 (First three quarters)		
Men	29 255	20 057
Women	31 461	33 582

There are two, not necessarily distinct and different, conclusions that can be drawn:

1. Women are not such good drivers as men when they come to sit their test.
2. Women are being evaluated less favourably than men.

Which conclusion would you agree with and why? How would you set about designing research to look at this issue?

Source: Driving Standards Agency, Department of Transport, Edinburgh.

Gold and Pringle's (1989) study of promotion in management shows that a major hindering factor for female managers was organizational attitudes to women in a male environment. Interestingly more of the 'successful' female managers attributed their progress to their own performance when compared with the men.

The male managers were more likely to invoke luck or opportunity as one of the reasons for their promotional success. Perhaps one explanation is that the women did have the pressure to outperform men in equivalent positions in order to be seen as equal.

The road to promotion is, for some, 'a golden pathway' (Davies and Rosser, 1986). A study of the National Health Service, one of the largest employers of female labour in Britain, shows that to remain on the pathway, mobility is essential, the optimum time in any one job being two years. The years before a candidate is 30 are crucial and the acquisition of additional professional educational qualifications very important. Stepping off the pathway severely jeopardizes the chances of being perceived as a senior manager. For women, who may plan to have children and/or with domestic commitments and the expectation of having to move for a male partner's career development, the obstacles are great. For a man marriage suggests stability and a sense of responsibility; for a woman it is seen as a liability.

The double standard

Men's weaknesses can be interpreted as strengths or ignored, while supposed female weaknesses are highlighted and used to exclude them. The following piece compares attitudes to men and women.

He's ambitious	She's pushy
He's having lunch with the boss: he must be doing well	She's having lunch with the boss: they must be having an affair
He gets on well with people at work	She's always gossiping
He's moving on—he must be a good worker	She's moving on—women are so unreliable

---

Source: Dawson (1986: 39)

Some jobs are considered to be 'men's jobs' requiring masculine characteristics, whereas others are labelled 'women's jobs' requiring feminine characteristics (Krefting and Berger, 1979). The current incumbents in the job and other characteristics of the context make salient particular stereotypes of the ratee. For example there is some evidence that raters are more likely to describe female ratees with stereotypic female traits when there are more female ratees in a situation than when there is an equal number of male and female ratees (Heilman, 1980).

Similarly, raters may be more likely to stereotype a job as a man's job or a woman's job depending on the proportion of men and women currently in the job.

They then judge performance in a job according to how well the person fits the stereotype of the ideal job holder. They are more likely to notice and remember information consistent with their expectations of the stereotype-fit. Those raters who discriminate unfairly do so for what they believe to be rational reasons, the ratee lacks the requisite characteristics—they do not fit the stereotype (Dipboye, 1985). Jobs are, then, sex-typed and the incumbent has to fit the stereotype.

This is what feminine looks like?

Despite almost 10 years of equal opportunities policy at the London Fire and Civil Defence Authority (LFCDA) there are only 47 women out of 6500 firefighters; outside London women firefighters are few. This is due, in part, to a height requirement of 5ft. 6in., you have to be physically fit and to the fact that the job has a male image. Positive action has been taken to train women and ethnic minorities through a pre-entry course which provides a taste of fire service work. The LFCDA has also bought some nursery school places to take the burden off women with children.

Source: *Everywoman*, June 1991: 166–117.

Is there a risk in hiring a woman for a job normally typed as male? People in selection positions operate under a reward system which praises them for a successful selection but would subject them to criticism for an unsuccessful one. The more important the job, the higher the risk, or as the noticability of failure increases. Shaw (1972) found that male applicants were preferred over females (for a male-typed position) where the risk of a bad selection was high, in an important job, rather than for a position where the risk was not so great. McKenna and Johnson (1981) also show that females are discriminated against in a female-oriented occupation in the presence of high selection risk. Selection risk may have a greater effect on sex discrimination than just sex-typing of jobs.

One result is that women are not hired for high-risk, high-profile jobs. Instead they find themselves in dead-end jobs. Kanter (1977) has argued that many of the negative traits ascribed to women managers may be a product of the dead-end roles they occupy. Powerless managers are those left out of critical decisions or easily bypassed in terms of their own competence. All too often this is the experience of a woman when more senior managers want to be kept informed of what she is doing, effectively encouraging those who should be reporting to her to go over her head. The experience of powerlessness corrupts, creating petty tyrants rather than leaders. It promotes the stereotype of women bosses and nagging housewives. In effect Kanter suggests that at least some of the personality traits which appear to be causes of female ineffectiveness as managers may themselves be the effects of the frustrating, ineffectual position in which aspiring women managers often find themselves. It is not that women do not know how to play in teams; it is just very hard to play in a team that does not want you in it!

One initially worrying piece of evidence about the evaluation of women and their work comes from a study by Goldberg (1967) of evaluations of male and female competence. A set of articles from different professional disciplines were presented to two groups of female subjects. Articles were identical in content for both groups but differed in the sex of the first name of the ascribed author. The results were that the ratings of the articles ascribed to women were consistently lower than those of male articles, regardless of the sexual association of the professional field. However, using Goldberg's original stimulus materials, or comparable ones, several investigators have been unable to find significant sex-of-author effects (Chobot et al., 1974; Gross and Geffner, 1980; Levenson et al., 1975; Panek et al., 1976).

Baruch (1972) showed that Goldberg's sample did not evaluate male and female competence differently and explained this by saying that major changes had taken place in attitudes with respect to women and that the Goldberg study drew on students at a traditionally oriented women's college. A woman may be evaluated as favourably for her achievements as a man if her performance is recognized by an authority (Pheterson et al., 1971). It is, then, a question of a woman's credibility, and the acknowledgement of achievement may therefore be especially important to women.

Baruch also supported a 'competence model hypothesis': that it is women whose mothers have not worked who devalue feminine competence. Career-related achievement is apparently defined as masculine by women who have not been exposed to a maternal model of work competence. This view was supported by Vogel et al. (1970) who found among female college students that the tendency to stereotype and differentiate the male and female sex roles, especially in the dimension of competence, was associated with a non-working mother; for these women competence was linked to masculinity and was not part of the feminine sex role.

Valuing achievement can have its penalties. It is thought that women who value achievement, higher education, and professional careers are especially likely to be obsessed with thinness and to suffer from eating disorders such as anorexia and bulimia. They occur when the level of discrimination against women is low enough to let women into higher education and the professions but when the level is not low enough to break the association between femininity and incompetence (Tavris, 1992: 32). This happens particularly to women who are insecure about their competence and who feel that their fathers did not think they were intelligent and did not support their ambitions. To resolve the dilemma they try to 'measure up', to become as thin as a man.

The research on women and how they are rated produces very mixed results. There is evidence to support Goldberg (e.g. Cline *et al.*, 1977). There is evidence showing bias against women, even in the skill with which they shelve library books (Schmitt and Lappin, 1980).

Despite this, and other evidence of the bias against women, a substantial number of studies have found no differences in rating men and women (Hall and Hall, 1976; Heilman and Guzzo, 1978; London and Stumpf, 1983) or have found that higher evaluations are given to women (Bigoness, 1976; Hamner *et al.*, 1974; Norton, *et al.*, 1977). Wallston and O'Leary (1981: 19) were able to conclude that 'although a number of studies have not found real differences in the level of competence exhibited by women and men in specific positions, differences are *perceived* to exist'. One explanation for this evaluation bias is the effect of sex as a status characteristic. Since the male sex is more highly valued, in management, men's behaviour is frequently valued more, even when compared to equally effective behaviour performed by women.

Lott (1992) concluded that the tendency to devalue a competent women, although not invariable, appears to be more the rule than the exception. The available data suggest that a competent woman is most likely to be devalued (when she is not actually known or known well by an evaluator) when judgements are made in a serious, believable, and realistic context, and when there are potential consequences for the evaluator. Negative evaluations of competent women are least likely in situations where persons are judging someone they know well, or with whom they have worked or interacted.

One study shows that women managers perceive themselves as being different to male managers. Myers and McCaulley (1985) reported systematic differences on the Myers–Briggs Type Inventory in a study of self-descriptions of 1051 men and 181 women attending management development programmes. The women more frequently typed themselves as predominantly intuitive and feeling, while the men more frequently typed themselves as predominantly sensing and thinking.

To make matters more complex, there are studies to show that women are rated as highly or higher than men when they both exhibit high levels of performance and less favourably when they both exhibit mediocre or poor levels of performance (Abramson *et al.*, 1978; Jacobson and Effertz, 1974; Madden and Martin, 1979; Pheterson *et al.*, 1971). Also Rosen and Jerdee (1974) and Mai-Dalton *et al.* (1979) found that females who act 'out of role' by behaving aggressively are evaluated more favourably than those who comply with the conventional sex role stereotype. How would you explain the inconsistent results (see Dipboye, 1985)?

Dress will influence a person's perception of you. The influence of clothing on the personal characteristics of the wearer has been well documented (Damhorst and Reed, 1980; Douty, 1963; Forsythe, 1987; Forsythe *et al.*; 1984, 1985; Hamid,

---

How do men wish to be perceived in the domestic sphere?

It may be advantageous for a man (I know this one particularly well!) to be perceived as 'hopeless' at household tasks. He might fill the dishwasher with clothes washing powder, go to the shops and forget most of the essential items on the list you have both compiled, and so on. Do you know of any of these strategies men might use?

The bank worker's tale

Lesley Wayne started as a teagirl for one of the major clearing banks at 16. Twenty-two years later, she has, she says, 'crawled into middle management' and is one of the three managers in a big branch ... She is one of the tiny minority; 6 per cent of the bank's managers are women, yet 57 per cent of its employees are women. It's been an uphill struggle and she is not surprised she has so few women colleagues. 'When I started in the late 1960s, men were paid more for the same job. When a women married it was presumed she would leave. Women worked in the back office and were only allowed to go on the counters on Saturday mornings as a sort of treat or reward.'

I got stuck in my twenties for six years on a junior clerical level—I'd married and the bank labelled me with the career potential assessment of a married woman—that meant a secretary for life. I went through a grievance procedure for 18 months to get myself re-assessed because only then was there any chance of getting the training I needed.'

Source: *The Guardian*, 29 October 1991. ©*The Guardian*, 1991.

1968). Forsythe *et al.* (1984) indicated that masculinity of women applicants' clothing had a positive effect on the perception of masculine management characteristics. A woman applicant's clothing may provide a means for her to convey management characteristics and so improve her opportunity for employment in management positions. The more masculine outfits result in more favourable hiring decisions (Cash, 1985; Forsythe *et al.*, 1985; Heilman and Saruwatri, 1979).

However, the masculinity of the costume does not affect the perception of feminine managerial traits. Female applicants will be rated highly on feminine management traits regardless of the outfit worn. It seems that women may be

---

Does how you look matter?

An employee of Price Waterhouse felt aggrieved when she was not granted partnership status, so she took her case to court. She was described by law partners as 'macho', harsh, and aggressive. One man advised her to 'walk more femininely, dress more femininely, wear make-up, have her hair styled, and wear jewellery'. Her supporters described her behaviour as outspoken, independent, self-confident, assertive and courageous. Her opposition interpreted the same behaviour as overbearing, arrogant, self-centred, and abrasive.

At the same time as this case was being taken to court a lawyer lost her job because she was too feminine. She favoured short skirts, designer blouses, ornate jewellery, and high heels. Her boss told her that she looked like a 'bimbo' and she was sacked after she complained about his remarks to the EEOC (Equal Employment Opportunities Commission).

Have you seen these pressures on women to be both feminine and masculine?

Under what kind of conditions is the negative stereotyping of women more likely to occur? Men are likely to behave like the Price Waterhouse partners in the case above when the woman (or other minority) is a token member of the organization; when the criteria used to evaluate women are ambiguous and when observers lack necessary information to evaluate the women's work.

Source: Adapted from Tavris (1992: 21–22).

perceived to possess feminine managerial traits regardless of the masculinity of costume, whereas a more masculine costume is necessary to enhance the perception of masculine managerial traits (Forsythe, 1987). The research suggests, then, that masculinity of clothing may be one way in which women can communicate masculine managerial traits and may help them in job interviews.

Looks seem to matter too. The retailer Asda employs a recruitment guide which instructs managers to avoid employing anyone overweight or with a poor complexion. The ideal look is a healthy, well groomed appearance and a pleasant expression (*Personnel Today*, 10 August 1993: 2). The accepted look is in the employer's mind. There may be differences in the way the standards are applied to men and women. For example, it is acceptable for women to wear pony-tails and some men chose to sport them. A man was sacked for wearing a pony-tail but won compensation for unfair dismissal in court (*Personnel Today*, 14 July 1992: 2).

Men do seem to have a head start. Good-looking men may have an

,ntage over less good-looking men for entry into managerial and clerical jobs, good looks may only work to the advantage of women with regard to clerical sitions. Attractive women may be penalized when being considered for manage- ient jobs (Heilman and Saruwatri, 1979).

Physical attractiveness is beneficial in performance evaluations and recom- mendations for promotion, merit pay rises, and bonuses in clerical positions. However, for a woman in a managerial job Heilman and Stopeck (1985a, b) have shown that attractiveness can be a disadvantage. In addition, a male assistant senior manager's career success was more likely to be attributed to ability and capability if the man was good looking; success of a good-looking female was more likely to be attributed to luck or connections. The attractive male was also seen as more likeable and to have more integrity, but the attractive female was rated as having less integrity.

Heilman proposed a 'lack of fit' model. Attractiveness enhances perceived masculinity and femininity and is an asset for both men and women. If a job is masculine sex typed, as managerial jobs seem to be, then masculine qualities are considered a prerequisite for success and attractiveness benefits only men. Attractive females, perceived as more feminine than less attractive ones, are more negatively evaluated for such jobs as they are perceived as having a less good person–job 'fit'. Good looks disadvantage females when being considered for stereotypically masculine jobs.

Contrary evidence can be found. Physically attractive women can find that more office doors are readily open to them and be granted longer interviews. Then (1988) found that in the judgement of 35 male and 37 female students in a simulation experiment, very attractive women were rated higher than the average- looking or unattractive women in their potential for promotion to top management. The unattractive women received the lowest ratings, despite their being seen as more masculine in their potential for promotion as well as more suitable as a co- worker or friend.

This issue of attractiveness is dealt with in detail in Naomi Wolf's *The Beauty Myth* (1990), in which it is argued that women's progress, in terms of liberation, has been stalled. Eating disorders rose exponentially during the 1980s while cosmetic surgery became the fastest growing medical speciality. Market manipulation in the USA has led to a diet industry worth $32 billion, a cosmetics industry of $20 billion, a $300 million cosmetic surgery industry and a $7 billion pornography industry. Thirty thousand American women told researchers that they would rather lose 10– 15lb than achieve any other goal. Women's magazines is one medium which provides the aspirational ideology to promote the myth.

Wolf argues that we are in the midst of a violent backlash to feminism that uses images of female beauty as a political weapon against women's advancement. The fixation on beauty in the 1980s was a direct consequence of, and a one-to-one check and balance upon, the entry of women into powerful positions. The beauty myth is social control; it keeps male dominance intact. The beauty myth is not about women but about men and power. Competition between women is part of the myth so that women will be divided from one another. What do you think? How do women fare in terms of perception when it comes to power?

WOMEN AND POWER

Discussion point

It is said that men debate and women manipulate. Do you think this is true? Are all stereotypes about women negative?

The concept of interpersonal power can be defined as the ability to influence another person to do or to believe something she or he would not necessarily have done or believed spontaneously (Johnson, 1978). Women have long been seen to be manipulators, who use indirect, devious strategies to get their way. Support for this view, however, cannot be based solely on sex differences because the issue of gender difference in power strategies is confounded with power inequality between the sexes (Miller, 1976). Differences in the strategies women and men use to exert influence may be more a function of power or status inequality than gender.

A person's view of their attributes will vary according to their position in the organizational power hierarchy (Fagenson, 1990; Kanter, 1977). Those occupying positions at the upper corporate levels have power and are in an advantageous position. Those in lower positions have little power. Those who have the advantage find that they also have the ability to satisfy their own needs and desires within the work situation. Those located high in the organizational power hierarchy think of themselves as more instrumental and masculine—forceful, strong, self-confident and independent; they can depend on themselves. In contrast, those outside this hierarchy are inhibited from acting on their own behalf and are dependent on others to meet their needs. They then see themselves as being more feminine or 'other-focused' (Kanter, 1977; Spence and Helmreich, 1978)—kind, warm, gentle, understanding, aware of others' feelings, and helpful to others.

Miller (1976) suggested that in most organizations power means the ability to advance oneself and simultaneously to control, limit if possible, destroy the power of others. This definition does not fit easily with how women see themselves as workers (Cassell and Walsh, 1993). The stereotypical base of women's power is 'relational' (Gilligan, 1982). Relational power is concerned with 'taking care', the supportive or facilitative aspects of women's behaviour. Although it is socially and culturally acceptable for women to express themselves in this way, the cost is that it does not fit easily with the definition of powerful behaviour expressed by Miller.

Women who have reached the higher echelons of management have used 'gender management strategies' (Cassell and Walsh, 1993: 111). They modify their behaviour to match organizational expectations which help them cope in male-dominated cultures (Franklin, 1985). They learn how to redefine and manage their 'femaleness' (Marshall, 1984). The most used strategy appears to be one of attempting to blend in with an existing organizational culture, trying very hard to be feminine enough while simultaneously being business-like and exhibiting stereotypically male characteristics such as rationality and instrumentality (Sheppard, 1989; Cassell and Walsh, 1991). Not managing your gender, not blending in can lead to exclusion (Fine, 1987).

Women are criticized for being feminine—talking incessantly, nagging, gossiping, being concerned with appearance, driving poorly (Kaschack, 1992). If this is how they are perceived, it is easy to see why men succeed in power wars. Women are unable to become powerful in organizations because definitions of power are inappropriate to women's experience; women are socialized into fearing power and using second-class power tactics to get what they want. These are pervasive barriers to advancement (Cassell and Walsh, 1993).

It is men who occupy the majority of jobs in the upper levels of organizations; women occupy the majority of lower-level jobs (Powell, 1988; Peitchinis, 1989). Men's perceived masculine characteristics and women's perceived feminine characteristics are associated with their organizational level, not with their sex. Individuals in the upper levels in the organizational power hierarchy are perceived as more masculine than those in the lower levels (Fagenson, 1990). Women, in the upper levels, see themselves as fitting the masculine profile inherent in managerial ideology (Brenner *et al.*, 1989; Massengill and DiMarco, 1985; Schein, 1973, 1975). Leventhal and Garcia (1991) show how male and female employees perceived their female bosses, and female bosses perceived themselves, to be high on the masculine scale and to have characteristics related to managerial success. The nature of the job was seen to be a critical factor in sex-role stereotyping. How, then, do they fare when it comes to appraisal?

WOMEN AND APPRAISAL

We saw earlier how Lott (1992) had shown that where women are less known to the evaluator, the perception is more likely to be negative. We would expect, then, that where women are known well, as in a situation where they are being appraised by someone they know, the evaluation would be more positive. But Thomas (1987) demonstrated that the words used to evaluate men and women in appraisals were different. Women were 'less competent, logical, and mature' and their performance warranted fewer recommendations and only nebulous praise. Poor evaluations of women employees in appraisal may be helping perpetuate lack of equal opportunities (Wilson and Beaton, 1992). Performance appraisal can turn staff into cynics and losers (*Personnel Today* 13–26 October 1992: 4). Performance-related pay systems can systematically disadvantage women employees; men at similar job levels with the same performance ratings as women were more likely to have been offered training and promotion opportunities (Institute of Manpower Studies, 1992). Raters can find their own self-esteem threatened by a high-performing female (Grube *et al.*, 1982)

Research by Corby (1982) highlights the difference in men's and women's appraisals in the British Civil Service. The men, generally, received critical feedback but the women were far more likely to receive innocuous, non-specific criticism, if any. This finding suggests that men feel discomfort in appraising female colleagues. If the information exchanged in the review process is to be used for development, then the quality of information exchanged for both sexes must be equal. If it's not, less women might be promoted—this was this case in the Civil Service.

A US laboratory experiment by Dobbins *et al.* (1988) showed that evaluations are dependent on how traditional the stereotype of women was for the appraisee. Female ratees were evaluated less accurately by raters with traditional stereotypes of women than by raters with non-traditional stereotypes. Women who are evaluated by raters with traditional stereotypes of women will be at a disadvantage in obtaining merit pay increases and promotions.

Alimo-Metcalfe (1993: 21) has also reported significant differences in the perceptions of women and men in the appraisal interview in an English context. Women found it more difficult than men to: talk freely about what they wanted to discuss; discuss their relationship with their appraiser; give feedback to their appraiser; and identify their areas of strength.

Of the general managers, twice the proportion of male general managers reported receiving the highest rating (on a five-point scale) than did female general managers. It is very important, then, that women benefit from the appraisal discussion and yet this does not seem to be the case.

The characteristics associated with a successful *manager* are more congruent with the traits attributed to men than women (Bernadin, 1982; Broverman *et al.*, 1975). Basil (1972) and Schein's studies (1973, 1975) showed that these beliefs were held equally strongly by female and male managers. Women are assumed to be less assertive, less ambitious and less career oriented that men (Kaufman and Fetters, 1980). A more recent study has shown that women's attitudes have changed, but men's have not (Schein and Mueller, 1990). A cross-cultural study shows that nothing has changed with respect to men's attitudes but female middle managers no longer sex stereotype the managerial job (Brenner *et al.*, 1989; Schein and Mueller, 1990; Schein *et al.*, 1989).

There is thus a persistent stereotype that associates management with being male. Whichever characteristics are considered important for managers, they appear to be the ones generally identified more closely with men than with women (Brenner *et al.*, 1989; Hearn and Parkin, 1988). Studies of management in different cultures have left untouched the myth that management responsibilities are best fulfilled by men so, for example, Laurent's sample of managers attending the INSEAD business school in France contains almost no women (Antal and Izraeli, 1993). The prevailing paradigm in the study of management can be summarized as 'think manager, think male' (Nkomo, 1988).

Women also perceive characteristics of managers to be those more closely ascribed to men than women. Schein (1989) has described this phenomenon as Nkomo does. Yet women are not less ambitious or career oriented. Alban-Metcalfe (1989), having conducted one of the largest surveys of managers and professionals working in Britain, was able to conclude that there is little foundation for the popular myth that women are less ambitious and career oriented than men. Indeed her data show the opposite might be true.

Researchers have, then, no problem in identifying bias against women in management. An instrument designed to measure this bias was developed by Peters et al. (1977). They developed a 21-item scale called the Women as Manager Scale (WAMS). Each item consists of a statement about women in business and the respondents are asked to indicate their level of agreement on a seven-point scale. Sex-role stereotyping, measured by WAMS, is related to discrimination in hiring (Terborg et al., 1977). Females receive significantly less favourable personnel decisions than males, though it must be noted that Cohen and Leavengood (1978) question the utility of WAMS in predicting behaviour.

Women are afraid of achievement?

If you are female, write a story which begins: 'After first term finals Anne finds herself at the top of her medical school class.' If you are male substitute, Anne for John. If there are differences in the stories men and women produce, could the result be interpreted as fear of success? An alternative explanation is that they are responding in terms of stereotyped expectations about what happens to women or men who succeed, and in the case of Anne, what happens to the women who succeed in a male-dominated and high-status occupation. Is the research merely tapping sex role stereotypes?

WOMEN ARE SEEN TO FEAR SUCCESS?

The concept of fear of success came along with the beginning of the contemporary women's movement and closely followed the publication of *The Feminine Mystique* (Freidan, 1963) and the formation of the American National Organization for Women. It was an idea, according to some writers 'whose time had come'.

Horner (1972) argued that women suffer from a fear of success in competitive achievement situations. For men, success in this situation is consistent with self-esteem and masculinity; for women, there are often overtones of aggression and masculinity which could lead to social rejection and disapproval, something on which women depend. Horner used a projective procedure to assess the presence or absence of fear of success. Women and men were given verbal cues and asked to complete the story as in the experiment above. The analysis was done scoring for presence or absence of fear of success imagery in the stories. In the initial study 65 per cent of females wrote 'fear of success' stories to the Anne cue; less than 10 per cent of male subjects wrote fear of success stories to the John cue.

A similar study, by Feather and Raphelson (1974), gave men and women both verbal cues. They found some support for Horner's findings in an Australian sample, but less support in an American group. While male students in the American sample saw Anne's success as more likely to have negative consequences than John's success, there was very little difference in the proportion of fear of success stories written by females in the American sample to the Anne and John cues. But males in both groups, however, wrote a larger proportion of fear of success stories to the Anne cue than to the John cue identifying potentially negative consequences for the female when she succeeded in a male-dominated occupation (being a doctor).

If the word 'medical' is changed to 'nursing' in Horner's first sentence, females' stories include less negative imagery (Alper, 1974). Success in non-traditional occupations is associated with negative consequences (Condry and Dyer, 1976). Both women and men recognize that successful females (and perhaps successful males in a non-traditionally masculine field like nursing) may experience obstacles and conflicts as a result of their occupational choices. Responses indicative of fear of success, therefore, may reflect expectations of 'punishment' for sex role deviancy.

Fear of punishment is highlighted in the work of Majorie Goodwin. Her research on children's play sheds light on why women might fear success. Sadly pre-teen and teenage girls were criticized for success, for appearing better than others in their group. One girl's offence was to skip a class in school and get A's on her report card; another incurred wrath from her classmates by wearing newer and more expensive clothes (Goodwin, 1990; Tannen, 1990: 217).

In a British study (see Haste, 1993: 152) students did not find success problematic but they anticipated some difficulties. Girls particularly expected conflict if they were successful in competition with their boyfriends. About half of each sex saw female success in positive terms, about half in negative terms. Male success was seen as unproblematic.

Other research has revealed that males exhibit as much fear of success in projective imagery as do females (see, for example, Brown *et al.*, 1974; Tresemer,

1974). Thus the findings reported by Horner are very much in doubt. Many researchers discarded the concept on the basis of its problematic scientific status (Fleming, 1982). The concept of fear has generated hundreds of studies and its scientific status is still debated (Betz and Fitgerald, 1987; Spence and Helmreich, 1983). But psycho-analysts have continued to embrace it as an explanation for client's problems. It refuses to be buried due to its intuitive appeal; it offers an explanation of why women have problems with accomplishment that is simple and satisfying (Mednick, 1989).

Here is another explanation. Olson (1988) reported that women were less self-confident than men and attributed their successes less often to their own abilities than to luck. They also reported less overall confidence in their present and future performance. They do this to appear modest, she says. But if we do not take the male as norm then this explanation can be turned around to read that men wish to appear self-confident and this inhibits them from making modest explanations of their abilities or acknowledging the help of others or the role of chance (Tavris, 1992: 28).

Discussion point

What are the accepted and appropriate achievements for both men and women among your student group?

In a longitudinal study of career planning among college women, Almquist and Angrist (1970) focused on career-oriented women who chose male-dominated occupations. They posed a 'deviance hypothesis' which suggested that these women are different from non-career-oriented women who choose traditionally feminine occupations, but this received little support. Instead they found support for an alternative hypothesis, stressing the effects of broadening and enriching experiences on career planning when data on the mother's work histories, the

---

Discussion point

Sometimes women become 'invisible' as managers in people's minds. Consider the following headline 'Why the best man doesn't always win: A firm's most effective man can often be passed over.'

It looks as though it is not only the best man that is passed over.

Can you think of other times when women have become 'invisible'?

Source: *Sunday Times*, 3 December 1989. © *Sunday Times*, 1989.

student's own work experience, and the influence of occupational role models were taken into account.

HOW DO WOMEN MANAGERS SEE THEMSELVES?

A study by Alban-Metcalfe and West (1991) (see also Alban-Metcalfe, 1987) has shown how women perceive themselves as more likely to show their feelings, more sociable, and more intellectual (which is not surprising if they were better academically qualified) than did men. They were less relaxed and less confident but felt more fulfilled than men. But there were more similarities than differences between the sexes; men and women were, in general, equally ambitious, controlling, forceful, creative, trusting, optimistic, happy, content with themselves, and had the same degree of dislike and uncertainty.

Women are more cautious than their male counterparts in fixing first-year targets when setting up in business but end up being more successful. They take a more realistic approach to financial forecasting, employ fewer people and are less likely to set up a limited company. Caution proves, then to be best for women (NOP Corporate and Financial survey reported in the *Daily Telegraph*, 12 October 1992: 29). Alison Hewlett, a director of the research company, reported: 'The research suggests women take a more prudent approach to business. Their estimations tend to be more conservative right from the start.'

WOMEN HAVE LOWER POWER NEEDS?

It has also been assumed that women have lower power needs than men. Power needs can be defined as the need to establish, maintain, or restore prestige or impact. The need for power has been shown to be closely linked with managerial success (Kotter, 1977; McClelland and Burnham, 1976). Research by Kanter (1977) has contradicted this assumption that women have lower power needs and that women would not be interested in positions of increased responsibility and influence. She found that decreased interest in responsibility and influence were functions of status power differences in organizational employment rather than a function of gender. Kanter concludes that where women workers are accepted as equals and given realistic advancement opportunities, they no longer take the role of low-status persons but interact actively with their co-workers and display ambition and task orientation in accordance with their abilities.

Kanter (1976) suggested that it is not gender which is the critical factor but number. This suggestion was supported by Taylor *et al.* (1977). Minority individuals are evaluated are more extremely and more likely to be cast in special, often stereotypical roles. Is women's motivation different to that of men? This is the topic for a later chapter.

What advice does the research offer to women about how they can be perceived favourably? Women managers need to ensure their superiors of their competence by earning the right credentials and receiving competitive job offers and outside acclaim (Wood, 1975). They need a network of contacts, particularly pragmatic business contacts (Cox, 1986). Learning how to befriend, and give and receive help from men without allowing it to become a sexual encounter is important. They need to know how to deal with sexual advances and sexual harassment. Female job applicants who combine a warm, co-operative style with goal-oriented leadership skills are the most likely to be preferred by their employers.

These are the issues with which women need to learn to deal. This chapter has described the perceptual errors women face. Standard organization behaviour texts and women in management texts rarely look at this topic in any depth. It is clear, however, that extensive organizational change is needed to alter the negative view of women at work. The perspectives, values, and prejudices of the decision makers need to be challenged. Management can play a central role. Where senior managers initiate and make a clear commitment to equal opportunities, coherent and consistent employment equity programmes will follow (Abella, 1984).

Men and women have learned to perceive women in this negative way but it is possible to question these perceptions, ignore what you do not like, change the gender rules, resist and challenge what is regarded as 'normal'. Gender rules, like any set of rules, are outcomes rather than fixed, immutable entities (see Mills and Murgatroyd, 1991: 94–96). We need to question what attitudes we think of as 'normal' and consider what the holders of social power wish to have accepted. What do we know of what men and women in organizations have already learned; what are the gender rules which have been learned? This is the topic for the next chapter.

Review Questions

Why does it matter what you wear?

Review why men and women are perceived differently and what the consequences may be.

Must women adopt male characteristics to succeed or is it men and organizations that need to change?

Does our culture prepare females for powerlessness? (See Lips, 1994.)

REFERENCES

ABELLA, R. S.. (1984) 'Equity in Employment' Report of the Royal Commission (Canada) Ministry of Supply and Services, Ottowa, Canada.

ABRAMSON, P. E., GOLDBERG, P. A., GREENBERG, J. H. and ABRAMSON, U. M. (1978) 'The Talking Platypus Phenomenon: Competency Ratings as a Function of Sex and Professional Status', *Psychology of Women Quarterly*, **2**, 114–124.

ALBAN-METCALFE, B. (1987) 'Male and Female Managers: An Analysis of Biographical and Self-concept Data', *Work and Stress*, **1**(3), 207–219.

ALBAN-METCALFE, B. (1989) 'What Motivates Managers: An Investigation by Gender and Sector of Employment', *Public Administration*, **67**(Spring), 95–108.

ALBAN-METCALFE, B. and WEST, M. (1991) 'Women Managers', Chapter 12 in J. Firth Cozens and M. West, (eds), *Women at Work*, Open University Press, Milton Keynes.

ALIMO-METCALFE, B. (1993) 'Women in Management: Organizational Socialization and Assessment Practices that Prevent Career Advancement', *International Journal of Selection and Assessment*, **1**(2), April, 68–83.

ALMQUIST, E. M. and ANGRIST, S. S. (1970) 'Career Salience and Atypicality of Occupational Choice among College Women', *Journal of Marriage and the Family*, May, 242–249.

ALPER, T. G. (1974) 'Achievement Motivation in College Women: A Now-you-see-it-now-you-don't Phenomenon', *American Psychologist*, **29**, 194–203.

ANTAL, A. B. and IZRAELI, D. N. (1993) 'A Global Comparison of Women in Management', Chapter 3 in E. A. Fagenson (ed.), *Women in Management*, Sage, Newbury Park, Calif.

ARCHIBALD, K. (1970) *Sex and the Public Service*, Public Service Commission, Ottowa, Canada.

BARUCH, G. K. (1972) 'Maternal Influences upon College Women's Attitudes toward Women and Work', *Developmental Psychology*, **6**(1) , 32–37.

BASIL, D. C. (1972) *Women in Management*, Dunellen, New York.

BELSEY, C. (1988) 'Marking by Numbers', *AUT Women*, **15**.

BERNADIN, H. J. (ED.) (1982) *Women in the Workforce*, Praeger, New York.

BERNARD, M. E., KEEFAUVER, W., ELSWORTH, G. and NAYLOR, F. D. (1981) 'Sex Role Behaviour and Gender in Teacher–Student Evaluations', *Journal of Educational Psychology*, **73**, 681–696.

BETZ, N. E. and FITZGERALD, L. F. (1987) *The Career Psychology of Women*, Academic Press, London.

BIGONESS, W. J. (1976) 'Effect of Applicant's Sex, Race and Performance on Employers' Performance Ratings: Some Additional Findings', *Journal of Applied Psychology*, **61**, 80–84.

BRADLEY, C. (1984) 'Sex Bias in the Evaluation of Students', *British Journal of Social Psychology*, **23**, 147–153.

BRENNER, O. C., TOMKIEWICZ, J. and SCHEIN, V. E. (1989) 'The Relationship Between Sex Role Stereotypes and Requisite Management Characteristics Revisited', *Academy of Management Journal*, **32**, 662–669.

BRONSTEIN, P., BLACK, L., PFENNIG, J. and WHITE, A. (1986) 'Getting Academic Jobs: Are Women Equally Qualified—And Equally Successful?', *American Psychologist*, March, 318–322.

BROVERMAN, I. K., VOGEL, S. R., BROVERMAN, D. M., CLARKSON, F. E. and ROSENKRANZ, P. S. (1972) 'Sex Role Stereotypes: A Current Appraisal', *Journal of Social Issues*, **28**(2), 59–78.

BROVERMAN, I. K., VOGEL, R., BROVERMAN, D. M., CLARKSON, F. E. and ROSENKRANZ, P. S. (1975) 'Sex Role Stereotypes: A Current Appraisal', in M. T. S. Mednick, S. S. Tangri and L. W. Hoffman (eds) *Women and Achievement: Social and Motivational Analyses*, Hemisphere, New York.

BROWN, M., JENNINGS, J. and VANIK, V. (1974) 'The Motive to Avoid Success: A Further Examination', *Journal of Research in Personality*, **8**, 172–176.

CASH, T. (1985) 'The Impact of Grooming Style on the Evaluations of Women in Management', in M. R. Solomon (ed.), *The Psychology of Fashion*, pp. 343–355, Heath, Lexington, Mass.

CASSELL, C. M. and WALSH, S. (1991) 'Towards a Woman-friendly Psychology of Work: Gender Power and Organizational Culture', paper presented to the BPS Annual Occupational Psychology Conferences, Liverpool, quoted in Cassell and Walsh (1993).

CASSELL, C. M. and WALSH, S. (1993) 'Being Seen But Not Heard: Barriers to Women's Equality in the Workplace', Working Paper, Sheffield Business School, published in the *Psychologist*, **6**(3), 110–113.

CHOBOT, D. S., GOLDBERG, P. A. and ABRAMSON, L. M. (1974) 'Prejudice Against Women: A Replication and Extension', *Psychological Reports*, **35**, 478.

CLINE, M. E., HOLMES, D. S. and WERNER, J. (1977) 'Evaluations of the Work of Men and Women as a Function of the Sex of the Judge and Type of Work', *Journal of Applied Social Psychology*, **7**, 89–93.

COHEN, S. L. and LEAVENGOOD, S. (1978) 'The Utility of the WAMS: Shouldn't it Relate to Discriminatory Behaviour', *Academy of Management Journal*, **21**(4), December, 742–748.

CONDRY, J. and DYER, S. (1976) 'Fear of Success: Attribution of Cause to the Victim', *Journal of Social Issues*, **32**, 63–83.

CORBY, S. (1982) *Equal Opportunities for Women in the Civil Service*, HMSO, London.

COX, M. (1986) 'Clearer Connections: The Nebulous Networks of the 70s Give Way to Pragmatic Business Contacts', *Wall Street Journal*, 24 March.

DAMHORST, M. I. and REED, J. A. P. (1980) 'Effect of Clothing Color on Assessment of Characteristics of Job Applicants'. Research Report at 71st Annual Meeting of American Home Economics Journal Association.

DAVIES, C. and ROSSER, J. (1986) *Processes of Discrimination: A Study of Women Working in the NHS*, DHSS, London.

DAWSON, R. (1986) 'And All That Is Unseen', Church House Publishing, London.

DEAUX, K. and EMSWILLER, T. (1974) 'Explanations of Successful Performance on Sex-linked Tasks: What is Skill for the Male is Luck for the Female, *Journal of Personality and Social Psychology*, **29**(1), 80–85.

DEAUX, K. and LEWIS, L. L. (1984) 'The Structure of Gender Stereotypes: Interrelationships among Components and Gender Labels, *Journal of Personality and Social Psychology*, **46**, 991–1004.

DEAUX, K. and TAYNOR, J. (1973) 'Evaluation of Male and Female Ability: Bias Works Two Ways, *Psychological Reports*, **32**, 261–262.

DENMARK, F. L. (1979) 'The Outspoken Woman: Can She Win?' paper presented at the New York Academy of Sciences, New York City, quoted in J. Bohan, (ed.), *Seldom Seen, Rarely Heard, Woman's Place in Psychology*, p. 175, Westview Press, Boulder, Colo., 1992.

DIPBOYE, R. L. (1985) 'Some Neglected Variables in Research on Discrimination in Appraisals', *Academy of Management Review*, **10**(1), 116–127.

DIPBOYE, R. L., ARVEY, R. B. and TERPSTRA, D. E. (1977) 'Sex and Physical Attractiveness of Raters and Applicants and Determinants of Resume Evaluations', *Journal of Applied Psychology*, **62**, 288–294.

DIPBOYE, R. L., FROMKIN, H. L. and WIBACK, J. K. (1975) 'Relative Importance of Applicant Sex, Attractiveness and Scholastic Standing in Evaluation of Job Applicant Resources', *Journal of Applied Psychology*, **60**, 39–43.

DOBBINS, G. H., CARDY, R. L. and TRUXILLO, D. M. (1988) 'The Effects of Purpose of Appraisal and Individual Differences in Stereotypes of Women on Sex differences in Performance Ratings: A Laboratory and Field Study', *Journal of Applied Psychology*, **73**(3), 551–558.

DOUGLAS, M. (1987) *How Institutions Think*, Routledge & Kegan Paul, London.

DOUTY, H. I. (1963) 'Influence of Clothing on Perceptions of People', *Journal of Home Economics*, **55**, 197–202.

FAGENSON, E. (1990) 'Perceived Masculine and Feminine Attributes Examined as a Function of Individuals' Sex and Level in the Organizational Power Hierarchy: A Test of Four Theoretical Perspectives', *Journal of Applied Psychology*, **75**(2), 204–211.

FEATHER, N. T. (1984) 'Masculinity, Femininity, Psychological Androgyny, and the Structures of Values', *Journal of Personality and Social Psychology*, **47**, 604–621.

FEATHER, N. T. and RAPHELSON, A. C. (1974) 'Fear of Success in Australian and American Students: Motive or Sex-role Stereotype?', *Journal of Personality*, **42**, 190–201.

FIDELL, L. S. (1970) 'Empirical Verification of Sex Discrimination in Hiring Practice in Psychology', *American Psychologist*, **25**, 1094–1098.

FINE, G. A. (1987) 'One of the Boys: Women in Male-dominated Settings', in M. S. Kimmel (ed.), *Changing Men: New Directions in Research on Men and Masculinity*, Sage, Newbury Park, Calif.

FLEMING, J. (1982) 'Projective and Psychometric Approaches to Measurement: The Case of Fear of Success', in A. J. Stewart (ed.), *Motivation and Society: A Volume in Honor of David C. McClelland*, pp. 63–95 Jossey Bass, San Francisco.

FORREST, A. (1989) 'Women in a Man's World', *Journal of Management Development*, **6**, 61–68.

FORSYTHE, S. (1987) 'Effect of Clothing on Perception of Masculine and Feminine Traits', *Perceptual and Motor Skills*, **65**, 531–534.

FORSYTHE, S. M., DRAKE, M. F. and COX, C. E. (1984) 'Dress as an Influence on Perceptions of Management Characteristics in Women', *Home Economics Research Journal*, **13**, 112–121.

FORSYTHE, S. M., DRAKE, M. F. and COX, C. E. (1985) 'Influence of Applicant's Dress on Interviewer's Selection Decisions', *Journal of Applied Psychology*, **70**, 374–378.

FRANKLIN, U. M. (1985) 'Will Women Change Technology or Will Technology Change Women?', Canadian Research Institute for the Advancement of Women, paper no. 9, quoted in Cassell and Walsh (1993).

FRIEDAN, B. (1963) *The Feminine Mystique*, Dell, New York.

GILLIGAN, C. (1982) *In a Different Voice: Psychological Theory and Women's Development*, Harvard University Press, Cambridge, Mass.

GOLD, U. and PRINGLE, J. (1989) 'Management Promotions: Gender-specific Factors', *Women in Management Review and Abstracts*, **4**(3), 5–10 (published in association with the Equal Opportunities Commission, MCB University Press, Bradford).

GOLDBERG, P. (1967) 'Misogyny and the College Girl', paper presented at the meeting of the Eastern Psychological Association, Boston, April.

GOLDBERG, P. (1968) 'Are Women Prejudiced Against Women?', *TransAction*, **5**, 28–30.

GOODWIN, M. H. (1990) *He-Said-She-Said: Talk as Social Organization Among Black Children*, Indiana University Press, quoted in Tannen (1990).

GROSS, M. M. and GEFFNER, R. A. (1980) 'Are the Times Changing? An Analysis of Sex-role Prejudice', *Sex Roles*, **6**, 713–722.

GRUBE, J. W., KLEINHESSELINK, R. R. and KEARNEY, K. A. (1982) 'Male Self Acceptance and Attraction Toward Women', *Personality and Social Psychology Bulletin*, **8**, 107–112.

GUTEK, B. A. and STEVENS, D. A. (1979) 'Effects of Sex of Subject, Sex of Stimulus Cue and Androgyny Level on Evaluations in Work Situations which Evoke Sex Role Stereotypes', *Journal of Vocational Behaviour*, **14**, 23–32.

HAEFNER, J. E. (1977) 'Sources of Discrimination among Employees: A Survey Investigation', *Journal of Applied Psychology*, **62**, 265–270.

HALL, F. S. and HALL, D. T. (1976) 'Effects of Job Incumbents' Race and Sex on Evaluations of Managerial Performance', *Academy of Management Journal*, **19**, 476–481.

HAMID, P. M. (1968) 'Style of Dress as a Perceptual Cue in Impression Formation', *Perceptual and Motor Skills*, **26**, 904–906.

HAMNER, W. C., KIM, J. S., BAIRD, L. and BIGONESS, W. J. (1974) 'Race and Sex as Determinants of Ratings by Potential Employers in a Simulated Work Sampling Task', *Journal of Applied Psychology*, **59**, 705–711.

HARRIMAN, A. (1985) *Women/Men Management*, Praeger, New York.

HASTE, H. (1993) *The Sexual Metaphor*, Harvester Wheatsheaf, Hemel Hempstead.

HEARN, J. and PARKIN, W. P. (1988) 'Women, Men and Leadership: A Critical Review of Assumptions, Practices and Change in Industrialized Nations', in N. J. Adler and D. N. Izraeli (eds), *Women in Management Worldwide*, Sharpe, New York.

HEILMAN, M. E. (1980) 'The Impact of Situational Factors on Personnel Decisions Concerning

Women: Varying the Sex Composition of the Applicant Pool', *Organizational Behaviour and Human Performance*, **26**, 386–395.

HEILMAN, M. E. (1984) 'Information as a Deterrent Against Sex Discrimination: The Effects of Applicant Sex and Information Type on Preliminary Employment Decisions', *Organizational Behaviour and Human Performance*, **33**, 1174–1186.

HEILMAN, M. E. and GUZZO, R. A. (1978) 'The Perceived Cause of Work Success as a Mediator of Sex Discrimination in Organizations', *Organizational Behaviour and Human Performance*, **21**, 346–357.

HEILMAN, M. E. and SARUWATRI, L. R. (1979) 'When Beauty is Beastly: The Effects of Appearance and Sex on Evaluations of Job Applicants for Managerial and Non Managerial Jobs', *Organizational Behaviour and Human Performance*, **23**, 360–372.

HEILMAN, M. E. and STOPECK, M. H. (1985a) 'Being Attractive: Advantage or Disadvantage? Performance Based Evaluations and Recommended Personnel Actions as a Function of Appearance, Sex and Job Type', *Organizational Behaviour and Human Decision Processes* **35,** 202–215.

HEILMAN, M. E. and STOPECK, M. H. (1985b) 'Attractiveness and Corporate Success: Different Causal Attributions for Males and Females', *Journal of Applied Psychology*, **70**(2), 379–388.

HORNER, M. S. (1972) 'Toward an Understanding of Achievement Related Conflicts in Women', *Journal of Social Issues*, **2**(2), 157–175.

INSTITUTE OF MANPOWER STUDIES (1992) *Merit Pay, Performance Appraisal and Attitudes to Women's Work*, Sussex University, Brighton.

JACOBSON, M. B. and EFFERTZ, J. (1974) 'Sex Roles and Leadership Perceptions of the Leaders and the Led', *Organizational Behaviour and Human Performance*, **12**, 383–396.

JOHNSON, P. B. (1978) 'Women and Interpersonal Power', in I. H. Frieze, J. E. Parsons, P. B. Johnson, D. N. Ruble and G. L. Zellman (eds), *Women and Sex Roles: A Social Psychological Perspective*, pp. 301–320, Norton, New York.

KANTER, R. (1976) 'Why Bosses Turn Bitchy', *Psychology Today*, May, 56–59, 88–91.

KANTER, R. (1977) *Men and Women of the Corporation*, Basic Books, New York.

KASCHACK, E. (1981) 'Another Look at Sex Bias in Student's Evaluations of Professors: Do Winners Get the Recognition that They Have Been Given?', *Psychology of Women Quarterly*, **5**, 767–772.

KASCHACK, E. (1992) *Engendered Lives: A New Psychology of Women's Experience*, Basic Books, New York.

KAUFMAN, D. and FETTERS, M. (1980) 'Work Motivation and Job Values among Professional Men and Women: A New Accounting', *Journal of Vocational Behaviour*, **17**, 251–262.

KIRCHLER, E. (1992) 'Adorable Women, Expert Man: Changing Gender Images of Women and Men in Management', *European Journal of Social Psychology*, **22**, 363–373.

KOTTER, J. P. (1977) 'Power, Dependence and Effective Management', *Harvard Business Review*, **55**, 125–136.

KREFTING, L. A. and BERGER, P. K. (1979) 'Masculinity–Feminine Perceptions of Job Requirements and their Relationship to Job–Sex Stereotypes', *Journal of Vocational Behaviour*, **1**, 164–174.

LANE, I. M. and MESSE, L. A. (1971) 'Equality and the Distribution of Rewards', *Journal of Personality and Social Psychology*, **20**, 1–7.

LEVENSON, H., BURFORD, B., BONNO, B. and DAVIS, L. (1975) 'Are Women Still Prejudiced Against Women? A Replication and Extension of Goldberg's Study', *Journal of Psychology*, **89**, 67–71.

LEVENTHAL, G. S. and ANDERSON, D. (1970) 'Self Interest and the Maintenance of Equity', *Journal of Personality and Social Psychology*, **15**, 57–62.

LEVENTHAL, G. and GARCIA, V. L. (1991) 'An Examination of Personal and Situational factors which Affect Female Managers and their Employees', *Psychological Reports*, **68**, 835–848.

LEWIN, A. Y. and DUCHAN, L. (1971) 'Women in Academia: A Study of the Hiring Decision in Departments of Physical Science', *Science*, **173**, 892–895.

LIPS, H. M. (1994) 'Female Power: A Case of Cultural Preparedness', in H. L. Radtke and H. J. Stam (eds), *Power and Gender: Social Relations in Theory and Practice*, pp. 89–107, Sage, London.

LOMBARDO, J. P. and TOCCI, M. E. (1979) 'Attribution of Positive and Negative Characteristics of Instructors as a Function of Attractiveness of Sex of Instructor and Sex of Subject', *Perceptual and Motor Skills*, **48**, 491–494.

LONDON, M. and STUMPF, S. A. (1983) 'Effects of Candidate Characteristics on Management Promotion Decisions: An Experimental Study', *Personnel Psychology*, **36**, 241–259.

LOTT, B. (1987) 'Feminist, Masculine, Androgynous or Human', paper presented at the meeting of the American Psychological Association, New York and cited in Mednick (1989).

LOTT, B. (1992) 'The Devaluation of Women's Competence', Chapter 6 in J. S. Bohan (ed.), *Seldom Seen, Rarely Heard, Women's Place in Psychology*, Westview Press, Boulder, Col.

MCCLELLAND, D. C. and BURNHAM, D. H. (1976) 'Power is a Great Motivator', *Harvard Business Review*, **54**, 100–110.

MCKENNA, D. J. and JOHNSON, D. A. (1981) 'Selection Risk, Sex-role Stereotyping and Sex Discrimination in Employment Decision', *Journal of Occupational Behaviour*, **2**, 223–228.

MACKE, A. S. and RICHARDSON, L. W. with COOK, J. (1980) 'Sex-typed Teaching Styles of University Professors and Student Reactions', Ohio University Research Foundations, Columbus, quoted in Tannen (1990).

MADDEN, J. M. and MARTIN, E. (1979) 'An Indirect Method of Attitude Measurement', *Bulletin of the Psychonomic Society*, **13**, 170–172.

MAI-DALTON, R. R., FELDMAN-SUMMERS, S. and MITCHELL, T. R. (1979) 'Effects of Employee Gender and Behavioural Style on the Evaluations of Male and Female Banking Executives', *Journal of Applied Psychology*, **64**, 221–226.

MAJOR, B. and DEAUX, K. (1982) 'Individual Differences in Justice Behaviour', in J. Greenberg and R. I. Cohen (eds), *Equity and Justice in Social Behaviour*, pp.43–76, Academic Press, New York.

MAJOR, B., MCFARLIN, D. B. and GAGNON, D. (1984a) 'Overworked and Underpaid: On the Nature of Gender Differences in Personal Entitlement', *Journal of Personality and Social Psychology*, **47**, 1399–1412.

MAJOR, B., VANDERSLICE, V. and MCFALIN, D. B. (1984b) 'Effects of Pay Expected on Pay Received: The Confirmatory Nature of Initial Expectations', *Journal of Applied Social Psychology*, **14**, 399–412

MARSHALL, J. (1984) *Women Managers: Travellers in a Male World*, Wiley, Chichester.

MASSENGILL, D. and DIMARCO, N. (1985) 'Sex Role Stereotypes and Requisite Management Characteristics: A Current Replication', *Sex Roles*, **5**, 561–570.

MEDNICK, M. T. (1989) 'On the Politics of Psychological Constructs', *American Psychologist*, August, 1119–1123.

MILLER, J. (1976) *Towards a New Psychology of Women*, Penguin, Harmondsworth.

MILLS, A. J. and MURGATROYD, S. J. (1991) *Organizational Rules: A Framework for Understanding Organizational Action*, Open University Press, Milton Keynes.

MYERS, I. B. and MCCAULLEY, M. H. (1985) *Manual: A Guide to the Development and Use of the Myer–Briggs Type Indicator*, Consulting Psychologists Press, Palo Alto, Calif.

NEWSTEAD, S. and DENNIS, I. (1993) 'Bias in Student Assessment', *Psychologist*, **6**(10), 451–452.

NKOMO, S. M. (1988) 'Race and Sex: The Forgotten Case of the Black Female Manager', in S. Rose and L. Larwood (eds), *Women's Careers: Pathways and Pitfalls*, Preager, New York.

NORTON, S. D., GUSTAFSON, D. P. and FOSTER, C. E. (1977) 'Assessment for Management Potential: Scale Design and Development, Training Effects and Rater/Ratee Sex Effects', *Academy of Management Journal*, **20**, 117–131.

OLSON, C. B. (1988) 'The Influence of Context on Gender Differences in Performance Attributions: Further Evidence of a "Feminine Modesty Effect"', paper presented at the annual meeting of the Western Psychological Association, San Francisco and cited in Tavris (1992).

PANEK, P. E., DEITCHMAN, R., BURKHOLDER, J. H., SPEROFF, T. and HAUDE, R. H. (1976) 'Evaluation of Feminine Professional Competence as a Function of Level of Accomplishment', *Psychological Reports*, **38**, 875–880.

PEITCHINIS, S. G. (1989) *Women at Work: Discrimination and Response*. McClelland & Stewart, Toronto, Ontario.

PERRY-LANGDON, N. (1990) 'Marking by Numbers: Evaluation of the Marking of Final Degree Examinations in the Faculty of Humanities and Social Studies', Internal Report, University of Wales, College of Cardiff, reported in Newstead and Dennis (1993).

PETERS, L. H., TERBORG, J. R. and TAYNOR, J. (1977) 'Women as Managers Scale (WAMS): A Measure of Attitudes Toward Women in Management Positions', *Journal of Applied Psychology*, **62**, 33.

PHETERSON, G. T., KIESLER, S. and GOLDBERG, P. A. (1971) 'Evaluation of the Performance of Women as a Function of their Sex, Achievement and Personal History', *Journal of Personality and Social Psychology*, **19**, 114–118.

POWELL, G. N. (1988) *Women and Men in Management*, Sage, Beverley Hills, Calif.

PUTNAM, L. and HEINEN, S. J. (1976) 'Women in Management: The Fallacy of the Trait Approach', *MSU Business Topics*, Summer, 47–53.

REIS, H. I. and JACKSON, I. A. (1981) 'Sex Differences in Rewards Allocation: Subjects, Partners and Tasks', *Journal of Personality and Social Psychology*, **40**, 465–478.

ROSEN, B. and JERDEE, T. H. (1974) 'The Influence of Sex-role Stereotypes on Evaluations of Male and Female Supervisory Behaviour', *Journal of Applied Psychology*, **59**, 9–14.

RUBLE, D. N. and RUBLE, T. L. (1982) 'Sex Stereotypes', in A. G. Miller (ed.), *In the Eye of the Beholder: Contemporary Issues in Stereotyping*, Praeger, New York.

SCHEIN, V. E. (1972) 'Fair Employment of Women through Personnel Research', *Personnel Journal*, **51**, 330–335.

SCHEIN, V. E. (1973) 'The Relationship between Sex Role Stereotypes and Requisite Management Characteristics', *Journal of Applied Psychology*, **57**, 95–100.

SCHEIN, V. E. (1975) 'Relationships between Sex Role Stereotypes and Requisite Management Characteristics among Female Managers', *Journal of Applied Psychology*, **60**, 340–344.

SCHEIN, V. E. (1989) 'Sex Role Stereotypes and Requisite Management Characteristics Past, Present and Future', paper presented at the Current Research on Women in Management Conference, Queens University, Ontario, Canada.

SCHEIN, V. E. and MUELLER, R. (1990) 'Sex Role Stereotyping and Requisite Management Characteristics: A Cross Cultural Look', paper presented at the 22nd International Congress of Applied Psychology, Kyoto, Japan.

SCHEIN, V. E., MUELLER, R. and JACOBSON, C. (1989) 'The Relationship Between Sex Role Stereotypes and Requisite Management Characteristics among College Students', *Sex Roles*, **20**(1/2), 103–110.

SHAW, E. A. (1972) 'Differential Impact of Negative Stereotypes in Employee Selection', *Personnel Psychology*, **25**, 333–358.

SCHMITT, N. and LAPPIN, M. (1980) 'Race and Sex as Determinants of the Mean and Variance of Performance Ratings', *Journal of Applied Psychology*, **65**, 428–435.

SHEPPARD, D. L. (1989) 'Organizations, Power and Sexuality: The Image and Self-image of Women Managers', in J. Hearn, D. L. Sheppard, P. Tancred-Sherif and G. Burrell (eds), *The Sexuality of Organization*, Sage, London.

SPENCE, J. T. and HELMREICH, R. L. (1978) *Masculinity and Femininity: Their Psychological Dimensions, Correlates and Antecedents*, University of Texas Press, Austin, Texas.

SPENDER, D. (1978) 'Educational Research and the Feminist Perspective', unpublished paper, British Educational Research Association Conference on Women, Education and Research, University of Leicester, quoted in L. Stanley and S. Wise (1983) *Breaking Out: Feminist Consciousness and Feminist Research*, p. 29, Routledge & Kegan Paul, London.

TANNEN, D. (1990) *You Just Don't Understand: Women and Men in Conversation*, Morrow, New York.

TAYLOR, M. S. and ILGEN, D. R. (1981) 'Sex Discrimination Against Women in Initial Placement Decisions: A Laboratory Investigation', *Academy of Management Journal*, **24**, 859–865.

TAYLOR, S. E., FISKE, S. T., CLOSE, N. M., ANDERSON, C. E. and RUDERMAN, A. J. (1977) 'Solo Status as a Psychological Variable: The Power of Being Distinctive', unpublished manuscript, Harvard University.

TERBORG, J. R. and ILGEN, D. R. (1975) 'A Theoretical Approach to Discrimination in Traditionally Masculine Occupations', *Organizational Behaviour and Human Performance*, **13**, 352–376.

TERBORG, J. R., PETERS, L. H., ILGEN, D. R. and SMITH, F. (1977) 'Organizational and Personal Correlates of Attitudes toward Women as Managers', *Academy of Management Journal*, **20**, 89–100.

THEN, D. A. (1988) 'Benefits of Beauty: The Impact of Physical Attractiveness, Sex and Education on Social and Work Evaluations', paper presented at the International Congress of Psychology, Sydney, Australia.

THOMAS, P. J. (1987) 'Appraising the Performance of Women: Gender and the Naval Officer', in B. A. Gutek and L. Larwood (eds), *Women's Career Development*, Sage, London.

TRESEMER, D. (1974) 'Fear of Success: Popular, but Unproven', *Psychology Today*, **7**, 82–85.

UNGER, R. and CRAWFORD, M. (1992) *Women and Gender: A Feminist Psychology*, McGraw-Hill, Temple University Press, Phil.

VOGEL, S. R., BROVERMAN, I. K., BROVERMAN, D. M., CLARKSON, F. and ROSENKRANZ, P. S. (1970) 'Maternal Employment and Perception of Sex Roles Among College Students', *Developmental Psychology*, **3**, 384–391.

WALLSTON, B. S. and O'LEARY, V. E. (1981) 'Sex Makes a Difference: Differential Perceptions of Women and Men', in L. Wheeler (ed.), *Review of Personality and Social Psychology*, vol. 2, pp. 9–41, Sage, Beverley Hills, Calif.

WEBB, J. (1991) 'The Gender Relation of Assessment', in J. Firth-Cozens and M.A. West (eds), *Women at Work*, Open University Press, Milton Keynes.

WILLIAMS, J. E. and BEST, D. L. (1990) *Measuring Sex Stereotypes: A Multination Study*, Sage, Newbury Park, Calif.

WILSON, F. M. and BEATON, D. (1992) 'The Theory and Practice of Appraisal: The Case of a Scottish University', paper presented to British Academy of Management Conference, Bradford, September and published in *Higher Education Quarterly*, **47**(2), 163–189.

WOLF, N. (1990) *The Beauty Myth*, Chatto & Windus, London.

WOODS, M. M. (1975) 'What Does it Take for a Woman to Make it in Management?', *Personnel Journal*, **54**, 38–41 and 66.

3 Learning and Socialization

Discussion point

A woman looks at things in a different light to what a man does.
A woman is happy when she is made a fuss of and protected.
There are a few women who want to be a boss. Women get more
emotional than men do—have different feelings. You get bad
news and a man takes it better than a woman. A woman gets
easily upset. Men show their feelings differently, by giving
things like a bunch of flowers. A woman shows her feelings by
fetching up a family, looking after the house.   (Alf, aged 89, a
retired commercial traveller, widowed, quoted in Walczak,
1988: 43)

Do you agree with this view? What experience has led you to accept or reject
the views? If you were to argue against this view, how would you do it?

THE BIOLOGY VERSUS CULTURE/SOCIALIZATION ARGUMENT

Do you believe that men and women are fundamentally different and that these
differences are fundamentally biological? Do you think that existing gender
divisions are natural and rooted in an eternal, unchanging biology? Do you think
that the sexes not only differ in physical form but also mentally? Do you think
men are stable whereas women are emotional due to the hormonal changes
associated with the menstrual cycle, pregnancy, childbirth, and the menopause?
Do you think that the 'natural order of things' is to have woman as man's
helpmate? If the answer to these questions was yes, you might be described as
subscribing to a 'common-sense' or 'traditional' or 'biological' view of men and
women.

The biological view stresses the differing intellectual and physical abilities men and women posses. This biological view can be encapsulated in one metaphor: Man the Hunter. The metaphor of Man the Hunter is an interesting one as it is widely available in common-sense and lay thought and is used to explain present-day behaviour. The key argument is that because we spent a long period in the hunter-gatherer state, there evolved psychological, social, and physical characteristics of which we are now the heirs. The metaphor gives us a script, a set of rules for male behaviour, motives, skills, and relations with others. This makes a lot of sense until you realize that the hard evidence for what went on during those millenia is scarce (Haste, 1993).

The idea that women are naturally less capable of intellectual endeavour than men because of the biological demands of childbearing was used in the nineteenth century as an argument against extending opportunities for higher education to women (Ehrenreich and English, 1979). Women were seen as weak in nature, subject to fainting fits, and lacking in stamina. More recently it has been said that males were superior in their mathematical abilities, were more aggressive, had greater visual-spatial ability, while females possessed superior verbal ability (Grusec and Lytton, 1988: 363–410; Maccoby and Jacklin, 1974).

The biological arguments are particularly relevant. Socially oppressed groups are more likely to have biological arguments levelled against them than are socially dominant groups. This is the case whether the division is based on gender, ethnicity, social class, or sexual preference (Birke, 1986: 10). The chief significance of biological arguments is that they reinforce relationships of power. The arguments are conservative, oppose the possibility of change, and deny the social context of our lives. We must challenge the assumption that the biological make-up of our bodies is the basis, foundation, framework, essence, or mould of the social relations of gender (Connell, 1987: 67). Further the biological arguments often involve massive generalizations that regard women as a homogeneous social group. At a simple biological level women do have much in common, but the experiences of different women are markedly different, including their experiences of the biological events themselves.

Views in the 1990s have changed. Nevertheless, many still hold on to the traditional view, stressing the differences between men and women. Research, however, shows little or no differences between the sexes. As far as mathematics is concerned there is no difference with regard to arithmetic and geometry but males may more readily deal with algebra. Girls tend to do as well as boys in maths classes but the difference is that girls opt out. By the time they reach adulthood, the percentage differences as well as maths ability between the sexes is considerable (Sonderegger, 1985). Basow (1992: 51) concluded that research findings reveal more similarities than differences between males and females in the cognitive area.

It is no longer believed that males have across the board superiority in visual-spatial ability. Men and women are less likely to be seen to be fundamentally different. Men and women can be equally aggressive, but for different reasons. Men are likely to initiate aggression and to respond to physical challenges; women are more likely to become angry because of unfair treatment (Powell, 1988). It is the conditions for acceptable behaviour for men and women that are different. If you are dominant and male, you will be more sexually attractive; if you are dominant and female the same will not be true (Kendrick, 1987). We have learned to believe that men and women are different, despite the fact that research has shown more similarities than differences. We have been socialized to be different, and we expect men and women to conform to that norm.

Expectations, acquired learning, and patterns of socialization do not, however, have to be frozen in time. The differences learned by men and women are not always resistant to change and inflexible. There is now more confidence that socialization and education can help individuals compete with members of either sex. Male and female abilities overlap considerably (Hyde, 1985). If the differences are not biological in origin, then it would appear that we have to look to learning and socialization to explain why the differences appear.

One view comes from social learning; a social learning theory, to explain sex differences, would focus on how rewards and punishments shape sex-role behaviours. Connell (1987) is particularly critical of role theory to explain why people are trapped into stereotypes. He accepts that people reward conformity to roles and punish departures from them: little boys are praised for being assertive and ridiculed for being girlish. But why do second parties apply the sanctions? This cannot be explained by *their* role expectations. The general assumption we are left with is that people choose to maintain existing customs.

Another view would look at the social identity of women where aspects of identity are derived from membership of the group women, which is distinguished from the identity of men. Intergroup relations between the sexes can be seen to be an important part of the social construction of gender identity. One way in which men and women are differentiated in this view is in terms of their communal or agentic styles. Women, it is said, are more likely to express a communal social identity than men, valuing personal relationships more and deriving greater social self-esteem through their social relationships with others, rather than in an individualistic fashion. (Williams, 1984). But, again using social identity theory, Skevington (1989) has argued that regardless of sex, people who work in a woman's world, e.g. nursing, have a predominantly communal social identity, and value relationships more with outgroups and third parties. Male-oriented groups express the agentic style which considers such relationships unimportant. We thus learn our social identities from the groups to which we belong.

Social identity theory says that a person needs a secure and satisfying social identity and will act to achieve it. People derive their self-concept from their knowledge of their group memberships together with the emotional significance attached to those memberships. If the social identity is unsatisfying the individual will seek to change the relevant group membership. Women who have been socially mobile have denied that their womanhood is central to their social identity and have appraised themselves in terms of male standards and adopted male roles and forms of behaviour where possible, thus gaining a positive social identity. But there are penalties. Men will feel threatened and will act to maintain the value and distinctiveness of their group. Where women seek assimilation, the institutions which accept them will lose status. When women claim that they possess characteristics of value, they will be ridiculed. The women may be labelled unnatural and unwomanly (see Breakwell, 1979). One is left wondering if women can achieve a positive social identity?

Yet another view comes from social cognition theory which identifies cognitive 'schemas' or 'scripts' as the core of sex-role development. Some merge these latter two analyses together. The result is a conditioning view which says that sex differences should not be seen in terms of female inadequacy or weakness but as the result of societal (male) pressures that have resulted in female subservience and underachievement (Archer and Lloyd, 1985). You have inherited your biological sex but your gender has been attributed to you on the basis of a variety of bodily and behavioural cues. (For an excellent review of the arguments on biology versus culture see Chapter 1 of Charles, 1993, or Kelly, 1991.)

Sex relates to the label male or female that identifies the individual. Gender refers to the characteristics, traits, and appropriate behaviour for members of each sexual group; they are social attributes passed on by parents and other influential people in your life. Gender is a context-dependent and highly flexible process; it cannot be viewed as a category. It would appear that Simone de Beauvoir was right when she said, 'One is not born a woman, but rather becomes a woman' (de Beauvoir,1952: 301). How is gender learned?

LEARNING TO BE MALE OR FEMALE

The birth of a child is an event in which a whole series of gender rules is reconstructed and regenerated: for example, colour coding for dressing babies; the child is given a gender-specific forename (Mills and Murgatroyd, 1991). Parents treat newborn baby boys and girls differently (White and Wollett, 1981) and describe them in gender-stereotyped ways (Rubin et al., 1974). Mothers react differently in a laboratory setting to the same baby depending on whether it is presented as a boy or a girl, whereas they report few differences in the handling of their own babies (Smith and Lloyd, 1978) and were unaware that they handled the babies in the laboratory setting differently according to gender (Culp et al., 1983). A baby dressed in pink and labelled a girl will be given dolls, seen as cuddly, weaker, softer, smaller, and more finely featured than a baby dressed in blue and labelled a boy (Sheppard-Look, 1982). If subjects have been told that a crying baby is a boy, they will think the baby is angry; if told the crying baby is a girl, they will think it is afraid (Condry and Condry, 1976). (We must be wary here, however, that we do not blame mothers for being solely responsible for early unconscious stages of socialization and for producing sexually stereotyped children; see Stanley and Wise, 1983: 89.)

Parents of school-age boys and girls show considerable differences in their treatment according to gender. For example, parents of sons are more concerned with punishment, negative sanctions, and with conformity to gender-stereotyped standards; fathers also provide more comfort to their daughters than sons. Boys will be taught how to do a task, and be praised for their independence and ability. Fathers, in particular, are found to stress competence, task performance, achievement, careers, and occupational success for their sons but to reinforce dependency behaviour in their daughters (Sheppard-Look, 1982). Parents give boys and girls different toys; boys are given more toy animals, vehicles, and live animals, whereas girls are given more dolls and doll's houses.

LEARNING FROM THE MEDIA

Socialization also comes from outside the family. Television programmes and commercials portray gender-stereotypical images. For example a study of Saturday morning children's television programmes found that 68 per cent of the major characters were male and that male characters engaged in more activity than female characters. Boys, then, had the greater opportunity to imitate same-sex models than girls. Also the sexes tended to appear in different roles. Females were more often presented in relationships with others such as family or friends, while males were more often portrayed in roles independent of others or at work.

Itzin (1986) undertook a review of media representations of women and cites surveys of pictorial representations that emphasize female sexuality, together with feature stories that represent women in terms of their sexuality, appearance, and domestic relations. Similarly a number of studies have examined the social representation of women in British television and radio advertising and have found women to be portrayed as domestic consumers, offering no argument or authority (Furnham and Schofield, 1986; Livingstone and Green, 1986).

In commercials males were presented as more knowledgeable and females as more bewildered. Males seem more important, deserve more attention, and are more in command of themselves and the situation. The majority of complaints received by the Independent Television Commission in 1991 were about how women were represented in television advertisements. A 1990 Broadcasting Standards Council survey found that twice as many men as women were featured in television advertisements, and women were consistently shown in decorative rather than professional roles (Faludi, 1992). Not surprisingly both adults and children who watch more television tend to be more aware of gender stereotypes, see themselves in more stereotypical terms, and hold more traditional attitudes toward men's and women's roles. (McArthur and Eisen, 1976; McGhee and Frueh, 1980; Morgan, 1982; Ross *et al.*, 1982).

LEARNING FROM SCHOOL

Many studies have claimed that classroom talk is discriminatory: boys dominate mixed-sex talk, and girls give away power. Boys take up more 'verbal space' than girls and have more say in what goes on (Swann, 1992: 68). Teachers may respond in a typical gender-stereotyped manner to boys and girls. Teachers consistently pay more attention to boys than girls. They usually favour boys at the expense of girls (Swann, 1992). They tend to reward males for independence and task performance, and females for passivity and dependence behaviour, thereby instilling learned helplessness in girls (Greenberg, 1988). Teachers talk less to girls. Gender differences and inequalities in classroom talk need to be considered, not only in the light of unequal relations between boys and girls but in the light of the increasing attention paid to the development of communication skills and the recognition of the role played by talk in pupils' learning. Such issues have become increasingly important in the United Kingdom with the advent of the National Curriculum in England and Wales and the Development Programme in Scotland.

Schools also often have sex-typed tracking systems, with a higher proportion of girls going into English, history, and social sciences, while boys tend towards the physical sciences and maths. Textbooks and texts also perpetuate traditional sex roles (Hahn *et al.*, 1988). The physical sciences and technology, like computing, tend to have a male image (see Wajcman, 1994).

Peer groups are another influence. One study found that children playing at gender-inappropriate activities were criticized and ostracized by their peers. The two genders tend to play independently of one another and are exposed to different models during play. There is, then, plenty of evidence of gender-stereotyped messages from a variety of sources available to boys and girls from an early age (Archer and Lloyd, 1985).

It is questionable whether these observed differences are ingrained. We can conclude that boys and girls do develop different styles of play and influences but they do not differ in passivity and activity in some consistent, trait-like way. Maccoby (1988) found that the behaviour depends on the gender of the child they are playing with. Girls are seldom passive with each other, but when paired with boys will, for example, stand on the sidelines and let the boys monopolize the toys. The gap between boys and girls seems to be fostered and rewarded.

Sex-role socialization in childhood influences the personality development of women and men. Gender differences are small in junior school: adolescent girls are found to be significantly more concerned with being liked and are more self-conscious; boys are more concerned with achievement and competence. Gilligan (1982) describes how childhood social contexts can account for the development of many psychological sex differences, particularly those reflecting the greater embeddedess of women in social contexts in contrast to the more individualistic, mastery-directed activities of men. These early influences form an important background against which to consider the personality variables investigated in the relationship to female achievement and career development.

Discussion point

Can women be socialized to be both feminine and intellectually competent? If a woman is intellectually competent, will her femininity be doubted? Academic excellence, achievement and femininity have historically not been viewed as compatible (Hyde, 1985).

> … many women internalize the belief that competence and
> achievement are incompatible with their femininity or with their
> being desired as a woman … if I am female and successfully act
> on my achievement orientation, I will be less attractive to men
> than women who do not because men prefer women who want
> to share a man's professional life and to raise his children.
> (Gilbert, 1983: 6)

Kate McKenzie Davey interviewed women in non-sex-stereotypical careers and reported that women have to chose between femininity, which is not seen as compatible with career success, and the 'privilege' of being 'one of the lads' at work (Davey, 1993).

What do you think? Do you agree with Lucia Gilbert, Kate McKenzie Davey, and Janet Hyde?

SOCIALIZATION IN ADULTHOOD

Sex-role socialization continues in adulthood. Magazine advertising conveys similar messages. Until recently women were rarely shown in working roles and never shown as executives or professionals. Several stereotypes of women's roles were there: women's place is in the home, women do not make important decisions, women are dependent and in need of men's protection, men regard women as sex objects.

We learned that it is men who have the voice of authority. Lucy Komisar (1972) pointed out that in advertising it is men who give instructions to women on how to do housework. Men tell women why one detergent or soap powder or floor polish is better than another. The reason, according to a leading advertising agency executive, was that the male voice is the voice of authority.

As early as 1963 Betty Friedan's thesis was that magazines and other media most often depict women in traditional sex roles such as homemakers or models of attractiveness. In doing so they nurtured a narrow and servile image of women. Women were often portrayed as happy and diligent homemakers, beautiful and dependent social companions, or most concerned with being blond, thin, or having other physical characteristics they did not possess (Sexton and Haberman, 1974). Women are portrayed in books, magazines, television, and films as passive, conforming, self-subordinating and less competent than men (Dominick, 1979; Harris and Voorhees, 1981; Kaiser, 1979; Seggar, 1975).

Discussion point

Has advertising changed since the 1970s? Think of an advertisement where there is a positive image of a woman as independent, out of the home, making decisions, and so on. Compare your positive images with others. Can you also think of an equal number of advertisements with the woman at home, in the supermarket, making trivial decisions? Can you think of any advertisement where the woman is not a beautiful and potentially dependent social companion?

More recently, Demarest and Garner (1992) have looked at a sample of articles in two women's magazines over the period 1954–1982. They found that traditional sex roles still dominate the pages of women's magazines. Even new magazines designed to satisfy the market created by the feminist movement (e.g. *New Woman*) seem to be more concerned with physical appearance than with equality of sexes (Kaiser, 1979). It may be that media coverage of feminist issues varies with fluctuations in the strength of the women's movement (Cancian and Ross, 1981; Weston and Ruggiero, 1986). There has been a slow, steady increase in stories with feminist themes and a decline in traditional themes of mother and homemaker between 1954 and 1982 (Demarest and Garner, 1992).

Society is like a gigantic prison of already constructed dimensions. Humans enter the world already shaped by gender, class, race, ethnicity, nationality, and existing socio-political systems. Your life is lived by learning from others, significant others telling you what you must do (Farganis, 1986). One set of significant others has been your teachers.

Those of you who are female and have been to single-sex schools may well have an advantage over those sent to co-educational schools. Girls at single-sex schools, as we saw in Chapter 1, are more educationally successful. Why? Women in single-sex settings are exposed to more leadership experiences, they are exposed to more females, and females of a higher status, they can demonstrate higher self-regard and self-confidence, hold higher levels of aspiration, and explore career options more fully than those in co-educational settings (Monaco and Gaier, 1992).

This chapter is designed to help you think through the learning and socialization you have experienced which has helped form your gender identity. The term gender refers, then, to the way, in a particular society, people are socially constructed to behave and experience themselves as women or men. You could argue that women are boxed in by the very structure of society in which their positions are the subordinate ones. There would need to be a fundamental transformation of the structure of society to liberate women. They would need to be released from their domestic and nurturing roles and the goals of the world of work and politics would also have to change.

Discussion point

Are women liberated? If they are, why do so many of us feel an embarrassed foolishness when we talk about women's liberation? Why does the word 'feminist' carry connotations of extremism and seem so alienating to many women?

How many times have you heard 'I'm not a feminist but ... '? Here is a quote from a female councillor who objected to funding Kilmarnock Rugby Club's 125th anniversary dinner unless they let women attend. 'I'm not a feminist but I don't think females have any lesser part to play than men' (*Daily Record*, 4 May 1993: 19).

Is she right? Why did she preface what she had to say? If you are female would you call yourself a feminist?

Cynthia Cockburn (1991) argues that feminism has been anathematized by men in an attempt to put a stop to its appeal to women. Do you agree?

One could argue that the structure of society has defined men's identity too (Collinson, 1988; Collinson *et al.*, 1990; Collinson and Hearn, 1994; Willis, 1977). Most discussions of masculinity treat it as if it is measurable. Some men have more of it, others less. Men who appear to lack masculinity are, by definition, sick or genetically inadequate (Brittan, 1989). Maybe we should not talk of masculinity but masculinities. There are a range of versions of masculinity which can change over time.

Barbara Ehrenreich (1983) has documented the changes in American men's attitudes to marriage from the 1950s to the 1980s. In the 1950s there was a firm expectation that required men to grow up, marry, and support wives.

> To do anything else was less than grown-up, and the man who willfully deviated was judged to be somehow 'less than a man'. ... But by the end of the 1970s and the beginning of the 1980s, adult manhood was no longer burdened with the automatic expectation of marriage and bread-winning. The man who postpones marriage even into middle age, who avoids women who are likely to become financial dependents, who is dedicated to his own pleasures, is likely to be found not suspiciously deviant but 'healthy'. (Ehrenreich, 1983: 11–12).

The fact that men might be rebelling against their role as breadwinners does not, however, entail the undermining of their dominance in the political and economic spheres. What has changed is not male power as such, but its form, its presentation, its packaging. The substance of male power does not change despite changes in male behaviour over time—wearing shoulder length hair in the 1960s, androgynous styles of presentation, a few men becoming house husbands. Masculinism is the ideology that justifies and naturalizes male domination. It takes for granted that there is a fundamental difference between men and women, assumes heterosexuality is normal, accepts the sexual division of labour, and sanctions the political and dominant role of men in both public and private spheres. It is the ideology of patriarchy (Brittan, 1989: 4). The concept of patriarchy refers to the structures through which male domination over women is established. Patriarchy is made possible by the near universality of mother-dominated nurturing which continuously reproduces the sexual division of labour.

Ideology has an important role to play in the structural view of society. An ideology is a set of ideas a person holds in order to make sense of the world in which they live. Ideologies are social constructs that are created in a society and only make sense to that society. They influence us all in our thinking; they tend to support the status quo and make existing power relations seem inevitable, serving the interests of those with power. We could talk, then, of a patriarchal ideology which prevents equality of opportunity for women and makes women's subordination seem natural.

Ideology can be said to inform organizational politics. Organizational politics is also usually treated as gender neutral but is premised on the dominance of one set of definitions and assumptions that are essentially gender based. The connection between language, symbolism, and other aspects of organizational culture and the gendered basis of power have been suggested by a number of writers (e.g. Mills, 1994; Riley, 1983; Wilson, 1992). Language is our most vital conceptual tool. One way in which the patriarchal ideology makes women's subordination seem natural is through sexism in the vocabulary we use and the very structure of language itself. The culture of an organizational language and style can be very masculine. Examples of male-associated signs include the use of male sports and military references and the use of demeaning and derogatory terms for women (e.g. 'a bitch of a machine', 'the girls in the office')

WOMEN AND MEN: THE LANGUAGE THEY HAVE LEARNT

Another example of this dominance in organizational culture and language is how the generic 'he', 'man' and 'mankind' has been used to include women. There are some good pragmatic reasons as to why such male-specific language should be banned. The first is that it is unclear when we are talking about all humans and when we are talking specifically about men. Using so-called generic terms hides the fact that it is often males who are being considered. At best it is highly confusing and inaccurate language. In addition it has been concluded that ' ... the linguistic form can be a cause of sexism as well as the reverse' (Moulton *et al.*, 1978: 1033). Using the terms 'mankind' and 'he' for both sexes perpetuates sex biases. Use of 'he' makes men and women think of males first, even when the context implies both sexes (Gastil, 1990; Moulton *et al.*, 1978). The generic masculine is not as generic as language 'authorities' claim it is.

Here is a quote from a book published in 1992 that shows how confusing this non-acknowledgement of gender can be:

> Vallins (1966) presented fraudulant information to his subjects. At times the subjects overheard bogus heart-rate information indicating that they were in a heightened state of arousal while viewing slides of semi-nude females. After viewing the stimuli, the subjects rated the attractiveness of the nudes. (Weiner, 1992: 307)

One assumes subjects are both male and female until you realize this is less likely to be the case and the subjects are probably men! A check of the original article proves the subjects were male undergraduate students.

A second aspect of language and culture concerns labels applied to men and women. The language used in organizations relegates women to the subordinate position (Spender, 1985). Titles used to address men and women debase women. Just think about the pairs of words used to refer to men and women in addressing them. Any female, for example, can be described as a lady, but lord is reserved for men of a certain status in British society, and deities. With sir/madam and master/

mistress we find that the female forms have been debased into words with sexual connotations. King retains its original meaning while queen has developed debased sexual connotations. Even with the word tramp there is a shift to the negative and sexual meaning when it is applied to females. There are more words for men in general, and more positive words for men than women. There are 220 words for a sexually promiscuous female and only 20 male equivalents (Spender, 1985). Key's (1975) *Male/Female Language* and Miller and Swift's (1978) *Words and Women* are two of the most important treatments of vocabulary differences in labels, descriptors, taboos, and asymmetrical word pairs. Language, then, embodies sexual inequality and it is not women who enjoy the advantage.

The practice of labelling women as married or single also serves supremely sexist ends. It conveniently signals who is 'fair game' from the male point of view (see Spender, 1985: 27). The current usage of Miss and Mrs is relatively recent; until the beginning of the nineteenth century Miss was usually reserved for young females while Mrs designated mature women: marital status played no role. But now these are labels of women for the convenience of men.

Foucault (1980) has argued that experience and knowledge do not exist outside the language in which they are talked about. Discourse creates the experience of which they talk. If medical discourse sees women in terms of their reproductive potential, they will talk about them in terms of their wombs, creating the term hysteria (from the Greek word for womb) and the condition itself. Thus as subjects of this nineteenth century discourse women became hysterical. This was a form of power used by the medical establishment over the minds and bodies of women.

When there are differences in behaviour to observe it is because people are playing out gender roles, roles where men have more power. These differences in behaviour are then reflected in the language differences. This is a third aspect of language and power. Lakoff (1975) characterized women's language as using different vocabulary, lacking forcefulness; they demonstrate politeness and uncertainty. Women, for example, use tag questions, which add a short phrase to declarative sentences (e.g. 'It's a nice day, isn't it?') and turn a statement into a question, making them seem less certain of their statements and weaker when speaking (Lakoff, 1975). This is something children do too, in play (Sachs, 1987). People expect women to use tags (Tannen, 1990: 228). The women may be trying to facilitate communication, so may not view this as a weakness, but men often interpret this as a means of avoiding conflict, as an indication that the speaker is unsure of herself or does not know the answer. Females who use tag questions and disclaimers are viewed as less intelligent and knowledgeable than men who use them. These language forms weaken women's image but not men's (Bradley, 1981).

Women also use more supportive language where men use more hostile verbs (Hyde, 1985). Women swear less, and use words like lovely, nice, and pretty more.

Men's speech tends to be harsher with more exclamations. It may be that these differences that have been observed are dependent on context, dependent on the gender of the person women are speaking to rather than on their own intrinsic conversational style. Carli (1990) found that women spoke more tentatively than men did only when they were speaking with men. With men they offered more disclaimers ('I'm no expert', 'I may be wrong', 'I suppose', 'I'm not sure'), used more hedges, moderating terms, and more tag questions. When a woman uses tentative language with a man she may be communicating that she has no wish to enhance her own status or challenge his which will make him more inclined to listen. Men were more influenced by a women who spoke tentatively. So it is no wonder that women can be tentative in speech. But this phenomenon is not limited to women's behaviour. Where a man's power has been diminished, where they are in a subordinate position in a relationship, e.g. a witness in a court-room, they will reveal the hesitations and uncertainties of so-called women's speech (Tavris, 1992: 299).

If a women is tentative in her speech, she may be signalling insecurity, doubt, and eagerness to please. The compliant speaker allows herself to be interrupted. She moves out of the way when someone approaches her. She smiles often to assure the goodwill of others. She maintains eye contact and listens attentively while others speak but averts her eyes when she is the focus of attention. In this way she communicates submissiveness and a relative lack of power (Borisoff and Merrill, 1985: 11).

Differences have also been found in intonation, with women using patterns of surprise, unexpectedness, cheerfulness, and politeness. Women have four levels of pitch, the fourth being the highest; men have three. Women's ability to use this fourth level is interpreted by men as making female speech seem overly emotional and high-pitched (Hyde, 1985: 214). If they used only three they would probably seen as tough and unlady-like. As long as there is a power imbalance, any way that women communicate that differs from men will be stigmatized as different and therefore worse (Lakoff, 1990).

Women also differ in story telling. One way linguists and anthropologists have looked at how men and women might differ is to look at how they talk about events in their lives and create different worlds. Barbara Johnstone looked at 58 narratives recorded by her students. The women's stories tended to be about community, while the men's were about contest. Johnstone concludes that men live in a world where they see power as coming from an individual acting in opposition to others and natural forces. Life is a contest and they want to avoid failure. But for women the source of power is the community, a community from which they fear being cut off (Johnstone, 1989; Tannen, 1990).

The stereotype is that women talk a lot. Dale Spender has suggested that the stereotype arose because more people feel instinctively (if not consciously) that women, like children, should be seen and not heard, so any amount of talk from them seems like too much. Women who talk are labelled 'too talkative' or 'too opinionated' even when they are not. Women who talk one-third of the time are perceived as talking half of the time, reported Hall (1986). If women talk more than that they are seen as dominating. The myth of the 'gabby' woman prevails in spite of overwhelming evidence to the contrary.

Voices being described as carping, nagging, shrill, strident, or grating are adjectives usually used to describe female speech and not male. Women bring these socially imposed stereotypes to public settings and then, not surprisingly, have a deeply rooted reticence to speak out. If a woman is, in contrast, soft spoken, she will not be heard. The soft-spoken woman is at a marked disadvantage if she attempts to negotiate a contract, persuade a jury, or present a report (Borisoff and Merrill, 1985: 9).

Studies have repeatedly shown that in identical settings, given the same question or situation (all other factors being identical), men talk for a longer time than women (Freed, 1985). For example, communications researchers Barbara and Gene Eakins (1978) taped and studied seven university faculty meetings. They found that, with one exception, men spoke more often and, without exception, for a longer time. The women's longest turns were still shorter than the men's shortest turns.

For most women the language of conversations is the language of rapport, a way of establishing connections and negotiating relationships. For most men talk is primarily a means to preserve independence and negotiate and maintain status in a hierarchical social order. This is done by exhibiting knowledge, skill, and by holding centre stage through verbal performance such as story telling, joking, or imparting information (Tannen, 1990: 77).

Candace West (see Smith, 1987: 33) has studied differences between single-sex and mixed-sex conversations, focusing on rights to speak. What she observed was a set of 'devices' used by men, apparently with women's consent, that served to maintain male control of the topics of conversation. Examples included men tending to complete women's sentences, to give minimal responses to topics initiated and carried by women, and to interrupt without being sanctioned.

Women get the 'shitwork' in conversations; women 'feed men the lines, draw them out, respond to the topics that men determine, and act as their audience' (Fishman, 1983: 117). Fishman found that, in studies of conversations between couples in their homes, women asked questions almost three times as often as men. The women initiated 62 per cent of the topics; men 38 per cent. None of the men's initiations failed to evolve into a conversation, whereas only 38 per cent of the topics women raised developed into a conversation.

Women use other verbal strategies to keep conversations going; they use more attention-getting devices than men and more conversation openings, e.g. 'Do you know what?' Children employ the same strategy. Women also use the phrase 'this is really interesting' and 'you know' more than men. This would fit with Carli's (1990) explanation that this is a strategy to make men more likely to listen.

Discussion point

The medical profession seem to be particularly adept at making women 'invisible'. We have all heard about the fact that taking small doses of aspirin can reduce the chances of a heart attack, but did you know there were no women in the study? Another research study used a sample of men to examine the effects of diet on breast cancer.

Can you think of other examples of the 'invisibility of women'?

Source: (Tavris, 1992: 94).

THE CULTURE AND IDEOLOGY WHICH INFORMS THE LEARNING

It may be that what is needed is an understanding of organizational culture in order to uncover the gendered nature of organizational theorizing. The feminist contention (see Oakley, 1972) is that gender is a cultural phenomenon. and that various elements of sexual discrimination are rooted in the culture of a society. We need, then, to examine the character of organizational culture and its part in the processes of sexual inequalities. Numerous article and books have been written on the subject (e.g. W. Ouchi's *Theory Z*, 1981) but most fail to deal with the issue of gender. Gender is presented as a non-gendered phenomenon and ignores the dominant role of men in the construction of the cultures of organizations. Ouchi's theory did note, however, that Japanese corporations exclude women from tenured jobs (Mills, 1994).

Albert Mills provides us with this definition of culture:

> Culture is essentially composed of a number of understandings and expectations that assist people in making sense of life. In organizations no less that other aspects of social life, such understandings have to be learned and they guide people in the appropriate or relevant behaviour, help them to know how things are done, what is expected of them, how to achieve certain things etc. Indeed, it is the very configuration of such 'rules' of behaviour that distinguishes one social organization or group from another, it is an essential part of their cultural identity. (Mills, 1988a: 360)

> The culture of an organization can ... be viewed as consisting simultaneously of a structured set of rules in which behaviour is bounded and of a process, or outcome, resulting from the particular character of the rule-bound behaviour of the actors involved.   (Mills, 1988b: 4)

Gender refers to patterned, socially produced distinctions between female and male, masculine and feminine (Acker, 1992: 250). Gender is a daily accomplishment that occurs in the course of our participation in organizations. This usually involves the subordination of women, either concretely or symbolically. Gender is a pervasive symbol of power (Scott, 1986).

Gender is a set of 'master' rules. Sense is made of each of a number of rules by reference to a broader, more or less coherent class of rules which coalesce in notions of gender. The gender-rule learning takes place thoughout the life of an individual; organizations play a crucial part in that learning. Some of these rules concern the attitude towards women in terms of their worth, segregated to a secondary labour market with low pay and low-status jobs. Women's entry into the labour force is restricted by a set of values (Wolpe, 1978). Women are filtered into a narrow range of occupations (Barron and Norris, 1976) that tend to mirror assumed domestic roles of carers, cleaners, and food preparers. Many women are excluded from working long and inflexible hours by their two roles—breadwinner and homemaker—but , as early as 1977 it was noted that the basic question of why women have two roles had not been discussed (Wolff, 1977: 20).

This idea of rules and ruling is to be found in many sources. From the perspective of sociology, Dorothy Smith (1987) believed that is necessary to take on the view of ruling and to view society and social relations in terms of the perspectives, interests, and relevances of men active in 'relations of ruling'. Relations of ruling is, she argued, a concept that grasps power, organization, direction, and regulation as more pervasively structured than can be expressed in traditional concepts provided by the discourses of power. The relations of ruling are rationally organized; they are objectified, impersonal, claiming universality. Their gender subtext has been invisible. We are looking at the gender organization of the apparently neutral and impersonal rationality of the ruling apparatus.

In considering the place of men and women in the world of work we can contrast public and domestic spheres of life. A number of writers, especially O'Brien (1981), Elshtain (1981), and Stacey and Price (1981), have critically attended to the public/private divide. The public has more cultural worth. Public life is predominantly important and gives authority and value to the roles and activities of men. Men dominate public situations and 'public thinking', including social and political theory and thereby organization theory. Most organizations remain patriarchal if only by virtue of their domination by men. There are few organizations composed of more men than women, yet how many are managed by women? Even all-women organizations can indirectly serve the interests of men (Cohen, 1979).

The domestic life and the work it affords is of little consequence—as typified by the woman who, when asked what she does, says 'I'm just a housewife.' The sense of domesticity is reinforced in those jobs labelled 'women's jobs'—nursing and childcare, or jobs that stress physical attractiveness like air hostesses, beauticians, department store sales personnel. Women are hired for their gender-based characteristics (Benson, 1986). In the airline industry the sexuality of advertising is shown in the flight attendant's job with adverts like 'Fly me, you'll like it'. The sexualized cabin atmosphere is expressly designed to diminish the male passenger's fear of flying: 'they figure mild sexual arousal will be helpful in getting people's minds off of flying' (Hochschild, 1983: 94). All this portrayal of women in feminine roles, in turn, reinforces male notions of female sexuality. The trainees are chosen for being able to act. They know the rules on how they act; they may also know how to resist. But there appears to be a human cost in all this emotional labour (see Hoschshild, 1983: 186).

Men and women learn their roles and act them out. It is surprising how many ways researchers have demonstrated male sexuality and dominance in aircraft. Here is one of the most unusual of experiments showing that 'male chauvinism transcends gravity'. Males seated next to females aboard airplanes are more likely to use their mutual armrest on a ratio of three to one, even when the experiment was controlled for males' larger body size (reported in Goodman, 1983).

Let us just go back for a moment to this idea that individuals know how to resist the rules. One element of the socialization process appears to be the development of cynicism. This was shown particularly by Bryan's (1965) study of apprenticeship call-girls. The rules they develop include regarding each customer as a 'mark' and avoiding any emotional involvement or pleasure with the client (see also Terkel, 1977). This is one way in which you can maintain self-respect (also see Davis's 1959 study of taxi drivers and Spradley and Mann's 1975 study of cocktail waitresses).

The culture and the rules that are learned mean, as we have seen, that women behave in certain ways, they are hired for their gender-based characteristics, and so certain jobs are labelled women's work. In addition a number of factors combine to ensure that women's work is rarely seen as skilled. Building upon gender divisions, the work of men has historically been valued higher than that of women and women are rarely recruited to jobs involving traditional skill training. What is shocking, as Jenny Firth-Cozen (1991) has noted, is how little has changed in the last 20 years. She believes there are three reasons why changes have failed to occur. The first is that economic forces have not necessitated change. The second is that men, who have the power in organizations, do not want the situation to change. The third is that women are reluctant, or at least ambivalent about helping change come about.

Kanter (1975) has suggested that work attitudes and behaviour are a function of the location of a person in organizational structures and not a function of sex differences. Men, as well as women, are in a disadvantaged position both in society and organizations but women are more disadvantaged. The structure of power in organizations ensures the concentration of women at the bottom, not gender attributes or characteristics. What do you think?

Let us look at some more examples of how ideology works. In the United Kingdom women are rarely given jobs which require physical strength. Women are thought to have less strength than men and to be unwilling to lift and carry. Women can come to find it difficult to believe in their own ability. Yet in most of the non-industrialized world where water needs to be carried, this task tends to be women's work. Here is another example.

As early as 1976, Wardle put women through tests of physical strength, energy, and endurance simulating the requirements of demanding jobs like mining. It was found that women possessed the capacities for most physically demanding jobs including mining and deep-sea fishing. A nurse's job was found to require as much expenditure of energy in a typical shift as mining and fishing. Of course not all women or men wish to pursue such work, but they ought to be offered the choice. So why have we not heard about this research? Why is it that we continue to believe in the myth of the weaker sex?

We can say that, on average, men possess a number of physical advantages as they are larger, stronger, and more muscular than women. They can carry higher concentrations of oxygen on the blood and are better equipped to deal with the waste products of physical exertion. These are only average differences, however, and, with the exception of height, are all characteristics that can be improved considerably with appropriate training (Lowe, 1982). We should not ignore the overlapping distribution of physical abilities in men and women and their potential for improvement as a result of training.

One area of work where women, through training, must have improved their physical strength is nursing. In this country, nursing is seen as primarily women's work as it is an extension of domestic caring; in the context of the home or in nursing no one questions whether or not women should be lifting or carrying children, lifting elderly relatives or patients.

The variation between cultures in the tasks assigned to each gender shows that particular gender roles are not biologically given (Oakley, 1972). Any differences in behaviour that do exist are induced by environmental pressures and the reality of the social and economic context. This knowledge has been available to us for a long time, yet many still hold on to the belief in gender roles being biologically determined in some way. There is no evidence which forces us to accept that men and women must behave differently because they are different biologically (Nicholson, 1984). Discrimination calls for psychological theories which justify inequality (Millet, 1971). Gender identities are not determined by a person's sex—as shown by cases where children have been wrongly assigned to a sex; these children assume their socially assigned gender identity rather than their biological sex (Money and Ernhardt, 1972).

Gender roles are socially constructed. In New Guinea, among the Tchambuli tribe, Margaret Mead (1963), the social anthropologist, observed that women looked after the children and did the heavy work while the men, adorned with paint, gossiped with each other and tackled less heavy tasks. She noted (1949: 7–8) that in every society there is a biological division of labour but there is great variety of ways in which the roles of the two sexes have been patterned. The biological division of labour is only very remotely related to the original biological differences so we find that there is considerable variability in sex roles across societies. The evidence accumulated by anthropologists suggests that no one pattern of sex role prevails across all societies, so it is unlikely that our 'traditional' conceptions of sex roles are the result of principles of evolution (see also Moore, 1994). To understand the relationship between the sexes we need to look elsewhere (Powell, 1988: 25).

The myth of women's inability to fulfil wider or more valued roles is challenged only when a drastic event disrupts the usual arrangements. Few questioned women's ability to do jobs labelled as men's and requiring strength in the shipbuilding and other manufacturing industry during the two world wars. Before 1914 as many as $5\frac{1}{2}$ million women were in employment, mainly in textile work, clerical, nursing and teaching jobs. During the 1914–1918 war the number of women in paid employment increased by nearly 2 million; the corresponding number for 1939–1943 was less than 1 million (Wilson, 1977). It is, then, very easy to overturn some of the basic tenets of how men and women's jobs are segregated.

Discussion point

Some researchers believe that our behaviour is biologically determined and we cannot change something that is fundamentally biological. Even if we could provide identical education for men and women, the basic biological imperatives would show through (see Wilson, 1978). Biological differences account for men's inability to load the dishwasher, according to Moir and Jesel (1989)! Biological differences, not social conditions, were held to be responsible for black children's underachievement in US schools (see Rose *et al.*, 1984, for a criticism of this argument). What do you think?

Biological arguments are still used, though, to justify why jobs are segregated. A biological determinist would argue that sex differences are due to biology and this cannot be changed. They would point to examples of animals and humans. (A popularist sociobiological view can be found in Morris (1981).) They help justify existing social organization. Sometimes the female can be evaluated as superior. Some renowned misogynists are not averse to claiming that women are superior to men. It excuses all sorts of bad behaviour, legitimates double standards, and does not disturb the expectations that women will care, feel, and nurture (Segal, 1987: 5).

The assumptions must still exist that what is biological or natural is somehow more real than what is social. The stereotypes still exist, showing impressive toughness and resilience. 'Social process has its own power to constrain, its own resistance to dissolution. And yet it is entirely human. The oppression of women and gays is a matter of human agency, not nature' (Connell, 1987: x).

Can you argue, then, that everything we are has been socially constructed? If you do, are you then likely to go down 'the slippery slope of social determinism: the well worn cry that the subjugation of women is all the result of conditioning?' (Lloyd, 1989: vii). It may seem like nonsense to argue that everything we are is socially and ideologically constructed, as though we have no body, no biology. We need to acknowledge biology as a fact, that our biological bodies are important components of what we are, but also say that their involvement is much more complicated and subtle than a biological determinist argument would have us believe (Birke, 1992: 75).

We can argue that we accept that women are different because we are socialized to believe this is the case. Socialization can, then, also help explain why women seem to accede to their own oppression and can show why equal opportunities will not be enough to create an equal society. Men and women's lives are formed by different experiences and expectations. Men and women cannot be expected to behave in the same way if offered equal opportunity and women are unlikely to fit into the roles for which men have been socialized.

Discussion point

Why do women appear to act to support the values which reinforce inequality? Why does latent conflict between men and women remain submerged? Is the status quo accepted because it is seen as the normal way of being (see Davies, 1985) and because women do not see men as oppressors? (Marshall, 1984). Is it because women oppose change (see Novarra, 1980)?

Should we argue that women's sexual difference from men results in a different life pattern, a different psychology, and different moral values (see Gilligan, 1982; Griffin, 1985)? Or should we say that women and men are more or less a blank slate on which gender identity is inscribed as we learn to be male or female (Epstein, 1988)?

Women's lives and ways of behaving are socialized as different. Women, for example, are found to cope differently with the anxieties and uncertainties of living. Women may look to union and co-operation to cope with uncertainty and threat. Men may change the environment to match preconceived ideas, creating a world of competition, seeking control and dominance (Marshall, 1984). But we must be careful not to see the socialization model as overly deterministic. People are not totally passive and malleable and entirely determined by society. We must leave room for change.

Men have been ascribed dominant status at birth and then use overt power to maintain this inequality between the sexes (Marshall, 1984). Dominant members are punished if they support a member of the subdominant group. The subdominant group is kept in place by being labelled substandard and being ascribed appropriate sex roles. The subdominant group accept the dominant group's definition of the relative status of each group and accommodate to the extent that they define their own aspiration in terms of the dominant group's goals.

> Once a group is defined as inferior, the superiors tend to label it as defective or substandard in various ways. These labels accrete rapidly. Thus blacks are described as less intelligent than whites, women are supposed to be ruled by emotion, and so on. In addition, the actions and words of the dominant group tend to be destructive of the subordinates. (Miller, 1978: 6)

We saw earlier, for example, how language has been 'man-made' and how that man-made language can be detrimental to the interests of women.

Subordinates are described, named, in terms of characteristics pleasing to the dominant group—submissiveness, passivity, docility, dependence, lack of initiative, inability, to decide, to think. If subordinates adopt these characteristics they are considered well adjusted. If they behave, say, assertively, they will be regarded as unusual or abnormal. Socialization prepares women for their current roles, not for challenging those roles.

Here is a quote that illustrates this point well:

> Women fear that if they act in an unfeminine manner, they will be isolated, avoided and ignored. Furthermore, women are confused because they are frequently chastised or punished for the very behaviours for which men are rewarded—for speaking loudly and forcefully, for example. (Borisoff and Merrill, 1985: 81)

Discussion point

Have you learned that there are no great women artists? What are the reasons as to why there are so few exceptional women in art? (See Nochlin, 1971.)

In their course of work on learning and student development Goldberger *et al.* (1987) were concerned about why women students so frequently spoke about problems and gaps in their learning and so often expressed doubts about their intellectual competence. Women often felt alienated in academic settings and experienced formal education as peripheral or irrelevant to their central interests and development. Girls and women tend to have more difficulty than boys and men in asserting their authority and considering themselves as authorities (West and Zimmerman, 1983); in expressing themselves in public so that others will listen (Sadker and Sadker, 1982); in gaining respect of others for their minds and ideas (Hall and Sandler, 1982); and in fully utilizing their capabilities and training in the world of work (Treichler and Kramarae, 1983).

> In private and professional life, as well as in the classroom, women often feel unheard even when they believe that they have something important to say. Most women can recall incidents in which they or their female friends were discouraged from pursuing some line of intellectual work on the grounds that it was unwomanly or incompatible with female capabilities ... women, like children, should be seen, not heard.   (Goldberger *et al.*, 1987)

Day-to-day interaction in all organizations can affect the success or failure of women trying to enter. Everyday conversation can bring women in or leave them outside the group. Being within is important to success. Any messages which stress that women are different, or directly or indirectly question their competence or raise doubts about their future, will exclude them. Action is needed by top management to help make women successful. Formal messages and actions from those in top positions must convey sustained support for women. Shared styles of discourse and manner need to be questioned so that women are not seen to differ from men and are not therefore excluded. Cox (1986) has argued that women presently have no choice but to adopt male styles in order to gain organizational power, since the male styles are the stereotyped image of competence, intelligence, and leadership. Without this style women will remain 'invisible' in terms of communication and therefore power.

Davidson and Cooper (1992) talk of the culture trap due to sex-role learning. The first trap women get caught up in is the 'low expectation trap' particularly when contemplating or performing a male-stereotyped task. Women begin to feel their abilities are not up to the task and so the vicious circle widens. The more a person feels their ability is not up to the task, e.g. managing other people, the lower the likelihood of success (Weiner *et al.*, 1977). Data from Northern Ireland show that women are four times as likely as men to turn down offers of promotion (Davidson and Cooper, 1992: 60).

Women have been expected and encouraged to pursue a dependent role in relation to men. Some suggest this makes them less self-reliant and more amenable to influence; others see women as less achievement oriented and less aggressive. This culture trap creates difficulties for women as most organizations are dominated by male values and behaviours.

Women are, according to Davidson and Cooper (1992: 62), on the horns of a dilemma when it comes to assertive, power-seeking behaviour. If a female manager does not display the kind of behaviour that is traditionally associated with successful management, then the male managers will not feel she is a very effective manager. However, if she does, many male and female colleagues will see her as hostile, maladjusted, and over-controlling.

However, research indicates that women managers who adopt modes of assertive behaviour report increased confidence and effectiveness. According to Davidson (1985), if other people cannot cope with assertive women, then that should be their problem, not a problem for the woman in question. Advice on assertion, a five stage approach, is outlined in by Langruish (in Davidson and Cooper, 1992: 62).

There is little chance of change when men are more likely than females to prefer occupations dominated by their own sex. Male-intensive occupations have less than 30 per cent women. One study found that 86 per cent of males aspire to male-intensive occupations; only 4 per cent aspire to female occupations. Little is going to change while this is the case. In contrast 53 per cent of females were found to aspire to female-intensive occupations and 35 per cent to male occupations (Marini and Brinton, 1986).

Sex-role identity, which seems to be more of a result of socialization than of basic sex differences, seems to have a substantial effect on the formation of occupational aspirations and expectations. Men are going to aspire to, and succeed in, more male-intensive occupations. When individuals make choices about the occupations in which they will work they are likely to be influenced by the distribution of male and female workers across occupations and their own socialization experiences. The fact that expectations mirror the sex segregation of occupations more than aspirations, particularly for females, shows the constraining nature of these influences (Powell, 1988).

You could try to argue again that this situation is changing by looking to different research and ideas. There is one argument that has just been touched on in this chapter and is to be found later in this book, in Chapter 6, which says that being androgynous, having both male and female characteristics, means being well adjusted. The androgynous concept of psychological health defines the ideal person as having a blend of interests, abilities and traits which are both expressive and instrumental. In an androgynous society people are not forced into roles or traits on the basis of gender. 'In time as the androgynous personality is recognised, gender could become irrelevant to the assignment of roles. Roles would depend overwhelmingly on individual characteristics' (Bardwick, 1980: 159).

There is some evidence to suggest that the traditional roles of men and women in marriage have changed. The anthropologist Geoffrey Gorer (1955, 1971) found that in 1950 great admiration was attached to the conventional male virtue of being a good provider, and female excellence at domestic and mothering skills. Nearly 20 years later, in 1969, he found that good communication and companionship were top of the list.

Women bear children and men do not; if this fact were to change the very definition of the sexes would be in question. In an equal society women and men would have equal capacity and desire to care for children; this might be the necessary step to the creation of the androgynous personality and a more equal society. Is reason that men seem to be unwilling to care for children due to the lack of social prestige and power attached to this task?

In defining men and women as different, Catherine McKinnon (1987: 3) has claimed that the social relation between the sexes is organized so that men dominate and women submit and this relation is sexual. 'Men in particular, if not men alone, sexualize inequality, especially the inequality of the sexes.' Gender is basically a difference, it is a bipolar distinction, each pole being defined in contrast to the other by opposed intrinsic attributes. This gender difference obscures and legitimates the way in which gender is imposed by force. The idea of gender difference keeps the reality of male dominance in place. Femininity and masculinity are ideological practices all the more effective because they appear as natural and inevitable results of biology or experience (Wetherell, 1986: 77). Gender is about power; differences between men and women are derived from that, rather than the other way round. Gender is an inequality of power, a social status that defines who can do what to whom.

Haste (1993) has used the idea that metaphors underlie our taken-for-granted assumptions about the world and permeate gender. Our conceptions of sex difference, sex roles, and sexual relations are couched in terms of metaphors that explain and justify. Metaphors derived from gender and sexuality invade vast other areas of life. The primary metaphor of gender is dualism and polarity which gains extra power from mapping other dualities on to gender, entwining masculinity and femininity with such dualities as active–passive, public–private, rational–intuitive. Metaphors also operate as analogies, so, for example, we describe male and female in terms of soft and hard. With the metaphor of dualism comes overtones of control. Femininity may sap masculinity, contaminate, undermine it: maintaining masculinity requires suppression of the feminine.

Some psychologists, theorists, and researchers have decried the idea of falling into the trap of viewing women as a homogeneous mass. Lott (1987) has recently affirmed this view, noting that women and men differ enormously in the conditions under which they live, most notably in their access to power and control of resources. Even in death, it seems, men have more power; their deaths are far more likely to be investigated—in the same way that the death of a middle-class individual is more likely to be investigated than a working-class death (Prior, 1987: 368). A person's level of autonomy or relatedness could depend on their position in the social hierarchy than on gender (Hare-Mustin and Marecek, 1986). People in power tend to focus on rules and rationality, whereas those with less power emphasize relatedness and compassion. The individual's behaviour cannot be predicted from gender alone.

Men, it could thus be argued, like women, cannot be viewed as a homogeneous mass either. Dominant forms of men and masculinities have been learned and are not 'natural' and unchangeable either. Men and masculinities are not unproblematic but are social constructions which need to be explored, analysed, and in some respects (e.g. as in the case of violence) changed (see Hearn and Morgan, 1990). Yet there is little sustained research on the male experience and the activities of men (Edley and Wetherell, 1993).

It is possible to argue, implicitly for women's difference from men. According to Cockburn (1991: 9–10), women need to keep this idea of women's difference in play, but on women's terms; women must be the ones to say when difference is relevant. Women are not just like men, but being different should not mean being less equal. 'We can also be the same and different from each other. What we are seeking is not in fact *equality*, but *equivalence*, not *sameness*, for individual women and men, but *parity* for women as a sex, or for groups of women in their specificity.'

Are women the same or different to men in terms of their motivation to work? The next chapter goes on to look at how women have been treated in the literature on motivation in organizational behaviour.

———————————— *Review Questions* ————————————

How do children learn the 'master rules of gender'? Have girls learned to be powerless? (See Lips, 1994.)

Some (e.g. Betz and Fitzgerald, 1987) regard the lack of a mathematics background as the 'critical filter', the factor that constitutes one of the major barriers to women's career development. What do you think?

How are men and women portrayed in advertising? Who has the voice of authority in advertising?

Do you think that women are portrayed as passive, conforming, self-subordinating, and less competent than men in films, novels, magazines, and television? Support your argument with published research studies.

How are we gender socialized in organizations? (See Cox, 1986; Mills,1988b,1993.)

What can we say about advertising and the issue of race?

What is the social identity of women? What is the social identity of men?

Is the language men and women use significantly different? Does it help us understand the concept of power in organizations? (See also Wilson, 1992.)

Many women in organizations, like universities, are reluctant to call themselves feminists. This may stem from the belief that men view feminists as angry, bitter women who hate men. What do you think? (see Berryman-Fink and Verderber, 1985; Condor, 1986; Griffin, 1989;Unger and Crawford, 1992: 6.)

Do you agree that there is a move towards accepting that being androgynous is best? What evidence can you find, from your own experience and reading, to support this argument? Or do you believe that masculine characteristics are still held to be more valuable and that this view ignores the domination and subordination we can witness?

REFERENCES

ACKER, J. (1992) 'Gendering Organisational Theory', Chapter 14 in A. J. Mills and P. Tancred, (eds), *Gendering Organisational Analysis*, Sage, London.

ARCHER, J. and LLOYD, B. (1985) *Sex and Gender*, Cambridge University Press, Cambridge.

BARDWICK, J. (1980) *Women in Transition*, Harvester, Brighton.

BARRON, R. D. and NORRIS, G. M. (1976) 'Sexual Divisions and the Duel Labour Market', in D. L. Barker and S. Allen (eds), *Dependence and Exploitation in Work and Marriage*, Longman, London.

BASOW, S. (1992) *Gender: Stereotypes and Roles*, 3rd edn, Brooks/Cole, Monterey, Calif.

BENSON, S. P. (1986) *Counter Cultures: Saleswomen, Managers and Customers in American Department Stores, 1890–1940.* University of Chicago Press, Urbana and Chicago, Ill.

BERRYMAN-FINK, C. and VERDERBER, K. S. (1985) 'Attributions of the Term Feminist: A Factor Analytic Development of a Measuring Instrument', *Psychology of Women Quarterly*, 9, 51–64.

BETZ, N. E. and FITZGERALD, L. F. (1987) *The Career Psychology of Women*, Academic Press, London.

BIRKE, L. (1986) *Women, Feminism and Biology: The Feminist Challenge*, Wheatsheaf, Brighton.

BIRKE, L. (1992) 'Transforming Biology', Article 2.1 in H. Crowley and S. Himmelweit (eds), *Knowing Women: Feminism and Knowledge*, Open University Press, Milton Keynes.

BORISOFF, D. and MERRILL, L. (1985) *The Power to Communicate: Gender Differences as Barriers*, Waveland, Prospect Heights, Ill.

BRADLEY, P. H. (1981) 'The Folk-linguistics of Women's Speech: An Empirical Investigation', *Communication Monographs*, **48**, 73–90.

BREAKWELL, G. N. (1979) 'Woman: Group and Identity', *Women's Studies International Quarterly*, **2**, 9–17.

BRITTAN, A. (1989) *Masculinity and Power*, Basil Blackwell, Oxford.

BRYAN, J. H. (1965) 'Apprenticeships in Prostitution', *Social Problems*, **12**, 287.

CANCIAN, F. M. and ROSS, B. L. (1981) 'Mass Media and the Women's Movement: 1900–1977', *Journal of Applied Behavioural Science*, **17**, 9–16.

CARLI, L. L. (1990) 'Gender, Language and Influence', *Journal of Personality and Social Psychology*, **59**, 941–951.

CHARLES, N. (1993) *Gender Divisions and Social Change*, Harvester Wheatsheaf, Hemel Hempstead.

COCKBURN, C. (1991) *In the Way of Women: Men's Resistance to Sex Equality in Organizations*, Macmillan Press, Basingstoke.

COHEN, G. (1979) 'Symbiotic Relations: Male Decision Makers–Female Support Groups in Britain and the United States', *Women's Studies International Quarterly*, **2**, 391–406.

COLLINSON, D. C. (1988) 'Engineering Humour: Masculinity, Joking and Conflict in Shop Floor Relations', *Organization Studies*, **9**(2), 181–199.

COLLINSON, D. C. and HEARN, J. (1994) 'Naming Men as Men', *Gender, Work and Organization*, **1**(1), 2–22.

COLLINSON, D. C., KNIGHTS, D. and COLLINSON, M. (1990) *Managing to Discriminate*, Routledge, London.

CONDOR, S. (1986) 'Sex Role Beliefs and Traditional Women: Feminist and Intergroup Perspectives', Chapter 6 in S. Wilkinson (ed.), *Feminist Social Psychology*, Open University Press, Milton Keynes.

CONDRY, J. and CONDRY, S. (1976) 'Sex Differences: A Study of the Eye of the Beholder', *Child Development*, **47**, 812–819.

CONNELL, R. W. (1987) *Gender and Power: Society, the Person and Sexual Politics*, Polity Press, Basil Blackwell, Oxford.

COX, M. G. (1986) 'Enter the Stranger: Unanticipated Effects of Communication on the Success of an Organizational Newcomer' in L. Thayer (ed.), *Organization Communication: Emerging Perspectives*, pp. 34–50, Ablex, Norwood, NJ.

CULP, R. E., CROOK, A. S. and HOUSLEY, P. C. (1983) 'A Comparison of Observed and Reported Adult–Infant Interactions: Effects of Perceived Sex', *Sex Roles*, **9**, 475–479.

DAVEY, K. MCKENZIE (1993) Study reported in *Mind Body and Power*, report on issues raised at the Psychology of Women Section and the Women in Psychology Society Annual Conference at the University of Sussex, 1993 and reported in *Psychologist*, **6**(9), 386.

DAVIDSON, M. J. (1985) *Reach for the Top: A Woman's Guide to Success in Business and Management*, Piatkus, London.

DAVIDSON, M. J. and COOPER, C. L. (1992) *Shattering the Glass Ceiling: The Woman Manager*, Chapman, London.

DAVIES, J. (1985) 'Why Are Women Not Where the Power Is? An Examination of the Maintenance of Power Elites', *Management Education and Development*, **16**(3), 278–288.

DAVIS, F. (1959) 'The Cabdriver and his Fare', *American Journal of Sociology*, **65**, 2, 158–165.

DE BEAUVOIR, S. (1952) *The Second Sex*, Vintage Books, New York.

DEMAREST, J. and GARNER, J. (1992) 'The Representation of Women's Roles in Women's Magazines Over the Past 30 Years', *Journal of Psychology*, **126**(4), 357–369.

DOMINICK, J. R. (1979) 'The Portrayal of Women in Prime Time: 1953–1977', *Sex Roles*, 405–411.

EAKINS, B. W. and EAKINS. R. G. (1978) *Sex Differences in Communications*, Houghton-Mifflin, Boston, Mass.

EDLEY, N. and WETHERELL, M. (1993) 'Constructing Masculinity', paper delivered at the Social Psychology Conference, Jesus College, Oxford, available from M. Wetherell, Social Sciences Faculty, Open University, Walton Hall, Milton Keynes.

EHRENREICH, B. (1983) *The Hearts of Men: American Dreams and the Flight from Commitment*, Pluto Press, London.

EHRENREICH, B. and ENGLISH, D. (1979) *For Her Own Good: 150 Years of the Experts' Advice to Women*, Pluto Press, London.

ELSHTAIN, J. B. (1981) *Public Man, Private Woman*, Robertson, Oxford.

EPSTEIN, C. F. (1988) *Deceptive Distinctions: Sex Gender and the Social Order*, Yale University Press, New Haven, Conn.

FALUDI, S. (1992) *Backlash: The Undeclared War Against Women*, Vintage Books, London.

FARGANIS, S. (1986) *The Social Reconstruction of the Feminine Character*, Rowman & Littlefield, Totowa, NJ.

FIRTH-COZENS, J. (with Michael West) (1991) 'Women at Work: Reflections and Perspectives', Chapter 15 in *Women at Work*, Open University Press, Milton Keynes.

FISHMAN, P. (1983) in J. L. Thompson, *Learning Liberation: Women's Response to Men's Education*, Croom Helm, London.

FOUCAULT, M. (1980) *The History of Sexuality: An Introduction*, trans. R. Hurley, Vintage Books, New York (Gallimard, Paris, 1976; Allen Lane, London, 1979).

FREED, A. (1985) 'What We Teach Kids About Language, About Themselves', *Star Tribune*, Minneapolis, quoted in Van Nostrand (1993: 49).

FRIEDAN, B. (1963) *The Feminine Mystique*, Dell, New York.

FURNHAM, A. and SCHOFIELD, S. (1986) 'Sex Role Stereotyping in British Radio Advertisements', *British Journal of Social Psychology*, **25**, 165–171.

GASTIL, J. (1990) 'Generic Pronouns and Sexist Language: The Oxymoronic Character of Masculine Generics', *Sex Roles*, **23**, 629–643.

GILBERT, L. A. (1983) 'Female Development and Achievement', *Issues in Mental Health Nursing*, **5**, 5–17. See also the *Counseling Psychologist*, 1982, **9**, 83–84.

GILLIGAN, C. (1982) *In a Different Voice: Psychological Theory and Women's Development*, Harvard University Press, Cambridge, Mass.

GOLDBERGER, N. R., CLINCHY, B. M., BELENKY, M. F., and TARULE, J. M. (1987) 'Women's Ways of Knowing: On Gaining a Voice', Chapter 8 in P. Shaver and C. Hendrick (eds), *Sex and Gender: Review of Personality and Social Psychology* Sage, Newbury Park, Calif.

GOODMAN, H. (1983) 'Up in Arms', *Psychology Today*, August, 78.

GORER, G. (1955) *Exploring English Character*, Cresset Press, London.

GORER, G. (1971) *Sex and Marriage in England Today*, Nelson, London.

GREENBERG, S. (1988) 'Educational Equality in Early Educational Environments', in S. S. Klein (ed.), *Handbook for Achieving Sex Equality Through Education*, pp. 457–469, Johns Hopkins University, Baltimore, Md.

GRIFFIN, C. (1985) *Typical Girls? Young Women from School in the Labour Market*, Routledge & Kegan Paul, London.

GRIFFIN, C. (1989) ' "I'm not a Women's Libber, but ... " Feminism, Consciousness and Identity', Chapter 9 in *The Social Identity of Women*, Sage, London.

GRUSEC, J. E. and LYTTON, H. (1988) *Social Development: History, Theory and Research*, Springer-Verlag, New York.

HAHN, C. L., BERNARD-POWERS, J. with HUNTER, L., GROVES, S., MACGREGOR, M. and SCOTT, K. P. (1988) 'Sex Equality in the Social Sciences', in S. S. Klein (ed.), *Handbook for Achieving Sex Equality Through Education*, p. 280, Johns Hopkins University, Baltimore, Md.

HALL, R. M. (1986) 'He Said, She Said: Gender and Classroom Climate', address to Gender and the Curriculum Project, St John's University, St Joseph, MN, in Van Nostrand, C. H. (1993) Gender-Responsible Leadership, Sage, London.

HALL, R. and SANDLER, B. R. (1982) 'The Classroom Climate: A Chilly One for Women?', project on the Status of Education of Women, Association of American Colleges, Washington, DC, quoted in Goldberger *et al.*, (1987).

HARE-MUSTIN, R. and MARACEK, J. (1986) 'Autonomy and Gender: Some Questions for Therapists', *Psychotherapy*, **23**, 205–212.

HARRIS, M. B. and VOORHEES, S. D. (1981) 'Sex Role Stereotypes and Televised Models of Emotion', *Psychological Reports*, **48**, 826.

HASTE, H. (1993) *The Sexual Metaphor*, Harvester Wheatsheaf, Hemel Hemstead.

HEARN, J. and MORGAN, D. (eds) (1990) *Men, Maculinities and Social Theory*, Unwin Hyman, London.

HOCHSCHILD, A. R. (1983) *The Managed Heart*, University of California Press, Berkley, Calif.

HYDE, J. S. (ed.) (1985) *Half the Human Experience: The Psychology of Women*, 3rd edn, Heath, Lexington, Mass.

ITZIN, C. (1986) 'Media Images of Women: The Social Construction of Ageism and Sexism', in S. Wilkinson (ed.), *Feminist Social Psychology: Developing Theory and Practice*, Open University Press, Milton Keynes.

JOHNSTONE, B. (1989) 'Community and Contest: How Women and Men Construct their Worlds in Conversational Narrative', paper presented at Women in America: Legacies of Race and Ethnicity, Georgetown University, Washington, DC, quoted in Tannen (1990).

KAISER, K. (1979) 'The New Women's Magazines: It's the Same Old Story', *Frontiers*, **IV**, 14–17.

KANTER, R. M. (1975) 'Women and the Structure of Organizations: Explorations in Theory and Behaviour', *Sociological Inquiry*, **45**, 3–74.

KELLY, R. M. (1991) *The Gendered Economy: Work, Careers and Success*, Sage, Newbury Park, Calif.

KENDRICK, D. T. (1987) 'Gender, Genes and Social Environment: A Biosocial Interactionist Perspective', in P. Shaver and C. Hendrick, *Sex and Gender*, Sage, Newbury Park, Calif.

KEY, M. R. (1975) *Male/Female Language*, Scarecrow Press, Metuchen, NJ.

KOMISAR, L. (1972) 'The Image of Women in Advertising' in V. Gornick and B. Moran (eds), *Women in a Sexist Society: Studies in Power and Powerlessness*, Signet Books, New York.

LAKOFF, R. (1975) *Language and Women's Place*, Harper & Row, New York.

LAKOFF, R. (1990) *Talking Power: The Politics of Language*, Basic Books, New York.

LIPS, H. M. (1994) 'Female Powerlessness: A Case of Cultural Preparedness?', Chapter 5 in H. L. Radtke and H. J. Stam (eds), *Power/Gender: Social Relations in Theory and Practice*, Sage, London.

LIVINGSTONE, S. and GREEN, G. (1986) 'Television Advertisements and the Portrayal of Gender', *British Journal of Social Psychology*, **25**, 149–154.

LLOYD, B. (1989) 'Forward to the Social Identity of Women', in S. Skevington and D. Baker (eds), Sage, London.

LOTT, B. (1987) 'Feminist, Masculine, Androgenous or Human', paper presented at an American Psychological Association Meeting, New York City, cited in Mednick, (1989) 'On the Politics of Psychological Constructs', *American Psychologist*, August, 1119–1123.

LOWE, M. (1982) 'Social Bodies: The Interaction of Culture and Women's Biology', in R. Hubard, M. S. Henifin and B. Fried (eds), *Biological Woman: The Convenient Myth*, Shenkman, Cambridge, Mass.

MCARTHUR, L. Z. and EISEN, S. V. (1976) 'Television and Sex-role Stereotyping', *Journal of Applied Social Psychology*, **6**, 329–351.

MACCOBY, E. E. (1988) 'Gender as a Social Category', *Developmental Psychology*, **24**, 755–765.

MACCOBY, E. E. and JACKLIN, C. N. (1974) *The Psychology of Sex Differences*, Stanford University Press, Stanford University, Stanford, CA.

MCGHEE, P. E. and FRUEH, T. (1980) 'Television Viewing and the Learning of Sex-role Stereotypes', *Sex Roles*, **6**, 179–188.

MCKINNON, C. (1987) *Feminist Unmodified: Discourse on Life and Law*, Harvard University Press, Cambridge, Mass.

MARINI, M. M. and BRINTON, M. C. (1986) 'Sex Typing in Occupational Socialisation in Sex Segregation in the Workplace', in B. F. Reskin and H. I. Hartmann (eds), *Women's Work, Men's Work, Sex Segregation on the Job*, National Academy Press, Washington, DC.

MARSHALL, J. (1984) *Women Managers: Travellers in a Male World*, Wiley, New York.

MEAD, M. (1949) *Male and Female*, Morrow, New York.

MEAD, M. (1963) *Sex and Temperament in Three Primitive Societies*, Morrow, New York.

MILLER, C. and SWIFT, K. (1978) *Words and Women*, Anchor Press, Garden City, NY.

MILLER, J. B. (1978) *Towards a New Psychology of Women*, Penguin, Harmondsworth.

MILLET, K. (1971) *Sexual Politics*, Rupert Hart Davis, London.

MILLS, A. J. (1988a) 'Organization, Gender and Culture', *Organization Studies*, **9**(3), 351–370.

MILLS, A. J. (1988b) 'Organizational Acculturation and Gender Discrimination', in P. K. Kresl (ed.), *Women and the Workplace*, International Council for Canadian Studies, Ottowa.

MILLS, A. J. (1993) 'Organizational Discourse and the Gendering of Identity', Chapter 8 in J. Hassard and M. Parker (eds), *Postmodernism and Organizations*, Sage, London.

MILLS, A. J. (1994) 'Organizational Culture', in K. M. Borman and P. Dubeck, (eds), *Encyclopedia of Women and Work*, Oakland, New York.

MILLS, A. J. and MURGATROYD, S. J. (1991) *Organizational Rules: A Framework for Understanding Organizational Action*, Open University Press, Milton Keynes.

MOIR, A. and JESSEL, D. (1989) *Brain Sex: The Real Difference Between Men and Women*, Michael Joseph, London.

MONACO, N. M. and GAIER, E. L. (1992) 'Single-sex Versus Co-educational Environment and Achievement in Adolescent Females', *Adolescence*, **27**(107), Fall, 579–594.

MONEY, J. and EHRHARDT, A. (1972) *Man and Woman, Boy and Girl: The Differentiation and Dimorphism of Gender Identity from Conception to Maturity*, Johns Hopkins University Press, Baltimore, Md.

MOORE, H. (1994) 'The Cultural Constitution of Gender', Chapter 1 in *The Polity Reader in Gender Studies*, Polity Press, Blackwell, Oxford.

MORGAN, M. (1982) 'Television and Adolescents' Sex Role Stereotypes: A Longitudinal Study', *Journal of Personality and Social Psychology*, **43**, 947–955.

MORRIS, D. (1981) *The Naked Ape*, Panther, London.

MOULTON, J., ROBINSON, G. M. and ELIAS, C. (1978) 'Sex Bias in Language Use. "Neutral" Pronouns that Aren't' *American Psychologist*, November, 1032–1036.

NICHOLSON, J. (1984) *Men and Women*, Oxford University Press, London.

NOCHLIN, L. (1971) 'Why Are There No Great Women Artists?' in V. Gornick and B. Moran (eds), *Women in a Sexist Society*, pp. 480–510, Basic Books, New York.

NOVARRA, V. (1980) *Women's Work, Men's Work*, Marion Boyars, London.

OAKLEY, A. (1972) *Sex, Gender and Society*, Temple Smith, London.

O'BRIEN, M. (1981) *The Politics of Reproduction*, Routledge & Kegan Paul, London.

OUCHI, W. (1981) *Theory Z*, Addison-Wesley, Reading, Mass.

POWELL, G. N. (1988) *Women and Men in Management*, Sage, Newbury Park, Calif.

PRIOR, L. (1987) 'Policing the Dead: A Sociology of the Mortuary', *Sociology*, **21**(3), 355–376.

RILEY, A. (1983) 'Structuralist Account of Political Culture', *Administrative Science Quarterly*, **28**, 414–437.

ROSE, S., KAMIN, L. and LEWONTIN, R. (1984) *Not in Our Genes*, Penguin, Harmondsworth.

ROSS, D. R., ANDERSON, D. R. and WISOCKI, P. A. (1982) 'Television Viewing and Adult Sex-role Attitudes', *Sex Roles*, **8**, 589–592.

RUBIN, J. Z., PROVENZANO, F. J. and LURIA, Z. (1974) 'The Eye of the Beholder: Parents' Views on the Sex of New Borns', *American Journal of Orthopsychiatry*, **44**, 512–519.

SACHS, J. (1987) 'Young Children's Language Use in Pretend Play', in S. Phillips, S. Steele and C. Tanz, (eds), *Language, Gender and Sex in Comparative Perspective*, pp. 178–188, Cambridge University Press, Cambridge.

SADKER, M. P. and SADKER, D. M. (1982) *Sex Equity Handbook for Schools*, Longman, New York.

SCOTT, J. (1986) 'Gender: A Useful Category of Historical Analysis', *American Historical Review*, **91**, 1053–1075.

SEGAL, L. (1987) *Is the Future Female? Troubled Thoughts on Contemporary Feminism*, Virago, London.

SEGGAR, J. F. (1975) 'Imagery of Women in Television Drama: 1974', *Journal of Broadcasting*, **19**, 273–282.

SEXTON, D. E. and HABERMAN, P. (1974) 'Women in Magazine Advertisements', *Journal of Advertising Research*, **14**(4), 41–46.

SHEPPARD-LOOK, D. I. (1982) 'Sex Differentiation and the Development of Sex Roles' in B. B. Wolman (ed.), *Handbook of Developmental Psychology*, Prentice Hall, Englewood Cliffs, NJ.

SKEVINGTON, S. (1989) 'A Place for Emotion in Social Identity Theory', Chapter 3 in S. Skevington and D. Baker (eds), *The Social Identity of Women*, Sage, London.

SMITH, D. (1987) *The Everyday World as Problematic: A Feminist Sociology*, Northeastern University Press, Boston, Mass.

SMITH, C. and LLOYD, B. B. (1978) 'Maternal Behaviour and Perceived Sex of Infant', *Child Development*, **49**, 1263–1265.

SONDEREGGER, T. B. (1985) *Psychology and Gender*, University of Nebraska Press, Lincoln.

SPENDER, D. (1985) *Man Made Language*, 2nd edn, Routledge & Kegan Paul, London.

SPRADLEY, J. P. and MANN, B. J. (1975) *The Cocktail Waitress*, Wiley, New York.

STACEY, M. and PRICE, M. (1981) *Women, Power and Politics*, Tavistock, London.

STANLEY, L. and WISE, S. (1983) *Breaking Out: Feminist Consciousness and Feminist Research*, Routledge & Kegan Paul, London.

SWANN, J. (1992) 'Girls' and Boys' Talk in the Classroom', Chapter 3 in *Girls, Boys and Language*, Blackwell, Oxford.

TANNEN, D. (1990) *You Just Don't Understand: Women and Men in Conversation*, Morrow, New York.

TAVRIS, C. (1992) *The Mismeasure of Woman*, Simon & Schuster, New York.

TERKEL, S. (1977) *Working*, Penguin, Hamonsworth.

TREICHLER, P. and KRAMARAE, C. (1983) 'Women's Talk in the Ivory Tower', *Communication Quarterly*, **31**, 118–132.

UNGER, R. and CRAWFORD, M. (1992) *Women and Gender: A Feminist Psychology*, Temple University Press, Phil.

WAJCMAN, J. (1994) 'Technology as Masculine Culture', Chapter 19 in the *Polity Reader in Gender Studies*, Polity Press, Blackwell, Cambridge.

WALCZAK, Y. (1988) *He and She, Men in the Eighties*, Routledge, London.

WARDLE, M. G. (1976) 'Women's Physiological Responses to Physically Demanding Work', *Psychology of Women Quarterly*, **1**, 151–159.

WEINER, B. (1992) *Human Motivation: Metaphors, Theories and Research*, Sage, Newbury Park, Calif.

WEINER, J., NEIRENBERG and GOLDSTEIN, (1977) in L. Larwood and M. M. Wood (eds), *Women in Management*, Lexington Books, London.

WEST, C. and ZIMMERMAN, D. H. (1983) 'Small Insults: A Study of Interruptions in Cross-sex Conversations between Unacquainted Persons', in B. Thorne, C. Kramarae, and N. Henley, *Language, Gender and Society*, Newbury House, Rowley, Mass.

WESTON, L. C. and RUGGIERO, J. A. (1986) 'The Popular Approach to Women's Health Issues: A Content Analysis of Women's Magazines in the 1970s', *Women and Health*, **10**, 47–62.

WETHERELL, M. (1986) 'Linguistic Repertoires and Literary Criticism: New Direction for a Social Psychology of Gender', Chapter 5 in S. Wilkinson (ed.), *Feminist Social Psychology: Developing Theory and Practice*, Open University Press, Milton Keynes.

WHITE, D. and WOLLETT, A. (1981) 'The Family at Birth', paper presented at the British Psychological Society London Conference, December.

WILLIAMS, J. A. (1984) 'Gender and Intergroup Behaviour: Towards an Integration', *British Journal of Social Psychology*, **23**, 311–316.

WILLIS, P. (1977) *Learning to Labour*, Saxon House, London.

WILSON, E. (1977) *Women in the Welfare State*, Tavistock, London.

WILSON, E. O. (1978) *On Human Nature*, Harvard University Press, Cambridge, Mass.

WILSON, F. M. (1992) 'Language, Power and Technology', *Human Relations*, **45**(9), 883–904.

WOLFF, J. (1977) 'Women in Organizations', in S. Clegg and D. Dunkerley (eds), *Critical Issues in Organizations*, pp. 7–20, Routledge & Kegan Paul, London.

WOLPE, A. (1978) 'Education and the Sexual Division of Labour', in A. Kuhn and A. Wolpe (eds), *Feminism and Materialism*, pp. 290–328, Routledge & Kegan Paul, London.

Motivation

In the case of motivation and job satisfaction, the conditions that faced employers and managers at the time the human relations movement emerged, after the First World War, and face them now, was ensuring that both men and women in the labour force turned out products of competitive price and quality. (Hollway, 1991: 8). The problem of motivating an individual emerged in order to create sufficient satisfaction with the job to produce adequate work. Supervisory relations, how to get supervisors to treat workers in such a way as not to bring about unrest, sabotage, or restriction of output, is a long-running problem. F. W. Taylor had created fragmented, routinized and control jobs and alienating work. Enough resisted to create a problem so there was a need to devise forms of control of work performance through human relations management.

F. W. Taylor's ideal worker was rational and essentially economistic in his motivation. Taylor's study was of the male manual worker in the steel and metal manufacturing processes, yet industrial sociology reviews have not thought it worthwhile to mention this male-centred focus of Taylor's work. This is yet another clear example of treating workers as unisex even though it is men who are being described (Dex, 1985).

The established textbook theories on motivation have little to say about women; they appear to assume that men and women are a homogeneous group in this regard. Little research has considered the importance of sex differences in motivation (Harriman, 1985). It is possible to find a literature, not quoted or used in organizational behaviour textbooks to date, which looks at women's work motivation. It is possible to look for differences between the sexes in terms of motivation, but an alternative may be to ask what social practices determine women's motivation at work?

'Why work?' is a question which is asked of women but rarely of men. The classic, much-quoted study by Morse and Weiss (1955) on working men which did ask this question concluded that for most men having a job serves other functions than that of earning a living. Even if they had enough money to support

themselves, they would still want to work. 'Work gives then a feeling of being tied into the larger society, of having something to do, of having a purpose in life. These other functions which working serves are evidently not seen as available in non-work activities' (p. 191.) We are left to assume that the same results may be found among women. Would the same results have been obtained from a group of women? Although more men would continue working irrespective of financial needs than women (Hakim, 1991), how far this reflects on women's actual experience of poorer working conditions and less rewarding jobs, and how far upon different life priorities in the first place is still open to debate (Kremer and Montgomery, 1993: 197).

When women are included in the studies, gender as a category of analysis is rarely included. This was the error in the studies at the Hawthorne plant, begun in the mid-1920s, in which the females in the relay assembly test room had been pressured into the experimental situation while the men in the bank wiring room were observed in normal conditions (see also Dex, 1985). When results from the two groups differed, gender was not a category of analysis. Subsequent analysis of the informal work group (such as those by Donald Roy and Michael Burawoy) focused on shop-floor behaviour and ignored the gender of the workers being studied.

Robert Blauner (1964) in *Alienation and Freedom*, while not ignoring women altogether, dismisses the women who make up almost half the workers in the textile industry he studied as a 'major safety valve against the consequences of alienation work conditions'. Women were to be found in the least skilled, most repetitive, and least free jobs, leaving men with the jobs with opposite attributes. Yet Blauner, without giving evidence, asserted that the women were not dissatisfied with the work and that it did not have the central importance and meaning in their lives that it had for men since women's most important roles were of wife and mother (Oakley, 1974: 20).

Women's tolerance of boring and repetitive work is part of industrial folklore. If this were the case female labour turnover would be as high in intrinsically satisfying jobs as those without. Wild and Hill's (1970) study of job satisfaction and labour turnover in the electronics industry shows that turnover rates have a high relationship with job satisfaction. Many women, like men, express a need for personally satisfying work, and the failure to find it is often a reason for changing jobs.

Women are, however, often recruited into roles in organizations which require passivity and compliance. There are unique mechanisms employed in organizations to control women (Acker and Van Houton, 1974). So we would expect that motivation of men and women may differ.

Let us look briefly at the theories usually presented, finding what they have to say about women, and then look at research focusing on women and motivation, then women and job satisfaction.

ABRAHAM MASLOW

Maslow's theory of motivation is derived from clinical experience (Maslow, 1970). Subjects are treated as individuals where gender is inconsequential. According to Maslow, we have five basic, innate needs which account for much or most human behaviour. These needs vary in their relative prepotency, or urgency for the survival of the individual, and are arranged hierarchically, in a pyramid. At the bottom are physiological needs, then come safety needs; these are followed by needs for love and esteem, and finally the need for self-actualization. As the most prepotent needs become reasonably well gratified, the less prepotent one (the higher-order needs) become increasingly more important.

Maslow notes that in most people the physiological needs are partly satisfied and partly unsatisfied. A realistic description of the hierarchy would be in terms of decreasing percentages of satisfaction as we go up the hierarchy. He estimated that the average working adult has satisfied about 85 per cent of their physiological needs, 70 per cent of safety, 50 per cent of social, 40 per cent, of esteem and 10 per cent of self-actualization needs. The hierarchy ought not, then, to be seen as a series of rigid steps where as one set of needs is satisfied it is shut off and another set of needs clicks into place.

The first two sets of needs, physiological and safety, are essential to human existence. The physiological needs include need for food, water, oxygen, warmth, and freedom from pain. If these needs are unsatisfied an individual's actions will be dominated by attempts to fulfil them. Ultimately if physiological and safety needs are not satisfied, we die. When they are more or less gratified, love and esteem start to have a comparatively greater influence on behaviour.

Love and esteem needs concern our requirement for friendship and affiliation. If these needs are satisfied we feel self-confident, competent, and adequate, and have a creditable place in our world. We need to have good interpersonal relationships. If these needs are not satisfied, they lead to feelings of inferiority and helplessness, and may lead to mental illness.

If all other needs are satisfied, then a new discontent and restlessness will develop unless the individual is doing 'what he is fitted for'. (Note that in common with most writers of his time, Maslow uses the male term). Self-actualization is the ultimate human goal. Self-actualization is about self-fulfilment. Personal development may be expressed in many ways—maternally, athletically, artistically or occupationally; or as Maslow put it: 'A musician must make music, an artist must paint, a poet must write, if he is to be ultimately at peace with himself. What a man can be, he must be. This need we may call self actualisation' (Maslow, 1943: 382).

Some individuals may never experience the desire to develop their potential. An individual who attains self-actualization will occasionally have peak experiences. A peak experience can best be described as a sense of euphoria that is not chemically induced. It can be felt as a sense of completeness or of oneness with the universe. Fully satisfied and self-actualizing people are, however, in the minority, according to Maslow. In studying self-actualizing individuals, Maslow selected personal acquaintances and friends, as well as public and historical figures.

The gender of the comptemporaries he chose are not mentioned but the historical figures included Lincoln, Jefferson, Einstein, Eleanor Roosevelt, and Jane Addams. In all there were 43 subjects. (Maslow used surnames only for men and full names for women).

It can be argued that self-actualization reflects stereotypical male traits and defines concepts such as risk-taking in ways that reflect male experiences (Cullen, 1992; Kasten, 1972). Self-actualization is the expression of male self that denies relatedness rather than the female self-in-relation (Chodorow, 1989), a self that thinks in terms of hierarchy rather than webs (Gilligan, 1982).

Maslow's theory has been widely adopted by organizations and is frequently used as the foundation for organizational development programmes such as participative management, job enrichment, and quality of work life. While it is widely accepted, there is little research evidence to support it (Wahba and Bridwell, 1976). And it takes little account of gender or gender differences, if they exist.

What do we know of Maslow's theory as applied to women? We might believe that women have been taught to seek gratification of their needs through someone else, usually husbands or fathers. Homemakers may never learn to gratify their own lower-level needs and will not, then, move on to satisfy higher-level needs. Betz (1982, 1984) tested this idea and found that homemakers were distinguished from working women by their higher scores on the lower-level security/safety and social needs. The need hierarchies of working women supported the ordering postulated by Maslow but homemakers diverged considerably (with high-level needs at both the top and bottom of their hierarchy and low-level needs falling in between). Homemakers reported greatest deficits in esteem needs, while employed women reported greatest deficits in meeting needs for autonomy.

In studies controlling for occupational level an overall pattern of gender similarity is found. There is some evidence that women's values are becoming more like men's over time. Both sexes value the opportunity for feelings of accomplishment, job security, income potential, and respect from others at work (Betz and Fitzgerald, 1987)

What about Maslow's theory as applied to women managers? Donnell and Hall (1980) found that women managers reported lower basic needs and higher needs for self-actualization. Compared with males, female managers are more concerned with opportunities for growth, autonomy, and challenge. Contrary to popular belief, females do not have a greater need to belong than do males. Thus there are sex-based differences in managerial work motivation and these differences favour the female managers. Donnell and Hall, concluded, however, that women, in general, do not differ from men, in general, in the way they administer the management process; both sexes emphasize the same goals and promote the same values. Women who have become managers may have been motivated by a higher need for achievement and self-actualization than male managers (Powell, 1988: 157).

FREDERICK HERZBERG

Herzberg's two-factor theory of work motivation is one of the most widely known and influential views on work motivation. As a part of a study on job satisfaction, Herzberg and his colleague originally interviewed 203 engineers and accountants from a variety of organizations in the Pittsburgh area of the United States (Herzberg et al., (1959). He was keen to show how universal his theory was and how it applied equally easily to both men's and women's jobs. Later studies were based on employees drawn from samples of 1685 in 12 different investigations and included lower-level supervisors, professional women, agricultural administrators, men about to retire from management positions, hospital maintenance personnel, manufacturing supervisors, nurses, food handlers, military officers, engineers, scientists, housekeepers, teachers, technicians, female assemblers, accountants, Finnish foremen, and Hungarian engineers (Herzberg, 1968).

Herzberg skirted the concern with motives and motivation and looked at what people value in their work. Using a semi-structured interview technique, he accumulated data on the factors that employees said had an effect on their feelings about their jobs. He asked two key questions 'Can you describe, in detail, when you felt extremely good about your job?' and 'Can you describe, in detail, when you felt exceptionally bad about your job?' Interviewees were able to recall such critical incidents for either their current or previous jobs. Two or three incidents, on average, were gathered from each interviewee.

Two distinct groups of factors emerged from the data. The intrinsic factors related to the immediate interaction between the worker and the job, and the extrinsic related to pay, benefits, working conditions, and other aspects of the job situation. Herzberg's research identifies motivators as factors producing good feelings in the work situation, and hygiene factors as arousing bad feelings.

Hygiene factors are concerned with the work environment rather than the work itself. Company policy and administration is a hygiene factor and was at least partly blamed for 31 per cent of the reported cases of dissatisfaction. Unhappy relationships with the supervisor appeared in 20 per cent of the stories, while poor interpersonal with peers was the critical factor in 15 per cent of cases. Hygiene factors also included supervision in general, work conditions, salary, personal life, relationships with subordinates, status, and security. Hygiene factors can prevent dissatisfaction but do not produce satisfaction; they could create dissatisfaction if not attended to.

It is the motivators that cause satisfaction and have the potential to motivate employees to higher levels of performance because they provide opportunities for satisfaction. Motivators include achievement (found in 41 per cent of instances of job attitudes), recognition (33 per cent), the work itself, responsibility, and growth and advancement. The absence of these factors would not make employees feel unhappy but would leave them feeling somewhat neutral toward their jobs. Managers should be able to build motivators into the job to positively promote job satisfaction. To minimize dissatisfaction, hygiene factors should be improved.

There are two main ways to enrich jobs in an attempt to make tasks more interesting and rewarding: (i) vertical loading—injecting more important and challenging duties into the job; and (ii) horizontal loading—job enlargement or job rotation where you increase the number or diversity of task activities.

Job enrichment experiments in the 1960s and 1970s showed some impressive results in the United States. AT & T were able to bring about a 27 per cent reduction in the termination rate and a production cost saving of $558,000 over a 12-month period. Texas Instruments, with an assembly-line work group of women, were able to reduce the assembly time. ICI increased production of sales staff by 19 per cent over the previous year, while sales staff in two control groups were producing 5 per cent less than in the previous year (Jackson, 1970). Some British companies experimented with job enrichment—ICI and United Biscuits experimented widely and Philips used the approach in various sites in Britain, including Hamilton in Scotland (Buchanan, 1987).

Critics of the two-factor theory argue that respondents in the interviews were acting in a way which protected their egos. People tend to give socially desirable answers to the questions asked, answers they think the researcher wants to hear or that sound 'reasonable'. Wall *et al.* (1971), were able to show that job applicants in a formal selection interview on the whole attributed their highly satisfying past experiences to motivators and highly dissatisfying experiences to hygiene factors. Yet when interviewed in an informal situation by an independent researcher, when the need to give socially acceptable answers was minimized, failed to give answers to the same questions to support Herzberg's hypothesis. Individuals would also be likely to report the good things that happened to them at work as being due to their own efforts while the bad things are due to external or environmental forces. It is easier to blame co-workers and company policy when things go wrong than to blame yourself.

Another criticism is that motivators and hygiene factors are a little too neatly packaged. The importance of intrinsic factors is stressed, but are employees not affected by extrinsic factors? An individual's expectations will be affected by both past social experience and learning, as well as present social cues and interactions.

Is pay only a hygiene factor or could it also be a motivator as it contributes towards personal pride and self-esteem? Herzberg classified salary as a hygiene factor because it related to more stories of long-term negative attitude shifts than to positive ones, but it did appear in more stories of job satisfaction than of dissatisfaction. Herzberg and his colleagues acknowledged that three of the motivators can also decrease job satisfaction and that satisfaction and dissatisfaction are not opposite sides of the same coin. Dunnette *et al.*, (1967) have criticized Herzberg's approach for gross oversimplification as the same factors can contribute to both satisfaction and dissatisfaction. Malinowsky and Barry (1965), Ewen (1967), Friedlander (1966), House and Wigdor (1967) and Payne (1970) have all come to a similar conclusion.

Do all workers respond positively to job enrichment? Do varied, complex, demanding jobs always equal job satisfaction? Job enlargement may be good for those who are not already alienated by their jobs. Some workers may not welcome an opportunity to become more involved in their work and to participate in decision making. If you were a women working as a packer on an assembly line and felt exhausted by the boredom of the job and the demands of home and family would you welcome job enrichment? Approximately 40 studies have been done to support or refute Herzberg's claims. They show methodological weaknesses and inconsistency with previous findings in research on satisfaction and productivity. Little research has been done using gender as a unit of analysis. Again, as with Maslow's work, there is little concern shown for gender differences. There is just one dimension being used for analysis, namely intrinsic versus extrinsic factors associated with the job itself.

What has been found when men and women are compared using Herzberg's ideas? Donnell and Hall (1980) found that compared with males, female managers were more concerned with opportunities for growth, autonomy, and challenge, and less concerned with the work environment and pay. These results support the notion that women managers possess traits superior to those of men, as women have had to overcome stereotypical attitudes about their unsuitability for management.

Men have been found to underestimate the importance of intrinsic motivation for women. Male and female university students were asked to rate the importance of 10 job characteristics for both themselves and the opposite sex (Siegfield *et al.*, 1981). The 10 characteristics reflected Herzberg's classification of five hygiene factors (extrinsic factors) and five motivators (intrinsic factors). Both sexes rated the motivators as important. However, the men tended to underestimate the motivators for women. If these attitudes are perpetuated by men as managers, then we can expect men to reinforce this belief in decisions about women's job performance.

DAVID McCLELLAND AND ACHIEVEMENT THEORY

David McClelland's initial theory of achievement concerned men as men were compatible with his theoretical predictions. When female subjects did not respond to the instructions designed to arouse their achievement motivation, it was suggested that they were less motivated than men (Veroff *et al.*, 1953). A different theory, McClelland suggested, would have to be developed for females (McClelland, 1966). The researchers did not seem to think it important that under relaxed conditions females actually scored higher than males in the achievment motivation test (Betz and Fitzgerald, 1987). For the next decade or so only males were used in achievement motivation research. Males tended to be treated as the norm and women regarded as members of a non-standard population of lesser interest (Spence *et al.*, 1985).

In his studies McClelland first tried to find people with a high need to achieve. He did this by presenting people with pictures that could arouse some different kinds of reaction. For example, the individuals would be presented with a picture of an executive sitting in his chair and they would be asked to say what was going on in the picture—what is the man thinking and what has led up to the situation? This is known as the Thematic Apperception Test (TAT) and supposedly revealed covert, unconscious complexes.

The following story could be written by a manager who had viewed the picture just described, and whom McClelland would describe as a high achiever. The person is a senior manager who intends to introduce a new and innovative product into his company's product range. He knows that other companies have been considering introducing a similar product but he knows of a new innovation that he can introduce that will allow his company to be the first to manufacture. The change can be made speedily and cheaply. This will make his company a market leader and will probably mean he will be awarded the promotion he feels he deserves. He is taking time now to think of how this will make him feel. The managing director, he thinks, will be pleased with the new innovation.

McClelland interpreted recurring themes of hard work and success in people's stories as signs of a high need to achieve. He then studied the high-achievement individuals in a variety of natural and laboratory settings.

McClelland and his colleagues were able to identify some factors that indicated a predisposition to strive for success. In general, high performance levels and executive success appear to be correlated with a high need for achievement. Entrepreneurs, as contrasted with teachers or lawyers, tend to be higher than average in achievement motivation and lower than average in affiliation motivation.

The interesting point is that it is chiefly men who are perceived as having achievement motive arousal. The TAT motive measure was not, then, valid for females, so females, tended to be neglected in early achievement research. The fact that females gave ample achievement imagery under relaxed conditions is particularly noteworthy in a society which attempts to inhibit the achievement-related tendencies of women (Fitzgerald and O'Crites, 1980). Furthermore, there are now data suggesting that the achievement motives of women are often experimentally suppressed in groups, especially mixed-sex groups, but are enhanced when women perform alone or are convinced that their achievements will not be noticed by or offend men (Stake, 1976).

Some studies did include females and combined the data from both sexes, but an equally large number of research investigations either did not test females or reported systematic data for the male but not the female subject (Weiner, 1992). Maybe we need to ask if achievement motivation is an adequate construct to explain women's career behaviour (Fitzgerald and O'Crites, 1980).

Astin (1985) did not believe that women's motivations are fundamentally different to those of men. Motivation is influenced by childhood socialization and structure of opportunities. Farmer (1985) presented a similar view of factors involved in achievement motivation. An in-depth interview technique to determine the level of need for achievement among black and white successful women (Boardman et al., 1987) found that 94 per cent of women were rated as having a strong need for achievement.

Leonard Chusmir showed that women managers had a higher need for achievement, a higher need for power, and a not significantly different need for affiliation than male managers. When the need for socialized power was separated from the need for personalized power, female managers had a greater need than male managers for socialized power and the same need for personalized power (Chusmir, 1985; Chusmir and Parker, 1984). Chusmir concluded by saying that the ideal male manager has been described as one who is high in the need for power, low in the need for affiliation, and moderately high in the need for achievement.

> Results from this study indicate that this motive profile better fits the executive women participants than their male counterparts. This implies that the women who enter management are likely to have greater management potential and may be more success-prone than the men managers.   (Chusmir, 1985: 158).

Another study reporting women to be high in power motivation, found women were 'less overtly assertive and competitive than men'. It was suggested that the stereotypic sex-role expectations for women cause the variation (House and Singh, 1987).

The achievement motive has been defined as a disposition or behavioural tendency to strive for excellence or success. From McClelland's work we know that managers manifest higher achievement needs and rate accomplishment as more important in their jobs than in most occupational groups (e.g. McClelland, 1961). Studies have found some sex differences in achievement needs. However, rather than women showing differences in absolute level of need to achieve, the context in which achievement needs are measured appears crucial. In one study, McClelland (1951) himself, as we have seen, found that women's need for achievement was higher that that of men in non-competitive situations, whereas under competitive conditions men's achievement needs were higher than those of women. Harlan and Weiss (1982) found that women who are attracted to management have high achievement needs and are especially likely to enjoy an environment where they are given substantial autonomy and independence.

Group dynamics may well contribute to the motivation to achieve. Being in a numerical minority inhibits members performance in a group situation, so women managers in a male-dominated managerial group may well be under-achieving. Finigan (1982) found that underachievement was particularly pro-nounced for females in male-dominant groups. This may be caused by the 'feminine modesty' effect.

To test your own need for achievement you could ask yourself the following questions:

1. Do you like situations where you must be responsible for finding solutions to problems?
2. Do you tend to set moderate goals and take moderate, thought-out risks?
3. Do you want specific feedback about how well you are doing? Do you spend time considering how to advance your career, how to do your job better, or how to accomplish important tasks?

If you responded yes to these questions then you probably have a high need for achievement. (McClelland also talks of need for affiliation and need for power. You may like to test your need for affiliation and power too.)

Self-motivated achievers prefer to set their own goals. They are seldom content to drift without purpose letting life happen to them. They are nearly always trying to achieve objectives. They are quite selective about the goals to which they commit themselves. They avoid choosing extremely difficult goals and prefer moderate goals that are neither so easy that attaining them provides no satisfaction, nor so difficult that attaining them is more a matter of luck than ability. They gauge what is possible and then select as difficult a goal as they think they can attain—the hardest practical challenge. They also need specific feedback on their performance, preferably immediate feedback because of the goal's importance to them.

The need for achievement partly determines how employees respond to challenge as persistence and acceptance of challenge are closely related to this need. High achievers are driven by the prospect of performance-based satisfaction rather than by monetary gain. For these people money is primarily a source of feedback on personal performance rather than an end in itself. High-need achievers perform well with or without financial incentives (Atkinson and Reitman, 1956).

According to McClelland, all motives are learned from experiences in which certain cues in the environment are paired with positive or negative consequences. The need for achievement is learned when opportunities for competing with standards of excellence become associated with positive outcomes. The origin of achievement motivation appears to lie in learning and socialization during early life. Parents who encourage early self-reliance in their children produce children who are more achievement-orientated later in life. This early independence training has to be teamed with supportiveness, which is crucial as the child must not feel that they have been abandoned.

McClelland proposed that a culture's growth is due to the level of need for achievement inherent in its population. His research indicates that increases in the level of need for achievement precede increases in economic activity. McClelland also believed that achievement motivation can be enhanced in adults who otherwise lack a high level.

Women's aspirations

A survey of 1011 women aged between 16 and 70 showed that getting on in a job was more important than having children for 76 per cent of women under the age of 35.

Among women of child-bearing age, few believed they needed a child or a stable relationship to feel fulfilled. But although 76 per cent of mothers of working age said they wanted to get on in their jobs or get a job, 40 per cent were doubtful of achieving their career goals . . . Less than half were satisfied with their career prospects. Nearly three-quarters of the women wanted more education.

Source: *The Guardian*, 25 November 1992: 7. Report on survey by Research International for the National Council of Women of Great Britain. ©*The Guardian*, 1992.

IS WOMEN'S MOTIVATION DIFFERENT TO THAT OF MEN?

When we look at women's educational and occupational achievements, women's intellectual capacities and talents are not reflected, so we might assume their motivation to be different. Women's career aspirations and choices are frequently far lower in level than are the aspirations of males with comparable levels of ability (Fitzgerald and O'Crites, 1980; Betz and Fitzgerald, 1987). Women are socialized to pursue the same roles due to their sex, regardless of individual capabilities and talents. Added to this is the fact that the adult role for the female is primarily family directed, whereas for the male it is primarily occupationally directed. The question for women, then, is how to manage home and career.

What about women whose aspirations are high? What of their managerial motivation? One of the determinants of motivation is the extent to which individuals believe in external versus internal control of events influencing them. Persons who are high on internal control, have an internal locus of control, feel they are able to influence their own destiny and are more likely to attribute success to their own skills, efforts, or abilities. Waddel (1983) showed that women who achieved higher-status positions tended to have an internal locus of control. Individuals in high-status, high-earning positions have a more internal locus of control than those in low-status, low-earning positions (Andrisani and Nestel, 1976; White *et al.*, 1992). In contrast, those who are high on external control feel that they have little influence over what happens to them with the result that they are more likely to attribute success to external factors such as luck or being in the right place at the right time.

Maccoby and Jacklin (1974), in a review of the literature of control, found a strong tendency for women to be externalizers, feeling that events affecting them were the result of chance rather than their own actions. Men were more likely to be internalizers. Later studies have shown that men are more likely to attribute success to their own actions but attribute failure to external events. Women are just the opposite: more likely to attribute failure to their own actions and success to external events (Kukla, 1972; McMahan, 1971). The perceived cause of success leads to different responses to that success. Rewards vary depending on whether they are due to internal or external causes as will decisions such as promotion or placement. This proposition is called into question by Harlan and Weiss (1982) who found that the majority of both men and women felt their success was due to their hard work and good performance of responsibilities. (See also Nelson and Quick, 1985, who look at gender, locus of control, and stress.)

Motivation can be a significant determinant of performance and the expectations that significant others have of you will affect the career opportunities you are offered. A study of nearly 800 female and 1500 male managers and professionals in Britain concerned with career development issues sought to find out what they thought to be important in a job (Alban-Metcalfe and Nicholson, 1984). The 17 items of the attitudes to work scale were derived from existing literature on motivation and so based substantially on male populations.

The top five motivators for women were identical to the top five for men though not identical in relative ranking order. The females obtained higher mean scores than did the males (controlling for age) in the following (Alban-Metcalfe, 1989):

■ Challenge
■ An opportunity to improve knowledge and skills
■ Being appreciated
■ Good-quality senior management
■ Autonomy.

The motivations of successful women were found by White *et al.*, (1992) to be very similar to those of male high-flyers (Cox and Cooper, 1988). Successful women were primarily motivated by the intrinsic desire to excel in their work. The demand for challenging and interesting work is stronger than the desire for promotion. They have a tendency to prefer challenging tasks, which could be interpreted as high 'mastery' (*sic*) motivation. Successful women have high aspirations and have made their career central to their lives, all which would indicate a high need for achievement.

The belief that senior managers, who are predominantly male, appear to hold in regard to what women want in a job would seem directly to contradict these findings. Doubtless the misperceptions affect male manager's decisions on opportunities for female career development and promotion and, in turn, women's motivation. The way women are treated in organizations affects their motivation. Women can be rendered virtually speechless in mixed-sex conversations (Zimmerman and West, 1975) by excessive interruption by men and in the woman's role as facilitators in mixed-sex conversations (Alban-Metcalfe, 1990: 16). If this is the case, how can women be evaluated fairly and motivated equally?

Much is also going to depend on how you define motivation and who is in the sample. When motivation to manage was defined as orientation towards authority, competiveness, assertiveness, comfort in exercising power, obtaining visibility, and taking care of detail, female MBA students obtained mean scores lower than their male counterparts in their motivation to manage. The data were collected in four periods between 1960 and 1980 (Miner and Smith, 1982). Among 232 MBA students the mean score for motivation to manage was 7.04 for males and 3.24 for females (Bartol and Martin, 1986). For samples of store managers and school administrators, however, Miner (1974) could find no difference between the men's and women's motivation to manage.

Miner (1965) found that the motivation of women changed with training and experience in a similar way to that of men. Comparable results were reported by Morrison and Sebald (1974). Female executives were similar to male executives in terms of self-esteem, motivation, and mental ability. Terborg (1977) concluded that, on the whole, women who become managers have similar motives to male managers.

According to Koff and Handlon (1975), women who are more likely to advance are motivated to do so. Their motivation is evidenced by their desire to achieve, their previous success, and their personal commitment to developing their careers. Those who are career oriented are divided, by the authors, into one of three categories: pioneering, sensitive to the climate, or needing support. The pioneers are innovative, initiators, risk-taking high achievers. They enjoy challenge and are not easily discouraged; they have a positive sense of self-worth and expect to be successful. They also expect to operate independently and autonomously and be rewarded for their achievements. The climate sensitives are more responsive to the psychological climate around them and to approval and recognition from top management. The support seekers need positive reinforcement and help; their upward path needs to be cleared of obstacles and resistance. These women are easily discouraged, readily lose confidence, and do not like to take risks. Support is necessary, however, for most women with successful careers in management.

What influence do families have? Despite the strength of the relationship between a satisfying family life, job satisfaction, and organizational success (Renshaw, 1976), and the obvious interplay between work and family spheres, little has been done to include the family as a variable affecting the world of men's work (Kanter, 1977; Portner, 1978). Pleck (1977) has noted that, for women, the demands of family life are permitted to intrude into the work role more than the work role is allowed to interfere with family roles. For men, the opposite is true. Is family life a determinant of motivation or job satisfaction? As we saw earlier, marriage and a family can be seen as assets for men and their careers but a liability for women (Bronstein *et al.*, 1987; Bryson *et al.*, 1978).

We need, it seems, to understand more about the meaning that women assign to motivation, the experience of motivation as articulated by women. Women managers are more susceptible to role stress and work overload due to the multiple role demands inherent in running a career, a home, and a family. According to Davidson and Cooper (1986), time demands impose a tighter schedule on the personal lives of executive women than of men, the women being less able to relax at the end of the day. Women with children tend to experience significantly greater amounts of 'internal strain', due to conflicting role demands on their time and energy (Lewis and Cooper, 1989).

Support for domestic commitments from a home-based partner is less likely for a married woman than for a married man. Male managers have, then, the advantage. The Alban-Metcalfe and West (1991) survey found that 90 per cent of women managers in their sample had partners in full-time employment compared with around 25 per cent of the men. Men thus perceive home as a refuge, a place to relax, whereas women see home life as a source of strain and stress, providing additional demands and loss of private time.

There are some other interesting features of family and home that are brought to work by women. Women's employment is inextricably linked to their position in the family. For example, Westwood (1985) in looking at women's informal socializing in a garment factory, describes the rituals surrounding weddings and engagements that take place at work or among work friends after hours. Westwood argues that women's culture offers a context of resistance to management through celebrations that confirm a traditional vision of femininity. Lamphere (1985) also discusses the birthday celebrations, pre-baby and wedding parties, and retirement parties, which 'bring the family to work', humanizing the workplace. She also notes how the common identity as women, wives, mothers enables communication. Through the social events and communication '... women workers make friends of strangers and bridge cultural and age divisions within the work force' (1985: 521) Women's family and gender roles provide some of the 'glue' that holds participants in a work culture together. Management may even orchestrate such events in order to build a loyal workforce.

What factors motivate mothers at work, especially those with young children? Research in the early 1960s indicated that for women important motivations for finding work outside the home are a need for achievement, competence, independence, and social contact (Hoffman, 1963). These findings are supported by Sobol (1963) who found that women's needs for accomplishment, in terms of career or doing something important, and the need to occupy time and meet people, were strong predictors of future work plans, stronger even than of financial need. Intrinsic rewards of a job are frequently far more important to women than extrinsic ones (Thompson, 1980). 'A need to achieve', 'a sense of competence', 'personal satisfaction' and 'interaction with other adults' emerge as important reasons for working (Harper and Richards, 1986; Hock et al., 1985; Hoffman and Nye, 1974; Ross, 1984; Wearing, 1984).

Hoffman (1963) has suggested that it is personality differences that are important in influencing who goes out to work and at what stage of the family cycle they work. Interestingly, it is the restriction of freedom felt by many mothers of pre-school children that may be, in itself, an important motive for employment. Pragmatic motivations such as 'to get out of the house' and 'to get away from the children' have also found to be important for many women (Harper and Richards, 1986).

The cost of working outside the home can, however, be considerable for mothers with young children. In a sample of non-employed women, 48 per cent said that either they, or their families, believed that they should be at home with the family (Ross, 1984). Traditional norms regarding the upbringing of children are incompatible with most forms of employment and the potential for role strain is considerable (Thompson, 1980). These pressures mean that a woman will take a job which is 'convenient' rather than one which is intrinsically interesting or for which she was trained.

A study in Northern Ireland showed that both men and women were likely to record the need for money as the single most important reason for working. Replies from part-time and full-time workers were similar (Kremer and Curry, 1986). Women's motivation to work does not come from partners or husbands. Only 8 per cent of women said they worked because their husband/partner liked them to work (Kremer and Montgomery, 1993: 198). The intrinsic reasons and motivators are extremely important for women and have become significantly more so over the last decade. Further, women's commitment to work appears to be far from short term or transient. These results 'challenge the view that women themselves conform to the traditional stereotype of marginal workers' (Kremer and Montgomery, 1993: 202).

The picture painted by Kremer and Montgomery is not one of a homogeneous group of women but a conglomeration of individual values and priorities.

Financial necessity is a reason for working which most find acceptable and few sanctions operate against the mother who has to work to support herself and her family. We should not be surprised, then, if the majority of women, when asked why they work, include 'for the money' as one of their reasons. Ross (1984) found that, of the non-working women in her sample who stated they might seek work, the main reasons, given by 53 per cent, were financial ones. Many more said they would work if their husbands were unemployed. Mothers with low labour force attachment, those with the lowest proportion of time worked since the birth of their first child, non-employed mothers with young children who would only work if in 'extreme financial need' see financial need as the strongest motive that would influence their returning to work (Ross, 1984; Cotton *et al.*, 1989). Money also contributes towards needs for self-esteem, self-worth, self-satisfaction, independence, and security.

It is interesting to note that the affluent worker studies (Goldthorpe *et al.*, 1968) pointed to an influence of women in male worker's orientations but this point was almost entirely lost (Dex, 1985: 33). For example, in comparing the economic position of 229 male manual workers with 54 white-collar workers, white-collar workers were found to have an advantage in family income but not in husband's income. This discrepancy resulted from the fact that more wives of white-collar men worked and this group had fewer dependent children. Men's orientations to work cannot be understood without reference to women and the same is true of women's orientations.

Why, then, are the studies on women's motivation to work not quoted by the mainstream texts on motivation? One reason may be that there are some difficulties in comparing studies that have investigated women's motivation to work outside the home. The samples in these studies vary considerably in terms of family structure, particularly the age of the youngest child. It is reasonable to predict that the needs and motives of mothers change over the family lifecycle so that what is salient at one time may not be at another. But the motives of men too will change over time and with circumstances.

A second difficulty is in the variety of techniques used. Some studies have used open-ended questions, others ask respondents to rank or rate a number of reasons in order of importance. But the same difficulty is to be found when comparing studies of men's motivation. Is there, then, a valid reason for ignoring the role of women's motivation?

JOB SATISFACTION

Kornhauser (1965) claimed that the main determinant of mental health of American male industrial workers was the amount of opportunity they had to use their skills and abilities. Since then skill utilization has been found to be the strongest predictor of job satisfaction (O'Brien, 1982). Similar studies on perceived job attributes and job satisfaction have generally concluded that the use of abilities and opportunities for learning at work are significant predictors of job satisfaction (Argyle, 1974; Locke, 1976; Warr and Wall, 1975).Women hold jobs that are, on average, inferior to those held by men (Berch, 1982; Featherman and Hauser, 1976) and you would therefore expect them to experience less job satisfaction.

Changes in job characteristics do affect employee reactions to their work. Employees on jobs that increased in motivating potential gained in internal work motivation and growth satisfaction; the reverse is true for employees whose jobs deteriorated in motivating potential (Hackman et al., 1978). But if we look at the job characteristics of women's jobs we find that they usually have less autonomy, closer supervision, and more limited promotional opportunities than men (Wolf and Fligstein, 1979).

Studies introducing gender as a salient variable have found an inverse relationship between age and work satisfaction. Young women have tended to report a greater degree of satisfaction with work than their older counterparts (Arnold and Feldman, 1982). Job satisfaction may be affected by how much discrimination is perceived. Age has been found to be significantly related to the respondent's perception of equality, with younger women reporting less discrimi-nation in pay and promotion than their older counterparts (Kissman, 1992). As education and training increase, so do the differences in pay between males and females with roughly equal credentials (Sanders and Wong, 1985).

It seems reasonable to assume that women's attitudes towards their jobs will be less favourable than those of men, and both equity and relative deprivation theories suggest that individuals should feel anger, resentment, and/or dissatisfac-tion when they perceive that their rewards are less than those received by a comparative person, e.g. others doing similar work. You would also expect that the constraints of family roles may well influence the job satisfaction of employed married women, especially mothers with dependent children, by impeding their ability to function and progress in their jobs.

Despite the fact that women are concentrated in lower-paying, lower-prestige jobs than men, and women are paid less than similarly qualified men doing comparable work, most studies of job and pay satisfaction have found little evidence that women are more dissatisfied than men with their pay or their jobs (e.g Crosby, 1982). One reason may be that women value social relations and comfortable working conditions more than men, who place pay and promotion higher on a list of features they value from their jobs (see Nieva and Gutek, 1981). But others (e.g. Golding et al., 1983) found no difference in job values of men and women in the same occupation. Research also shows similarity between the job satisfaction scores of part-time and full-time women workers (Beechey and Perkins, 1987; Kremer and Montgomery, 1993).

There is also evidence that women report higher job satisfaction than men (e.g. Veroff *et al.*, 1981). One reason for women reporting greater levels of job satisfaction may be, as we have seen above, that they are interested in different aspects of work than men (Kanter, 1977). They may, as a consequence of a history of occupational and wage discrimination, have lower pay expectations than men. (For example a study of students on management courses found that women students expected lower pay than men students, not only at the entry level but at the peak of their careers as well; Major and Konar, 1984.)

Or women may use different reference groups than men in evaluating their jobs (Kessler and McRae, 1982). If women who stay at home and do housework have poorer mental health than those who are employed, and women at home are the reference point, then paid employment will look relatively positive. Or they may compare themselves to other working women rather than men and may not feel relatively deprived. Crosby (1982) reported that most workers compare themselves to someone of the same sex in appraising their jobs. Women are found to report greater levels of job satisfaction if they are employed in female-type occupations where comparisons with male workers are not readily available (Hodson, 1989). Women who had mothers who did not work outside the home, and are employed in female-type occupations, will be slightly more satisfied (Hodson, 1989). This is probably because the reference point is women who work at home and may make paid work outside the home seem relatively desirable, regardless of its limitations.

An alternative explanation might focus on differences in gender socialization to express discontent. If women are socialized to be more passive than men, they will be less likely to express their discontent at work. Glenn and Feldberg (1977: 60) noted that employers rely on deskilled female clerical workers to 'act like ladies and continue to be loyal, dependable, and polite'.

Perhaps working women have made adjustments in their responses to work because of family responsibilities (Hodson, 1989). Women may derive satisfaction from their role as homemakers and therefore place less emphasis on job satisfaction (Veroff *et al.*, 1981). One study looked at how family support for employment and conflict between family and work roles influences wife/ mother job satisfaction (Andrisani, 1978). Andrisani hypothesized that personal characteristics that reflect productivity potential and family circumstances would also influence the job satisfaction of women. It was found that black women were less satisfied with their jobs than white women. Conflicting demands between responsibilities at home and at work appeared to result, for both black and white women, in lower than average levels of job satisfaction, the source of greatest conflict being a husband who had an unfavourable attitude to the wife working.

At least two studies have found a relationship between job satisfaction of married women and other life satisfactions. McKenry *et al.*, (1985) found that the best predictors of the satisfaction of rural employed mothers were job duties, progress, and performance. Sekaran (1983) found that job satisfaction was related to life satisfaction in the same way for both men and women. Job satisfaction was directly related to lack of stress from multiple roles, and recognition and support for being both a career and family person. The most useful variable in explaining variation in job satisfaction was workload—the extent to which the respondents perceived their total workload to interfere with how well they carried out both household and employment responsibilities (Rudd and McKenry, 1986).

Quinn *et al.*, (1974) and Hodson (1989) found that working women with children under six are less satisfied than those without young children. Other research findings indicate that children feel more positive about maternal employment when it presents a minimum conflict for their mothers (Baruch, 1972), or when the work is personally satisfying (Trimberger and MacLean, 1982). But women appear to have a low expectation for help from husbands and children and rarely receive more than minimal assistance (Rudd and McKenry, 1986; Smith and Reid, 1982).

The maternal role is likely to conflict with work outside the home and the welfare of children is likely to be the source of guilt and anxiety for employed mothers. The dual roles of homemaker and wage earner tend to overlap and create a stressful situation when performance in one of these roles is thwarted by the demands of the other (Astin, 1985). Family pressures can prevent some women from pursuing employment with as much commitment as they would like and thus can lead to lower job satisfaction. Lower job satisfaction is associated with other aspects of life. But jobs that have a positive impact on women, providing responsibility, security, and autonomy, may also impact positively, in turn, on families. Job satisfaction could be enhanced by increasing family support for women's employment.

Full-time mothers are at greatest risk of developing clinical depression, whether single or married (Brown and Bifulco, 1990). Part-time workers are at less risk than non-workers or full-timers. The full-timers' health risk was associated with a 'crisis' such as domestic strain, caused, for example, by deviant behaviour in child or partner. The authors argue that these crises were particularly stressful for full-time mothers because they could be interpreted as motherhood failure or a sense of being trapped in an unrewarding situation.

Martin and Roberts (1984) found the presence of children to be the single most important feature in whether working women had coping difficulties or not; single mothers were more likely to have difficulty in coping, particularly if they worked full time. The risk of multiple role strain and work overload exists where there is lack of substantial support from home and workplace, particularly with regard to childcare. The unsupported single mother is most at risk, more so if she is also working full time.

A study of black female managers and job satisfaction (Wright *et al.*, 1987) found that organizational authority was the most important predictor of job satisfaction. This finding is supported by an earlier study of black male managers (Fernandez, 1975). Those individuals who perceive themselves as having some degree of decision-making authority and responsibility will be more satisfied than those whose jobs lack these features.

If managers see themselves as lacking authority and responsibility, they will have fewer opportunities to exercise meaningful control over the work environment and confirm their skills. Also, and similarly, where managers see themselves as having opportunities for advancement within the organization, they will feel more satisfied. These are variables that can be affected by the organization; they can create procedures and policies that will lead to increased perceptions of these features of jobs.

Researchers (e.g. Quick and Quick, 1984; Walshok, 1981; Yogev and Brett, 1985) have identified some of the obstacles and facilitators associated with work tenure and managerial positions. Emotional support and competence are the facilitators. Networking, for example, can enhance the sense of competence that women often lack (Cooper and Davidson, 1982). Females have been found to be much more likely to request support and they find social support more helpful and available than do men (Butler, 1985). Moreover the buffering effects of social support in mediating work stress have been well documented (House, 1980; Pines *et al.*, 1981).

The obstacles include discrimination in pay and promotion, role conflict, and sexual harassment. Sexual harassment is a particularly severe obstacle to work satisfaction among blue-collar workers (Walshok, 1981; Kissman, 1992). Sexual harassment will be explored in a subsequent chapter. First let us look at leadership and then personality.

Review Questions

Are women less satisfied with their jobs than men? Review the sources cited here (see also Major, 1987) and see what you can conclude.

We have seen here how women's achievement motive may be affected by whether or not it will be noticed by, or offend, men. Do you think this is true? What evidence can you find to support and refute the view? (See Betz and Fitzgerald, 1987; Stake,1976 and others.)

If you were a single parent, living in a tower block, what would your priorities be in terms of what you needed from work? Is self-actualization or job enrichment derived from work what you would need from work? Or is group support from those in a similar position of more use?

What research would you draw on to answer these questions?

What effect do families have on women's motivation and job satisfaction? Is family life a determinant of motivation or job satisfaction?

Freidlander (1966) discusses the difference in motivation between white and blue collar workers and concludes that it is possible that the cultural norms of blue-collar workers are sufficiently different to white collar and each group behaves in accordance with its individual principles. Generalizations concerning the motivation–performance relationship cannot be made from one cultural group to another. Can they then be made from men to women?

We have looked at the question of 'why work?' here but that begs the question of 'why not work?' and the issue of unemployment. Studies of women's unemployment and redundancy paint a complex picture. Some women will have similar experiences of unemployment as men; others will be different. What do the studies show of women's experience of unemployment? (See Dex, 1985, Chapter 3.)

REFERENCES

ACKER, J. and VAN HOUTON, D. R. (1974) 'Differential Recruitment and Control: The Sex Structuring of Organizations', *Administrative Science Quarterly*, **19**(2),152–163.

ALBAN-METCALFE, B. (1989) 'What Motivates Managers: An Investigation by Gender and Sector of Employment', *Public Administration*, **67**(Spring), 95–108.

ALBAN-METCALFE, B. (1990) 'Gender, Leadership and Assessment', adapted from a paper presented to the 3rd European Congress on the Assessment Centre Method, Working Paper, Nuffield Institute, University of Leeds.

ALBAN-METCALFE, B. and NICHOLSON, N. (1984) *The Career Development of British Managers*, British Institute of Management Foundation, London.

ALBAN-METCALFE, B. and WEST, M. (1991) 'Women Managers', Chapter 12 in J. Firth Cozens and M. West, *Women at Work*, Open University Press, Milton Keynes.

ANDRISANI, P. J. (1978) 'Job Satisfaction Among Working Women', *Signs: Journal of Women in Culture and Society*, **3**, 588–607.

ANDRISANI, P. and NESTEL, G. (1976) 'Internal–External Control as a Contributor and Outcome of Work Experience', *Journal of Applied Psychology*, **62**, 156–165.

ARGYLE, M. (1974) *The Social Psychology of Work*, Penguin, Harmondsworth.

ARNOLD, H. A. and FELDMAN, D. C.. (1982) 'Negative Relationship Between Age and Turnover Intention: A Multivariate Analysis of Determinants of Job Turnover', *Journal of Applied Psychology*, **67**, 350–360.

ASTIN, H. S. (1985) 'The Meaning of Work in Women's Lives: A Socio-psychological Model of Career Choice and Work Behavior', *Counseling Psychology*, **12**, 117–126.

ATKINSON, J. W. and REITMAN, W. R. (1956) 'Performance as a Function of Motive Strength and Expectancy of Goal Attainment', *Journal of Abnormal Social Psychology*, **53**, 361–366.

BARTOL, K. M. and MARTIN, D. C. (1986) 'Women and Men in Task Groups', in R. D. Ashmore and F. K. Del Boca (eds), *The Social Psychology of Female–Male Relations: A Critical Analyses of Central Concepts*, Academic Press, London.

BARUCH, G. K. (1972) 'Maternal Influences Upon College Women's Attitudes Toward Women and Work', *Developmental Psychology*, **6**, 32–37.

BEECHEY, V. and PERKINS, T. (1987) *A Matter of Hours: Women, Part-time Work and the Labour Market*, Polity Press, Cambridge.

BERCH, B. (1982) *The Endless Day: The Political Economy of Women and Work*, Harcourt Brace Jovanovich, New York.

BETZ, E. L. (1982) 'Need Fulfilment in the Career Development of Women', *Journal of Vocational Behavior*, **20**, 53–66.

BETZ, E. L. (1984) 'Two Tests of Maslow's Theory of Need Fulfilment', *Journal of Occupational Behavior*, **24**, 204–220.

BETZ, N. E. and FITZGERALD, L. F. (1987) *The Career Psychology of Women*, Academic Press, London.

BLAUNER, R. (1964) *Alienation and Freedom*, University of Chicago Press, Chicago.

BOARDMAN, S. K., HARTINGTON, C. C. and HOROWITZ, S. V. (1987) 'Successful Women: A Psychological Investigation of Family Class and Educational Origins', in B. A. Gutek and L. Larwood (eds), *Women's Career Development*, Sage, Beverly Hills, Calif.

BRONSTEIN, P., BLACK, L., PFENNIG, J. L. and WHITE, A. (1987) 'Stepping onto the Academic Career Ladder: How are Women Doing?' in B. A. Gutek and L. Larwood (eds), *Women's Career Development*, Sage, London.

BROWN, G. W. and BIFULCO, A. (1990) 'Motherhood, Employment and the Development of Depression. A Replication of a Finding?', *British Journal of Psychiatry*, **156**, 169-179.

BRYSON, R., BRYSON, J. B. and JOHNSON, M. F. (1978) 'Family Size, Satisfaction and Productivity in Duel Career Couples', *Psychology of Women Quarterly*, **3**, 67–77.

BUCHANAN, D. (1987) 'Job Enrichment is Dead: Long Live High-performance Work Design!' *Personnel Management*, May, 40–43.

BURAWOY, M. (1978) *Manufacturing Consent: Changes in the Labor Process under Monopoly Capitalism*, University of Chicago Press, Chicago.

BUTLER, T. (1985) 'Gender and Sex-role Attributes as Predictors of Utilization of Natural Support Systems During Personal Stress Events', *Sex Roles*, **13**, 515–524.

CHODOROW, N. J. (1989) *Feminism and Psychoanalytic Theory*, Yale Universtiy Press, New Haven, Conn.

CHUSMIR, L. H. (1985) 'Motivation of Managers: Is Gender a Factor?', *Psychology of Women Quarterly*, **9**, 153–159.

CHUSMIR, L. H. and PARKER, B. (1984) 'Dimensions of Need for Power: Personalized vs. Socialized Power in Female and Male Managers', *Sex Roles*, **11**, 759–769.

COOPER, C. L. and DAVIDSON, M. J. (1982) 'The High Cost of Stress on Women Managers', *Organizational Dynamics*, **10**, 44–53.

COTTON, S., ANTILL, J. K. and CUNNINGHAM, J. D. (1989) 'The Work Motivations of Mothers with Pre-school Children', *Journal of Family Issues*, **10**(2), 189–210.

COX, C. and COOPER, C. L. (1988) *High Flyers*, Basil Blackwell, Oxford.

CROSBY, F. (1982) *Relative Deprivation and Working Women*, Oxford University Press, New York.

CULLEN, D. (1992) 'Sex and Gender on the Path to Feminism and Self Actualisation: Women in Management', paper presented at the annual meeting of the Administrative Sciences Association of Canada (ASAC).

DAVIDSON, M. J. and COOPER, C. L. (1986) 'Executive Women Under Pressure', *International Review of Applied Psychology*, **35**, 301–326.

DEX, S. (1985) *The Sexual Division of Work*, Harvester Wheatsheaf, Brighton.

DONNELL, S. M. and HALL, J. (1980) 'Men and Women as Managers: A Significant Case of No Significant Difference', *Organizational Dynamics*, **8**, 60–77.

DUNNETTE, M., CAMPBELL, J. and HAKEL, M. (1967) 'Factors Contributing to Job Satisfaction and Job Dissatisfaction in Six Occupational Groups', *Organizational Behaviour and Human Performance*, **21**, 143–174.

EWEN, R. B. (1967) 'Weighting Components of Job Satisfaction', *Journal of Applied Psychology*, **LI**, 68–73.

FARMER, H. S. (1985) 'Mode of Career and Achievement Motivation for Women and Men', *Journal of Counseling Psychology*, **32**(3), 363–390.

FEATHERMAN, D. L. and HAUSER, R. M. (1976) 'Sexual Inequalities and Socioeconomic Achievement in the US, 1962–1973', *American Sociological Review*, **41**, 462–483.

FERNANDEZ, J. P. (1975) *Black Managers in White Corporations*, Wiley, New York.

FINIGAN, M. (1982) 'The Effects of Token Representation on Participants in Small Decision-making Groups', *Economic and Industrial Democracy*, **3**, 531–550.

FITZGERALD, L. F. and O'CRITES, J. O. (1980) 'Towards a Career Psychology of Women: What Do We Know? What Do We Need to Know?' *Journal of Counseling Psychology*, **27**(1), 44–62.

FRIEDLANDER, F. (1966) 'Motivations to Work and Organizational Performance', *Journal of Applied Psychology*, **50**(2), 143–152.

GILLIGAN, C. (1982) *In a Different Voice*, Harvard University Press, Cambridge, Mass.

GLENN, E. N. and FELDBERG, R. L. (1977) 'Degraded and Deskilled: The Proletarianization of Clerical Work', *Social Problems*, **25**(1), 52–64.

GOLDING, J., RESNICK, A. and CROSBY, F. (1983) 'Work Satisfaction as a Function of Gender and Job Status', *Psychology of Women Quarterly*, **1**, 286–290.

GOLDTHORPE, J. H., LOCKWOOD, D., BECHOFER, F. and PLATT, J. (1968) *The Affluent Worker: Political Attitudes and Behaviour*, Cambridge University Press, Cambridge.

HACKMAN, J. R., PEARCE, J. L and WOLFE, J. C. (1978) 'Effects of Changes in Job Characteristics on Work Attitudes and Behaviours: A Naturally Occurring Quasi-Experiment', *Organizational Behaviour and Human Performance*, **21**, 289–304.

HAKIM, C. (1991) 'Grateful Slaves and Self-made Women: Fact and Fantasy in Women's Work Orientations', *European Sociological Review*, **7**(2), 101–121.

HARLAN, A. and WEISS, C. L. (1982) 'Sex Differences in Factors Affecting Managerial Career Advancement', Chapter 4 in P. Wallace (ed.), *Women in the Workplace*, Auburn House, Boston, Mass.

HARPER, J. and RICHARDS, L. (1986) *Mothers and Working Mothers*, Penguin, Ringwood, Victoria.

HARRIMAN, A. (1985) *Women/Men Management*, Praeger, New York.

HERZBERG, F. (1968) 'One More Time: How Do You Motivate Employees', *Harvard Business Review*, January–February, 53–62.

HERZBERG, F., MAUSNER, B. and SNYDERMAN, B. (1959) *The Motivation to Work*, 2nd edn, Wiley, New York.

HOCK, E., MORGAN, K. and HOCK, M. (1985) 'Employment Decisions Made by Mothers of Infants', *Psychology of Women Quarterly*, **9**, 383–402.

HODSON, R. (1989) 'Gender Differences in Job Satisfaction: Why Aren't Women more Dissatisfied?', *Sociological Quarterly*, **30**(3), 385–399.

HOFFMAN, L. (1963) 'The Decision to Work', in F. I. Nye and L. W. Hoffman, (eds), *The Employed Mother in America*, pp. 18–39, Rand McNally, Chicago.

HOFFMAN, L. and NYE, F. (1974) *Working Mothers*, Jossey Bass, San Francisco.

HOLLWAY, W. (1991) *Work Psychology and Organizational Behaviour*, Sage, London.

HOUSE, J. S. (1980) *Work Stress and Social Support*, Addison-Wesley, Reading, Mass.

HOUSE, R. J. and SINGH, J. V. (1987) 'Organizational Behaviour: Some New Directions for I/O Psychology', *Annual Review of Psychology*, **38**, 673–678

HOUSE, R. J. and WIGDOR, L. A. (1967) 'Herzberg's Duel Factor Theory of Job Satisfaction and Motivation: A Review of the Evidence and a Criticism', *Personnel Psychology*, **20**, 369–389.

JACKSON, R. (1970) 'Job Enrichment, Challenge of the 70s', *Training and Development Journal*, June, 7–9.

KANTER, R. M. (1977) *Men and Women of the Corporation*, Basic Books, New York.

KANTER, R. M. (1978) 'Work in the New America', *Daedalus*, **107**, 47–78.

KASTEN, K. (1972) 'Toward a Psychology of Being: A Masculine Mystique', *Journal of Humanistic Psychology*, **12**(2), 23–24.

KESSLER, R. C. and MCRAE, J. A. (1981) 'Trends in the Relationship Between Sex and Psychological Distress, 1957–1976', *American Sociological Review*, **46**(4), 443–452.

KISSMAN, K. (1992) 'Women in Blue-collar Occupations: An Exploration of Constraints and Facilitators', *Journal of Sociology and Social Welfare*, **17**, 139–149.

KOFF, L. A. and HANDLON, J. H. (1975) 'Women in Management—Key to Success or Failure', *Personnel Administration*, **20**, 22–28.

KORNHAUSER, A. (1965) *The Mental Health of the Industrial Worker*, Wiley, New York.

KREMER, J. and CURRY, C. A. (1986) 'Attitudes towards Women in Northern Ireland', Equal Opportunities Commission, Northern Ireland, March.

KREMER, J. and MONTGOMERY, P. (1993) *Women's Working Lives*, Equal Opportunities Commission for Northern Ireland, HMSO.

KUKLA, A. (1972) 'Attribution Determinants of Achievement-Related Behaviour', *Journal of Personality and Social Psychology*, **21**, 166–174.

LAMPHERE, L. (1985) 'Bringing the Family to Work: Women's Culture on the Shop Floor', *Feminist Studies*, **11**(3) 519–540.

LEWIS, S. and COOPER, C. L. (1989) *Career Couples*, Unwin Hyman, London.

LOCKE, E. (1976) 'The Nature and Causes of Job Satisfaction', in M. Dunnette, (ed.), *Handbook of Industrial and Organizational Psychology*, Rand McNally, New York.

MCCLELLAND, D. C. (1951) *Personality*, Dryden Press, New York.

MCCLELLAND, D. C. (1961) *The Achieving Society*, Van Nostrand, Princeton, NJ.

MCCLELLAND, D. C (1966) 'Longitudinal Trends in the Relation of Thought to Action', *Journal of Consulting Psychology*, **30**, 479–483.

MCKENRY, P. C., HAMDORF, K. G., WALTERS, C. M. and MURRAY, C. I. (1985) 'Family and Job Influences on Role Satisfaction of Employed Rural Mothers.', *Psychology of Women Quarterly*, **9**, 242–257.

MCMAHAN, I. D. (1971) 'Sex Differences in Causal Attributions Following Success and Failure', paper presented at the meeting of the Eastern Psychological Association, April.

MACCOBY, E. E. and JACKLIN, C. N. (1974) *The Psychology of Sex Differences*, Stanford University Press, Stanford University.

MAJOR, B. (1987) 'Gender, Justice and the Psychology of Entitlement', Chapter 5 in P. Shaver and C. Hendrick (eds), *Sex and Gender*, Review of Personality and Social Psychology, vol. 7, Sage, Newbury Park, Calif.

MAJOR, B. and KONAR, E. (1984) 'An Investigation of Sex Differences in Pay Expectations and their Possible Causes', *Academy of Management Journal*, **27**, 77–793.

MALINOWSKY, M. R. and BARRY, J. R. (1965) 'Determinants of Work Attitudes', *Journal of Applied Psychology* **XLIX**, 446–451.

MARTIN, J. and ROBERTS, C. (1984) *Women and Employment: A Lifetime Perspective*, HMSO, London.

MASLOW, A. (1943) 'A Theory of Human Motivation', *Psychological Review*, **50** (4), 370–396.

MASLOW, A. (1970) *Motivation and Personality*, Harper & Row, New York.

MINER, J. B. (1965) *Studies in Management Education*, Springer-Verlag, New York.

MINER, J. B. (1974) 'Motivation to Manage Among Women: Studies of Business Managers and Educational Administrators', *Journal of Vocational Behaviour*, **5**, 197–208.

MINER, J. B. and SMITH, N. R. (1982) 'Decline and Stabilization of Managerial Motivation Over a 20 Year Period', *Journal of Applied Psychology*, **67**, 297–305.

MORRISON, R. F. and SEBALD, M. (1974) 'Personal Characteristics Differentiating Female Executives from Female Non-executive Personnel', *Journal of Applied Psychology*, **59**, 656–659.

MORSE, C. and WEISS, R. S. (1955) 'The Function and Meaning of Work and the Job', *American Sociological Review*, **20**, 191–198.

NELSON, D. J. and QUICK. J. C. (1985) 'Professional Women: Are Distress and Disease Inevitable?', *Academy of Management Review*, **10**(2), 206–218.

NIEVA, V. F. and GUTEK, B. A. (1981) *Women and Work: A Psychological Perspective*, Praeger, New York.

OAKLEY, A. (1974) *The Sociology of Housework*, Martin Robertson, Oxford.

O'BRIEN, G. E. (1982) 'The Relative Contribution of Perceived Skill-utilization and Other Perceived Job Attributes to the Prediction of Job Satisfaction: A Cross-Validation Study', *Human Relations*, **35**(3), 219–237.

PAYNE, R. (1970) 'Factor Analysis of a Maslow-type Need Satisfaction Questionnaire', *Personnel Psychology*, **23**, 251–268.

PINES, A., RANSON, A. and KADRY, D. (1981) *Burnout: From Tedium to Personal Growth*, Free Press, New York.

PLECK, J. H. (1977) 'The Work–family Role System', *Social Problems*, **24**, 417–427.

PORTNER, J. (1978) 'Impacts of Work on the Family', Minnesota Council on Family Relations, Minneapolis.

POWELL, G. N. (1988) *Women and Men in Management*, Sage, Newbury Park, Calif.

QUICK, J. C. and QUICK, J. D. (1984) *Organizational Stress and Preventive Management*, McGraw-Hill, New York.

QUINN, R., STAINES, G. and MCCULLOUGH, B. C. (1974) *Job Satisfaction: Is There a Trend?* US Government Printing Office, Washington, DC.

RENSHAW, J. R. (1976) 'An Exploration of the Dynamics of the Overlapping Worlds of Work and Family', *Family Process*, **15**, 143–165.

ROSS, R. (1984) 'Married Women and the Market Work: How Much Choice?, *Australian Quarterly*, **56**, 227–238.

ROY, D. (1952) 'Restrictions of Output in a Piecework Machine Shop', Ph.D. dissertation, University of Chicago.

RUDD, N. M. and MCKENRY, P. C. (1986) 'Family Influences on the Job Satisfaction of Employed Mothers', *Psychology of Women Quarterly* **10**, 363–372.

SANDERS, J. M. and WONG, H. Y. (1985) 'Graduate Training and Initial Job Placement', *Sociological Inquiry* **55**, 154–169.

SEKARAN, V. (1983) 'How Husbands and Wives in Duel-career Families Perceive their Family and Work Worlds', *Journal of Vocational Behaviour*, **22**, 288–302.

SIEGFIELD, W. D., MCFARLANE, I., GRAHAM, D. B., MOORE, N. A. and YOUNG, P. L. (1981) 'A Re-examination of Sex Differences in Job Preferences', *Journal of Vocational Behaviour*, **18**, 30–42.

SMITH, A. D. and REID, W. J. (1982) 'Family Role Revolution', *Journal of Education for Social Work*, **18**, 51–57.

SOBOL, M. (1963) 'Commitment to Work', in F. Nye and L. Hoffman (eds), *The Employed Mother in America*, pp. 40–63, Rand McNally, Chicago.

SPENCE, J. T., DEAUX, K. and HELMREICH, R. L. (1985) 'Sex Roles in Contemporary American Society', Chapter 17 in G. Lindzsey and E. Aronson (eds), *Handbook of Social Psychology*, Random House, New York.

STAKE, J. E. (1976) 'The Effect of Information Regarding Group Perfomance Norms on Goal Setting in Males and Females', *Sex Roles*, **2**, 23–28.

TERBORG, J. R. (1977) 'Women in Management: A Research Review', *Journal of Applied Psychology*, **62**, 647–664.

THOMPSON, E. (1980) 'The Value of Employment of Mothers of Young Children', *Journal of Marriage and the Family*, **42**, 551–566.

TRIMBERGER, R. and MCLEAN, M. J. (1982) 'Maternal Employment: The Child's Perspective', *Journal of Marriage and the Family*, **44**, 469–475.

VEROFF, J., DOUVAN, e. and KULKA, R. A. (1981) *The Inner American*, Basic Books, New York.

VEROFF, J., WILCOX, S. and ATKINSON, J. W. (1953) 'The Achievement Motive in High-school and College Age Women', *Journal of Abnormal and Social Psychology*, **48**, 108–119.

WADDEL, F. T. (1983) 'Factors Affecting Choice, Satisfaction and Success in the Female Self Employed', *Journal of Vocational Behaviour*, **23**, 294–304.

WAHBA, M. A. and BRIDWELL, L. G. (1976) 'Maslow Reconsidered: A Review of Research on the Need Hierarchy Theory', *Organizational Behaviour and Human Performance*, **15**, 212–240.

WALL, T. D., STEPHENSON, G. M. and SKIDMORE, C. (1971) 'Ego-involvement and Herzberg's Two-factor Theory of Job Satisfaction: An Experiential Field Study', *British Journal of Social and Clinical Psychology*, **10**, 123–131.

WALSHOK, M. Z. (1981) *Blue-collar Women: Pioneers on the Male Frontier*, Anchor Books, New York.

WARR, P. and WALL, T. (1975) *Work and Well-being*, Penguin, New York.

WEARING, B. (1984) *The Ideology of Motherhood*, Allen & Unwin, Sydney.

WEINER, B. (1992) *Human Motivation: Metaphor, Theories and Research*, Sage, Newbury Park, Calif.

WESTWOOD, S. (1985) *All Day, Every Day*, University of Illinois Press, Urbana–Champaign, Ill.

WILD, R. and HILL, A. B. (1970) *Women in the Factory: A Study of Job Satisfaction and Labour Turnover*, Institute of Personnel Management, London.

WHITE, B., COX, C. and COOPER, C. (1992) *Women's Career Development: A Study of High Flyers*, Blackwell, Oxford.

WOLF, W. C. and FLIGSTEIN, N. D. (1979) 'Sex and Authority in the Workplace: The Causes of Sexual Inequality', *American Sociological Review*, **44**, 235–252.

WRIGHT, R., KING, S. W., BERG, W. E. and CREECY, R. F. (1987) 'Job Satisfaction among Black Female Managers: A Causal Approach', *Human Relations*, **40**(8), 489–506.

YOGEV, S. and BRETT, J. (1985) 'Patterns of Work and Family Involvement Among Single and Duel-earner Couples', *Journal of Applied Psychology*, **70**, 754–768.

ZIMMERMAN, D. H. and WEST, C. (1975) 'Sex Roles, Interruptions, and Silences in Conversation', in B. Thone and N. Henley (eds), *Language and Sex: Difference and Dominance*, Newbury House, Rowley, Mass.

5 *Leadership*

We should not be surprised to learn that the study of leadership or of power rarely included sex or sex roles as organizationally significant variables. The male as normal assumption is unchallenged and all leaders are not only male but quite masculine (Harriman, 1985). Very little research has looked at the relationship between masculinity or femininity and leadership. Women and leadership is not a topic discussed in other chapters on leadership in the main texts (e.g. Bass, 1990), but segregated into a chapter of its own. There is, then, little integration of research on women and leadership in the leadership literature. Research on the impact of gender on the leadership of groups is relatively new and most research has been conducted by male investigators whose subjects are men in groups led by men (Dion, 1985; Reed, 1981). Leadership analysis has historically focused only on male leaders.

Leadership is often conceived of as a skill. If you think management is about asking what problems have to be solved and thinking about the best ways of achieving results so that people will continue to contribute to the organization, then leadership is simply a practical effort to direct affairs. Alistair Mant (1983) reported that when he asked which bosses were recalled with gratitude and affection as really good, the most common formulation was 'Tough (or firm) but fair'.

Stop! Think of bosses you recall with gratitude and affection who were tough but fair. Are they men, women, or both?

Leadership might be about simply being a good manager; it might take persistence, tough-mindedness, hard work, intelligence, analytical ability, tolerance, and goodwill to be a manager. A male view of leadership might define it in terms of dominance, aggression, and other stereotypically male attributes. A non-stereotypical definition of leadership might include the ability to negotiate, to be considerate to others, and to help others resolve conflicts without confrontation (Denmark *et al.*, 1988).

Another view of leadership might assume that only great people are worthy of leadership. 'Here leadership is a psychodrama in which a brilliant, lonely person

must gain control of himself or herself as a precondition for controlling others' (Zaleznik, 1992: 127). Is there any way great leaders can be trained to be, for example, persistent and tough-minded? Are these the traits needed for leadership or is leadership about charisma, something which cannot be taught? Are women as likely as men to be perceived as possessing charisma?

Stop! What traits do you think make for a good manager? Are these traits different from those of a good leader? Do the traits you think of have masculine or feminine stereotypes attached to them?

TRAIT THEORIES OF LEADERSHIP

If leaders are endowed with superior qualities that differentiate them from followers, it should be possible to identify those qualities. There are some important reviews of literature on personality traits and leadership to be found in Smith and Kreuger (1933), Jenkins (1947), and Stogdill (1948). Most of the leadership studies from 1930 through much of the 1940s used a trait-theory approach. Trait theorists assume that leaders possess characteristics not found in followers. Leaders tend to be tall, of high socioeconomic status, intelligent, exhibit superior judgement, knowledge, and verbal ability, be decisive, and have good interpersonal skills and a high need for achievement (Aldag and Brief, 1981). This tells us something of why women are less likely to be chosen as leaders. On average women are shorter than men, and are perceived (stereotypically) as less intelligent, decisive, and motivated. They may have good interpersonal skills but they are not seen are being powerful or influential.

Stogdill found that the following conclusions are supported by uniformly positive evidence from 15 or more studies surveyed:

a. The average person who occupies a position of leadership exceeds the average member of his group in the following respects (1) intelligence, (2) scholarship, (3,) dependability in exercising responsibilities (4) activity and social participation, and (5) socio-economic status

Stop! Would you want to select potential leaders of departments within your organization with these particular traits? If not, why not? How would you determine whether or not the individual possessed the required traits?

b. The qualities, characteristics, and skills required in a leader are determined to a large extent by the demands of the situation in which he is to function as a leader.

According to Stogdill, it is not especially difficult to find persons who are leaders. It is quite another matter to place these persons in different situations where they will be able to function as leaders. Leadership is not about possessing a combination of traits; it is about developing a working relationship among members of a group in which the leader acquires status through active participation and demonstration of his or her capacity for carrying co-operative tasks through to completion.

The problem of selecting leaders should be much less difficult than that of training non-leaders to become leaders. Those who have observed the fruitless efforts of socially isolated individuals to gain group acceptance or leadership status would be aware of this problem. As Bass (1990: 96) has concluded, to emerge as a leader, one must participate; to remain acceptable to others as a leader, one must exhibit competence. These are not traits as such, but about the interaction between leader and group.

Discussion point

You saw how Stodgill only used the term 'men' in the context of leadership. Here is a quotation from a 1947 management manual:

> He [the leader] knows that the master of men has physical energies
> and skills and intellectual abilities, vision and integrity, and he
> knows that, above all, the leader must have emotional balance
> and control. The great leader is even-tempered when others rage,
> brave when others fear, calm when others are excited, self-controlled
> when others indulge.

It is hard, when this language is used, to see a woman in this description. Many at this time, and during the 1960s, believed that women were 'temperamentally unfit' for management because they were too emotional (Bowman *et al.*, 1965).

Have views changed? Marking exam papers and essays of undergraduate students today leads me to think that few question the validity of using the term 'men' and 'he' meaning to include women. Few question the stereotype that women are more emotional than men. What do you think? (See Swan, 1994.)

Evidence suggests that people tend to view men as more appropriate than women for task leadership (Lorber, 1984; Martin *et al.*, 1983). In a study by Bowman *et al.*, (1965), 51 per cent of managers agreed that women were 'temperamentally unfit for management'. The stereotypes of the typical man and the typical manager tend to have almost identical traits, revealing, among other factors, greater competence but less warmth and emotionalism (Larwood and Wood, 1977: 36). If the judges who define the typical manager are male managers and male business students, then it is hardly surprising that good managers come out looking like good men (Hale, 1987: 497).

Gilmer (1961) found that over 65 per cent of the male managers in his study felt that women would be inferior to men in supervisory positions. Effective leadership is perceived to require traits stereotyped as masculine (Brenner *et al.*, 1989; Powell and Butterfield, 1979, 1984, 1989; Schein, 1973, 1975). Maleness has traditionally conferred higher status on a person than femaleness (Brown, 1965; Mussen, 1969; Broverman *et al.*, 1970). Cecil, *et al.* (1973) asked business students to evaluate 50 variables in terms of what an interviewer would consider important in interviewing a particular candidate 'for a job as a white-collar worker'. The results indicated that candidates with female names tended to be perceived as potential clerical workers, while candidates with male names were seen as potential administrative management employees.

Indeed we know that men occupy a disproportionate number of positions of authority. The public sphere is for men, while a woman's 'natural habitat' is the private sphere, 'privatized' by the process of reproduction (see Elshtain, 1981; O'Brien, 1981). Leadership, especially leadership that is labelled political, naturally inhabits the so-called public domain. Women have been consigned to the private realm and as 'natural' inhabitants of that they are aliens in the public realm where 'political leadership' is exercised. Crosby (1988) has argued strongly that we should rethink conceptions of public and private as every human being is inherently a public being in need of varying degrees of privacy. We need to adopt a more seamless view of public and private and jettison language that obscures that view.

We have noted, in Chapter 2, how women's performance is more critically judged than men's (Goldberg, 1968) and that Broverman *et al.* (1972) have found that people describe most leadership behaviours, including competence, as masculine attributes. But in societies and organizations where a male culture is prevalent, and power rests in the hands of men, women must conform to the masculine model if they want to 'keep their heads' (Bourantas and Papalexandris, 1991; Cixous, 1981; Grant, 1988). One argument is that women who want to move up the organizational hierarchy are forced to adopt a male model of managerial behaviour and eliminate their feminine traits. They imitate the male managerial model in order to achieve success. Therefore we should not be surprised if no differences emerge between male and female managers.

Wright (1976) and Beauvais (1976) found that the leader's gender affects people's perceptions of those in authority, with both men and women viewing men in positions of authority more positively. Costrich *et al.*, (1975) found that women exhibiting assertive or aggressive behaviour towards others are more unpopular and judged as poorly adjusted psychologically. Women occupying positions of authority may, then, face conflict between that which is expected of and attributed to them based on their gender and that based on their work roles.

Exercise

The smart ones among you might have noted that the most negative findings concerning women and leadership, women and perception, are from the studies of the early 1970s. You might argue that attitudes have changed. What evidence, apart from that to be found in this book, can you find to support that argument? You might use this question for a project and, taking a methodology developed in the 1970s, use the questionnaires again to find if attitudes have changed.

Davidson and Cooper (1983), as we saw earlier, explained the problems faced in leadership roles by drawing heavily on the concept of culture trap, borrowed from Larwood and Wood (1977). The managerial role is seen as essentially masculine, calling for competitiveness, assertiveness, and aggression, which are antithetical to female socialization. Female managers are thus prone to sex-role conflict and the combined disadvantage of low expectations, fear of success, heightened dependency needs, indecisiveness, fear of taking risks, lack of self-confidence, and inability to delegate responsibility. Compounding these traits is career ambivalence and conflict between work and family responsibilities, especially when geographic mobility is required by the job. The consequence is stress, reflected in symptoms such as smoking, tiredness, migraines, and dizzy spells (Davidson and Cooper, 1983).

Women managers show significantly higher detrimental work performance scores on six behaviour items compared with men. These items included being unable to cope well in conflict situations, being unable to sell themselves in competitive situations, lacking self-confidence in their ability to do the job, or to put views forward, reacting too emotionally when faced with problems at work, and feeling unable to be successful (Davidson and Cooper, 1983: ch. 7).

As we have noted earlier, Davidson and Cooper talk of women being in a cultural trap. There is a lack of appropriate female role models and so the male role model prevails in which women are at a cultural disadvantage appearing either as failing to conform or as unfeminine. As a direct consequence of their token status they tend to be viewed as symbols rather than as individuals, stereotyped according to the oft-repeated four variants of (i) mother earth—the passive, nurturing type; (ii) pet—a decoration at meetings with clients; (iii) seductress or sex object; or (iv) iron maiden or too successfully masculine. None of these is seen as valuable manager material (Davidson and Cooper, 1983: 23–25). Women who try to distance themselves from other women, in order to avoid these female stereotypes, become 'queen bees'.

BEHAVIOURAL THEORIES

An alternative approach would be to focus on leader behaviour. Behavioural theories have looked at what leaders do. Research programmes were begun at the University of Michigan (Likert, 1967) and the Ohio State University (Hemphill and Coons, 1957) in the late 1940s. Both were able to identify behavioural differences in leaders. In the Ohio State studies the dimensions which helped differentiate between leader's behaviours were referred to as initiating structure and consideration (Halpin and Winer, 1957). They only describe leadership styles; they do not prescribe the most effective style. These dimensions are to be found today in the path goal model of leadership (House, 1971) and help diagnose the degree of initiating structure and consideration employed by leaders in organizations.

We saw earlier how the behaviour of men and women managers is seen to differ, women seeking co-operation, and men power and dominance. Is this gender difference reflected in leadership style? Are there implicit differences between men and women's leadership style? These are questions that do not seem to have been addressed by organizational behaviour textbooks.

Consider the following definitive statements to be found in Eagly and Johnson (1990): 'The preponderance of available evidence is that no consistently clear pattern of differences can be discerned in the supervisory style of female as compared to male leaders' (Bass, 1981: 499). 'Contrary to notions about sex specialization in leadership styles, women leaders appear to behave in similar fashion to their male colleagues' (Nieva and Gutek, 1981: 91). 'There is as yet no research evidence that makes a case for sex differences in either leadership aptitude or style' (Kanter, 1977: 199). In general, comparative research indicates that there are few differences in the leadership styles of female and male designated leaders. Some studies, especially those conducted in the laboratory, have been able to find differences, but more have not (Osborn and Vicars, 1976).

If we implicitly believe that men and women do have differences in style, then this may be due to the stereotypical images we have about men and women.

Bryman (1987) has contested the approach to consideration and initiating structure that uses questionnaires on leader behaviour. He argued that people have implicit theories of leadership which underpin individual's descriptions of leaders when answering batteries of questions. When people describe leaders they use 'information simplification heuristics' (Phillips, 1984: 126). Their perceptions are affected by knowledge of their performance. It is the implicit theories that are being measured rather than the behaviours of leaders as such. Gender of leader or follower appears to be immaterial but is it fundamental to how leaders are going to be described?

Let us now look at the behavioural differences between leaders and how they can be described.

AUTOCRATIC VERSUS DEMOCRATIC LEADERSHIP

The democratic approach is advocated for the fostering of effectiveness and satisfaction. Human relations theorists (e.g. Argyris, 1957; McGregor, 1960) support this view. The evidence suggests that in specified circumstances, an authoritarian approach may result in heightened productivity in the short term, but overall the democratic approach is likely to be more effective, and under most conditions working for a democratic supervisor will be more satisfying (Bass, 1990: 421). Strong evidence in favour of democratic management has been accumulated from over 500 studies completed between 1950 and 1977. In the long run the democratic approach tends to generate larger improvements in an organization's productivity as well as in the satisfaction of its employees.

Borrowing heavily from the original experimental concepts and results of Lewin and Lippitt (1938), Likert (1961) conceived of four systems of interpersonal relationships in large organizations:

1. Authoritative autocratic
2. Benevolent autocratic
3. Consultative
4. Democratic

Likert proposed and demonstrated that moving the organization away from systems 1 and 2 and towards 3 and 4 would result in increases in both productivity and satisfaction of employees. In more than 500 studies positive associations have generally been found between the measure of organizations' performance and whether they are closer to democratic systems 3 and 4 than to autocratic systems 1 and 2.

Profile of organizational characteristics

Organizational variables	System 1	System 2	System 3	System 4
How much confidence + trust is shown in subordinates	Virtually none	Some	Substantial amount	A great deal
How free do they feel to talk to their superiors about the job?	Not very free	Somewhat free	Quite free	Very free
How often are subordinates' ideas sought and used constructively?	Seldom	Sometimes free	Often	Very frequently
Is predominant use made of: (1) fear, (2) threats, (3) punishment, (4) rewards, (5) involvement	1, 2, 3, occasion- ally 4	4 and some 3	4, some 3, and 5	5, 4, based on group
Where is responsibility felt for achieving organizational goals?	Mostly at top	Top and middle	Fairly general	At all levels
How much co-operative teamwork exists?	Very little	Relatively little	Moderate amount	Great deal
What is the usual direction of information flow	Downward	Mostly downward	Down and up	Down, up, and side- ways
How is downward communication accepted	With suspicion	Possibly with suspicion	With caution	With a receptive mind
How accurate is upward communication?	Usually inaccurate	Often inaccurate	Often accurate	Almost always accurate
How well do supervisors know problems faced by subordinates?	Not very well	Rather well	Quite well	Very well
At what level are decisions made?	Mostly at top	Policy at top, some delegation	Broad policy at top, more delegation	Through- out, but well integrated

Organizational variables	System 1	System 2	System 3	System 4
Are subordinates involved in decisions related to their work?	Almost never	Occasionally consulted	Generally consulted	Fully involved
What does decision-making process contribute to motivation?	Not very much	Relatively little	Some contribution	Substantial contribution
How are organizational goals established?	Orders issued	Orders, some comments invited	After discussion by orders	By group action (except in crisis)
How much covert resistance to goals is present?	Strong resistance	Moderate resistance	Some resistance at times	Little or none
How concentrated are review and control functions?	Very highly at top	Quite highly at top	Moderate delegation to lower levels	Widely shared
Is there an informal organization resisting the formal one?	Yes	Usually	Sometimes	No—same goals as formal
What are cost, productivity, and other control data used	Policing, punishment	Reward and punishment	Reward, some self-guidance	Self-guidance, problem solving

Employees can assess their organization and its leadership processes by using the profile of organizational characteristics. Assess organizations to which you belong or have belonged, comparing and contrasting those where there was female or male management.

Source: adapted from Rensis Likert, *The Human Organization: Its Management and Value*, Appendix 11 ©1967 McGraw-Hill Book Company.

An employee should be able, from the profile, to assess where their organization is perceived to lie on the dimensions between systems 1 and 4. In the consultative and democratic systems (3 and 4) supervisors and subordinates trust each other a great deal, supervisors are very supportive, very easy to talk to, and virtually always ask for subordinates' ideas to try to make use of them. Economic and achievement motivation and personal worth are emphasized. The subordinates' participation in goal setting is encouraged along with bottom-up communication. Subordinates are influential in determining goals, tasks, and methods. Decisions and controls are decentralized.

In contrast, in the autocratic system (1) there is an emphasis on threats, fear, and punishment with some promise of reward; in the benevolent autocrat system (2) there is more positive and less negative reinforcement. Top-down communication is stressed. Subordinates have little influence on goals and methods. Decisions and controls are centralized and are made person-to-person. Are organizations where women predominate in management more consultative and democratic?

CONCERN FOR PEOPLE OR PRODUCTION?

Stogdill's (1948) call to researchers to adopt a contingency approach to investigation leadership went unheeded until Fiedler (1964) developed his contingency model of leadership, focusing on attitudes, rather than behaviour. This has been the most widely researched leadership model (Bass, 1990: 494).

Instead of emphasizing leader behaviours, Fiedler's least-preferred co-worker (LPC) scale measured the affective reaction of a leader to his or her least-preferred co-worker with a series of bipolar items. Gender is, again, ignored in these theories. Leaders with low LPC scores are assumed to be task oriented, whereas leaders with high scores are relationship oriented. Like the Ohio State studies the emphasis is on work and worker orientations.

In its standard version the individual is asked to think of everyone with whom they have ever worked and then to describe the person with whom they could work least well. This is done through marking 16 items as shown in the box.

The model states that task orientation (as measured by LPC) works best in situations that are either extremely favourable or extremely unfavourable to the leader or in which the leader has very high or very low control. Relations orientation works best in situations that are moderately favourable to the leader or in which the leader has moderate control.

Two other models of leadership use a task versus people orientation. Blake and Mouton's (1978) managerial grid model incorporates two dimensions: concern for people and concern for production. They recommend that effective leaders should have a high emphasis on both concern for people and production. There is, then, one best way to achieve effective leadership. Their managerial grid is based on the idea that managers and leaders vary from 1 to 9 in their concern for people (the vertical axis on the grid) and from 1 to 9 in their concern for production (horizontal axis). It is team leadership (9,9) that is prescribed. This is attained by participation, openness, trust, respect, involvement, commitment, open confrontation to resolve conflicts, consensus, mutually determined management by objectives, and mutual support, change, and development through

The least-preferred co-worker scale

Think of the person with whom you can work *least* well. This person may be someone you work with now or someone you knew in the past. This person does not have to be the person you like least well, but should be the person with whom you had the most difficulty in getting a job done.

Please describe this person as he or she appears to you by putting an 'X' in the appropriate space on the following scales:

Pleasant	— — — — — — — —	Unpleasant
Friendly	— — — — — — — —	Unfriendly
Rejecting	— — — — — — — —	Accepting
Helpful	— — — — — — — —	Frustrating
Unenthusiastic	— — — — — — — —	Enthusiastic
Tense	— — — — — — — —	Relaxed
Distant	— — — — — — — —	Close
Cold	— — — — — — — —	Warm
Co-operative	— — — — — — — —	Uncooperative
Supportive	— — — — — — — —	Hostile
Boring	— — — — — — — —	Interesting
Quarrelsome	— — — — — — — —	Harmonious
Self-assured	— — — — — — — —	Hesitant
Efficient	— — — — — — — —	Inefficient
Gloomy	— — — — — — — —	Cheerful
Open	— — — — — — — —	Guarded

Source: F. Fiedler, *A Theory of Leadership Effectiveness* (1967: 41). © McGraw-Hill Book Company

feedback. Managers who achieve the 9,9 style are more likely than those with other dominant styles to advance further in their careers (Blake and Mouton, 1964; Hall, 1976).

Hersey and Blanchard's (1973) tri-dimensional leader effectiveness model includes task behaviour and relationship behaviour, in addition to follower maturity. They pay more attention, in common with Fiedler, to the situation before prescribing a leadership style.

If, as a manager, you believe people are inherently poor workers who have to be controlled and directed, then they will, in your view, be uplifted by authority. You might have a very orderly and consistent workforce. If, on the other hand, you believe people should be given the freedom to learn, grow, and overcome problems as workers, they need a different style of leadership. If you want to see commitment,

Should a manager be democratic, autocratic, or in-between?

Which of these statements about leadership would you agree with?

I believe in my subordinates. I merely serve as a catalyst and I mirror back the group's thoughts and feelings so they understand them. They know how to do the job and I have faith in them.

I don't believe one person should make all the decisions. I always discuss issues with my subordinates but I make it clear I have the final word.

Once I have decided what we are doing and how we are doing it, I sell my ideas to my employees.

I am being paid to lead. If I let other people make decisions I should be making, I am not worth my salt.

I believe in getting things done. Democracy is time consuming. Someone has to make the decisions and I think it should be me.

Each of these statements represents a point of view about what good leadership is about. You can find considerable support, experience, factual data, and theoretical principles to support each statement even though they seem to be inconsistent when placed together. These contradictions point to one of the dilemmas frequently faced by managers.

increased loyalty, and improved involvement and satisfaction, then your workforce needs a democratic and egalitarian leadership style. There is, then, a dilemma for each manager to face.

Here is another way of looking at the dilemma. There will be times when a manager will be torn between helping a group make a decision and taking over because the manager understands the problem better than the group and therefore should make the decision. The manager remains unsure when a group decision is really appropriate or when holding staff meetings serves merely as a device for avoiding their own decision-making responsibility.

Stop! As you were reading the above passage how were you envisaging this mythical manager? What gender were they?

DIRECTIVE VERSUS PARTICIPATIVE LEADERSHIP? IT ALL DEPENDS...

Tannenbaum and Schmidt (1958) presented their classic view of leadership in 1958 which provides a framework to help the manager in grappling with the dilemma of strong and permissive leadership. They present a continuum of possible leadership behaviour available to a manager (Fig. 5.1). Each type of action is related to the degree of authority used by the boss and to the amount of freedom available to the subordinates in reaching decisions. The actions on the extreme left characterize the manager who maintains a high degree of control; those on the extreme right represent the manager who releases a high degree of control. Neither extreme is absolute as authority and freedom are not without their limitations. The continuum does not offer a choice between two styles of leadership—democratic and authoritarian—instead it sanctions a range of behaviours. It is designed to help managers analyse their own behaviour and review that behaviour within a context of other alternatives without saying whether or not a style is right or wrong.

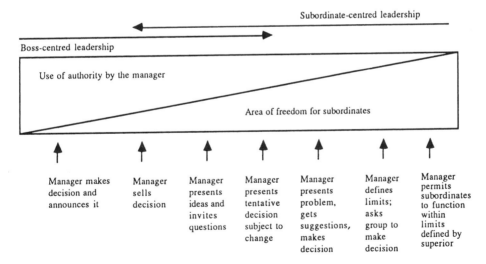

Figure 5.1 Continuum of possible leadership behaviour (Source: Tannenbaum and Schmidt (1958) © 1958 by the President and Fellows of Harvard College. All rights reserved.

Another prescriptive model that has been popular is that by Vroom and Yetton (1973). Again the model details the situations in which practising managers should be directive or participative to maximum satisfaction and effectiveness. The leadership decision style that is most conducive to effectiveness in the Vroom–Yetton model depends on the demand characteristics of the situation. Particularly important is whether the leader is aiming for a high-quality decision or for the subordinates' acceptance of the decision. Vroom and Yetton (1973: 13) lay out a direction–participation continuum, a decision tree, which offers a choice of directive, consultative, participative, and delegative. Situational demand characteristics and the requirements of the problem for the leader depend on how they answer a series of seven questions. Seven rules are then imposed to limit various styles of leadership to those feasible sets that can be deduced to protect the quality of the solution and acceptance of the decision. Vroom and Jago (1984) added to these questions. According to Vroom and Yetton (1973), on average, managers would use the same decision style as the decision tree model in about 40 per cent of situations. In two-thirds of situations the managers' behaviour was consistent with the feasible set of styles proposed in the model.

Situational leadership theory (SLT) developed from the writings of Reddin (1967). His three-dimensional management style posits the importance of a manager's relationship and task orientation in conjunction with effectiveness. From the interplay of these three dimensions Reddin proposed a typology of management styles (e.g. the autocrat, the missionary, the deserter). The style should be matched to the situation, but Reddin did not specify situational attributes that could be explicitly incorporated into a predictive scheme.

Hersey and Blanchard (1969) built on this suggestion and proposed a lifecycle theory of leadership. Here task orientation and relationship orientation are examined in conjunction with the dimension of follower maturity to account for leader effectiveness. As the level of follower maturity increases, effective leader behaviour will involve less structuring (task orientation) and less socio-emotional support (relationship orientation). The decline in need for both these leader behaviours is, however, not straightforward. During the early stages of employment a low level of relationship orientation coupled with high task orientation is considered to be ideal. As the employee(s) gain in maturity the need for supervisory social-emotional support increases while the need for structuring declines. Beyond a certain level of maturity the need for both social-emotional support and structuring declines. At the highest levels of employee maturity, supervisory task and social behaviours become superfluous to effective employee performance. In later editions (1982) Hersey and Blanchard provide greater precision and suggest that follower maturity can be broken down into benchmark categories of high, moderate, and low, and that appropriate leader style can be summarized in terms of a leader primarily telling, selling, participating, or delegating in relations with subordinates.

There are similarities to be drawn between Hersey and Blanchard (1982) and motivation–leadership theory—McGregor's Theory X and Y (1960), Argyris's (1957) maturity-immaturity continuum, Likert's (1967) management systems, Maslow's (1954) need hierarchy, Herzberg's (1966) two-factor theory, and McClelland's (1961) achievement theory.

Investigations of the theoretical and empirical robustness of SLT have been rare (Vecchio, 1987). Vecchio finds support for the theory in the low-maturity condition. Employees who are relatively lacking in task-relevant knowledge or commitment should require more structuring on the part of their supervisor. 'Displays of considerateness by superiors for low-maturity subordinates would be tantamount to sending improper signals to such subordinates' (1987: 449) For subordinates of moderate maturity it is unclear what style of supervision works best, and for high-maturity employees the theory is unable to predict.

Goodson *et al.*, (1989) tested the prescriptions for effective leadership as specified by Hersey and Blanchard's (1969, 1982, 1988) SLT. Their results indicate that styles involving high consideration (selling and participating) are associated consistently with higher levels of employee satisfaction. This finding closely parallels the results of several decades of research (e.g. Fleishman and Harris, 1962; Yukl, 1981). High consideration (participating) was also important or enhancing general job attitudes. But they fail to support SLT as a prescriptive theory. Yukl concludes 'Hersey and Blanchard provide little evidence in support of their theory' (1981: 143). The most valuable contribution which evolved from the SLT was its emphasis on leader flexibility or adaptability. Managers should, then, avoid making definitive judgements regarding appropriate leader behaviours that are based on the unsupported prescriptions of a largely untested leadership theory.

SOME OTHER RECENT VIEWS OF LEADERSHIP

We said earlier that charisma is a facet of leadership which cannot be taught. It is a feature of great leaders which seems to emerge regularly. Until the 1980s there was much commentary on charismatic leadership but little empirical research. Bass (1990) says that there are two attributes essential for the charismatic relationship: the leader must be a person of strong convictions, determined, self-confident, and emotionally expressive; and his or her followers must want to identify with that leader as a person, whether or not in a crisis. Whether the charismatic leader is self-aggrandizing or pro-social, he or she generates extraordinary performance in the followers.

> ## *Discussion point*
>
> How would you describe charisma and how would you try to measure it?

Bass (1985) developed a charismatic leadership scale of 10 items dealing with the behaviour of leaders and the reactions of followers. All the subjects seem to have been men. The highest correlations with charisma came from the following items:

- I have complete faith in him.
- Is a model for me to follow.
- Makes me proud to be associated with him.
- Has a special gift of seeing what it is that is really important for me to consider.
- Has a sense of mission that he transmits to me.

Maybe leadership is only about people having power? A popular way of looking at power, particularly at supervisory level, came from French and Raven (1959). In the box opposite is a list of statements that can be used to test individual's descriptions of their supervisors.

Let us look at each of the bases of power proposed in more detail, considering the issue of gender. Expert power, the ability to influence because you possess superior skills or knowledge, is more likely to be perceived as belonging to men. Referent power is charismatic power and the ability to get another to change behaviour. Referent power is again seen to be possessed more by men. A study of role models (cited in Kahn, 1984) found that while both sexes typically listed a member of their own sex as a role model, females listed a male role model 10 times more frequently than males listed a female role model.

Reward power refers to the ability to mediate rewards such as money, food, promotion, and affection in order to obtain change. Since men are more likely to work, are paid more for doing equal work, we can expect men to have more monetary reward than women and to have more reward power. The personal rewards such as affection should be equally available to men and women.

Coercive power refers to the ability to mediate punishment. Since men are, on average, larger and stronger than women and have more rewards to withhold, men typically possess more coercive power. Men also have more legitimate power as men are socialized to believe they have the right to influence and this is supported by our language, laws, and institutions which privilege the male.

Men, then, presently have more power than women in organizations and use that power to control and dominate women and thus maintain their power. Male power, especially power over females, appears to be central to many men's definitions of themselves. With power they are men; without it they are no better than women (Kahn, 1984). It is therefore unlikely that men will hand over their power as this will, for many men, mean they must hand over their self-images and the basis for their self-esteem.

My supervisor can . . .

1. *Expert power*
   Give me good technical suggestions.
   Share with me his/her considerable experience and/or training.
   Provide me with sound job-related advice.
   Provide me with needed technical knowledge.

2. *Referent Power*
   Make me feel valued.
   Make me feel like he/she approves of me.
   Makes me feel personally accepted.
   Makes me feel important.

3. *Reward Power*
   Increase my pay level.
   Influence my getting a pay rise.
   Provide me with special benefits.
   Influence my getting promotion.

4. *Coercive power*
   Give me undesirable job assignments.
   Makes my work difficult for me.
   Makes things unpleasant here.
   Make being at work distasteful.

5. *Legitimate power*
   Make me feel that I have commitments to meet.
   Make me feel like I should satisfy my job requirements.
   Give me the feeling I have responsibilities to fulfil.
   Make me recognize that I have tasks to accomplish.

Source: adapted from Hinkin and Schriesheim (1989). © American Psychological Association. Adapted by permission.

Bass (1990) has argued that power is not synonymous with leadership and the concept of power leaves unexplained much of what is involved in the leadership role. Yet power and leadership do seem to be closely connected, particularly where women are concerned. Kanter (1979) argues that women in management have found their opportunities in more routine, low-profile jobs where they have little power and responsibility. They are more likely than men to be rendered structurally powerless as they have few favours to trade, are kept out of the mainstream organization, information, and support networks, and are seen as 'different'. Many women are overprotected by more senior managers or, alternatively, given so little support that they are rendered powerless. When a woman exhibits powerlessness people assume that she does so 'because she is a woman'. A striking difference is that when a man engages in the same behaviour, people assume the behaviour is a matter of his own individual style and characteristics and so do not conclude that it reflects on the suitability of men for management.

The view of women as leaders is not all bleak; a more positive view of women as leaders and managers seems to have evolved too. There is evidence to show that females are just as successful as males in most leadership situations (e.g. Brown, 1979; Dobbins and Platz, 1986; Powell, 1988; Rice et al., 1984, Trempe et al., 1985) but the overlap persists between the stereotypes of a 'good manager' and a 'typical male'. This finding is particularly intriguing given the consistent finding that effective leader behaviour requires a blend of styles from two independent dimensions (Fleishman, 1973; Blake and Mouton, 1978). Is it therefore possible to argue that there are no differences between men and women as leaders?

There are a substantial number of studies reporting no significant gender-related difference in leadership behaviour. For example, a study of 273 female and male supervisors found no significant difference in the power bases they used to influence subordinates. They used the same three power bases in the same order: expertise, legitimate power, and reward power (Vilkinas, 1988).

Women who are experienced managers show no differences in leadership abilities from their experienced male counterparts (Caudrea, 1975). There are no differences to be found in the personal values or preferred decision-making styles of 108 male and 108 female business managers of the same age (Boulgarides, 1984). Evidence of sex differences are transitory evidence of the woman's lack of familiarity with the leadership tasks involved. With experience the sex differences disappear (Larwood and Wood, 1977). With societal change the differences in traits of men and women that are of consequence to leadership may disappear.

Stop! What are the consequences of accepting this argument? Does this mean that women's personality traits and leadership styles will become the same as those of men?

Pfeffer and Shapiro (1978) observed that managerial women are different from women in general; they are less likely to have traditional female characteristics and are more like, either by temperament or by accommodation, the stereotyped male (Hennig, 1971)—analytical, rationally oriented, and personally competitive. The interests of women leaders were found (Casey, 1975) to vary significantly from those of non-leaders. The leaders indicated a preference for positions of eminence, freedom of thought, challenge, and interpersonal contact; the non-leaders favoured artistic activities.

THE ANDROGYNOUS MANAGER IS BEST?

Studies to look at the different characteristics men and women bring to leadership roles show that a blend of masculine and feminine skills creates a more effective manager (e.g. Sargent, 1981) and that reliance on solely masculine or feminine characteristics might be counterproductive to organizational success (Bem, 1975). Sargent advocated that managers of each sex adopt 'the best' of the other sex's qualities to become more effective, androgynous managers. Individuals with androgynous gender roles are more flexible and the flexibility requirement between leadership behaviours and effectiveness is well documented in leadership theories (e.g. Bass, 1981). Spence (1992) found that those individuals who were classified as androgynous were highest in self-esteem. Cann and Siegfried (1990) say that effective leaders, those who can respond successfully to the variety of demands and situations encountered by leaders, must be behaviourally androgynous.

Exercise

Have a look at the lists of leadership qualities in the following table. How would you label the columns? Would you say that one column described feminine, one masculine, and one neutral traits? If you were a leader which traits would you have? Would there be a preponderance from one column?

Column 1	*Column 2*	*Column 3*
Ambitious	Affectionate	Adaptable
Independent	Gentle	Conscientious
Confident	Appreciative	Conventional
Aggressive	Sensitive	Helpful
Assertive	Emotional	Reliable
Dominant	Sentimental	Sincere
Forceful	Dependent	Solemn
Autocratic	Excitable	Tactful
Stern	Mild	Truthful
Tough	Submissive	Predictable
Analytical	Compassionate	Systematic
Competitive	Understanding	Efficient

Source: table adapted from Cann and Siegfried (1990) but has been selected from previous research by Bem (1974) and Williams and Bennet (1975). Column 1 is labelled masculine, 2 is feminine and 3 is neutral.

Is it possible to learn the sex-role behaviour of the opposite sex in order to perform more effectively as a manager (Sleeth and Humphreys, 1980)? There is no relationship between one sex-role behaviour and managerial success (Bem, 1974). The androgynous manager, then, one exhibiting both masculine and feminine characteristics, is likely to perform more effectively.

The study of sex-role behaviour and managerial leadership effectiveness have tended to use a self-assessment of sex-role behaviour (e.g. Moore and Rosenthal, 1984; Swenson and Ragucci, 1984). Some have suggested that the perception the subordinates have of the leader is important in understanding group effectiveness (e.g Lawless 1979). Hersey and Blanchard (1972) argued that the followers' perceptions are likely to have a strong impact on the leader's effectiveness. This is the research methodology adopted by Bushadt *et al.* (1987) who found no relationship between sex-role behaviour and leadership; they found that no universal style of sex-role behaviour was particularly effective and that followers appeared to adapt to the leader's sex-role behaviour.

Some researchers have argued that there is no difference between males and females in effectiveness but males are often evaluated as more effective in laboratory settings (see Goktepe and Scheiner, 1988). Spillman *et al.* (1981) caution that personality variables influence leadership emergence only during the initial stages of group interaction. How do men and women describe their own leadership styles?

MEN AND WOMEN BRING DIFFERENT QUALITIES TO LEADERSHIP?

Quantitative reviews of research on sex differences, primarily performed by social psychologists, have established the presence rather than the absence of overall sex differences (see Eagly, 1987; Hall, 1984). Although not usually large, these differences tend to be comparable in magnitude to most other findings reported in social psychological research. Sex appears to be a variable that has neither especially impactful nor especially weak effects on social behaviour and that produces findings consistent with people's ideas about how the sexes differ.

Rosener (1990) has differentiated between men and women's leadership performance and how they say they influence people at work. The traditional leadership style to be found in organizations she describes as male and as a command-and-control style. When asked about their leadership style, the men are more likely to describe themselves in ways that characterize 'transactional leadership'—they view job performance as a series of transactions with subordinates, exchanging rewards for services rendered or punishment for inadequate performance. The men are also more likely to use power that comes from their organizational position and formal authority.

The women respondents described themselves in ways that characterize 'transformational' leadership—getting subordinates to transform their own self-interest into the interest of the group through concern for a broader goal. They ascribe their power to personal characteristics like charisma, interpersonal skills, and hard work or personal contacts, rather than to organizational stature. Rosener called this an 'interactive' leadership style because these women actively work to make their interactions with subordinates positive for everyone involved. Women encourage participation, share power and information, enhance other people's self-worth, and infuse others with excitement about their work. All this reflects their belief that allowing employees to contribute and to feel powerful is important for a win–win situation—good for the employees and the organization.

A study of British male and female managers and their preference for one of five different leadership styles—described as traditionalist, visionary, catalyst, trouble-shooter, and negotiator, found that the largest proportion of men were traditionalist. The women, while not displaying clear preferences for any particular style, were far more likely to be catalysts or visionaries (Vinnicombe, 1987). But is this how men and women's leadership styles are perceived by the subordinates?

Research suggests that while subordinates may not perceive males and females to differ in their use of specific behaviours (Bartol, 1978; Cohen *et al.*, 1978; Day and Stogdill, 1972) subordinates often respond differently to the behaviour depending on whether it is exhibited by a male or female leader. Consideration behaviours, for example, displayed by a female rather than a male leader tend to be more favourably evaluated (Bartol and Butterfield, 1976) with subordinates reporting greater job satisfaction (Petty and Lee, 1975), greater satisfaction with their supervisor, and less propensity to leave (Petty and Miles, 1976). Women subordinates prefer a more democratic style of leadership and there is a need to improve the level of job satisfaction of women employees by increasing their perceived involvement in making decisions (Savery, 1991)

There seems to be some agreement that the styles of leadership female leaders exhibit are either accommodative (Wexley and Hunt, 1974) or affiliative (Deaux, 1976)—whereby they attempt to minimize distance between themselves and those persons with whom they interact. Women's affiliation needs are stronger than self-enhancement needs (Gilligan, 1987; Grant, 1988). Female leaders have been found to be more self-disclosing (Hyman, 1980), and have greater ease in expressing their vulnerability, their lack of self-confidence, and their emotions (Grant, 1988; Miller, 1987). They offer more positive effect, encouragement, support, and information to subordinates (Baird and Bradley, 1979), and behave in a non-assertive manner (Siegler and Siegler, 1976).

Women tend to be seen as better communicators (Hyman, 1980). In an assessment of 42 AT&T managers (Howard and Bray, 1988) women were superior in one of their oral presentations and scored slightly higher than the men on a test of verbal ability. The women also had better written communication skills. A laboratory experiment (Steckler and Rosenthal, 1985) showed that female voices were perceived to sound more competent verbally when women were speaking to their peers. Also women have been found to be superior in encoding and decoding non-verbal cues (Hall and Halberstadt, 1981). Howard and Bray (1988) found that their women subjects were judged as more sensitive and socially objective.

Women have more co-operative behaviour, something important in terms of consultation and democratic decision-making processes (Grant, 1988). They perceive power differently to men, less as domination or ability to control and more as a liberating force in the community (Grant, 1988; Hartsock, 1983; Kilpatrick, 1975). Women, then, are more oriented than men towards a democratic or participative leadership style. They are expected to be non-aggressive (Hilgard and Atkinson, 1967) and to be concerned for the welfare of others (Miner, 1965).

In contrast, male leaders are said to tend to maintain distance in order to assert status (Denmark, 1977). Men more frequently initiate non-reciprocated touching of women which declares their dominance and higher status. They employ a style referred to as instrumental, task oriented, or structuring, while female leaders employ a socio-emotional orientation or a style of consideration. Male leaders are more dominant, self-assured, directive, precise, and quicker to challenge the ideas of others (Baird and Bradley, 1979).

One explanation for this comes for the sex-role congruency hypothesis on the perceived congruence between sex-role norms and the leader style exhibited (Nieva and Gutek, 1981). Subordinates may react more favourably to consideration behaviours demonstrated by a female leader because the behaviours may be seen to be more congruent with a feminine role. For female supervision, the more traditionally incongruent the situation, the more unfavourable the reaction (Cohen et al., 1978). Subordinates may have, then, different expectations of the behaviours appropriated and appropriate situations for male and female leaders. They will, for example, respond favourably when the leader's style is consistent with the expectations and unfavourably when the leader's style is incongruent with the expectations. Yet there is little research to demonstrate this conclusively (Russell et al., 1988).

There are studies which contradict the stereotypical view of men and women's differing management styles. Ferrarrio (1990), for example, in a study of 124 female and 95 male managers, found that despite the widely held assumption that women are more people oriented and men more task oriented, the women obtained significantly higher self-report scores on both dimensions of consideration and initiating structure. Scase and Goffee (1990) have argued that the preferred managerial styles of both men and women are inevitably linked to prevailing fashions about effective management. In the 1980s more assertive interpersonal skills became highly valued. Consequently the pressures facing women managers may have encouraged them to be more directive and autocratic. Eighty eight per cent of those women managers in their survey referred to the need to be tough, aggressive, firm, and assertive, while less than 50 per cent mentioned the desirability of a more open, co-operative, and consultative approach.

It may be that a laboratory setting produces stereotypical results (Eagly and Johnson, 1990). Having reviewed 162 studies of leadership and gender, Eagly and Johnson concluded that men and women do not differ in style (task oriented or interpersonally oriented) in organizational studies. However, these aspects of leadership style were more gender stereotypic in laboratory experiments and assessment studies. Women were found to adopt a more democratic or participative style and a less autocratic or directive style than men. Women's social skills might enable them to perform managerial roles differently than men. Interpersonal behaviour that is skilful, in terms of understanding other's feelings and intentions, should facilitate a managerial style that is democratic and participative (see Johnson, 1993 for a fuller discussion of the conditions under which male and female leaders may act similarly and why).

Women may be adopting differing roles as a response to cultural reservations about their capability for leadership. Further, they may adopt the collaborative mode to win acceptance from others, gain self-confidence, and thereby be effective. As we saw earlier, women who are assertive and aggressive can be unpopular.

In marriage men generally occupy the role of leader and women the role of follower. Gerber (1988) tested the hypothesis that these leader–follower roles determine the way in which gender stereotype traits are assigned to men and women. In one situation the man was described as the leader in the marriage, in another the traditional power relationship was reversed and the woman was described as the leader. Regardless of sex, the leader was perceived as strong in agency and weak in communion (agency = defends one's own beliefs, independent, assertive, has strong personality, forceful, has leadership abilities, willing to take risks, makes decisions easily, dominant, willing to take a stand, aggressive, acts as a leader, individualistic, ambitious; communion = cheerful, affectionate, sympathetic, sensitive to the needs of others, understanding, compassionate, eager to soothe hurt feelings, warm, tender, loves children, and is gentle). The follower was perceived as strong in communion and weak in agency. A man and a woman who were described as equal leaders did not differ in the strength of their agentic and communal traits (For a critique of agency and communion, see Wetherell, 1986.)

IT ALL DEPENDS ...?

Eskilson and Wiley (1976) found that both men and women assumed leadership roles more easily and effectively when their followers were of the same gender as the leader. The women had the most difficulty leading men because the men would not allow the leader to exercise her authority. The men had the most difficulty leading mixed gender groups as the men would compete by challenging the leader's suggestions. The context of leadership determines the salience of sex-role stereotypes in task situations.

Much seems to have to do with the situation and whether you are a subordinate or superior. From the point of view of a superior, masculine traits are valued more highly; superiors perceive a need for highly directed behaviours. From a subordinate's position the highly valued traits are feminine qualities, emphasizing the employee-oriented aspects of leader's behaviour. Subordinates, as the primary beneficiaries of employee-centred behaviours, are more concerned with consideration from their leaders. Superiors, on the other hand, value the more directive or structuring behaviours designed to ensure task completion (Cann and Siegfried, 1987).

A study of the impact of gender on learning in groups (Correa et al., 1988) found that those who worked with women consultants reported higher levels of learning despite these consultants being younger and less experienced than their male counterparts. Earlier, Reed (1979) had found that, in experiential training, although groups led by women were considered more stressful than those led by men, participants of both genders felt they learned more in self-study groups led by women. Thus when it comes to learning in groups, women may be more appropriate leaders, though this was not, as we have noted, the conclusion of Wright (1976)!

We saw earlier, in Chapter 2, how important it was to understand how people look. In the leadership literature the theme arises again. How people look will affect how they are expected to be as leaders. Physically attractive individuals are believed to be more socially skilled and more successful (Miller, 1970; Dion et al., 1972). Individuals who look mature are believed to be more socially, physically, and intellectually competent (Berry and McArthur, 1985). These schemata are consistent with people's expectations that the leader be ambitious, competent, and socially skilled (Lord et al., 1984). It seems as though more attractive and mature-faced individuals emerge as leaders (Cherulnik et al., 1990). These findings challenge the view that the search for traits that differentiate leaders from non-leaders has been futile.

Stop reading for a moment and picture a socially skilled, physically attractive, successful, and intellectually competent person. Then ask yourself, what gender are they?

What can be concluded? Should we say that expecting women to be equal in leadership can be described as akin to 'waiting for fish to grow feet'? (Alimo-Metcalfe, 1994)? Can differences in leadership style produce differences in effectiveness? Experts on leader effectiveness ordinarily maintain that effectiveness of leadership styles is contingent on the features of the group or organizational environment (Fiedler, 1967; Vroom and Yetton, 1973), and it cannot be concluded that one style is any greater advantage or disadvantage. No doubt a democratic style enhances a leader's effectiveness under some conditions and an autocratic style enhances it under other circumstances.

Recently, however management consultants have criticized traditional management practices for being over-hierarchical and rigidly bureaucratic (Kanter, 1983; Ouchi, 1981; Peters and Waterman, 1982). Employment would be less alienating if workplaces were less hierarchical and were characterized by co-operation and collaboration between collegial groups of co-workers. Organizational theorists such as Handy (1989) and Kanter (1989) maintain that large organizations will become smaller, flatter, and decentralized, relying on people working across functions to work in project teams where there will be an emphasis on informal open communication. Organizational change is advocated towards the more democratic and participative leadership styles that Eagly and Johnson's (1990) analysis of leadership studies shows to be more prevalent among women than men.

This is not, as Alimo-Metcalfe (1993) has noted, simply a vision of the future but is already a reality. Barnham *et al.*, (1988) undertook a survey of leading-edge companies in Europe and their findings paint a picture of managers as developers, encouraging informal communication and adopting a participative style. Leaders need to be visionaries encouraging change and challenge to the status quo, transforming cultures and people, making them co-operative, caring, and receptive. These are qualities closely associated with women (Vinnicombe, 1987; Rosener, 1990).

What can we conclude about men and women in leadership. Perhaps we should give up this view of women leaders being in a culture trap in which they and men are socialized for certain roles and say that managers need male characteristics. Instead we need to look at some women as having positive qualities that complement and enhance those more masculine traits exhibited by the androgynous men and women then look towards the reality of women's everyday lives. Focus on how well women make do in spite of all the obstacles set up by work, families, and the wider society, and how that remains invisible from the discourse about women. Instead of looking at women's failure to cope, look at what they cope with. The very prevalence of an analysis that has passed such negative judgements and blame on women reflects the domination of the 'oppressor's language', or more accurately, the oppressor's method of speaking over the discourse (Smith, 1982). We need to understand more of the behaviour of female managers, not by some sex-related variable, but by their work conditions, which apply equally to men (Hale, 1987).

Perhaps we should consider giving up social action and organization based on hierarchy and therefore surrender the use of concepts such as leader and subordinate? Co-operatives, social movement organizations, and some parts of the voluntary sector are places where the differentials between members can be reduced. Helen Brown (1992) describes situations where there is a commitment to egalitarian values and where there is the intention to organize without hierarchy and leaders. But non-hierarchical organization does not occur spontaneously. Social orders based on collectivist-democratic and non-hierarchical forms of co-operation have to be constantly negotiated and struggled for to create forms of organization which embody and enhance the values of collectivism (Brown, 1992). There does seem to be some emphasis in the organizational literature on promoting 'flatter', less hierarchical forms of organization which emphasize autonomy, flexibility, and collaboration (Barnham *et al.*, 1988; Morgan, 1986).

Discussion point

Would the sexual stereotypes—women fail to assert themselves, women fear success and are unable to speak in public—apply to the women in your group? If the theories do not apply, why are we still using them?

An alternative is to note how there is a myth of leadership which claims to represent knowledge about what leadership is and what leaders do. Deconstructing leadership permits us to question the limits of our knowledge of the concept of leadership and look at how the concept is presented in the literature on organizations. Calas and Smircich (1991), through using feminist deconstructive strategies, have shown how organizational leadership has been sustained as a seductive game. Leadership, they say, is a form of seduction and a game. Examining the rhetoric of the leadership literature exposes the seductive game. They take the work of Barnard, McGregor, Mintzberg and Peters, and Waterman and show how the texts trace a circle of seduction. With this comes a constant recycling of a masculine self-image; the male writers reproduce strong manifestations of the homosocial order by repeating seduction as truth. Calas and Smircich ask if this homosocial, élitist, monologic leadership is the desired seduction for organized life at present. Henry Mintzberg, in a letter which follows the Calas and Smircich (1991) article, produces an interesting reply.

Let us look in some more detail at the features of personality that might affect leadership, being a manager, or just help understand more about behaviour in organizations.

———————————— *Review Questions* ————————————

Should managers be men?

What does it take to be a good leader? Is having the right traits or qualities what counts?

Is it possible to reveal the nature of what might constitute a 'good leader' through the systematic empirical investigation of the attitudes and behaviour of leaders?

Are managerial women or women who are leaders different from women in general?

What effect does the structure of organizations have on women as leaders?

What style should a woman manager adopt and what will be the advantages and disadvantages of any one style?

REFERENCES

ALDAG, R. J. and BRIEF, A. P. (1981) *Managing Organizational Behaviour*, West Publishing, St Paul, MN.

ALIMO-METCALFE, B. (1993) 'Women in Management: Organizational Socialization and Assessment Practices that Prevent Career Advancement', *International Journal of Selection and Assessment*, 1(2), 68–83.

ALIMO-METCALFE, B. (1994) 'Waiting for Fish to Grow Feet! Removing Organizational Barriers to Women's Entry into Leadership Positions', Chapter 2 in M. Tanton (ed.), *Women in Management: A Developing Presence*, Routledge, London.

ARGYRIS, C. (1957) *Personality and Organization*, Harper & Row, New York.

ASHRIDGE MANAGEMENT COLLEGE (1988) 'Management for the Future', Ashridge Management Research Group/Foundation for Management Education.

BAIRD, J. E. and BRADLEY, P. H. (1979) 'Styles of Management and Communication: A Comparative Study of Men and Women', *Communication Monographs*, **46**, 101–111.

BARNHAM, K., FRASER, J. and HEATH, L. (1988) 'Management for the Future', Ashridge Management Research Group/Foundation for Management Education, cited in Alimo-Metcalfe (1993).

BARTOL, K. M. (1978) 'The Sex Structuring of Organizations: A Search for Possible Causes', *Academy of Management Review*, **3**, 805–815.

BARTOL, K. M. and BUTTERFIELD, D. A. (1976) 'Sex Effects in Evaluating Leaders', *Journal of Applied Psychology*, **61**, 446–545.

BARTOL, K. M. and MARTIN, D. C. (1986) 'Women and Men in Task Groups', in R. D. Ashmore and F. K. Del Boca (eds.), *The Social Psychology of Female-Male Relations: A Critical Analyses of Central Concepts*, Academic Press, London.

BASS, B. M. (1981) *Stogdill's Handbook of Leadership: A Survey of Theory and Research*, Free Press, New York.

BASS, B. M. (1985) *The Multifactor Leadership Questionnaire—Form 5*, State University of New York, reported in Bass (1990).

BASS, B. M. (1990) *Bass and Stogdill's Handbook of Leadership*, Free Press, New York.

BEAUVAIS, C. (1976) 'The Family and the Work Group: Dilemmas for women in authority', unpublished doctoral dissertation, City University of New York.

BEM, S. L. (1974) 'The Measurement of Psychological Androgyny', *Journal of Consulting and Clinical Psychology*, **42**, 155–162.

BEM, S. L. (1975) 'Sex Role Adaptability: One Consequence of Psychological Androgyny', *Journal of Personality and Social Psychology*, **31**(4), 634–643.

BERRY, D. S. and MCARTHUR, L. Z. (1985) 'Some Components and Consequences of a Babyface', *Journal of Personality and Social Psychology*, **9**, 272–279.

BLAKE, R. R. and MOUTON, J. S. (1964, 1978) *The New Managerial Grid*, Gulf, Houston.

BOWMAN, G. W., WORTHY, N. B. and GREYSER, S. (1965) 'Are Women Executives Really People?', *Harvard Business Review*, **43** (July-August), 14–17.

BOULGARIDES, J. D. (1984) 'A Comparison of Male and Female Business Managers', *Leadership and Organizational Development Journal*, **5**(5), 27–31.

BOURANTAS, D. and PAPALEXANDRIS, N. (1991) 'Sex Differences in Leadership: Leadership Styles and Subordinate Satisfaction', *Journal of Managerial Psychology*, **5**(5), 7–10.

BRENNER, O. C., TOMKIEWICZ, J. and SCHEIN, V. E. (1989) 'The Relationship Between Sex Role Stereotypes and Requisite Management Characteristics Revisited', *Academy of Management Journal*, **32**, 662–669.

BROVERMAN, I. K., BROVERMAN, D. M., CLARKSON, F. E., ROSENKRANZ, P. S. and VOGEL, S. R. (1970) 'Sex Role Stereotypes and Clinical Judgements of Mental Health', *Journal of Consulting and Clinical Psychology*, **34**, 1–7.

BROVERMAN, I. K. VOGEL, S. R., BROVERMAN, D. M., CLARKSON, F. E. and ROSENKRANZ, P. S. (1972) 'Sex Role Stereotypes: A Current Appraisal', *Journal of Social Issues*, **25**(2), 59–78.

BROWN, H. (1992) *Women Organising*, Routledge, London.

BROWN, R. (1965) *Social Psychology*, Free Press, New York.

BROWN, S. M. (1979) 'Male Versus Female Leaders: A Comparison of Empirical Studies', *Sex Roles*, **5**, 595–611.

BRYMAN, A. (1987) 'The Generalizability of Implicit Leadership Theory', *Journal of Social Psychology*, **127**(2), 129–141.

BUSHARDT, S. C., FOWLER, A. and CAVENY, R. (1987) 'Sex-role Behaviour and Leadership: An Empirical Investigation', *Leadership and Organizational Development Journal*, **8**(5), 13–17.

CALAS, M. B. and SMIRCICH, L. (1991) 'Voicing Seduction to Silence Leadership', *Organization Studies*, **12**(4), 567–601.

CANN, A. and SIEGFRIED, W. D. (1987) 'Sex Stereotypes and the Leadership Role', *Sex Roles*, **17**, 401–408.

CANN, A. and SIEGFRIED, W. D. (1990) 'Gender Stereotypes and Dimensions of Effective Leader Behaviour', *Sex Roles*, **23**(7/8), 413–419.

CASEY, T. J. (1975) 'The Development of a Leadership Orientation Scale on the SVIB for Women', *Measurement and Evaluation Guide*, **8**, 96–100.

CAUDREA, P. A. (1975) 'Investigations of Sex Differences Across Job Levels', *Dissertation Abstracts International*, **36**, 1957B.

CECIL, E. A., PAUL, R. J. and OLINS, R. A. (1973) 'Perceived Importance of Selected Variables Used to Evaluate Male and Female Job Applicants', *Personnel Psychology*, **26**, 397–404.

CHERULNIK, P. D., TURNS, L. C. and WILDERMAN, S. K. (1990) 'Physical Appearance and Leadership: Exploring the Role of Appearance-based Attribution in Leader Emergence', *Journal of Applied Social Psychology*, **20**(18), 1530–1539.

CIXOUS, H. (1981) 'Castration or Decapitation', *Journal of Women in Culture and Society*, **7**(1), 41–55.

COHEN, S. L., BUNKER, K. A., BURTON, A. L. and MCMANUS, P. D. (1978) 'Reactions of Male Subordinates to the Sex Role Congruency of Immediate Supervision', *Sex Roles*, **4**(2), 297–311.

CORREA, M. E., KLEIN, E. B., STONE, W. N., ASTRACHAN, J. H., KOSSEK, E. E. and KOMARRAJU, M. (1988) 'Reactions to Women in Authority: The Impact of Gender on Learning in Group Relations Conferences', *Journal of Applied Behavioural Science*, **24**(3), 219–233.

COSTRICH, N., FEINSTEIN, J., KIDDER, L., MARECEK, J. and PASCALE, L. (1975) 'When Stereotypes Hurt: Three Studies of Penalties for Sex Role Reversals', *Journal of Experimental Social Psychology*, **11**, 520–530.

CROSBY, B. C. (1988) 'Women: New Images of Leadership', *Social Policy*, **19**, 40–44.

DAVIDSON, M. J. and COOPER, C. L. (1983) *Stress and the Woman Manager*, Martin Robertson, Oxford.

DAY, D. R. and STOGDILL, R. M. (1972) 'Leader Behaviour of Male and Female Supervisors: A Comparative Study', *Personnel Psychology*, **25**, 353–360.

DEAUX, K. (1976) *The Behaviour of Women and Men*, Brooks/Cole, Monterey, Calif.

DENMARK, F. L. (1977) 'Styles of Leadership', *Psychology of Women Quarterly*, **2**, 99–113.

DENMARK, F., RUSSO, N. F., FRIEZE, I. H. and SECHZER, J. A. (1988) 'Guidelines for Avoiding Sexism in Psychological Research: A Report of the Ad Hoc Committee on Nonsexist Research', *American Psychologist*, **43**, 582–85.

DION, K. (1985) 'Sex, Gender and Groups: Selected Issues', in V.O'Leary, R. K. Unger and B. Strudler-Wallston (eds.), *Women, Gender and Social Psychology*, Erlbaum, Hillsdale, NJ.

DION, K. K., BERSCHEID, E. and WALSTER, E. (1972) 'What is Beautiful is Good', *Journal of Personality and Social Psychology*, **24**, 285–290.

DOBBINS, G. H. and PLATZ, S. J. (1986) 'Sex Differences in Leadership: How Real are They?', *Academy of Management Journal*, **11**, 118–127.

EAGLY, A. H. (1987) *Sex Differences in Social Behaviour: A Social-role Interpretation*, Erlbaum, Hillsdale, NJ.

EAGLY, A. H. and JOHNSON, B. T. (1990) 'Gender and Leadership Style: A Meta-Aanalysis', *Psychological Bulletin*, **108**(2), 233–256.

ELSHTAIN, J. B. (1981) *Public Man, Private Woman*, Martin Robertson, Oxford.

ESKILSON, A. and WILEY, M. G. (1976) 'Sex Composition and Leadership in Small Groups', *Sociometry*, **39**, 183–194.

FERRARIO, M. (1990) 'Leadership Style of British Men and Women Managers', unpublished M.Sc. Dissertation, University of Manchester, Faculty of Management Science, cited in B. Alimo-Metcalfe, 'Women in Management: Organizational Socialization and Assessment Practices that Prevent Career Advancement', *International Journal of Selection and Assessment*, **1**(2), 68–83 (1993).

FIEDLER, F. E. (1964) 'A Contingency Model of Leadership Effectiveness', in L. Berkowitz (ed.), *Advances in Experimental Social Psychology*, vol. 1, pp. 150–199, Academic Press, New York.

FIEDLER, F. E. (1967) *A Theory of Leadership Effectiveness*, McGraw-Hill, New York.

FLEISHMAN, E. A. (1973) 'Twenty Years of Consideration and Structure', in E. A. Fleishman and J. G. Hunt (eds), *Current Developments in the Study of Leadership*, Southern Illinois University, Carbondale, Ill.

FLEISHMAN, E. A. and HARRIS, E. F. (1962) 'Patterns of Leadership Behaviour Related to Employee Grievance and Turnover', *Personnel Psychology*, **15**, 43–56.

FRENCH, J. R. P. and RAVEN, B. (159) 'The Bases of Social Power', in D. Cartwright (ed.), *Studies in Social Power*, University of Michigan, Institute of Social Research, Ann Arbor, Mich.

GERBER, G. L. (1988) Leadership Roles and the Gender Stereotype Traits', *Sex Roles*, **18**(11/12), 649–668.

GILLIGAN, C. (1987) *In a Different Voice: Psychological Theory and Women's Development*, Harvard University Press, New Haven, Conn.

GILMER, B. (1961) *Industrial Psychology*, McGraw-Hill, New York.

GOKTEPE, J. R. and SCHNEIER, C. E. (1988) 'Sex and Gender Effects in Evaluating Emergent Leaders in Small Groups', *Sex Roles*, **19**(1/2), 29–35.

GOLDBERG, P. (1968) 'Are Some Women Prejudiced Against Women?' *Transaction*, April, 28–30.

GOODSON, J. R., MCGEE, G. W. and CASHMAN, J. F. (1989) 'Situational Leadership Theory: A Test of Leadership Prescriptions', *Group and Organization Studies*, **14**(4), 446–461.

GRANT, J. (1988) 'Women as Managers: What They Can Offer to Organizations', *Organizational Dynamics*, **16**, 23, 56–64.

HALE, S. M. (1987) 'The Documentary Construction of Female Mismanagement', *Canadian Review of Sociology and Anthropology*, **24**(4), 489–513.

HALL, J. (1976) 'To Achieve or Not: The Manager's Choice', *California Management Review*, **18**, 5–18.

HALL, J. A. (1984) *Nonverbal Sex Differences: Communication Accuracy and Expressive Style*, Johns Hopkins University, Baltimore, Md.

HALL, J. A. and HALBERSTADT, A. G. (1981) 'Sex Roles and Nonverbal Communication Skills', *Sex Roles*, **7**, 273–287.

HALPIN, A. W. and WINER, B. J. (1957) 'A Factorial Study of the Leader Behavior Descriptions', in R. M. Stogdill and A. E. Coons (eds.), *Leader Behavior: Its Description and Measurement*, pp. 39–51, Bureau of Business Research, Ohio State University, OH.

HANDY, C. (1989) *The Age of Unreason*, Penguin Business Books, London.

HARRIMAN, A. (1985) *Women/Men Management*, Praeger, New York.

HARTSOCK, N. (1983) *Money, Sex and Power*, Northeastern University Press, Boston, MA.

HEMPHILL, J. K. and COONS, A. E. (1957) Development of the Leader Behavior Description Questionnaire in R. M. Stogdill and A. E. Coons (eds.) *Leader Behavior: Its description and measurement*, pp. 39–51, Bureau of Business Research, Ohio State University, OH.

HENNIG, M. (1971) 'What Happens on the Way Up' *MBA*, March, 8–10.

HERSEY, P. and BLANCHARD, K. (1969) 'Life-cycle Theory of Leadership', *Training and Development Journal*, **23**, 26–34.

HERSEY, P. and BLANCHARD, K. H. (1973) *Leader Effectiveness and Adaptability Description-self*, Center for Leadership Studies, Escondido, Calif.

HERSEY, P. and BLANCHARD, K. (1972, 1982) *Management of Organizational Behaviour: Utilizing Human Resources*, Prentice Hall, Englewood Cliffs, NJ.

HERZBERG, F. (1966) *Work and the Nature of Man*, World Publishing, New York.

HILGARD, E. and ATKINSON, R. (1967) *Introduction to Psychology*, Harcourt Brace and World, New York.

HINKIN, T. R. and SCHRIESHEIM, C. A. (1989) 'Development and Applications of New Scales to Measure the French and Raven (1959) Bases of Social Power', *Journal of Applied Psychology*, **74**, 561–567.

HOUSE, R. J. (1971) 'A Path-goal Theory of Leadership Effectiveness', *Administrative Science Quarterly*, **16**, 334–338.

HOWARD, A. and BRAY, D. W. (1988) *Managerial Lives in Transition: Advancement in Age and Changing Times*, Guildford Press, New York.

HYMAN, B. (1980) 'Responsive Leadership: The Woman Manager's Asset or Liability?', *Supervisory Management*, **25**, 40–43.

JENKINS, W. O. (1947) 'A Review of Leadership Studies with Particular Reference to Military Problems', *Psychological Bulletin*, **44**, 54–79.

JOHNSON, C. (1993) 'Gender and Formal Authority', *Social Psychology Quarterly*, **56**(3), 193–210.

KAHN, A. (1984) 'The Power War: Male Response to Power Loss Under Equality', *Psychology of Women Quarterly*, **8**(3), Spring, 235–246.

KANTER, R. M. (1977) *Men and Women of the Corporation*, Basic Books, New York.

KANTER, R. M. (1979) 'Power Failure in Management Circuits', *Harvard Business Review*, **57**(4), 65–75.

KANTER, R. M. (1983) *The Change Masters: Innovations for Productivity in the American Corporation*, Simon & Schuster, New York.

KANTER, R. M. (1989) *When Giants Learn to Dance*, Simon & Schuster, London.

KILPATRICK, J. (1975) *Political Women*, Basic Books, New York.

LARWOOD, L. and WOOD, M. M. (1977) *Women in Management*, Lexington Books, Lexington, Mass.

LAWLESS, D. J. (1979) *Organizational Behavior: The Psychology of Effective Management*, Prentice Hall, Englewood Cliffs, NJ.

LEWIN, K. and LIPPITT, R. (1938) 'An Experimental Approach to the Study of Autocracy and Democracy: A Preliminary Note', *Sociometry*, **1**, 292–300.

LIKERT, R. (1961) *New Patterns of Management*, McGraw-Hill, New York.

LIKERT, R. (1967) *The Human Organization*, McGraw-Hill, New York.

LORBER, J. (1984) *Women Physicians: Status and Power*, Methuen, London and New York.

LORD, R. G., FOTI, R. J. and DEVADER, C. (1984) 'A Test of Leadership Categorization Theory: Internal Structure, Information Processing and Leadership Perceptions', *Organizational Behaviour and Human Performance*, **34**, 343–378.

MCCLELLAND, D. C. (1961) *The Achieving Society*, Van Nostrand, Princeton, NJ.

MCGREGOR, D. (1960) *The Human Side of Enterprise*, McGraw-Hill, New York.

MANT, A. (1983) *Leaders We Deserve*, Martin Robertson, Oxford.

MARTIN, P. Y., HARRISON, D. and DINITTO, D. (1983) Advancement for Women in Hierarchical Organizations: A Multi-level Analysis of Problems and Prospects', *Journal of Applied Behavioural Science*, **19**, 19–33.

MASLOW, A. (1954) *Motivation and Personality*, Harper & Row, New York.

MILLER, A. G. (1970) 'Role of Physical Attractiveness in Impression Formation', *Psychometric Science*, **19**, 241–243.

MILLER, I. B. (1987) *Toward a New Psychology of Women*, Boston Press, Boston, Mass.

MINER, J. (1965) *Studies in Management Education*, Springer-Verlag, New York.

MOORE, S. M. and ROSENTHAL, D. A. (1984) 'Balance Versus Effects Androgyny: Their Relationship to Adjustment in Three Ethnic Groups', *Psychological Reports*, **54**, 475–481.

MORGAN, G. (1986) *Images of Organization*, Sage, Beverley Hills, Calif.

MUSSEN, P. H. (1969) 'Early Sex Role Development', in D. Goslin (ed.), *Handbook of Socialization Theory and Research*, pp. 703–731, Rand McNally, New York.

NIEVA, V. F. and GUTEK, B. A. (1981) *Women and Work: A Psychological Perspective*, Praeger, New York.

O'BRIEN, M. (1981) *The Politics of Reproduction*, Routledge & Kegan Paul, Boston.

OSBORN, R. N. and VICARS, W. M. (1976) 'Sex Stereotypes: An Artifact in Leader Behaviour and Subordinate Satisfaction Analysis?', *Academy of Management Journal*, **19**, 439–449.

OUCHI, W. G. (1981) *Theory Z: How American Business Can Meet the Japanese Challenge*, Addison-Wesley, Reading, Mass.

PETERS, T. J. and WATERMAN, R. H. (1982) *In Search of Excellence: Lessons from America's Best Run Companies*, Harper & Row, New York.

PETTY, M. M. and LEE, G. K. (1975) 'Moderating Effects of Sex of Supervisor and Subordinate on Relationships between Supervisory Behaviour and Subordinate Satisfaction', *Journal of Personality and Social Psychology*, **60**, 624–628.

PETTY, M. M. and MILES, R. H. (1976) 'Leader Sex-role Stereotyping in a Female Dominated Work Culture', *Personnel Psychology*, **29**, 393–404.

PFEFFER, P. and SHAPIRO, S. J. (1978) 'Personal Differences in Male and Female MBA Candidates', *Business Quarterly*, **43**, 77–80.

PHILLIPS, J. S. (1984) 'The Accuracy of Leadership Ratings: A Cognitive Categorization Perspective', *Organizational Behaviour and Human Performance*, **33**, 125–138.

POWELL, G. N. (1988) *Women and Men in Management*, Sage, Newbury Park, Calif.

POWELL, G. N. and BUTTERFIELD, D. A. (1979) 'The "Good Manager": Masculine or Androgynous?', *Academy of Management Journal*, **22**, 395–403.

POWELL, G. N. and BUTTERFIELD, D. A. (1984) 'If "Good Managers" are Masculine, What are Bad Managers?', *Sex Roles*, **10**, 477–484.

POWELL, G. N. and BUTTERFIELD, D. A. (1989) 'The "Good Manager": Did Androgeny Fare Better in the 1980s?', *Group and Organization Studies*, **14**, 216–233.

REDDIN, W. J. (1967) 'The 3–D Management Style Theory', *Training and Development Journal*, **21**, 8–17.

REED, B. G. (1979) 'Differential Reactions by Male and Female Group Members to a Group Experience in the Presence of Male and Female Authority Figures', unpublished doctoral dissertation, University of Cincinnati.

REED, B. G. (1981) 'Gender Issues in Training Group Leaders', *Journal for Specialists in Group Work*, **6**, 161–170.

RICE, R. W., INSTONE, D. and ADAMS, J. (1984) 'Leader Sex, Leader Success and Leadership Process: Two Field Studies', *Journal of Applied Psychology*, **69**, 12–31.

ROSENER, J. B. (1990) 'Ways Women Lead', *Harvard Business Review*, November–December, 119–125.

RUSSELL, J. E. A., RUSH, M. C. and HERD, A. (1988) 'An Exploration of Women's Expectations of Effective Male and Female Leadership', *Sex Roles*, **18**(5/6), 279–287.

SARGENT, A. G. (1981) *The Androgynous Manager*, AMACOM, a division of the American Management Association, New York.

SAVERY, L. (1991) 'Perceived and Preferred Styles of Leadership', *Journal of Managerial Psychology*, **6**(1), 28–32.

SCASE, R. and GOFFEE, R. (1990) 'Women in Management: Towards a Research Agenda', *International Journal of Human Resource Management*, **1**(1), 107–125.

SCHEIN, V. E. (1973) 'Relationship between Sex Role Stereotypes and Requisite Management Characteristics', *Journal of Applied Psychology*, **57** (April), 95–100.

SCHEIN, V. E. (1975) 'The Relationship Between Sex Role Stereotypes and Requisite Management Characteristics Among Female Managers', *Journal of Applied Psychology*, **60**, 340–344.

SIEGLER, D. and SIEGLER, R. (1976) 'Stereotypes of Males' and Females' Speech', *Psychological Reports*, **39**, 167–170.

SLEETH, R. G. and HUMPHREYS, L. W. (1980) 'Influence on Managerial Attitudes: Sex and Androgeny', *Proceedings of the Southern Management Association*, pp. 269–271.

SMITH, D. E. (1982) 'Women and the Politics of Professionalism', mimeograph, quoted in Hale (1987).

SMITH, H. L. and KREUGER, L. M. (1933) 'A Brief Summary of Literature on Leadership', *Bulletin School Education Indiana University*, **9**, 4.

SPENCE, J. (1992) Study quoted in H. Crowley and S. Himmelweit (eds), *Knowing Women, Feminism and Knowledge*, p. 24, Open University Press, Milton Keynes.

SPILLMAN, B., SPILLMAN, R. and REINKING, K. (1981) 'Leadership Emergence: Dynamic Analysis of the Effects of Sex and Androgeny', *Small Group Behaviour*, **12**(2), 139–157.

STECKLER, N. A. and ROSENTHAL, R. (1985) 'Sex Differences in Nonverbal and Verbal Communication with Bosses, Peers and Subordinates', *Journal of Applied Psychology*, **70**, 157–163.

STOGDILL, R. M. (1948) 'Personal Factors Associated with Leadership: A Survey of the Literature', *Journal of Psychology*, **25**, 35–71.

SWAN, E. (1994) 'Managing Emotion', Chapter 6 in M. Tanton (ed.), *Women in Management: A Developing Presence*, Routledge, London.

SWENSON, E. V. and RAGUCCI, R. (1984) 'Effects of Sex-role Stereotypes and Androgynous Alternatives on Mental Judgements of Psychotherapists', *Psychological Reports*, **54**, 475–481.

TANNENBAUM, R. and SCHMIDT, W. H. (1958) 'How to Choose and Leadership Pattern', *Harvard Business Review*, **36**(2), 95–101.

TREMPE, J., RIGNEY, A. and HACCOUN, R. (1985) 'Subordinate Satisfaction with Male and Female Managers: Role of Perceived Supervisory Influence', *Journal of Applied Psychology*, **70**, 44–47.

VECCHIO, R. P. (1987) 'Situational Leadership Theory: An Examination of a Prescriptive Theory', *Journal of Applied Psychology*, **72**(3), 444–451.

VILKINAS, T. (1988) 'Do Women Use Different Influences?', *Women in Management Review*, **3**(3), 155–160.

VINNICOMBE, S. (1987) 'What Exactly are the Differences in Male and Female Working Styles?', *Women in Management Review*, **3**(1), 13–21.

VROOM, V. H. and JAGO, A. G. (1984) 'Leadership and Decision Making: A Revised Normative Model', paper, Academy of Management, Boston, Mass.

VROOM, V. H. and YETTON, P. W. (1973) *Leadership and Decision Making*, University of Pittsburgh Press, Pittsburgh, Penn.

WETHERELL, M. (1986) 'Linguistic Repertoires and Literary Criticism: New Direction for a Social Psychology of Gender', Chapter 5 in S. Wilkinson (ed.), *Feminist Social Psychology: Developing Theory and Practice*, Open University Press, Milton Keynes.

WEXLEY, K. N. and HUNT, P. J. (1974) 'Male and Female Leaders: Comparison of Performance and Behavior Patterns', *Psychological Reports*, **35**, 867–872.

WILLIAMS, J. E. and BENNETT, S. M. (1975) 'The Definition of Sex Stereotypes via the Adjective Checklist', *Sex Roles*, **1**, 327–337.

WRIGHT, F. (1976) 'The Effects of Style and Sex of Consultants in Self-study Groups', *Small Group Behaviour*, **7**, 433–456.

YUKL, G. A. (1981) *Leadership in Organizations*, Prentice Hall, Englewood Cliffs, NJ.

ZALEZNIK, A. (1992) 'Managers and Leaders: Are They Different?', *Harvard Business Review*, March–April, 126–135.

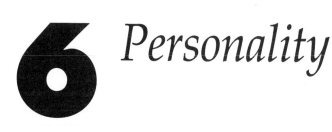

6 *Personality*

We have seen how men and women have learned to be different. What differences in personality could we observe? What features of men and women's personalities might it be useful to examine in order to understand more about behaviour in organizations? In Chapter 5 we touched on some of the personality features that contribute to differences between men and women in leadership styles and behaviours. In this chapter we build on that work and look at other aspects of personality.

We looked at how women were perceived and how they perceive themselves in Chapter 2. We have seen in Chapter 4 on motivation that an individual's need for achievement, which is a feature of a person's personality, can contribute to their motivation. It appears to be common sense to believe that the perceptions you hold about yourself affect what you do and how you behave. If you think of yourself as successful, you will act in ways which bring you success (Deaux, 1976). If you believe in yourself and your abilities, this will bring success. Psychologists have tested this idea through defining self-efficacy. Self-efficacy, the conviction you have in yourself and your abilities to exercise control, can effect how you feel, think, and act. An optimistic sense of personal efficacy has been identified as a precursor to human attainment and positive well-being (Bandura, 1986). The stronger a person's self-efficacy, the more career options they will think possible, the greater the interest they show in them, and the better prepared educationally they become for the different options (Betz and Hackett, 1986).

Personality inventories test self-esteem, self-acceptance and self-confidence. There are no consistent differences between men and women but career-oriented women have more positive self-concepts and higher levels of self-esteem than home-oriented women (e.g. Tinsley and Faunce, 1980). High levels of self-esteem are particularly charactersitic of women in male-dominated occupations (Betz and Fitzgerald, 1987: 114). However, when you look at levels of academic self-esteem, you find that women are lower in this. Women also tend to underestimate their abilities and their probable levels of future performance, even when their performance is objectively better than that of males (Betz and Fitzgerald, 1987:115).

Individuals who perceive that they possess characteristics that are relevant for a particular job seek that job (Heilman, 1983). The sex-role characteristics you

hold are, to some extent, barometers of how well you fare. But it is harder for women to have positive images of themselves and their attributes due to negative stereotyping of female traits and due to their lower academic self-esteem. Having feminine characteristics can be, as we saw, detrimental to your career.

Women's lack of self-efficacy may explain their lack of representation in traditional male occupations. According to White *et al.* (1992), the need for achievement is mediated by self-efficacy beliefs. Individuals with a high need for achievement will be motivated to tackle only those goals for which there is a moderate probability of success. The high self-efficacy beliefs held by successful women will increase the expectancy of success for challenging goals. The more you believe in yourself, the more likely you are to be successful in an organization.

Some have argued that what was needed for success was a mix of both male and female personality traits. Until the mid-1970s masculinity and femininity were generally believed to be opposites. If a person was high in masculinity then they must be low in femininity and vice versa. But instead of masculinity and femininity being the opposite ends of the same scale, perhaps they can be defined as separate and independent sets of characteristics so that you could be high in masculinity or low in masculinity; high in femininity or low in femininity.

ANDROGENY

Research on androgyny—the possession of a more or less equal balance of both masculine and feminine characteristics—has focused on differences in attitudes and behaviour between androgynous and non-androgynous individuals. A more androgynous view of oneself has been associated with greater maturity in one's moral judgements (Block, 1973), assertiveness (Bem, 1975a), a higher level of self-esteem, (Spence *et al.*, 1975), and flexibility in behaviour (Bem, 1975a,b). Being androgynous was clearly of benefit to men as well as women. Gutek and Stevens (1979) found, however, that androgyny level had no effect on how men and women were evaluated in Rosen and Jerdee's in-basket exercise. Male and female subjects responded in a sex-role stereotyped manner.

The idea of androgyny has attracted considerable interest. At least three scales have been developed to measure it, and it has spawned numerous dissertations (Bem, 1974; Bem and Lenney, 1976; Block, 1973; Spence and Helmreich, 1978). The concept was personified in male rock musicians like Boy George, Michael Jackson, and Prince. Female examples might include Sinéad O'Connor and Annie Lennox.

Serious questions were raised about the scientific merit of androgyny, even by the authors of two of the most widely used measures of androgyny (Bem, 1981; Lott, 1987). To explain her personal views on the labels male and female, Bem says that she does not label herself as heterosexual, lesbian, or bisexual. These three categories are irrelevant to her:

Although some of the (very few) individuals to whom I have been attracted during my forty-eight years have been men and some have been women, what those individuals have in common has nothing to do with either their biological sex or mine—from which I conclude, not than I am attracted to both sexes, but that my sexuality is organized around dimensions other than sex' (Bem, 1993: vii).

These cultural categories (male and female, masculine and feminine) construct and constrain social reality by providing the historically specific conceptual framework through which we perceive our social world. Bem originally focused on androgyny because it seemed to challenge the traditional categories of masculine and feminine as never before. But by the late 1970s and early 1980s it had focused so much attention on being both masculine and feminine that it reproduced the gender polarization that it sought to undercut. Bem's attempt to discover gender as a literal state rather than to treat it as a metaphorical device could have served to bolster the very ideological practice she hoped to diffuse (Wetherell, 1986). She now believes that masculinity and femininity are merely constructions of the cultural schema or lens that polarizes gender.

Others have been critical for different reasons. Some argue that androgyny produces a 'hollow identity' (Sarbin and Scheibe, 1983; Morawski, 1987; Mednick, 1989). It subsumes the feminine identity. (For further criticism, see Wetherell, 1986 and Haste, 1993.) It took for granted traditional descriptions of masculine and feminine traits, rather than eliciting more accurate reflections of men's and women's sexual identity. In this sense it was closer to rationalist reconstruction than to finding new authenticity (Haste, 1993: 13)

PERSONALITY AND STEREOTYPES

Sex and gender differences remain, bolstered mainly by sex-role stereotyping. We saw in Chapters 3 and 5 that women may have learned to be co-operative, whereas men compete, seeking power and dominance. There seems to be some common agreement that the sexes do differ in personality characteristics; they have learned to 'do gender' (Rakow, 1986). There appears to be a strong belief in sex differences, particularly those congruent with stereotypes (Deaux and Major, 1987; Greeno and Maccoby, 1986). The distinction which usually appears is between what are often labelled instrumental qualities versus expressive qualities, calling on Parsons's (1955) distinction between men's instrumental roles and women's expressive roles. The more recent work of Bem (1974) and Spence, et al. (1975) makes similar distinctions. We have witnessed the tenacity of these stereotypes and how artificial the rigid distinctions are between men and women.

Men are said to possess in greater abundance than women self-directing, goal-oriented characteristics such as independence, assertiveness, and decisiveness—qualities which allow them to discharge effectively their roles in both family and extra-familial settings. Women are said to possess interpersonally oriented, emotive qualities such as kindness, sensitivity to others, emotional responsiveness, and need for affiliation. Women's greater expressiveness allows them to perform their domestic roles and their lesser instrumentality results in their being less achievement oriented and less temperamentally suited than men to demanding positions of leadership. It is possible that there are some innate differences in temperament or ability between men and women, but if these do exist we can say, quite confidently, that they are not the basis of major social institutions (Connell, 1987: 71).

As we have seen, a sociobiologist would say, while not entirely dismissing the contribution of experiential and learning factors, that inborn temperamental differences between the sexes are great and lack malleability. Others, particularly psychologists, deny or play down the role of direct biological causation, proposing that the different socialization received by boys and girls in anticipation of their adult roles and the models of gender-appropriate behaviour they are expected to emulate, bring about the differences. Feminists (e.g. Stanley and Wise, 1983: ch. 4) would argue that these models are overly deterministic, non-reflexive, and embody the power divisions of a sexist society. The search for a universalized theory has meant that there has been no time, and little respect, for individual experience and variation.

The trait stereotype literature indicates that the sexes are currently perceived as differing in degree, not in kind. On average the typical female is not regarded as being non-instrumental but as being less instrumental than the typical male. Conversely the typical male is not regarded as being unexpressive but as being less expressive than the typical female (Spence et al., 1985). Much depends on how traditional your view is and sex-role attitudes have become more liberal. Connell (1987) has provided a useful critique of masculinity/femininity scales and says that femininity and masculinity need not be treated as polar opposites but each as separate scales: the same person might get high scores on both. He concluded that the kind of psychology which uses gender scaling that polarizes the characteristics, participates in a process of reification. Nevertheless the male–female distinction tends to be preserved by both sexes, i.e. that men should be more instrumental than women and women should be more expressive than men.

It is possible to find studies which identify sex differences in personality traits. Sheldon (1990) videotaped pre-school children settling disputes and found that girls made more effort to maintain connection by 'asking for or giving clarification about behaviour, wishes, or intent ' (p. 9). Boys argued longer, focused on self, insisted on getting their own way, and tried to assert their position of dominance through the use of language.

Discussion point

In 1993 the University of St Andrews Student Counselling Service carried out a survey of undergraduates in the university to gain information on who used the service and how the service was perceived. Fifteen per cent of women said they were users of the service compared to 7 per cent of men. Seventy-two per cent of women and 64 per cent of men would consider using the service. The interesting question is why do so many fewer men than women go to use the service? What do you think is the explanation? Is there a cultural expectation which militates against some men seeking help, especially on emotional issues? Do males have a 'pride' that makes them deal with problems themselves rather than finding someone with whom to talk?

Girls are more likely to take steps to avoid quarrels and to take themselves out of situations of high dominance or conflict; boys are inclined to seek them out (Gilligan, 1982). Reviews of multiple studies of sex differences in nurturance and aggressiveness show that females tend to be more nurturing as adults as well as in childhood, and that in a variety of cultures males are consistently found to be more aggressive, physical and dominance oriented (Grusec and Lytton, 1988). Basow (1992) has reported, however that males compared to females tend to be more aggressive, dominant, competitive and non-conforming, but the gender differences that exist are so small and are overshadowed by situational and sex typing. Gender differences in social behaviours are found when personal and situational variables maximize the salience and importance of gender role conformity. We must not, then, think of men being aggressive and females as being unaggressive or submissive. It is all a matter of relativity, and degree, not opposition (Denmark et al., 1988; Tavris, 1992).

Experiments, games, and observations of small group interaction find that women, when talking, use 'co-operative verbal strategies', turn-taking, and rotating speakers. In contrast men utilize competitive strategies where a hierarchy of speakers is established and challenged through verbal duelling (Aries, 1976). Women tend to talk to each other about relationships while men talk about themselves and tell stories that emphasize aggressiveness and combat. Women's co-operative strategies seem to be based on a respect for and competence in listening (Spender, 1980) and their discussions reveal more interest in achieving a 'fair outcome' than in determining winners and losers. The reverse is usually the case for men (Baird, 1976; Stoll and McFarlane, 1973).

Marshall (1987: 18) described how many women managers have recognized this problem and were aware that the low key relational style they preferred had disadvantages in the competitive environments they now inhabited ... Their style left them vulnerable to attack from others; their achievements were not always apparent because others had been collaboratively involved and sometimes their reluctance to act politically meant that desired job outcomes were not attained.

It is important to understand the differences in experience of females and males. Both have been recruited, as small children, to appropriate the gender ideals of their own sex. Children self-regulate the process of gender identity by monitoring their own and others' conduct with regard to its gender implications. Gender differences become objective facts. They have taken on a gender identity that they strive to maintain (West and Zimmerman, 1987). While males may be ridiculed and humiliated for behaving or sounding or looking like a female, so may females. Women are subject to censure not only for behaving too much like men, but for behaving too much like women. If women who exhibit assertive, decisive, and initiating behaviour are chastised for being unfeminine, bitchy, bossy, or pushy (we can all conjure up examples of hurtful criticism of women being masculine—castrating, dominating; for empirical examples see also Eichler, 1980; Kelly, 1991), it is not surprising they resort to other, more relational behaviours.

Women are seen by some psychologists, for example Carol Gilligan, as different. It was Gilligan who described women (as we saw in Chapter 2) as using a relational power base, where women are seen to take care and be supportive or facilitative of aspects of women's behaviour. Women are seen to base moral decisions on compassion and care (who is going to be hurt least?) whereas men base theirs on abstract principles of justice (what is the fairest thing to do?) (Gilligan, 1982: 100). Women feel 'the moral imperative' to care for others. Men wish to protect the rights of others. Gilligan does not say that women's moral reasoning is better than men's, only that it is different and that both styles have their strengths and weaknesses. There is, however, little empirical support for Gilligan's ideas. Men and women use both care-based and justice-based reasoning and there is no average difference in the kind of moral reasoning men and women apply (e.g. Thoma, 1986).

MEN AND WOMEN IN CONVERSATION

What about the topic of conversations? Are these different? Women have more conversations than men about personal issues that involve expressions of feelings about themselves and their close relationships (Aries and Johnson, 1983). Men focus their conversations more on sports, work, or issues external to the individual. Conversation is viewed by women friends as being more central to their relationships, as a source of support, encouragement, and self-validation (Johnson and Aries, 1983).

A study by Deakins (1989), in a dining-room where bank officials had lunch, noted that when no women were present, men talked mostly about business, then food, sport, and recreation. When women talked alone they talked mostly about people—friends, children, partners—then business, and third health including weight control. When men and women got together they tended to avoid the topics each group liked best and settled on topics of interest to both. But in discussing those topics they followed the style of men alone. Deborah Lange's (1988) tape recordings of conversations among teenagers also found that when boys and girls were together they talked more or less the way boys talked when no girls were present.

These studies show that male–female conversations are like men's conversations; the women make adjustments. Women are at a disadvantage as they have less practice in conducting conversations in the way they are conducted in these groups. This helps explain why women are dissatisfied with communications in their relationships with men while men, who are party to the same conversations express less dissatisfaction.

Gossip between women is the language of intimacy. It functions as an exchange of information and resources connected with the female role, as a catharsis for the expression of anger at women's restricted role, as entertainment, and as emotional sustenance through intimate mutual self-disclosure. But men gossip too. Women devote a larger proportion of their conversations to gossip than men, although they are not more derogatory in these discussions than men. Women are more likely to gossip about close friends and family, whereas men are more likely to talk about celebrities including sports personalities and acquaintances (Levin and Arluke, 1985).

Some believe that women are also reluctant to engage in politics (e.g. Arroba and James, 1987). Women feel they lack competence in political skill, so they lack confidence and they feel distaste for politics. They see the political arena as foreign and so avoid getting involved.

Desjardins (1989) has suggested that females are more apt to operate in a 'response mode'; this mode values connection rather than competition, caring rather than being objective; females try to synthesize and bridge, to co-operate and nurture. Many women have learned to establish their identities through affiliation and 'often the only forms of affiliation that have been available to women are subservient affiliations' (Rigby-Weinberg, 1986: 199). Their need to connect may be so efficient that they put other's needs first. As so much depends on building and maintaining successful relationships with others, their greatest fear is that they will be abandoned. The task for many women is to separate and be autonomous.

In contrast, males tend to operate in a 'justice/rights mode' that values autonomy rather than intimacy, analysis rather than synthesis; as a result they tend to prefer to interact with others through competition and power. They see power as having influence over others. Males establish their identities through separation, making sure they are not similar to, or influenced by females. In spite of their divergent paths, both men and women have a need to belong, but they choose different strategies (Rigby-Weinberg, 1986).

Desjardins (1989) warns that no behaviour is gender specific. But there does seem to be a need to define the personality differences between men and women. Other writers use similar terms to label women's behaviour, like 'connecting', 'accommodation', 'receptivity'. Receptivity and the other labels are seen as female personality traits, related to biological and physical factors, but Obsatz (1975: 5) has argued that it is a socialized trait. 'Women work at clarification, explication, and expression. Women work at relationships.' Women are afraid of being pushed away; men are afraid of being pushed around (Tannen, 1990).

Researchers in education have determined that women do not learn well in a competitive/adversarial environment (Belenky *et al.*, 1986). When women are with men in a classroom, or similar mixed group, men benefit more than women (Latour, 1987). Men interrupt more, control topics of conversation, and determine the parameters of talk. In a normal co-educational world, boys act like boys and women act in a hospitable fashion (Van Nostrand, 1993: 80). If a woman does try to contribute she is frequently seen as aggressive and dominating.

Women do not benefit as much as men from the 'advocacy mode' in which every point must be debated and defended (Keith, 1987). Females are not socialized to be as competitive as males. When most of the daily interchange of an organization is conducted in a competitive mode, women often feel ignored, invisible, and excluded. But co-operative learning, advantageous to women, can also be so for men too (Johnson and Johnson, 1988).

There appears, then, to be certain stereotypical male communication patterns that set up communication barriers and disrupt groups. Often the males will have more air-time than women, particularly if the subject is not personal. Males tend to answer questions while females will ask questions. Males will interrupt each other, and females, more than women do, indicating that they are not really listening. Instead they are listening only to the first part of another's statement and then formulating a response in preparation for competition in the conversation. Males will find fault; women will 'add a thought' (Thompson, 1985).

You would think that a person who did not have expertise in a conversation topic would spend more time offering agreement and support the person who did have expertise. This turned out to be true except in cases where a woman was the expert and her non-expert partner was a man. Here the women experts showed support far more than the non-expert men they were talking to. Observers often rated the male non-expert as more dominant and more controlling of the conversation than the female expert (Leet-Pellegrini, 1980). The women here did not wield their expertise as power, but tried to play it down almost as if their expertise was something to hide. Competent women appear to compensate for their power with social-emotional behaviours and avoidance of dominant responses.

PERSONALITY AND JOB-FIT

Women and men, as we have seen, are socialized into and by work. Social psychologists have been criticized for assuming that an individual's personality is reflected in the job they do, that personality is formed before careers begin, that people seek out and retain jobs which suit their dispositions, and that they mould their conditions of work to match these qualities. Personality is going to be important in job selection, but Kohn *et al.* (1983) emphasize a reverse phenomenon, saying that job conditions mould personality. The consequence is that many individuals move onto jobs more consonant with their personalities which have been influenced by their previous occupation. If two individuals of equal intellectual flexibility were to start their careers in jobs which differed in complexity, the person with the more complex job would be more likely to outstrip the other in intellectual growth. The job you do can affect your values, cognitive functioning, and concept of self.

Your personality is going to affect your attitudes towards men and women at work. The more traditional your attitudes, the more likely you are to see working men and women in stereotypical terms. Personal characteristics affect attitudes. Older and more educated individuals have less traditional attitudes towards women. The more frequently people attend church, the more traditional their attitudes towards women (Baker and Terpstra, 1986).

Women with high self-esteem hold less traditional attitudes than those with less self-esteem. This may be because those low in esteem lack the confidence necessary to adopt non-traditional roles in society or advocate them for other women. Androgynous men and women, likely to be high in self-esteem, tend to hold less traditional values but those who have sex-role identities agreeing with gender stereotypes tend to hold more traditional views (Harrison *et al.*, 1981; Motowidlo, 1982).

Time and experience are also factors. For example, the longer male fire-fighters worked with women fire-fighters, the less traditional their attitudes and the more positive their evaluation of female fire-fighters (Craig and Jacobs, 1985). The sex ratio of the group also affects attitude to women (Kanter, 1977). If, for example, the group is skewed in favour of men, women members will be highly visible and face additional performance pressures. Many token women report having to work twice as hard as men in their groups to have their competence recognized and their achievements noticed (see Powell, 1988: 111–115 for a good discussion of token women).

There is, however, little evidence that a clear-cut relationship between a particular type of personality and success in senior management. Cox and Cooper

(1988), for example, found that their group of successful chief executives showed a very wide range of different personalities. They scored slightly higher on intelligence, assertiveness, emotional stability, and self-sufficiency—but this is not too surprising.

Betz and Fitzgerald have summarized the individual, background, educational and lifestyle variables that they believe are generally found to enhance the quality of women's career choices and the extent of their career achievements. As you will see it is a very varied list and personality factors play only a small part.

Individual variables	*Background variables*
High ability	Working mother
Liberated sex-role values	Supportive father
Instrumentality	Highly educated parents
Androgenous personality	Female role models
High self-esteem	Work experience as adolescent
Strong academic self-concept	Androgynous upbringing
Educational variables	*Adult lifestyle variables*
Higher education	Late marriage or single
Continuation of maths	No or few children
Girls schools and women's colleges	

Source: Betz and Fitzgerald (1987: 143)

PERSONALITY AND BEHAVIOUR IN GROUPS

As research has supported the existence of a basic sex difference in aggressiveness, we might expect it to be manifested in groups. Evidence suggests that in groups men engage in more dominating behaviour than women. They express anger, talk frequently, interrupt others, and invade others' personal space (Radecki and Jennings, 1980). Women as well as men can have a tendency to dominate and we might expect individuals who are high on the tendency to dominate to emerge as leaders. But the gender stereotype of males as dominating is found to prevail over the female's tendency to be dominant, if little information is given about those involved. (Powell, 1988: 108). So more men than women are chosen as leaders.

If, however, more information is available about group members, about their competence at the task, a high dominance competent female would be chosen as the leader more often than a low dominance male. Information about task competence led to the selection of the more competent person, male or female, as leader, rather than the selection of the male on the basis of gender stereotypes (Fleischer and Chertkoff, 1986).

Sex-role identity seems to be key in this kind of decision making. Individuals high on masculinity, whether male or female, perform in a more active, instrumental manner in a group than those low in masculinity. Androgynous women and men tend to share leadership in mixed-sex task groups, particularly if given social support. In groups where men were masculine and women feminine, men tend to dominate the leadership role (Kelly *et al.*, 1982; Porter *et al.*, 1985). Sex-role identity has an important affect on behaviour in groups.

Do women show more empathy than men? You might say, intuitively, that it would appear so; women have a greater reputation for altruism and empathy than do men, and women accept the validity of this reputation. Some researchers have agreed (e.g. Hoffman, 1977). Females have traditionally been socialized to acquire expressive traits such as compassion. Females may also be more strongly affected by signs of affection or rejection from others. Females are also more likely to experience guilt than males if they have caused distress in others. One might conclude that this, like other differences in personality traits in the sexes, is due to socialization and expectation. When psychologists ask people to rate themselves on their empathic skills, women tend to score higher than men because women think they have the advantage. But when studies have looked at actual physical responses to another person's suffering or unhappiness, or looked at whether someone does something to help another person in distress, the gender differences vanish. There is therefore little basis for the conclusion that the self-described sex difference in empathy is due to an innate mechanism or predisposition (Eisenberg and Lennon, 1983). When gender differences do occur in showing empathy and altruism 'they are typically weak, partial, and buried in qualifications' (Kohn, 1990: 82).

Human beings have a capacity for empathy, the ability to see things from another person's perspective, but its expression is a learned skill, according to Tavris (1992). If you look at the history of motherhood, watch harried mothers in supermarkets, or observe your own behaviour as a harried mother, you will quickly lose the belief in a maternal instinct. Throughout time women have been as likely as men to abuse, reject, or simply fail to understand their own children (Tavris and Wade, 1984).

Are women more emotional than men? There is very little evidence to support the view that women are more emotional. However, they do tend to pay more attention than men to other people's emotions; they are more affected by them and perhaps may be regarded as more emotionally sensitive than men— though that view is speculative (Strongman, 1987: 24).

Do women have the same access to informal interactions and communications in organizations as men? Women may be excluded from, or may exclude themselves from the development of informal relationships which may help them gain power. It would appear that women are as adept, if not more so, than men at building informal networks, especially with other women. But because the women's networks are segregated, and less central than men's, they have less access to the dominant coalition. As a result they are less influential than men and receive disproportionately fewer promotions than men (Brass, 1985).

MEN, WOMEN AND NON-VERBAL BEHAVIOUR

Many gender differences have been established in non-verbal behaviour. Women smile more, gaze more, are approached more closely than men, and assume less relaxed, expansive body positions (Hall, 1984). It is interesting to find that gender differences are most pronounced in single-sex interactions; if these gender differences were simply expression of power and status, you would expect them to be maximized in male–female encounters, but this is not the case.

Women are also better at decoding non-verbal cues (Hall, 1979). Women seem to be more sensitive than men. The cause may be the subordinate status of women in our society, leading them to develop greater ability to sense another person's feelings in order to protect their own interests (Snodgrass, 1985: 148). Women are more 'tuned in' and responsive to men than to women (Weitz, 1976). Again, how traditional the women's views were seems to be an important variable. The less traditional women were better than the more traditional women at decoding women, whereas the more traditional women were somewhat better at decoding men (Hall and Halberstadt, 1981).

Social support can be very important for women and men. It is a very effective way of coping with stress. Women are often able to make more use of support as they tend to talk to one another as a way of coping. Women, more than men, tend to value friendship and invest in interpersonal relationships (Greenglass et al., 1990). Data also suggest that women have greater interpersonal social competence, are more responsive and interpersonally sensitive (Greenglass, 1991: 570).

IS THERE REALLY A DIFFERENCE?

A study by Risman (1987) is illustrative of how men and women may not differ in attitudes and behaviour. Risman examined how family roles and gender differ in their influence on attitudes and behaviour. She compared a group of widowed or deserted single fathers, living alone with young children, with a group of single mothers with married mothers and fathers. She found that in some respects, the single fathers were more similar to the mothers in both groups than to the married fathers. Having responsibility for childcare was as strongly related to 'feminine' traits, such as nurturance and sympathy, as being female was. She interpreted this as raising serious doubts about arguments for women's or men's true nature.

A similar study of 150 men (Kaye and Applegate, 1990) spending up to 60 hours a week caring for parents or wives found that the men provided just as much emotional support as women traditionally do. The men were found to spend as much time as women doing nurturant things, e.g., holding the sick relative's hands, listening, and showing concern. Behaviour is not dependent on sex but on what the individual needs to do.

Maybe what is needed is a different methodology using more qualitative methods. Condor (1986), for example, used open-ended interviews to understand the basis of group membership for 'traditional' women. Others have used discourse analysis (tape recordings of conversations, scientific and literary documents, media accounts, and so on). Wetherell (1986) advocated discourse analysis as a means of establishing a more fluid and fragmentary picture of gender identity rather than one based on fixed categories such as feminine/masculine and agency/communion. She believes that by looking at how people talk about their gender we may find that contradictory and inconsistent categorizations underlie gender identity and that its meaning changes from one situation to another.

> A homogeneous or consensual model of gender identity loses the ability to account for creativity and resistance. It recognizes the production of different gender practices only as deviance resulting from inadequate or aberrant socialization (Connell, 1987: 194)

Agencies of socialization cannot be sure of their results. Children may, for example, refuse heterosexuality, though gay autobiographies show it often takes a long time to construct a positive alternative as a homosexual. Socialization is not always a smooth and successful process.

PERSONALITY AND STRESS

Numerous studies have been carried out on individual personality and behaviours associated with stress-related diseases, particularly coronary heart disease (see Taylor and Cooper, 1989). Early Canadian studies using male subjects found that individuals who held more taxing jobs were particularly prone to type A behaviour, behaviour showing extreme levels of competitiveness, aggressiveness, striving for achievement, haste, impatience and pressures of time and responsibility. Male managers were found to consume large quantities of alcohol, tranquillisers, and sleeping pills. They experienced exhaustion, were overweight, lacked exercise, and had high blood pressure and family problems (Burke and Weir, 1980).

There has, however, been a scarcity of research on personality traits and stress for British female managers (Davidson and Cooper, 1992). Those women in higher occupational levels and more demanding jobs than other women are more prone to type A behaviour and suffer from the same symptoms of stress as male managers. A study of top female executives in Britain found that women generally did not report a high incidence of physical ill health, although a quarter did experience migraines. Tiredness, irritation, and anxiety were experienced by over half. Like male managers, most did not like admitting they suffered from some form of stress-related illness and tried to hide it from colleagues (Cooper and Davidson, 1992).

Two factors are associated with stress in female managers: coping ability, and type A coronary-prone behaviour. Being able to cope with pressure is an important factor in managerial success; most of the senior female executives in Davidson and Cooper's (1987) survey believed they coped better with stress than their subordinates of both sexes. A successful coping strategy is to change the demands of the role; this can also increase satisfaction with your career. Women who had tried to meet the demands of wife, mother, and worker were those at most risk of stress-related illnesses (Davidson and Cooper, 1992: 72). Studies of successful professionals frequently show that high achieving men are married, whereas high-achieving women tend to be unmarried (Houseknecht *et al.*, 1987).

In contrast, however, Canadian researchers, Long *et al.*, (1992) note that women managers who maintain traditional lifestyles (married with children) and traditional beliefs see occupational stressors as less threatening. It may be that they have invested less in their careers (Betz and Fitzgerald, 1987). Further, marriage may buffer women's psychological distress (Repetti *et al.*, 1989). Verbrugge and Madans (1985) found that the healthiest women have multiple roles: worker, wife, and mother. Cross-national data indicate that women who occupy more roles generally have better health (Froberg *et al.*, 1986; Sorenson and Verbrugge, 1987). Multiple roles can provide multiple sources of competence, resources, and increase a person's social standing. We saw earlier, in Chapter 4, how employed married women enjoy better mental health than homemakers (see also Waldron, 1980; Nathanson, 1980).

Some female managers are better able to cope with stressors than others. Some are psychologically predisposed to stress and are unable to adapt to stress-provoking situations. In the early 1960s Friedman and Rosenman demonstrated a relationship between behavioural patterns and the prevalence of coronary heart disease. Those with behavioural patterns named type A were more prone to coronaries than type B. Type A were described as extremely competitive, striving for achievement, aggressive, hasty, impatient, restless, hyper-alert, explosive in speech, have tense facial muscles, and feel under pressure of time and under the challenge of responsibility. People like this were often so involved and committed to their work that other aspects of their lives became relatively neglected. It was found that type As between the ages of 39 and 49 had 6.5 times the incidence of coronary heart disease than type Bs.

Three negative features of the type A personality are anger, hostility and aggression (Speilberger *et al.*, 1985). Hostile aggression is higher in some type A personalities than in others (Check and Dyck, 1986). Research by Hecker *et al.* (1988) lent support to the idea that it is the hostility component in type A that is the most coronary prone. Anger too is a strong risk factor. An in-depth study of men and women who had had heart attacks found that for men negative characteristics associated with masculinity (such as arrogance, hostility, cynicism, and anger) were related to having had more severe attacks, whereas men who were more empathic and nurturing were more likely to have had less severe heart attacks and better relationships. The extreme of masculinity, then, can be unhealthy. But so can being too feminine. Women who were the sickest were those who had become over-involved with others to the exclusion of caring for themselves (Helgeson, 1990).

Working women who score high on type A behaviour are twice as likely to develop coronary heart disease as their type A males (Waldron *et al.*, 1977). Pressures on top women executives come from male-dominated policy making, feelings of isolation, conflict demands between career and marriage/family, and coping with prejudice and discrimination (Lewis and Cooper, 1989). Frustration, irritation, and anxiety were the three psychological symptoms which were found to contribute the most to higher type A scores. Further, according to Dembroski and McDougall (1978), type A individuals are more likely to choose to work alone when put under high stress; as a result they have an increased workload and stress levels. This, in turn, reduces the opportunity for support from colleagues and subordinates and so contributes towards feelings of frustration. Much of the work overload associated with anxiety, high stress levels, and poor stress-related coping ability may be self-imposed by the type A person. Davidson and Cooper (1992: 76) go as far as to say that type A women may doubt their ability to cope with stress in managerial positions, this will negatively affect their motivation, work performance and success and chances of promotion.

Review questions

How can you explain why British research has shown that women managers with husbands and children are most at risk from stress and American research suggests the opposite? Is the clue in the 'traditional attitudes' the American women managers in the study held? Examine the literature using the references you find here, and those in the references themselves, and see what you can conclude.

Do men and women differ in the way they communicate? Using the references here (and a review by Aries, 1987), look at the evidence and draw your own conclusions. Maybe you could set up your own experiment with a student group to see if there are gender differences in mixed-sex and single-sex conversations.

REFERENCES

ARIES, E. (1976) 'Interaction Patterns and Themes of Male, Female and Mixed Groups', *Small Group Behaviour*, **7**, 7–18, in Spender, (1980), *Man Made Language*, p. 27, Routledge & Kegan Paul, London.

ARIES, E. (1987) 'Gender and Communication', Chapter 6 in P, Shave and C. Hendrick (eds), *Sex and Gender, Review of Personality and Social Psychology*, Sage, Newbury Park, Calif.

ARIES, E. and JOHNSON, F. (1983) 'Close Friendship in Adulthood: Conversational Content Between Same-sex Friends', *Sex Roles*, **9**, 1183–1196.

ARROBA, T. and JAMES, K. (1987) 'Are Politics Palatable to Women Managers? How Can Women Make Wise Moves at Work?', *Women in Management Review* **10(3)**, 123–130.

BAIRD, J. E. (1976) 'Sex Differences in Group Communication: A Review of Relevant Research', *Quarterly Journal of Speech*, **62**, 179–192.

BAKER, D. D. and TERPSTRA, D. E. (1986) 'Locus of Control and Self Esteem Versus Demographic Factors as Predictors of Attitudes Towards Women', *Basic and Applied Social Psychology*, **7**, 163–172.

BANDURA, A. (1986) *Social Foundation of Thought and Action: A social Cognitive Theory*, Prentice Hall, Englewood Cliffs, NJ.

BASOW, S. (1992) *Gender: Stereotypes and Roles*, 3rd edn, Brooks/Cole, Monterey, Calif.

BELENKY, M. F., CLINCHY, B.M., GOLDBERGER, N. R. and TARULE, J. M. (1986) *Women's Ways of Knowing: The Development of Self, Voice and Mind*, Basic Books, New York.

BEM, S.L. (1974) 'The Measurement of Psychological Androgeny,' *Journal of Consulting and Clinical Psychology*, **42**, 155–162.

BEM, S. L. (1975a) 'Androgeny vs. the Tight Little Lives of Fluffy Women and Chesty Men, *Psychology Today*, September, 59–62.

BEM, S. L. (1975b) 'Sex Role Adaptability: One Consequence of Psychological Androgyny' *Journal of Personality and Social Psychology*, **31**, 634–643.

BEM, S. L. (1981) 'Gender Schema Theory: A Cognitive Account of Sex Typing' *Psychological Review*, **88**, 354–364.

BEM, S. L. (1993) *The Lenses of Gender: Transforming the Debate on Sexual Equality*, Yale University Press, New Haven, Conn.

BEM, S. L. and LENNEY, E. (1976) 'Sex-typing and the Avoidance of Cross-sex Behaviour', *Journal of Personality and Social Psychology*, **33**, 48–54.

BETZ, N. E. and HACKETT, G. (1986) 'Applications for Self Efficacy Theory to Understand Career Choice Behaviour,' *Journal of Social and Clinical Psychology*, **4**, 279–289.

BETZ, N. E. and FITZGERALD, L. F. (1987) *The Career Psychology of Women*, Academic Press, San Diego, Calif.

BLOCK, J. H. (1973) 'Conceptions of Sex Role, Some Cross-cultural and Longitudinal Perspectives', *American Psychologist*, **28**, 512–526.

BRASS, D. J. (1985) 'Men's and Women's Networks: A Study of Interaction Patterns and Influence in an Organization', *Academy of Management Journal*, **28(2)**, 327–343.

BURKE, R. J. and WEIR, T. (1980) 'The Type A Experience: Occupational and Life Demands, Satisfaction and Well Being', *Journal of Human Stress*, **6(4)**, 28–38.

CHECK, J. V. P. and DYCK, D. G. (1986) 'Hostile Aggression and Type A Behaviour', *Journal of Personality and Individual Difference*, **7(6)**, 819–827.

CONDOR, S. (1986) 'Sex Role Beliefs and "Traditional" Women: Feminist and Intergroup Perspectives', in S. Wilkinson (ed.), *Feminist Social Psychology*, Open University Press, Milton Keynes.

CONNELL, R. W. (1987) *Gender and Power: Society, the Person and Sexual Politics*, Polity Press, Basil Blackwell, Oxford.

COOPER, C. L. and DAVIDSON, M. J. (1982) 'The High Cost of Stress on Women Managers', *Organizational Dynamics*, **10(4)**, 44–53.

COX, C. and COOPER, C. L. (1988) *High Flyers*, Basil Blackwell, Oxford.

CRAIG, J. M. and JACOBS, R. R. (1985) 'The Effects of Working with Women on Male Attitudes Towards Female Fire-fighters', *Basic and Applied Social Psychology*, **6**, 61–74.

DAVIDSON, M. J. and COOPER, C. L. (1987) 'Female Managers in Britain—A Comparative Review', *Human Resource Management*, **26**, 217–242.

DAVIDSON, M. J. and COOPER, C. L. (1992) *Shattering the Glass Ceiling*, PCP, London.

DEAKINS, A. H. (1989) 'Talk at the Top: Topics at Lunch', ms. English Department, William Paterson College, quoted in Tannen (1990).

DEAUX, K. (1976) 'A Perspective on the Attribution Process', in J. Harvey, W. J. Ickes and R. F. Kidd (eds), *New Directions in Attribution Research*, Vol. 1, Erlbaum, Hillsdale, NJ.

DEAUX, K. and MAJOR, B. (1987) 'Putting Gender into Context: An interactive Model of Gender-related Behaviour', *Psychological Review*, **94**, 369–384.

DEMBROSKI, T. M. and MCDOUGALL, J. M. (1978) 'Stress Effects on Application Preferences among Subjects Possessing the Type A Coronary-prone Behaviour Pattern', *Journal of Personnel and Social Psychology*, **36(1)**, 23–33.

DENMARK, F., RUSSO, N. F., FRIEZE, I. H. and SECHZER, J. A. (1988) 'Guide-lines for Avoiding Sexism in Psychological Research', *American Psychologist*, **43**, 582–585.

DESJARDINS, C. (1989) 'The Meaning of Gilligan's Concept of "Different Voices" for the Learning Environment', in C. Pearson, D. Shavlik and J. Touchton (eds), *Educating the Majority: Women Challenging Tradition in Higher Education* , pp. 134–146, Macmillan, New York.

EICHLER, M. (1980) *The Double Standard: A Feminist Critique of Feminist Social Science*, Croom Helm, London.

EISENERG, N. and LENNON, R. (1983) 'Sex Differences in Empathy and Related Capacities', *Psychological Bulletin*, **94**, 100–131.

FLEISCHER, R. A. and CHERTKOFF, J. M. (1986) 'Effects of Dominance and Sex on Leader Selection in Dyadic Work Groups', *Journal of Personality and Social Psychology*, **50**, 94–99.

FROBERG, D., GJERDINGEN, D. and PRESON, M. (1986) 'Multiple Roles and Women's Mental and Physical Health: What Have We Learned?', *Women and Health*, **11**, 79–96.

GILLIGAN, C. (1982) *In a Different Voice: Psychological Theory and Women's Development*, Harvard University Press, Cambridge, Mass.

GREENGLASS, E. R. (1991) 'Burnout and Gender: Theoretical and Organizational Implications', *Canadian Psychology*, **32(4)**, 563–572.

GREENGLASS, E. R., BURKE, R. J. and ONDRACK, M. (1990) 'A Gender-role Perspective of Coping and Burnout', *Applied Psychology: An International Review*, **39**, 5–27.

GREENO, C. G. and MACCOBY, E. E. (1986) 'How Different is the "Different voice"?', *Signs*, **11**, 310–316.

GRUSEC, J. E. and LYTTON, H. (1988) *Social Development: History, Theory and Research*, Springer-Verlag, New York.

GUTEK, B. A. and STEVENS, D. A. (1979) 'Effects of Sex of Subject, Sex of Stimulus Cue and Androgyny Level on Evaluations in Work Situations which Evoke Sex Role Stereotypes', *Journal of Vocational Behaviour*, **14**, 23–32.

HALL, J. A. (1979) 'Gender, Gender Roles and Non-verbal Communication Skills' in R. Rosenthal (ed.), *Skill in Nonverbal Communication: Individual Differences*, pp. 32–67, Oelgeschlager, Gunn and Hain, Cambridge, Mass.

HALL, J. A. (1984) *Nonverbal Sex Differences: Communications Accuracy and Expressive Style*, Johns Hopkins University Press, Baltimore, Md.

HALL, J. A. and HALBERSTADT, A. G. (1981) 'Sex Roles and Nonverbal Communication Skills', *Sex Roles*, **7**, 273–287.

HALL, R. (1986) 'He Said, She Said: Gender and Classroom Climate', Address, quoted in Van Nostrand (1993: 49).

HARRISON, B. G., GUY, R. F. and LUPFER, S. L. (1981) 'Locus of Control and Self-esteem as

Correlates of Role Orientation in Traditional and Non-traditional Women', *Sex Roles*, **7**, 1175–1187.

HASTE, H. (1993) *The Sexual Metaphor*, Harvester Wheatsheaf, Hemel Hempstead.

HECKER, M. H. L., CHESNEY, M. A., BLACK, G. W. and FRAUTSCHI, I. N. (1988) 'Coronary-prone Behaviours in the Western Collaborative Group Study', *Psychosomatic Medicine*, **50**, 153–164.

HEILMAN, M. (1983) 'Sex Bias in Work Settings: The Lack of Fit Model', in L. L. Cummings and B. Staw (eds), *Research in Organizational Behaviour*, vol. 5, pp. 269–298, JAI Press, New York.

HELGESON, V. S. (1990) 'The Role of Masculinity in a Prognostic Predictor of Heart Attack Severity', *Sex Roles*, **22**, 755–774.

HOFFMAN, M. L. (1977) 'Sex Differences in Empathy and Related Behaviour,' *Psychological Bulletin*, **84(4)**, 712–722.

HOUSEKNECHT, S. K., VAUGHAN, S. and STRATHAM, A. (1987) 'The Impact of Singlehood on Career Patterns of Professional Women', *Journal of Marriage and the Family*, **48**, 353–366.

JOHNSON, D. W. and JOHNSON, R. T. (1988) 'Cooperative Classroom, Cooperative Schools', University of Minnesota, Cooperative Learning Center, Minneapolis.

JOHNSON. F. and ARIES, E. (1983) 'The Talk of Women Friends, *Women's Studies International Forum*, **6**, 353–361.

KANTER, R. M. (1977) 'Some Effects of Proportions on Group Life: Skewed Sex Ratios and Responses to Token Women', *American Journal of Sociology*, **82**, 965–990.

KAYE, L. W. and APPLEGATE, J. S. (1990) 'Men as Elder Caregivers: A Response to Changing Families', *American Journal of Orthopsychiatry*, **60**, 86–95.

KEITH, S. (1987) 'A Strategy for the Female Math Student in the Battle', in H. L. Nelson and M. Rengel (eds), *Gender and the Curriculum: Theory and Practice, Selected Papers*, pp. 87–95, College of Saint Benedict/ St John's University, St Joseph/Collegeville, Minn.

KELLY, J. A., WILDMAN, H. E. and UREY, J. R. (1982) 'Gender and Sex Role Differences in Group Decision-making Social Interactions: A Behavioural Analysis', *Journal of Applied Psychology*, **12**, 112–127.

KELLY, R. M. (1991) *The Gendered Economy: Work, Careers and Success*, Sage, Newbury Park, Calif.

KOHN, A. (1990) *The Brighter Side of Human Nature: Altruism and Empathy in Everyday Life*, Basic Books, New York.

KOHN, M. L., SCHOOLER, C., MILLER, J., MILLER, K. A., SCHOENBACH, C. and SCHOENBERG, R. (1983) *Work and Personality: An Inquiry into the Impact of Social Stratification*, Ablex, Norwood, NJ.

LANGE, D. (1988) 'Using Like to Introduce Constructed Dialogue: How Like Contributes to Discourse Coherence', masters thesis, Georgetown University, quoted in Tannen (1990).

LATOUR, T. (1987) 'Language and Power: Issues in Classroom Interaction', *Women and Language*, **10(2)**, 29–32.

LEET-PELLEGRINI, H. M. (1980) 'Conversational Dominance as a Function of Gender and Expertise', in H. Giles, W. P. Robinson and P. M. Smith (eds), *Language: Social Psychological Perspectives*, Pergamon Press, Oxford.

LEVIN, J. and ARLUKE, A. (1985) 'An Exploratory Analysis of Sex differences in Gossip', *Sex Roles*, **12**, 281–286.

LEWIS, S. and COOPER, C. L. (1989) *Career Couples*, Unwin Hyman, London.

LONG, B. C., KAHN, S. E. and SCHUTZ, R. W. (1992) 'Causal Model of Stress and Coping: Women in Management', *Journal of Counseling Psychology*, **39(2)**, 227–239.

LOTT, B. (1987) 'Feminist, Masculine, Androgynous or Human', Paper presented at the meeting of the American Psychological Association, New York and cited in Mednick (1989)

MARSHALL, J. (1987) 'Issues of Identity for Women Managers', in D. Clutterbuck and M. Devine (eds), *Business Woman: Present and Future*, Macmillan, Basingstoke.

MEDNICK, T. (1989) 'On the Politics of Psychological Constructs', *American Psychologist*, **44(8)**, 1118–1123.

MORAWSKI, J. G. (1987) 'The Troubled Quest for Masculinity, Femininity and Androgeny', in P. Shaver and C. Hendrick (eds), *Sex and Gender*, Sage, Newbury Park, Calif.

MOTOWIDLO, S. J. (1982) 'Sex Role Orientation and Behaviour in a Work Setting', *Journal of Personality and Social Psychology*, **42**, 935–945.

NATHANSON, C. A. (1980) 'Social Roles and Health Status Among Women: The Significance of Employment', *Social Science and Medicine*, **14A**, 463–471.

OBSATZ, M. (1975) 'Boy Talk: How Men Avoid Sharing Themselves', unpublished manuscript cited in *Gender Responsible Leadership: Detecting Bias, Implementing Interventions*, C. H. Van Nostrand (1993), Sage, Newbury Park, Calif. .

PARSONS, T. (1955) 'Family Structure and the Socialization of the Child', in T. Parsons and R. F. Bales (eds), *Family, Socialization and the Interaction Process*, Free Press, Glencoe, Ill.

PORTER, N., GEIS, F. L., COOPER, E. and NEWMAN, E. (1985) 'Androgyny and Leadership in Mixed-sex Groups', *Journal of Personality and Social Psychology*, **49**, 808–823.

POWELL, G. (1988) *Women and Men in Management*, Sage, Newbury Park, Calif.

RADECKI, C. and JENNINGS, J. (1980) 'Sex as a Status Variable in Work Settings: Female and Male Reports of Dominance Behaviour', *Journal of Applied Social Psychology*, **10**, 71–85.

RAKOW, L. F. (1986) 'Rethinking Gender Research in Communication', *Journal of Communications*, **36(4)**, 11–26.

REPETTI, R. L., MATTHEWS, K. A. and WALDRON, I. (1989) 'Employment and Women's Health: Effects of Paid Employment on Women's Mental and Physical Health', *American Psychologist*, **44**, 1394–1401.

RIGBY-WEINBERG, D. N. (1986) 'A Future Direction for Radical Feminist Therapy', in D. Howard (ed.), *Guide to Dynamics of Feminist Therapy*, 2nd edn, Harrington, New York.

RISMAN, B. J. (1987) 'Intimate Relationships from a Microstructural Perspective: Men Who Mother', *Gender and Society*, **1**, 6–32.

SARBIN, T. R. and SCHEIBE, K. E. (1983) 'A Model of Social Identity' in T. R. Sarbin and K. E. Scheibe (eds), *Studies in Social Identity*, Pareger, New York.

SHELDON, A. (1990) 'Pickle Fights: Gendered Talk in Preschool Disputes', in D. Tannen (ed.), *Language and Gender*, Special Issue: *Discourse Processes*, **13(1)**, 5–31.

SNODGRASS, S. E. (1985) 'Women's Intuition and Subordinate Role', *Journal of Personality and Social Psychology*, **49(1)**, 146–155.

SORENSON, G. and VERBRUGGE, L. M. (1987) 'Women, Work and Health', *Annual Review of Public Health* **8**, 235–251.

SPENCE, J. T., HELMREICH, R., and STAPP, J. (1975) 'Ratings of Self and Peers on Sex Role Attributes and their Relation to Self-esteem and Conceptions of Masculinity and Femininity', *Journal of Personality and Social Psychology*, **32**, 29–39.

SPENCE, J. T. and HELMREICH, R. L. (1978) *Masculinity and Femininity: Their Psychological Dimensions, Correlates and Antecedents*, University of Texas Press, Austin.

SPENCE, J. T., DEAUX, K. and HELMREICH, R. L. (1985) 'Sex Roles in Contemporary American Society', Chapter 17 in G. Lindzsey and E. Aronson (eds), *Handbook of Social Psychology*, Erbaus, Random House, New York.

SPENDER, D. (1980) *Man Made Language*, Routledge & Kegan Paul, London.

SPIELBERGER, C. D., JOHNSON, E. H., RUSSELL, S.F., CRANE, R. S., JACOBS, G. A. and WORDEN, T. J. (1985) 'The Experience and Expression of Anger: Construction and Validation of an Anger Expression Scale', in M. A. Chesney and R. H. Rosenman (eds), *Anger and Hostility in Cardiovascular and Behavioral Disorders*, Hemisphere/McGraw-Hill, New York.

STANLEY, L. and WISE, S. (1983) *Breaking Out: Feminist Consciousness and Feminist Research*, Routledge & Kegan Paul, London.

STOLL, C. S. and MCFARLANE, P. T. (1973) 'Sex Differences in Game Strategy' in C. S. Stoll (ed.), *Sexism: Scientific Debates*, Addison-Wesley, Reading, Mass.

STRONGMAN, K. T. (1987) *The Psychology of Emotion*, 3rd edn, Wiley, Chichester.

TANNEN, D. (1990) *You Just Don't Understand: Women and Men in Conversation*, Morrow, New York.

TAVRIS, C. (1992) *The Mismeasure of Women*, Simon & Schuster, New York.

TAVRIS, C. and WADE, C. (1984) *The Longest War: Sex Differences in Perspective* 2nd edn, Harcourt Brace Jovanovich, San Diego, Calif.

TAYLOR, H. and COOPER, C.L. (1989) 'The Stress-prone personality: A Review of the Research in the Context of Occupational Stress', *Stress Medicine*, **5(17)**, 18–26.

THOMA, S. J. (1986) 'Estimating Gender Differences in the Comprehension and Preference of Moral Issues', *Developmental Review*, **6**, 165–180.

THOMPSON, D. C. (1985) *As Boys Become Men: Learning New Male Roles—A Curriculum for Exploring Male Role Stereotyping*, Irvington, New York.

TINSLEY, D. J. and FAUNCE, P. S. (1980) 'Enabling, Facilitating and Precipitating Factors Associated with Women's Career Orientation', *Journal of Vocational Behavior* **17**, 183–194.

VAN NOSTRAND, C. H. (1993) *Gender Responsible Leadership*, Sage, Newbury Park, Calif.

VERBRUGGE, L. M. and MADANS, J. H. (1985) 'Social Roles and Health Trends of American Women', *Milbank Memorial Fund Quarterly/Health and Society*, **63**, 691–735.

WALDRON, I. (1980) 'Employment and Women's Health: An Analysis of Causal Relationships', *International Journal of Health Services*, **10**, 435–454.

WALDRON, I., ZYANSKI, S. and SHEKELLE, R. B. (1977) 'The Coronary-prone Behaviour Pattern in Employed Men and Women', *Journal of Human Stress*, **3**, 2–18.

WEITZ, S. (1976) 'Sex Differences in Nonverbal Communication', *Sex Roles*, **2**, 175–184.

WEST, C. and ZIMMERMAN, D. H. (1987) 'Doing Gender', *Gender and Society*, **1(2)**, 125–151.

WETHERELL, M. (1986) 'Linguistic Repertoires and Literary Criticism: New Directions for a Social Psychology of Gender', in S. Wilkinson (ed.), *Feminist Social Psychology*, Open University Press, Milton Keynes.

WHITE, B., COX, C. and COOPER, C. (1992) *Women's Career Development: A Study of High Flyers*, Blackwell, Oxford.

7 *Sexuality in Organizations*

Discussion point
Women who wear low-cut, backless, or short items of clothing are seen as provocative. If a woman who wears such clothes is harassed, assaulted, or raped the response might be 'Well she asked for it.' Is this a fair or reasonable response?
What is the equivalent situation for a man? If a man wears fitted jeans, for example as in the Levi advertisement, or ripped T-shirts, as the Chippendales dress, is this provocative? Can you imagine that men would ever be assaulted for such behaviour? Would they be accused of being provocative?

Sexuality has been strangely absent from organizational theory (Burrell, 1984); there is a 'booming silence' around the subject (Hearn and Parkin, 1987). But sexuality at work in organizational settings is embedded (Hearn and Parkin, 1987; Pringle 1989). Sexuality has a power and a potential power of its own as work organizations construct sexuality and are constructed by and through sexuality; organizations are arenas of sexual practices.

Sexuality pervades organizations and not only in the more obvious ways. Some organizations, such as the pornography industry, may have sexual goals; others use sex, e.g. advertising. Military organizations promote a particular kind of aggressive heterosexual masculinity, the tough image helping attract recruits. Sexuality is ever present yet difficult to pin down. It makes itself felt through ambiguities, innuendo, gossip, and joking. The language and imagery of a predominantly male workplace can all serve to make women feel uncomfortable while affirming men's sense of shared masculinity. The rituals of back-slapping, sexist joking, and constant reminders of heterosexuality can also serve to exclude homosexual men (Borrowdale, 1993).

Most writing on sexuality in organizations tends to assume heterosexuality as a given. 'Heterosexual' (like 'white', 'male', or 'able-bodied') is always a silent term (Kitzinger *et al.*, 1992). Most women are willingly enmeshed in sexual relationships with men which some writers view as being 'more or less oppressive' (e.g. Ramazanoglu, 1989: 163). But heterosexual relations do not have to be expressions of male power, nor does heterosexuality need to be taken as a given. Lesbianism and male homosexuality need to be acknowledged as existing and sometimes are. At best, however, they are acknowledged as 'alternative lifestyles', and at worst as 'pathological perversions.'

To gain more insight into the taken-for-granted nature of heterosexuality in organizational thinking perhaps we need to ask ourselves a set of questions. For example: What is heterosexuality and why is it so common? Are you a 'generic' woman or man, rather than 'heterosexual'? Have lesbian feminists a political identity that heterosexual feminists lack? How does heterosexual activity affect a person's identity, their sense of self, and their relationships with others in organizations? How does being lesbian or homosexual affect that person's identity in an organization?

Why is heterosexuality taken as a given? One answer to this question comes from Adrian Rich (1980) who argues that heterosexuality is overtly and covertly forced upon us through, for example, the socialization of women to feel that the male sexual 'drive' amounts to a right, the idealization of heterosexual romance, and sexual harassment. Homosocial relations are organized in the ways they are precisely in order to produce the gender differences heterosexuality requires. Heterosexual sex equates with the expression of power and powerlessness—sex as male domination and female submission (Kitzinger *et al.*, 1992).

Men deploy or use their sexuality at work far more than women and yet it is women's workplace identity that is frequently saturated with sexuality (Gutek, 1989). Maybe this is because men are establishing their difference from women and their power over them. Male sexuality is privileged and enfused in organizational practices, so, for example, managers tend to be either blind to, tolerate, or even accept traditional forms of male sexuality. Talk of the male sexual drive serves to exclude women from sexualized male spaces and maintain men's dominant positions and use of hierarchical power. Men find it difficult to desexualize women. Women find that they must behave like men in order to succeed but not be men, and behave unlike women and yet be women (Witz and Savage, 1992). Modes of dress have to be gendered (skirts) and yet not sexualized (skirts too short).

If men and women have not learned the rules of how to behave as men and women, or resist the rules, then they may not 'fit in' at work. The pervasiveness of the masculine identity at work has been noted by a number of researchers (Collinson, 1988; Livingston and Luxton, 1989; Willis, 1979). It is seen as something of a stigma to be seen as 'less than a man'. At work, joking is often used to remind people of the masculine expectations of the workplace culture. The major forms of joking centre around three rules of sexuality: the ideal, typical, real man; definitions of males as not-female; and the normalcy of heterosexuality. Men who fall short of the ideal are in danger of being characterized as effeminate. Alongside the jokes, other aspects of workplace culture remind men of their sexuality. Examples include suggestive horseplay, pictures of nude women, and bragging about sexual activity.

Morgan and Knights (1991) provide some good examples of how the male gender identity is used by men to keep women out of the jobs as sales representatives in the insurance industry. Men did the selling while women were employed in back office functions doing routine clerical and administrative work, e.g. working as cashiers. The female cashiers and tellers passed referrals to the sales representatives. The women did not initially become sales representatives themselves. The men could not envisage women as sales representatives; they could not see women indulging in the bouts of communal drinking and the male sports which accompanied it; they played golf and snooker together as men. The social events would have been disrupted by the presence of a female sales representatives, and what would the wives think about their husbands working with a 'dolly bird'? Women were either 'dolly birds' without children, few responsibilities, and therefore inherently less reliable; or they were married in which case there was an assumption that they had a husband's income to support them and would not be driven to seek high commissions. If they were divorced there was a tinge of danger both managerial and moral about employing them to join a team of 'respectable' married men. There was, then, no comfortable fit for any woman. The self-image or identity subscribed to by the sales force or management personnel constructed a male culture. For the sales representatives women were to be manipulated and used to gain them customers, but the women were not passive in this process and were capable of effectively sabotaging their selling process.

Where men and women work together, romances are likely to flourish. We like and are attracted to people who are like us. There is abundant evidence that individuals tend to prefer others of similar attitudes over those with dissimilar attitudes (Smith *et al.*, 1993). Romances will occur at work. Organizational romances, relationships which develop between men and women who work together, are controversial. Margaret Mead (1980) has argued that, much like the taboos against sexual expression in the family that are necessary for children to grow up safely, taboos against sexual involvements at work are necessary for men and women to work together effectively. Some argue that both individuals should be sacked, or the organization should get rid of the less useful of the two employees (e.g. Collins, 1983). Relationships which involve some trade-off between sexual adventure and ego satisfaction for one participant and job or career advancement for the other violate the co-worker's sense of equality and provokes extreme negative reactions (Quinn and Lees, 1984). Others argue that people do not need the protection of taboos but need respect for individual freedom and rights. The creativity of the two people involved can be enhanced by the romance (Horn and Horn, 1982).

Studies from the United States show that sexual intimacy with clients, or the case of the professional who exceeds the boundaries of friendship, are common problems. One anonymous survey of graduate students indicated that 17 per cent had had sexual contact with at least one of their teachers during their training (Glaser and Thorpe, 1986). Most organizational romances were between higher-status males and lower-status females.

A survey of romances in white-collar settings reported that 62 per cent involved a man in a higher position, 30 per cent involved men and women at the same level, and only 8 per cent involved a woman in a higher position. A large majority of organizational romances involve a power differential (Anderson and Hunsaker, 1985), reflecting vertical occupational segregation. Organizational romances invoke issues of power and dependency (Mainiero, 1986).

Reports of women (and men) advancing their careers as a result of romantic relationships at work (or 'sleeping their way to the top') are less prevalent than many imagine. In Warfield's (1987) study of female managers, less than one-third of the respondents noted a case in their firm in which a woman successfully advanced her career through sexual encounters with her seniors. There were a number of negative effects noted, such as co-worker resentment, ruined credibility, and limited likelihood of future advancement.

Gutek (1985) similarly found little evidence of women using their sexuality to gain organizational goals. Only one woman out of 800 in her sample said she used sex to achieve her current position; many more reported that they were sacked or left after becoming involved with a man at work (see Mainiero, 1993).

An American survey reported that 13 per cent of therapists had had sexual contact with current or recent clients (Holroyd and Brodsky, 1977). The majority of sexual liaisons involved men in the powerful professional role and women in the less powerful student or patient role. Pope (1988) notes that 8.3 per cent of male therapists reported engaging in sex with their clients, compared with 1.7 per cent of female therapists. Such behaviour is likely to be exploitative and unethical within professional guidelines. The range of harmful consequences for the client includes an inability to trust, anger and confusion, depression and an increased risk of suicide (Pope, 1988).

It would appear that the key to the argument lies in the issue of power. Hemming (1985) argues that the psychodynamics of sexual harassment maintains an unequal power structure between the sexes, forcing women into compliance with nurturant or sexual aspects of the traditional sex role. Some forms of sexual intimacy may be acceptable if they are not extreme, have no adverse effects on productivity (Powell, 1988: 123–124), or are wanted. Women see less positive value in sexual intimacy than men. This is not surprising as women are more likely to have seen sexual harassment in the workplace and be concerned about it.

News?

A senior Intercity executive responsible for implementing the network's new anti-sexual harassment guide-lines in Scotland, has resigned from his post after allegations that he sexually harassed female staff.

Source: *Scotland on Sunday*, 3 November 1991.

During the 1980s there was a growing awareness that sexual harassment is a widespread problem (Hadjipotiou, 1983). Stories of sexual harassment are becoming popular in the press. A general practitioner writing in the *British Medical Journal* (1992) wrote of her experience of harassment. In previous encounters with aspiring rapists she had outrun one, knocked another unconscious, and hit another hard, where it hurt, (she gives the medical location). The local flasher had once hurriedly rezipped himself after she scorned the size of his organ.

What had happened that made her write of this experience of sexual harassment was an incident that took place in her surgery with one of her patients. She, finishing the 20-minute consultation, had recommended taking more rest. He leaned forward so his knee was touching hers and said 'My idea of a good rest, my dear, is lying between silk sheets and making love to a sweet young lady such as yourself.' Interpreting her numb silence as encouragement, he continued, 'I'm sure a gorgeous girl like you isn't short of offers ... you probably never thought of me as good in bed.' His hand closed over hers. She was nearly twice the size of her current aggressor, ten years his senior, and trained in martial arts. But this incident reduced her 'to a crimson, trembling wreck'.

In each case of sexual harassment, we have a perpetrator who feels powerful and a victim who feels powerless. All the evidence suggests that sexual harassment is disproportionately perpetuated by male supervisors or managers upon female subordinates (Rubenstein, 1988). It is estimated that 94 per cent of harassers are supervisors or members of management (Labour Research Department 1987). Kremer and Marks (1992: 14), from their study, were able to conclude that 'As regards perpetrators, harassers were without exception men and were normally in positions of authority over the person who was harassed.'

The organization and hierarchy must, then, be seen as a structure of gender power. Men are in locations where power resides, women where there is none. Sexual harassment can even occur in mentoring relationships; mentoring can then lead to women's underachievement at work (Paludi, 1990).

Sexual harassment and the police

Police Constable Tracey Scanlon claimed in an industrial tribunal she had received suggestive mail at work and obscene telephone calls at home. She had been plagued by rude noises on her police radio and denied promotion. What is more, her bosses have refused to investigate properly she claims.

Four out of five policewomen have experienced sexual harassment from male officers, a leaked report has found.

Source: *Personnel Today*, 13–26 October 1992 p. 13; 23 February–8th March 1993.

HOW DO WE DEFINE SEXUAL HARASSMENT?

Most sources agree that the term first came into use around 1974 and referred to male coercion—behaviour presented in the form of sexual initiative and frequently backed up by the force of higher rank at work. There is no single and precise definition of sexual harassment. The European Commission sorts sexual harassment into five categories:

- Non-verbal (e.g. pin-ups, leering, whistling and suggestive gestures)
- Physical (unnecessary touching)
- Verbal (unwelcome sexual advances, propositions or innuendo)
- Intimidation (offensive comments about dress, appearance, or performance)
- Sexual blackmail

The TUC defines it as

repeated and unwanted verbal or sexual advances, sexually explicit derogatory statements or sexually explicit remarks made by someone in the work-place which are offensive to the worker involved, which causes the worker to feel threatened, humiliated, patronised or harassed, or which interfere with the worker's job performance, undermine job security, or create a threatening or intimidating work environment. (Davidson and Earnshaw, 1990)

A single, isolated incident would not substantially affect the environment; a substantial number of incidents creates a hostile environment. Sexual harassment is power expressed sexually.

Which of the eight following types of behaviour should be defined as harassment?

1. Sex-stereotyped jokes or pictures.
2. Teasing remarks of a sexual nature.
3. Unwanted suggestive looks or gestures.
4. Unwanted letters or telephone calls.
5. Unwanted leaning or cornering.
6. Unwanted pressure for dates.
7. Unwanted touching.
8. Unwanted pressure for sexual activity.

Source: adapted from Kenig and Ryan (1986).

All eight types of behaviour in the box above are sexual harassment. As Halson (1989) points out, sexual harassment can take many forms. It may involve physical contact as when someone is patted, stroked, or held against their will. Being pinched, squeezed, grabbed, groped, and more serious sexual assaults all constitute sexual harassment. It may be verbal or psychological: staring, leering, standing too close for comfort, being followed, threatening body postures, sexual remarks or taunting, obscene gestures or jokes, explicit conversations about sex which causes offence as well as subtle or explicit pressure for sexual activity. What distinguishes sexual harassment from friendly sexual banter or flirtation is that it is not mutual; it is not welcome, it offends, and it threatens. It might appear to be about sexual attraction but it is primarily about men exercising power over women.

Wise and Stanley (1987: 71) support this view, but go one step further in their definition of sexual harassment which is

> minimalistic and yet all embracing ... all sexual harassment be-haviours are linked by the way they represent an unwanted and unsought intrusion by men into women's feelings, thoughts, be-haviours, space, time, energies and bodies.

Sexual harassment 'works' by treating women as powerless objects to men's powerful subjects. Most sexual harassment is small, mundane, and accumulating, permeating women's lives.

> Like a dripping tap these intrusions wear us down by always
> sounding in our consciousness so that we never get away from them;
> and the celestial plumber never changes the washer so we cope as
> best as we can. (Wise and Stanley, 1987: 114)

The EC code of practice draws attention to the fact that sexual harassment 'pollutes' the working environment; millions of women, and some men, suffer. As a result of this pollution employees take time off, are less efficient, and, in the worst cases, leave their jobs. It is well documented that sexual harassment damages the victim's health (Rubenstein, 1988). It results in anxiety, tension, irritability, depression, inability to concentrate, sleeplessness, fatigue, headaches, and other manifestations of stress at work. A person under stress is likely to work more erratically and make more mistakes. In short, sexual harassment has a direct impact on a company's profitability. Sandroff (1988) reported that sexual harassment cost a typical Fortune 500 company approximately $6.7 million each year as a result of lowered productivity, low morale, and increased absenteeism and turnover.

HOW PREVALENT IS THE PROBLEM?

Sexual harassment takes place in all sorts of work situations including government agencies (Ray, 1976), military units (Meyer *et al.*, 1981; Rogan, 1981), and religious organizations (Meyer *et al.*, 1981). It also happens among staff in the academic world as an article in *The Times Higher Education Supplement* (1 November 1991) shows. The author believes that the perpetrators are insecure. The insecurity

> turns itself into unmitigated and unwarranted malice. One man,
> terrified of women and especially of being contradicted by them,
> scornfully refers to senior female staff in canine terms as the pit bull
> terriers, the doberman, the rottweiller etc. Another publicly intro-
> duces a female colleague (whom he otherwise ignores) to new
> students as the member of staff 'who will soothe you' (if other women
> are present) or 'who will bite your balls off', if not.

In Scotland reports of sexual harassment are at record levels (*The Sunday Times Scotland*, 19 April 1992). The number of cases being brought is proportionally higher than in England and so decisions made in favour of victims in Scotland are being quoted as precedent in England. Industrial tribunal statistics show a 120 per cent rise in the number of sexual harassment cases taken to tribunal, from 88 in 1986 to 193 in 1991. An insurance broker, providing legal protection in cases of sexual harassment, says there has been an 81 per cent increase in the number of enquiries to their help-line. Under present sexual discrimination law it is a company's responsibility to ensure all reasonable action has been taken to prevent harassment taking place at work, so it is in employers' interests to protect themselves.

Studies seeking to document the existence and extent of harassment have indicated that it is a pervasive problem, as can be seen in the following table.

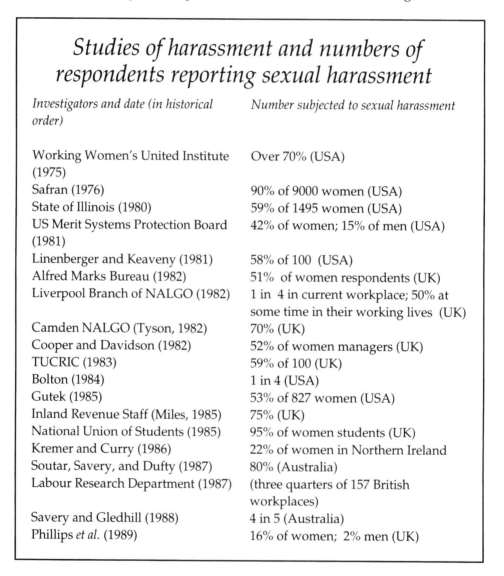

Studies of harassment and numbers of respondents reporting sexual harassment

Investigators and date (in historical order)	Number subjected to sexual harassment
Working Women's United Institute (1975)	Over 70% (USA)
Safran (1976)	90% of 9000 women (USA)
State of Illinois (1980)	59% of 1495 women (USA)
US Merit Systems Protection Board (1981)	42% of women; 15% of men (USA)
Linenberger and Keaveny (1981)	58% of 100 (USA)
Alfred Marks Bureau (1982)	51% of women respondents (UK)
Liverpool Branch of NALGO (1982)	1 in 4 in current workplace; 50% at some time in their working lives (UK)
Camden NALGO (Tyson, 1982)	70% (UK)
Cooper and Davidson (1982)	52% of women managers (UK)
TUCRIC (1983)	59% of 100 (UK)
Bolton (1984)	1 in 4 (USA)
Gutek (1985)	53% of 827 women (USA)
Inland Revenue Staff (Miles, 1985)	75% (UK)
National Union of Students (1985)	95% of women students (UK)
Kremer and Curry (1986)	22% of women in Northern Ireland
Soutar, Savery, and Dufty (1987)	80% (Australia)
Labour Research Department (1987)	(three quarters of 157 British workplaces)
Savery and Gledhill (1988)	4 in 5 (Australia)
Phillips et al. (1989)	16% of women; 2% men (UK)

The figures have to be treated with some caution as they reflect the number of respondents and not the number given questionnaires. Those who respond are more likely to have been harassed. They are a self-selected group. Much also depends on what behaviours are included in questionnaires, how situations are defined, and respondent characteristics (Brewer, 1982).

Equally you could argue that the incidence of harassment cannot be measured by the number of formal complaints because of a person's anxieties about the consequences of voicing their unease, particularly in the absence of an established grievance procedure. Perhaps we need more qualitative studies of sexual harassment. Farley (1978) referred to the use of tape recordings during job interviews to discover the existence of sexual harassment. There have been reports of how a secretary kept a diary which logged more than 100 incidents of sexual harassment by her boss against her (Corless, 1983).

Barak *et al.* (1992) have taken findings for various types of harassment in various settings, and conclude that a female worker or student has at least a 40 per cent chance of encountering some form of sexual harassment in her place of work or study.

Sexual harassment happens to men as well as women, but rarely. As seen in the table above, a survey by the US Merit Systems Protection Board (1981) found that 15 per cent of males reported having been sexually harassed during the preceding 24 months. A British Alfred Marks Bureau report (1982) showed that 51 per cent of women, compared with a third of men, responding to their national survey, had experienced sexual harassment at some point in their working lives. (It would appear that a good proportion of the studies are British but there is far more in-depth survey evidence from the United States.) But most surveys have shown that harassment is predominantly perpetrated by men against women. Gutek and Nakamura (1982) estimated that perhaps 1–2 per cent of men will experience sexual harassment in their working lives. A Labour Research Department survey (1987) confirmed this, noting that an insignificant number of workplaces mention harassment by women of men.

One group of men who might be thought of as unlikely harassers are judges. Yet Marina Angel (1991: 817) finds that judges have solicited sexual favours from criminal defendants, civil litigants, lawyers, law clerks, law students, court employees, job applicants, probation officers, juvenile court wards, and jurors. Some have demanded sex for favourable treatment and have retaliated when their demands were not met. A New Jersey Task Force (1984) reported that 25 per cent of responding women attorneys had experienced unwelcome sexual advances from judges. A Maryland survey of female attorneys found that 19 per cent had been subjected to verbal and physical sexual advances by judges. Yet men and women may like to deny that this is the case. The boxes on the next page shows how men and women respond to the information that women attorneys are subjected to these advances in a (1986) New York survey.

When a 1989 survey in Washington asked if male judges subjected female judges to verbal sexual advances, 13.3 per cent of women judges reported they were, but 96.3 per cent of male judges responded that it never happened.

Do judges subject women attorneys to verbal or physical sexual advances?

Frequency	Female respondents (%)	Male respondents (%)
Sometimes or often	16	3
Rarely	31	10
Never	–	82

Despite the seriousness of this the sanctions are light; in a typical case the judge receives no more that a censure, reprimand, or admonishment. A few, however, have been removed from office; even fewer have been criminally prosecuted. (For an excellent view of US law and sexual harassment, see MacKinnon, 1979.)

The Linenberger and Keaveny (1981) study showed that the most frequently faced form of harassment was sexual remarks and teasing, while the next most frequent was touching, brushing against, and grabbing, which has been experienced by 53 per cent of the respondents. Nine per cent had suffered actual sexual assaults. In the Soutar *et al.* survey (1987) one in 16 reported actual physical attacks. The Labour Research report found 10 per cent of all replies indicating physical assault.

Similar results can be found of the type and severity of sexual harassment in the survey by Savery and Gledhill (1988). The most common form of harassment was jokes or conversations about women which the person found offensive. Sixty-six per cent of respondents had experienced this type of harassment and 20 per cent had experienced it frequently. The least frequently experienced (in about 2 per cent of cases) was the most severe form—an attempt by a male co-worker to force the respondent to have sexual intercourse.

It is not only workers who are harassed. Students are sexually harassed too. A survey of 776 women students at Cambridge University carried out in 1989 found that one in ten had suffered unwanted sexual attention from academic staff, most of it mild—suggestive looks and remarks, sexual jokes, and being 'eyed up'. However, 2 per cent said the harassment had taken the form of requests for dates or sex and unwanted kissing, touching, and grabbing.

Carter and Jeffs (1992), drawing from research with staff, students, and ex-students from social work and youth and community work courses in English universities and polytechnics, concluded that the problem of sexual exploitation is extensive, far more so than they had ever imagined. Management in these institutions comprehensively protect those staff who engage in sexual exploitation of students; they 'leave the bottle uncorked'. A British survey of psychology Ph.D.

students showed that 6 per cent of female postgraduates had been sexually harassed by their male supervisors (Hatton, 1994). Another study (Crocker, 1983: 700) estimated that 53 169 women are victims of physical assault by their professors each year.

In the United States, according to Dziech and Weiner (1984: 15), 'again and again 20–30 percent of women students report they have been sexually harassed by male faculty during their college years'. Michele Paludi (1990: 13) reported that the most reliable figures 'indicate that 30 per cent of women students are sexually harassed by at least one instructor in college'. This figure is supported by Benson and Thomson (1982) and Adams *et al.* (1983).

Some US studies have found substantially larger percentages of women students experiencing sexual harassment. A 1981 study at the University of Iowa (Dziech and Weiner, 1984) found that 65 per cent of women students had been the target of sexist comments by faculty members. A survey by the Association of American Colleges found that 70–90 per cent of female college students reported they had experienced sexual harassment (National On-Campus Report, 1989). The most common type of harassment encountered by women university students is joking remarks about women's anatomy (Maihoff and Forrest, 1983).

Discussion point

If you are a male student, would you expect to be harassed by a woman teacher? If yes, why? If no, why not?

Women academics are highly unlikely to date or initiate sexual relationships with their male students. The great majority of their interaction with students involves mentoring or friendship behaviours, most of which involve women students (Fitzgerald and Weitzman, 1990: 137). It is extremely rare for a woman to hold the organizational power that would allow her to reward a man for sexual co-operation, or punish him for withholding it. Women virtually never become sexually involved with their students but one in four men do.

Sexual harassment also happens in British schools and universities but there is still little documented evidence. (For British research in schools see Halson, 1989, 1991; Jones, 1985; Mahony, 1985: for other non-work settings see Hey, 1986; Wise and Stanley, 1987.) Sexual harassment is a problem for women and girls wherever it occurs. Halson (1989, 1991) reported how sexual harassment was experienced by schoolgirls; these experiences in public places, from strangers, induced real fear. By far the majority of incidents involved people they knew; the girls were especially vulnerable in mixed-sex schools where they were harassed by teachers, other 'trusted' adults, and boys. These interactions are both a product of and a reproduction of power differences between men and women.

Jones (1985) has questioned the safety of mixed-sex schooling for girls. Female teachers and girls experience sexual violence at school. Their strategies for dealing with it depend on the length of time they have been at the school. The longer the woman has been teaching, or the older the girl, the less likely she is to report cases of assault, knowing that she is unlikely to be believed or that the boys would be inadequately punished. Sexual harassment is not recognized as a problem because the males do not experience it; it becomes invisible. As so few incidents are reported, the men in positions of authority are able to argue that sexual harassment is not a problem in the school.

We have seen in Chapter 2 how women are perceived in organizations. Here is how women are perceived by a group of fourth-year boys in a co-educational school in the Midlands:

> 'Scum that paints her face', 'something to kick when you are drunk', 'a thing to beat about the house', 'an ugly thing that increases population', 'a moaner', 'a slave', 'an object of ridicule' and 'a thing to use in clearing away the empty beer cans'.   (see Mahoney, 1989)

A commonly held belief is that sexual assaults are committed by men who are serious criminals or mentally ill, but the American literature suggests that large numbers of ordinary male college students have victimized women through coercion or force (Garrett-Gooding and Senter, 1987; Kanin 1985; Koss, 1981; Koss *et al.*, 1987). There is a continuum of misogyny that includes sexually harassing behaviours (sexist jokes and put-downs), intimidation, coercion, and sexual assault (Reilly *et al.*, 1982). Assaulters are more often intimates or acquaintances than strangers (Hughes and Sandler, 1987; Koss *et al.*, 1988).

Perhaps this is the most disturbing finding. Approximately one-third of men have said to researchers that if they were assured of not being reported, they might behave in a sexually assaultive manner (Briere and Malamuth, 1983; Check and Malamuth, 1983; Lotte *et al.*, 1982; Reilly *et al.*, 1982). More than half the men in Malamuth *et al.*'s (1980) study indicated some likelihood that they themselves would rape if assured of not being punished.

HOW IS SEXUAL HARASSMENT JUDGED BY EMPLOYEES AND STUDENTS?

It would appear from the results below that American university staff and students are more aware of behaviours that can be perceived as sexual harassment. Women are more likely to define the behaviour as harassing than men. Trade unionists in

Northern Ireland are more aware than managers there. There is a reluctance among all groups to label non-contact behaviour as sexual harassment.

Discussion point

If you are male, imagine this situation. You are being harassed, not by an attractive female colleague, but by a male superior in the work hierarchy. You report to this man; he controls your terms and conditions and promotion prospects. He makes appreciative comments about your physical attributes. When you enter his office he undresses you with his eyes and frequently puts a caressing arm around you. He habitually brushes up against you and then threatens that you will lose you job if you do not have sex with him. How would you react?

Here is how faculty and undergraduate students in an American university judge if the behaviour was sexual harassment (per cent)

Behaviour	Tenured faculty		Undergraduate students	
	Male	Female	Male	Female
1. Sex-stereotyped jokes or pictures	43	54	33	35
2. Teasing remarks of a sexual nature	61	80	60	58
3. Unwanted suggestive looks or gestures	81	93	71	89
4. Unwanted letters or telephone calls	97	100	98	98
5. Unwanted leaning or cornering	85	93	89	95
6. Unwanted pressure for dates	90	91	76	83
7. Unwanted touching	95	92	93	97
8. Unwanted pressure for sexual activity	99	100	99	98

Source: from Kenig and Ryan (1986: Table 11).

Here is how employers and unions in a Northern Ireland study defined acts of sexual harassment

Act	Definitely yes (%)	
	Employers	Trade unions
Suggestive remarks or other verbal abuse	44	82
Offensive pin-ups, calendars	36	64
Sexist or patronizing behaviour	41	71
Leering or eyeing up a person's body	49	71
Sexual propositions/compromising invitations	79	96
Demands for sexual favours	90	100
Unnecessary touching/unwanted contact	79	86
Physical assault	90	96

Source: adapted from Kremer and Marks (1992: 10). Adapted with permission of British Psychological Society.

The behaviour that an individual defines as sexual harassment depends on their gender, with women consistently defining more experiences as harassing than men (Collins and Blodgett, 1981; Gutek, 1985; Powell, 1983) In the Gutek (1985) survey, sexual touching showed the largest gender gap with 84 per cent of women compared with 59 per cent of men considering it to be sexual harassment. Furthermore individuals differ widely in their personal definitions; complimentary comments and suggestive remarks constitute sexual harassment for some individuals, for others they do not (Gutek, 1985; Powell, 1983).

Actions or statements on the part of the instructor suggesting coercion or threat were seen as the most harassing experiences by students (Reilly et al., 1982; Weber-Burdin and Rossi, 1982). Female students were found to rate sex-stereotyped jokes as more harassing than males did (Kenig and Ryan, 1986).

Female students also rate verbal sexual harassment, e.g. the use of obscene language, as more harassing and more inappropriate than do male students (Gervasio and Ruckdeshel, 1992). This is not surprising as men have always had more license in matters of taboo language (Preston and Stanley, 1987), more participation in naming games (Jay, 1980), and more power over women. A male harasser may well cling to the idea that his behaviour is not sexually harassing (Pryor and Day, 1988).

Sexual harassment is a complex social problem, one reason being that it is difficult to construct a consensus about what behaviours are and are not harassing. Most employees view sexual behaviour at work as benign or even positive. Men are more likely than women to view sexual behaviour at work favourably (Gutek *et al.*, 1983). In general employees tend to believe that people will be flattered by sexual overtures from the other sex and men will be somewhat more flattered than women. The same is true for students evaluating an incident of possible sexual harassment (Cohen and Gutek, 1985). Students tend to focus on the positive aspects of the encounter. For example, if a person walking down a passageway passes someone of the other sex and pats that person on the rear end, students tend to believe that the two people are friends or dating. They tend to assume that whatever happens is agreeable to both parties. It does not readily occur to them that they may be witnessing sexual harassment.

People tend to think positively about sex; sexual encounters affirm your sexual desirability. They also see social sexual encounters as interpersonal rather than as organizational; sexual overtures are not a product of the organization's culture or norms (Gutek, 1989). Individual women may want to preserve their right to set their own boundaries and contexts for sexual encounters. One might argue that Madonna has pushed and set her own boundaries, the 'Madonna paradigm' serving as a touchstone for discussions on issues of morality and gender relations; but she has inscribed herself on public consciousness in multiple and contradictory ways, appearing to some as whore or witch, others as feminist (free to be sexy, sensual, and in control of her life), and to yet others as antifeminist (see Schwichtenberg, 1993; Haste, 1993: 172–176). Not all women interpret sexual behaviour in the same way. What can be defined as harassing for one may be exciting for another. There does need to be a recognition of women's right to define their own sexuality. But we cannot escape the demands of social order and contest for power, and sexual harassment is a form of social control in the workplace and threatens the individual's autonomy. Sexuality is often used to punish women who are seen to violate gender or organizational norms (Sheppard, 1992: 157)

Sexual harassment is particularly complex in university or college settings because romantic affiliations between staff and students are going to occur and students who were complicit up to a point, are unsure about the academic's intent, have been afraid to say to their superior that their advances are unwelcome, will be reluctant to make complaints. This would help explain why only about 5 per cent of those harassed in universities in the United States have reported the harassment or filed a grievance (Fitzgerald, 1986). On average only between 2 and 7 per cent of undergraduates report confronting their harassers (UCLA Survey, 1985; Koss, 1990).

We should not be surprised if women do not complain of an experience of sexual harassment. Fitzgerald *et al.* (1988a) have indicated that undergraduate women typically do not label their experiences as sexual harassment despite the fact their experiences meet legal definitions and 30–70 per cent of these women experience one or more types of sexual harassment (gender harassment, seductive behaviour, sexual bribary, sexual coercion, and sexual imposition) each year by one or more of their male professors or graduate teaching assistants.

Another US university survey found that 75 per cent of students thought that most female students would be reluctant to report a professor's sexually harassing conduct. None of those surveyed who considered themselves harassed reported such harassment to a university official (Keller, 1990: 81). More than one-third of harassment victims in Jenson and Gutek's (1982) survey reported that they did not file a grievance against their professors because they 'thought it would be held against [them] or that [they] would be blamed' (p. 128). A lack of sexual harassment reports, then, does not necessarily indicate an absence of such a problem.

The structure of the university interacts in particular ways with psychological dynamics to increase women's susceptibility to seductive behaviour and makes it difficult for female students to see male academic behaviour as harassment (Zalk et al., 1990: 106). Many victims attempt to deny that unwanted sexual advances took place. When the coercive nature of the sexual advances cannot be denied, the relationship becomes a source of distress. Students attempt to ignore or trivialize unwanted sexual advances for as long as possible (Benson and Thomson, 1982).

There is also ample evidence to suggest that women experience an enormous amount of guilt and self-blame over harassment (Dziech and Weiner, 1984; Koss, 1990; Rabinowitz, 1990). The power that academics wield can also create an atmosphere of tension and fear. Psychologists have reported that the physiological arousal accompanying fear can mistakenly be interpreted as love (Middlebrook, 1974: 437).

Male faculty members typically do not label their behaviour as sexual harassment despite the fact they report they frequently initiate personal relationships with women students. Male faculty denied the inherent power differential between faculty and students as well as the psychological power conferred by this differential (Fitzgerald and Weitzman, 1990: 121). Pryor (1987) reported that the men who are most likely to initiate severe sexually harassing behaviour are those who emphasize male social dominance and who demonstrate insensitivity to other people's perspectives.

Male faculty who sexually harass students cross all ages, ranks, disciplines, and family situations (Fitzgerald et al., 1988b; Sandler, 1981). Why do they do it? One reason is that all the power lies with the faculty member, not the student. The student can feel singled out and special. Male teachers believe that female students are drawn to them 'as necessary and desirable guides to maturity', and the students are portrayed as needing their touch for intellectual and sexual vitality (Dziech and Weiner, 1984). The greatest power of teachers lies in their capacity to enhance or diminish their students' self-esteem.

It would be wrong to imply that all university teachers who engage in sexual relationships with female students are deceptive and manipulative men who consciously use their position of power for the explicit purpose of exploiting female students. There are always anecdotal stories to be told of marriages resulting from such relationships. But they are the exception and make for a weak defence or explanation of the dynamics underlying student–faculty sexual relations (Zalk, 1990).

Sexual harassment guidelines should, then, acknowledge that sexual harassment is more than isolated misconduct and define it as discrimination. They need to refer to a full range of harassment from subtle innuendoes to assault and to ways in which the context of open and mutual academic exchange is polluted by sexual harassment, recognizing that sexual harassment occurs between people who have unequal power (Crocker, 1983).

INTRODUCTION OF A SEXUAL HARASSMENT POLICY: EFFECT ON PREVALENCE

Organizations such as universities that introduce sexual harassment policies can initially expect reported incidents to rise in number. One study (Robertson *et al.*, 1988) showed that institutions with sexual harassment policies and procedures reported more complaints, probably indicating a heightened awareness. Two-thirds of respondents confidently believed that the grievance policy had reduced sexual harassment. This is a surprising result when one learns that only 37 per cent of those educational institutions had kept statistics on the number of complaints received and only 14.2 per cent had conducted a survey. Informal methods were most often used to deal with harassment and few sanctions were imposed. Robertson *et al.* (1988) concluded that harassers have little to fear from present sexual harassment grievance procedures and little is done to redress student complaints.

A longitudinal study by Williams *et al.* (1992) of the impact of a university policy on the sexual harassment of female students, however, showed more positive results. Their analysis suggested that the sexual harassment policy and grievance procedure at the University of Massachusetts helped to decrease reported levels of faculty/staff sexual harassment of female undergraduates, although there was an increase in reported levels of peer sexual harassment (harassment of women students by other students). The decrease in harassment, particularly in the first three years, is probably due to the educational campaign and the fact that the first claims were brought against university employees. In nearly every case formally pursued the faculty or staff member was found to have violated the policy and sanctions were imposed on the offender.

HOW IS SEXUAL HARASSMENT VIEWED BY MANAGERS?

According to a survey of 110 British companies (Davidson and Earnshaw, 1990, reported in *New Woman*, May 1992), 61 per cent of women have experienced some form of sexual harassment at work. Yet over one-third of personnel directors of top British companies do not regard sexual harassment as a serious management issue. As can be seen in the table below, less than half the personnel directors who responded classified offensive pin-up calendars and jokes with sexual connotation as amounting to sexual harassment. (A survey by Kremer and Jones, 1992, found that only two-thirds of union representatives saw offensive pin-ups and calendars as a form of sexual harassment.)

Percentage of personnel directors who regarded incidences as amounting to sexual harassment	
Incidence	*Percentage*
Unwanted physical contact	100
Demands for sexual favours in return for promotion, etc.	100
Physical assault	95.4
Asking intimate questions about a person's sex life	93.4
Unwanted propositions	92.6
Leering	76
Suggestive remarks	74
Offensive pin-up calendars	40
Jokes with sexual connotations	36.8

Source: Davidson and Bernshaw (1990)

Of those personnel directors, 88 per cent did not issue a policy statement on this subject for their companies. Only 30 per cent are in favour of stronger legislation and 54 per cent say that when a case is brought to their attention, the harasser never faces dismissal. As a solution it is more likely to be the victim, rather than the offender, who is moved to a new office.

A survey by Ford and McLaughlan (1988) found that of the 247 responding human resource managers, more than half indicated they had received either formal or informal complaints of sexual harassment in the past year. Of those complaints the most common were informal charges of comments, innuendoes, and jokes of a sexual nature. The most frequently alleged offenders were managers or supervisors and the most frequent complainers were office and clerical workers.

Ford and McLaughlan also reported that less than half the personnel managers they questioned agreed that it is harassment if the situation is 'an employee touching non-intimate parts of her body', or 'one female alleging another female got a raise, promotion, or better job assignment because the other woman and the boss were intimate'. All three of these, especially the first, could create a hostile environment and be a potential case of sexual harassment.

It would appear also that a claimant has to be able to demonstrate consistency of behaviour. A 'co-worker repeatedly asking for dates after some acceptances' is considered harassment by only 16.5 per cent of the managers. If, however, the co-worker repeatedly asked for dates after refusal, this would be considered harassment by 57.3 per cent. There is a general feeling that once the claimant has accepted a date, the legitimacy of a later complaint of sexual harassment, if further dates are requested and refused, is not as readily acknowledged.

The most common punishment, according to Labour Research (1987), for someone found guilty of harassment is a warning by management (22 per cent). The next most likely outcome, unfortunately, is 'no action'. Only two of 157 cases had gone to tribunal. Both harassers and victims left their jobs. In eight cases the victim left the job or was relocated. It may well be that women do not want disciplinary action to be taken against harassers. Brighton Borough Council, for example, found that none of the women reporting their experiences of sexual harassment wanted disciplinary action taken; they wanted the action simply to stop (Labour Research, May 1992: 18).

WHY IS SEXUAL HARASSMENT SUCH A PROBLEM TO DEAL WITH?

The first reason that makes the problem so difficult is that not all cases will be reported and so the breadth of the problem goes unrecorded. Interestingly Barak *et al.* (1992) found, in common with much previous research, that women commonly report *objectively* defined sexual harassment experiences but rarely *perceived* themselves as having been sexually harassed.

Women who have strong needs for social approval, who are repressors and erotophobic (generally disposed to respond to sexual content negatively and to avoid it), were less likely to report objectively defined experiences of sexual harassment. Women who were younger, and women who had experienced less extreme forms of objectively defined sexual harassment, were less likely subjectively to perceive they had been sexually harassed. These, then, are the individuals who are motivated to ignore (not notice, not report) objectively defined experiences of sexual harassment.

Sexual harassment is a subjective experience. Drawing the line between acceptable and unacceptable behaviour is not always easy. There is a thin line between harassment and teasing. Individuals may doubt their reactions or be embarrassed to report incidents of an intimate nature. They may fear ridicule or disbelief. The incidents might be difficult to perceive and think about: it is not always easy to see what is happening until it has happened. There is confusion and often the victim is ashamed; they might think they are just imagining what they see or they might feel that they have asked for it and it is their own fault for making themselves vulnerable. As a result they can be left with feelings of self doubt, inadequacy, and guilt and stress.

The pattern of guilt adds to the reluctance to lodge an official complaint even when the person recognizes that they have been subjected to harassment. When it comes to lodging a complaint they are frightened of hurting the person and their family as the accused is going to be in a very difficult position. Complaining might involve accusations against someone in authority. They are also scared about the effect it will have on them as they might be labelled a trouble maker. They feel demoralized and undermined. The case can involve one employee's word against another and often there are no witnesses.

As a result many victims react passively and keep silent. The majority of incidents of sexual harassment will not be reported. Kingsmill (1989) refers to a London School of Economics survey which found that only 25 per cent of incidents had been reported, while the TUCRIC survey showed that only 4 per cent had reported the incident through official channels. Phillips *et al.* (1989) found that only 27 per cent of incidents were formally reported and in 26 per cent of cases the individual who was harassed did nothing. A survey by Alfred Marks (reported in *Personnel Today*, 13–26 October 1992: 13) claimed that while 88 per cent of respondents have experienced sexual harassment at work, 71 per cent of victims do nothing, hoping the offender will stop of his own accord. The individual fears not being taken seriously, does not want to challenge the seniority of the harasser, or fears reprisals. In the 1987 US Merit Systems Protection Board survey, 52 per cent of the female respondents and 42 per cent of the males reported that they 'ignored' sexual harassment. Four per cent of the women and 7 per cent of the men reported that they simply 'went along' with it.

Two-thirds of a group of victims of sexual harassment reported apparent retaliation. They said they were criticized unduly or held up for ridicule before subordinates or clients, refused promotions, kept out of training programmes, and denied letters of reference (Crull, 1982). The experience of another group who filed complaints included prolonged harassment, retaliation by the harasser or organization in the form of psychological abuse, lowered evaluations, being denied promotion or dismissal, shunning by co-workers, withdrawal of social support previously derived from the work group (Koss, 1987: 77). It is not surprising that women are frightened of the consequences of speaking out. Those who file formal complaints or seek legal help experience 'dramatically' higher rates of physical and psychological symptoms compared to those who do not file charges (Livingston, 1982).

Among 88 cases of sexual harassment filed with one employer, almost half the complainants were fired and an additional quarter left their jobs in fear or frustration (Coles, 1986). The costs of leaving a job under these conditions mean loss of confidence, income, seniority, a disrupted work history, problems with references, and often a failure to qualify for unemployment benefit.

For university students the impact takes a different form. Dzeich and Weiner (1984) claimed that harassment often forces a student to forfeit work, research, educational comfort, or even a career. In a 1983 study conducted at Harvard University 15 per cent of the graduate and 12 per cent of the undergraduate students who experienced harassment changed their academic major or educational programme as a result (cited in Fitzgerald and Schullman, 1987). Adams *et al.* (1983) report that 13 per cent of the women students they surveyed said they had avoided taking a class or working with certain professors because of the risk of being subjected to sexual harassment.

Although the British EOC received 151 complaints of sexual harassment in 1988, most complainants felt unable to face pursuing the matter in a tribunal. Financial compensation may not be an acceptable remedy if all the victim needed was for the harassing to stop.

The study by Davidson and Earnshaw (1990) concluded that the vast majority of incidents are not reaching the ears of management because victims, who are predominantly female, are unlikely to report incidents, especially to men, unless they are sure their complaints will be dealt with seriously and sympathetically. Many believe they will not be listened to sympathetically and lack of action by management leads them to believe it is not worth reporting incidents of harassment.

Leaving the workplace is the only alternative. But some do not leave voluntarily. An Australian survey shows that in almost half of cases the complainant had 'either been sacked or resigned because of pressure or distress' (McCarthy and Stone, 1986: 318). Others claim that the majority of those who experience sexual harassment are either forced to leave or are sacked if they fail to comply with the harasser's requests (Coles, 1986; Terpestra and Cook, 1985).

WHY IS IT HAPPENING?

Sexual harassment has been socially acceptable behaviour, Lin Farley (1978) has argued. Evidence of this can be found in the numerous cartoons and jokes on the subject. Real feelings of the women involved are ignored, as if irrelevant. Even if women do not like it, there is no escape from it. 'The humour is both a function of our identification with power in a male supremacist culture and a mask for hiding the widespread damage done to the majority of working women as a result of sexual harassment' (Farley, 1978: 15).

Sexual harassment is an act of aggression and contributes to the ultimate goal of keeping women subordinate at work. Men maintain patriarchy, in part, through etiquette. Sexual harassment is about dominance. As Goffman (1956) explained, superordinates can often be identified by the exercising of familiarities which the subordinate is not allowed to reciprocate. He cites familiarities such as touching, teasing, informal demeanour, using familiar address, and asking for personal information.

Michael Argyle (1967) has given further clues to the communication of power which include bodily contact, physical proximity and position, gestures, posture, nodding or smiling, and silences and interruption. It is generally agreed that those who communicate dominance will initiate standing closer, precipitate touching, and interrupt freely. Some try to argue that this is only an expression of male sexual interest but have to agree that there is a status overlay; for example, if you are a student, waitress, barmaid you are more likely to witness male dominance behaviour than if you were royalty, the prime minister, or a boss.

Organizations, as Hearn and Parkin (1987) have noted, both those of paid work and those serving other purposes, are obvious places for the development of sexual relationships. Two surveys have reported fairly high levels of explicit sexual activity at work. Half of those men replying to a questionnaire in *Cosmopolitan* admitted to making sexual advances at work (McIntosh, 1982). A second survey of 645 readers of *Wedding Day* found that a quarter had met their marriage partners at work, school, or college (Parry, 1983). Dixons, the high street retailer, sacked three area managers for harassment but says that it does not want to turn the company into some 'puritanical place', and claims that more than half the population meets their future partner at work (*Personnel Today*, 10 August, 1993). An audience selection survey of 349 husbands and wives found that 'the most common place for affairs to start is at work' (Laming, 1985).

Harassment is more serious. In that *Cosmopolitan* survey 11 per cent of women workers reported that they had been subject to persistent, unwanted advances. Sexual harassment is allowed to survive in a web of discrimination. It thrives on collaboration and acceptance. Perpetrators only break the rules and harass where they think they can get away with it. As a practice it mostly singles women out for special treatment which adversely affects and burdens their status as employees. Two employment standards are created—one for women and one for men.

Stockdale (1986) found that the primary motives underlying sexual harassment were perceived to be sexual desire and power-play—gaining, asserting, or maintaining power and status. Whereas men were twice as likely to attribute sexual harassment to sexual desire rather than to power-play, the reverse was true for women. The harassers were seen as entirely responsible for initiating the behaviour in over three-quarters of the incidents (Phillips *et al.*, 1989). In some cases the work atmosphere was seen to encourage harassment (18 per cent), for example when 'macho' behaviour was the norm and harassment was widely accepted or when its friendly atmosphere led to a confusion of signals, or the person harassed believed they were partly at fault (11 per cent), by their failing to be more assertive or inadvertently encouraging comments or advances.

There are a number of theories or explanatory models about why sexual harassment is happening (Paludi, 1990). The first is an organizational model and, as we have noted, results from the opportunities presented by power and authority relations which derive from the hierarchical structure of organizations. Thus sexual harassment is an issue of organizational power. Institutions provide the opportunities to make harassment possible. This also explains why women may feel less comfortable, and receive less professional support and fewer intellectual challenges from male colleagues.

The second model is the socio-cultural model which posits that sexual and gender harassment is only one manifestation of the much larger patriarchal system in which men are the dominant group. Harassment is an example of men asserting their personal power, based on sex. Sex would be a better predictor of both recipient and initiator status than would organizational position. Women are more likely to be victims of sexual harassment.

Gutek (1985) has argued that sexual harassment is best thought about in relation to sex-role spillover, defined as the carry-over of gender-based expectations, that are usually irrelevant or inappropriate, about behaviour from other domains in the workplace. When the sex ratio at work is skewed in either direction, sex-role spillover occurs. Thus women in male-dominated work experience one kind of sex-role spillover. They are role deviants who will be treated differently from other (male) work-role occupants; they are aware of this differential treatment and they think it is directed at them as individual women rather than as work-role occupants. This is supported by evidence that women who enter male preserves are the most likely to be sexually harassed (ACOA, 1983: 39; DiTomaso, 1989). Men fear losing their privileged place in the labour force. Carothers and Crull (1984) have confirmed that male workers are overtly hostile to women who challenge or compete with them for jobs and that this hostility is expressed in terms of sexual harassment. In this way sexual harassment serves to reinforce the segregation of the labour market, keeping the majority of women in low-paid, low-status, often service occupations.

Women in female-dominated work also experience sex-role spillover, but this time sex role and work role are practically identical. These women are treated similarly to other (female) work-role occupants so are unaware that their treatment is based on sex role and think it is a function of their job; the job itself is sexualized. The individual's attitudes towards women, sexuality, gender, and interpersonal relations will all be significant factors, alongside their employee's commitment to the issue of sexual harassment.

This spillover hypothesis is not incompatible with the power-differential perspective on sexual harassment, as Gutek and Morasch (1982) have acknowledged. The power-differential hypothesis is particularly helpful to help place sexual harassment in the context of male–female relations. The spillover hypothesis places more emphasis on the structural variables of work-role, sex-role spillover, and sex ratios, and in the context of work behaviour.

It would appear that men and women are perceiving the same situations differently. Educational programmes need, then, to acknowledge the different understanding of the concept of harassment. Truax (cited in Fitzgerald, 1986) claimed that

> men's perceptions of what their behaviour means are vastly different from women's. ... We find, in working with victims of sexual harassment that there is often little disagreement with what has happened between student and professor, but rather, with what the conduct means. Professors will try to justify their behaviour on the grounds that they are just friendly and trying to make a student feel welcome, or they thought that the student would be flattered by the attention.

However, the interpretation given to the professor's behaviour by women students is not flattery or friendliness.

Abbey (1982) showed that men are more likely to perceive the world in sexual terms and to make sexual judgements than women are. Males seem to perceive friendliness from females as seduction. Saal (1992) carefully replicated and extended Abbey's work and showed how men perceived significantly more sexuality as flirtatiousness, promiscuity, and seductiveness, than did the women. Men have a more 'sensitive' threshold for perceiving sexy behaviour on the part of women. As Saal *et al.* (1989) explained:

> as a woman's interpersonal behaviour varies along a continuum ranging from very unfriendly and distant to very friendly and outgoing (as well it might, as a woman becomes more familiar with and comfortable in a given social setting), ... men will be quicker than women to label that increasingly friendly behaviour as 'sexy'. They *might* then respond in a variety of ways that the woman in question may construe as sexual harassment.

Gutek *et al.* (1983) found that men were likely to label any given behaviour as sexual; thus a business lunch becomes a 'date' if it is with a women. Fitzgerald and Weitzman (1990) reported how one professor stated he knew a student was interested in having sex with him because of 'the way she sat' and the fact that she made an appointment to see him shortly before the end of the working day. One of Gutek's (1985: 79) subjects noted 'We were at the lunch table. I was contacted under the table. She stepped on my foot. That told me she was interested in sexual relations'. This tendency to sexualize their experiences makes it difficult to interpret men's reports of seductive advances.

In all of the examples discussed so far, the woman has occupied a position in the organizational hierarchy that was either equal to the man's or inferior. A study by Johnson *et al.* (1987) reversed roles and portrayed a more powerful woman and a less powerful man. But the study suggests that the sex difference in perceptions of women's intentions in various organizational settings is not limited to situations where the woman is in an inferior position to the man. Whether the woman was presented in the role of student or professor, she was still perceived by male subjects as trying to be more sexual than she was perceived by female subjects.

Further findings suggest that men (mis)perceive friendliness on the part of women as a sign of sexiness or sexual availability, and are then more likely to tolerate, endorse, and ultimately engage in sexual harassment behaviours. Jensen and Gutek (1982) found that men are more likely than women to blame women for being harassed. Among women it is the victims that are less likely than others to blame women for being sexually harassed. Women who have traditional sex-role beliefs are more likely to blame themselves than other victims of sexual harassment.

We have seen how the psychologists explain why and how sexual harassment happens, but what of wider, less experimental and everyday view?

Exercise

We saw earlier how Wise and Stanley (1987) defined sexual harassment as an everyday experience and like a dripping tap. If you are female, think about the last 24 hours and see how many incidents you can recall where you have seen male power exerted. If you are male think about the incidents where you have exerted your power.

There is a masculine sway exerted over women and men alike by cultural means and force of ideas. Everyday examples of this can be found in our own experiences and are illustrated well in Cockburn's (1991) book on men's resistance to sexual equality. Cockburn showed how sexuality and difference are defined in male terms. She provided an example of a sexual regime in business that exists in a high street retail shop. The sales assistant must please while the manager must impress, placate, and control. The company's advertising and shop windows are full of idealized, 'attractive' women, men, and children, representing a caring and domestic lifestyle. A strict dress code exists for women, who are made to feel ill at ease wearing trousers or flat shoes. Male managers and office workers had created a male social world within and outside work for which women were excluded. In contrast to this exclusion is where women are included but marginalized and controlled—women are included in sexual jokes. If they 'give as good as they get' their behaviour is seen as distasteful. A woman cannot operate by men's rules and get away with it. What is funny coming from a man is obscene coming from a woman.

Everything in our culture is continually addressed in terms of patriarchal discourse. Women and men conspire to maintain the culture of woman as exploited. Women are not forced to accept such a belief. As Dorothy Smith (1987: 34) says

> At the interpersonal level it is not a conspiracy among men that they impose on women. It is a complementary social process between women and men. Women are complicit in the social practices of their silence.

As we saw in Chapter 1, there is a set of extra-organizational rules about gender that are brought into organizational life (Mills, 1992).

Now let us turn to more serious intrusions on women: sexual assaults. Two emotions involved in sexual assault are anger and lust (Lakoff, 1987). An analysis of a collection of interviews *Men on Rape* (Beneke, 1982), reported and analysed in Lakoff (1987), shows how a mild-mannered librarian would justify rape.

> Let's say I see a woman and she looks really pretty, and really clean and sexy and she's giving off very feminine, sexy vibes. I think, 'Wow, I would love to make love to her', but I know she's not really interested. It's a tease. A lot of times a woman knows she's looking really good and she'll use that and flaunt it, and it makes me feel like she's just laughing at me and I feel *degraded*. ... If I were actually desperate enough to rape somebody, it would be from wanting that person, but it would be a very spiteful thing, just being able to say, 'I have power over you and I can do anything I want with you'; because really I feel that *they* have power over *me* just by their presence. Just the fact that they can come up to me and just melt me and make me feel like a dummy makes me want revenge. They have power over me so I want power over them.   (Beneke, 1982: 43–44)

Lust and anger can go hand in hand and have serious consequences for the victim.

During 1991, 320 rapes and about 200 attempted rapes were recorded by police in Scotland. Researchers argue that rape is far more common than the statistics acknowledge. Some studies have shown that some 1 in 10 women are raped during their lifetimes. More than a third of those, and possibly half, are domestic assaults (*Scotland on Sunday*, 24 January, 1993: 34.). Other surveys show larger numbers of women who have experienced rape. For example 27.5 per cent of a national sample of US women university students had either been raped or subject to attempted rape (Koss *et al.*, 1987). A similar figure of 25.3 per cent can be found in a survey of New Zealand undergraduate university students (Gavey, 1991). In survey studies about half of all women report submitting to unwanted sexual intercourse because of male pressure, social status, or physical force (Koss *et al.*, 1987; Johnson *et al.*, 1992), although most do not apply the label 'rape'. The ultimate pragmatic reason for apparently 'consenting' to sex is to avoid being raped (Gavey, 1992).

There are many similarities between rape and sexual harassment (Quina, 1990). Rape and sexual harassment are both about power. Rape is a violent way to achieve a sense of power (Groth, 1979). A similar psychological mechanism is found among sexual harassers. While the rapist uses physical strength, a gun, or a knife, the sexual harasser uses age, social position, economic power, or authority. Both rely on the fear and vulnerability of their victims.

By their own admission rapists believe in, and act out, extreme versions of the cultural stereotype of masculinity as dominance over women (Beneke, 1982). There is evidence that sexual harassers hold the same stereotypes and desire the same macho image (Dziech and Weiner, 1984). Both kinds of offenders hold extreme stereotypes about women, including images of women as masochistic and secretly desiring their attentions. Cultural demands on women to be feminine—passive, submissive, helping, nurturing—increases the likelihood of them being victims of rape or harassment (Bart, 1985). Cameron and Frazer (1994) argue that male violence against women is political as it does not purely express individual anger and frustration but is a collective and culturally sanctioned misogyny which is important in maintaining the collective power of men.

Sexual abusers are habitual offenders and carry out their offences in a highly stereotypical fashion. Each assault is part of a pattern; victims can look for that pattern and identify others who have shared the experience and pursue a group grievance.

Eradicating sexual harassment involves a major challenge to attitudes. Formal procedures for dealing with such complaints have to be devised. Positive measures are needed to ensure that effective redress is not only available but will take place in all instances of harassment.

HOW ARE EMPLOYERS IN BRITAIN LIABLE?

Employers are liable for acts of harassment conducted by employees. Employers have responsibilities towards their employees under both common law and statute, including the Equal Pay and Sex Discrimination Acts, Race Relations Act, Employee Protection Acts and Health and Safety Acts. This means that the legal redress a woman or man takes would usually be against the employer. It is probably worth noting that the Sex Discrimination Act 1975 (Section 41) specifically states that the employer is liable for discrimination carried out by an employee, whether or not it was done with the employer's knowledge or approval, unless the employer took such steps as were reasonably practicable to prevent it.

What have companies done to try to prevent harassment? The most activity in combating harassment seems to have taken place in the public sector, for example the BBC, Birmingham City Council, the Royal Mail, and British Rail. A survey in May 1991 (reported in *Personnel Today*, 10 March 1992) showed that private-sector employers with policies are in the minority. Out of 521 companies surveyed, only 21 per cent had formal written policies for dealing with harassment. A survey by Kremer and Marks (1992) in Northern Ireland shows that only 16 per cent of private sector firms had company policy related to sexual harassment, compared with 60 per cent in the public sector. Seventy-six per cent of trade unions had agreed policies.

Sexual harassment is considered to be direct discrimination under the Sex Discrimination Act. The Act says that if a woman is treated less favourably, because of her sex, by her employer and the treatment subjects her to a 'detriment', then she can use the act to obtain compensation from her employer and have the discriminatory conduct ended. For a claim to succeed, the discrimination must be found to be unlawful, and generally leads to dismissal because the victim refuses to comply with demands.

The first successful case, which developed the law on sexual discrimination at work to include sexual harassment, was a Scottish case which occurred in 1986 (Porcelli *v*. Strathclyde Regional Council). It was a Court of Session ruling and was therefore binding on all lower Courts in Scotland and on all Industrial and Employment Appeal Tribunals within Britain. It also, under common law, had to be taken into account by the courts in England and Wales. Ms Porcelli had suffered a campaign of sexual harassment by two male colleagues.

Alternatively, using the Employment Protection (Consolidation) Act 1978, the victim of harassment can walk out of their job and claim constructive dismissal in that the employer has committed a serious breach of the employment contract. Their employer's implied duty of trust and confidence in the employment relationship was broken when sexual harassment was tolerated, encouraged, or committed by the employer. The case of Bracebridge Engineering Ltd *v*. Darby in 1990 showed that a single incident of sexual harassment, provided it was sufficiently serious, can amount to unlawful sex discrimination and that an employer's failure to treat seriously a complaint of sexual harassment can give grounds for constructive dismissal.

Otherwise, if someone has been dismissed because they objected to conduct towards them which they found unacceptable, or if they resigned because of a fundamental breach of contract by or on behalf of their employer, they may bring a complaint of unfair dismissal to an industrial tribunal. The complaint must be brought within three months of the termination of the employment and the person must have completed two years' continuous employment if they worked between 8 and 16 hours a week. There are other routes to taking a case to law, e.g. using common law, and all options should be considered.

It has recently been argued that sexual harassment could be considered under the employer's duty to ensure, as far as is reasonably practicable, the health, safety, and welfare of employees. If this is the case employers could face prosecution as well as civil proceedings but this interpretation of the Health and Safety At Work Act has not yet been tested in court. If the act was so serious that it amounted to unlawful assault, this would give rise to civil or criminal liability. Indecent assault is a serious criminal offence.

The levels of compensation are high in Britain and indicate the seriousness with which tribunals view harassment.

Employer	Harasser	Outcome
North Shore Meat Packers	Male co-workers	£8000
South Wales Newspapers	Manager	£3000
Co-op Garage	Manager	£6000
Strathclyde Regional Council	Male co-workers	£3000
William Rutter Management Holdings	Manager	£2255

Source: Labour Research Department (1987).

A study of the outcomes of court decisions from the United States shows that at first courts ruled that harassment could only be considered a form of discrimination if the victim had lost tangible benefits (e.g. employment, promotion) as a result of the harassment. Psychological damage was not sufficient to prove discrimination occurred. However, later rulings considered psychological damage as sex discrimination (Livingston, 1982). Further research on court decisions shows that these were related to the severity of the behaviour involved, presence of witnesses, whether the complainant had supporting documents, whether the complainants had notified their companies of the harassment before filing charges, and whether the organizations had taken action (Terpstra and Baker, 1992). This, then, can help us think through what individuals can and should do in cases of sexual harassment.

Here are some ideas about what can be done at work? As a group, can you think of other strategies?

What can be done?

1. Ask the harasser to stop or make it clear that the behaviour is unwelcome. Once the person knows the behaviour is unwelcome, this could be enough to stop it. It may be preferable to write to the harasser describing the offensive behaviour and asking for it to end. If this is done a copy of the letter should be kept to make it clear that further action will be taken if the behaviour persists. If a more subtle behaviour is required, leave an article, from a newspaper or magazine near the offender and see if they pick up the message. If there is policy on harassment, leave that at the harassers' workstation.
2. Should the behaviour continue, do what Wise and Stanley recommend—go public. Women have traditionally undermined sexual harassment by turning private experience into public knowledge through sharing it with other women. Talk to your manager or supervisor. If they are the source of harassment, speak to someone further up the hierarchy. Seek support from your colleagues, personnel officer, sexual harassment counsellor, the union official, or anyone you feel might lend personal support. If none of these options are open to you, you can seek help from a Citizens' Advice Bureau or the Equal Opportunities Commission. Ask for help in documenting the harassment and in finding similar cases. Seek a resolution with the help of those in authority.
3. Keep a diary of incidents of harassment. If any of your colleagues are being harassed by the same person, ask them to keep records too.
4. Pursue a formal grievance procedure. This might mean making a formal complaint.
5. Refuse to work next to the person.
6. Seek protection from colleagues; work in pairs if possible.
7. Put the matter 'fictionally' to the harasser and see if they agree such actions are wrong.
8. Introduce a sexual and racial harassment policy (see Rubenstein, 1991). The policy should include a workable definition of sexual harassment which informs employees that certain behaviours, whether intended or

---

not, are recognized by the organization as unacceptable and damaging to the victim's work and personal well-being.

If a sexual harassment policy has the status of a local agreement and is incorporated into the contract of employment, then this gives the employee strength. This gives the complainant a contractual right to have the matter dealt with through the agreed machinery and a right of action for breach of contract should the employer fail to use it. All employees should know how serious the consequences are. Clauses can be added, for example, it will be the harasser that is moved, and not the complainant. Procedures should commit management to prompt corrective action and be designed to maintain confidentiality at all times.

For the policy to work well there should be a confidential but effective source of advice, guidance, and support. There needs to be training of sexual harassment counsellors, or a panel and managers responsible for investigatory hearings. Panels need clear terms of reference. There should be strict time limits so that, for example, initial investigations by a panel or a designated officer should take place within days.

Men and women at all levels in an organization need to see 'the reality' of sexual harassment: men are made aware of the impact of imposed sexual attention and women perceive they have the right to challenge such behaviour.

Here are some ideas about what can be done at university or college. As a group, can you think of other strategies?

1. As in the previous example, simple solutions can be used, e.g. ask the harasser to stop or make it clear that the behaviour is unwelcome and go public.
2. If you have been harassed, find others and collectively tell the offender that their behaviour is unwanted and ask them not to repeat the behaviour.
3. Use teaching evaluation forms to make clear to staff which behaviours e.g. sexist comments, you find unacceptable.
3. The names of chronic harassers can be made public or passed through the student grapevine. Embarrassment over such exposure might motivate change.
4. Ask for key individuals to be trained e.g. wardens in residences, tutors, lecturers, faculty supervisors.
5. Write a pamphlet for distribution among students on what harassment is, how to avoid it and what their rights, as students, are. Make sure student

handbooks contain such information. The students newspaper can be urged to publish articles on sexual harassment. May be they could be encouraged to run a competition for 'Sexist Remark of the Year'.

Source: adapted from Biaggio *et al.*, 1990.

Organizational affiliations and romances are going to occur and it is sometimes hard for both the participants to see that the situation has developed into harassment. There will almost always be issues of power and dependency within the relationship. We can conclude that there appear to be a variety of individual interpretations as to what constitutes good practice and how sexual harassment should be defined. Sexual harassment is so difficult to deal with because it is difficult to construct a consensus on what behaviours are and are not harassing. Women are more likely to define behaviour as harassing than men, yet are unlikely to complain of an experience of sexual harassment.

Whether men are using sexual harassment to keep a junior woman 'in her place' or to warn a more senior woman of her proper place, it is a controlling gesture to diminish any sense of a woman's power. Men's sexuality and organizational power are inextricably linked (Collinson and Collinson, 1989: 107). Sexual harassment can be seen as a form of victimization or a display of power. It is an inappropriate use of power; it undermines, isolates, and degrades. As the perpetrator is normally a man, it can be seen as a product of, and reflects men's attitudes towards women in society. Harassment is inextricably linked with women's disadvantaged status at work and subordinated position in society. A case of sexual harassment appears in the Appendix.

As we have seen, Gutek (1985) has argued that sexual harassment is best thought of as in relation to sex-role spillover. The individual's attitudes towards women, sexuality, gender, and interpersonal relations are all be significant factors, alongside their employer's commitment to the issue of sexual harassment. The commitment to banishing sexual harassment does not seem to be present in the workplace or in the wider world. Complaints are not therefore going to be brought to attention.

--- *Review Questions* ---

Do you think consensual relationships between staff and students in your college/university should be banned? (See in particular, pp. 115–140 of Powell, 1988.)

What causes sexual harassment to happen?

Why is it so difficult to deal with? (Have a look at 'Anne's Experience' in the Appendix), p. 260.

How would you go about trying to investigate sexual harassment in an organization? How would you try to stop sexual harassment happening?

What are the similarities between rape and sexual harassment?

How are the images Madonna presents to men and women multi-faceted and contradictory?

REFERENCES

ABBEY, A. '(1982) Sex Differences in Attribution for Friendly Behavior: Do Males Misperceive Female's Friendliness?', *Journal of Personality and Social Psychology*, **42**, 830–838.

ADAMS, J. W., KOTTKE, J. L. and PADGITT, J. S. (1983) 'Sexual Harassment of University Students', *Journal of College Student Personnel*, **24**, 484–490.

ACOA (ADMINISTRATIVE AND CLERICAL OFFICERS' ASSOCIATION) (1983) 'Sexual Harassment in the Workplace: A Union Perspective', ACOA, Brisbane.

ALFRED MARKS BUREAU (1982) 'Sex in the Office: An Investigation into the Incidence of Sexual Harassment', London.

ANDERSON, C. I. and HUNSAKER, P. L. (1985) 'Why There's Romancing at the Office and Why It's Everybody's Problem' *Personnel*, **62**(2), 57–63.

ANGEL, M. (1991) 'Sexual Harassment by Judges', *University of Miami Law Review*, **45(4)**, 817–841.

ARGYLE, M. (1967) Psychology of Interpersonal Behaviour, Cox & Wyman, London.

BARAK, A., FISHER, W. A. and HOUSTON, S. (1992) 'Individual Difference Correlates of the Experience of Sexual Harassment Among Female University Students', *Journal of Applied Social Psychology* **22**(1), 17–37.

BART, P. (1985) *Stopping Rape: Successful Survival Strategies*, Pergamon Press, Elmsford, NY.

BENEKE, T. (1982) *Men on Rape*, St Martin's Press, New York.

BENSON, D. J. and THOMSON, G. E. (1982) 'Sexual Harassment on a University Campus: The Confluence of Authority Relations, Sexual Interest and Gender Stratification', *Social Problems*, **29**(3), 236–251.

BIAGGIO, M. K., WATTS, D. and BROWNELL, A. (1990) 'Addressing Sexual Harassment: Strategies for Prevention and Change', Chapter 11 in M. Paludi, *Ivory Tower: Sexual Harassment on Campus*, State University of New York Press, Albany.

BOLTON, M. (1984) 'One Woman in Four Suffers Work Harassment', *The Age*, 25, January, 14.

BORROWDALE, A. (ed.) (1993) 'Sex and Sexism in the Workplace', Chapter 6 in *A Woman's Place . . . ? Women and Work*, St Andrew Press, Edinburgh.

BREWER, M. (1982) 'Further Beyond Nine to Five: An Integration and Future Directions', *Journal of Social Issues*, **38**(4), 1149–1158.

BRIERE, J. and MALAMUTH, N. M. (1983) 'Self-reported Likelihood of Sexually Aggressive Behavior: Attitudinal Versus Sexual Explanations', *Journal of Research on Personality*, **17**, 315–323.

BRITISH MEDICAL JOURNAL (1992) 'Heartsink and Roses', **304**, 15 February, 450.

BURRELL, G. (1984) 'Sex and Organizational Analysis', *Organization Studies*, **5**(2), 97–110.

CAMERON, D. and FRAZER, E. (1994) 'Masculinity, Violence and Sexual Murder', Chapter 25 in *The Polity Reader in Gender Studies*, Polity Press, Blackwell, Cambridge.

CAROTHERS, S. C. and CRULL, P. (1984) 'Contrasting Sexual Harassment in Female and Male Dominated Occupations', in K. Brodkin-Sacha and D. Remy (eds), *My Troubles Are Going to Have Trouble with Me*, pp. 219–228. Rutgers University Press, New Brunswick, NJ.

CARTER, P. and JEFFS, T. (1992) *The Hidden Curriculum: Sexuality in Professional Education*, Chapter 18 in P. Carter, T. Jeffs and M. K. Smith (eds), *Changing Social Work and Welfare*, Open University Press, Milton Keynes.

CHECK, J. V. P. and MALAMUTH, N. M. (1983) 'Sex Role Stereotyping and Reactions to Depictions of Stranger Versus Acquaintance Rape', *Journal of Personality and Social Psychology*, **45**, 344–356.

COCKBURN, C. (1991) *In the Way of Women: Men's Resistance to Sex Equality in Organizations*, Macmillan, Basingstoke.

COHEN, A. F. and GUTEK, B. A. (1985) 'Dimensions of Perceptions of Social-sexual Behavior in a Work Setting', *Sex Roles*, **13**, 317–327.

COLES, F. S. (1986) 'Forced to Quit: Sexual Harassment Complaints and Agency Response', *Sex Roles*, **14**(1/2), 81–95.

COLLINS, E. G. (1983) 'Managers and Lovers', *Harvard Business Review*, **61**(5), 142–153.

COLLINS, E. G. and BLODGETT, T. B. (1981) 'Sexual Harassment: Some See It . . . Some Won't', *Harvard Business Review*, **59**(2), 76–95.

COLLINSON, D. L. 1988) 'Engineering Humour: Masculinity, Joking and Conflict in Shop Floor Relations', *Organizational Studies*, **9**(2), 181–199.

COLLINSON, D. L. and COLLINSON, M. (1989) 'Sexuality in the Workplace: The Domination of Men's Sexuality', in J. Hearn *et al.* (eds), *The Sexuality of Organizations*, Sage, London.

COOPER, C. and DAVIDSON, M. J. (1982) *High Pressure:, Working Lives of Women Managers*, Fontana, London.

CORLESS, F. (1983) 'The 100 Sexy Secrets of a Secretary's Diary', *Daily Mirror*, 5 October.

CROCKER, P. L. (1983) 'An Analysis of University Definitions of Sexual Harassment', *Signs*, Summer, 696–707.

CRULL, P. (1982) 'Stress Effects of Sexual Harassment on the Job: Implications for Counseling', *American Journal of Orthopsychiatry*, **52**, 539–544.

DAVIDSON, M. J. AND EARNSHAW, J. (1990) 'Policies, Practices and Attitudes towards Sexual Harassment in UK Organizations', *Personnel Review*, **19**(3), 23–27.

DITOMASO, N. (1989) 'Sexuality in the Workplace: Discrimination and Harassment', Chapter 5 in J. Hearn *et al.* (eds), *The Sexuality of Organizations*, Sage, London.

DZIECH, B. W. and WEINER, L. (1984) *The Lecherous Professor*, Beacon Press, Boston.

FARLEY, L. (1978) *Sexual Shakedown: The Sexual Harassment of Women on the Job*, Melbourne House, London/McGraw-Hill, New York.

FITZGERALD, L. F. (1986) 'The Lecherous Professor: A Study in Power Relations', paper presented at the American Psychological Association, August, Washington, DC and quoted in Paludi (1990).

FITZGERALD, L. F. and SCHULLMAN, S. L. (1987) 'The Development and Validation of an Objectively Scored Measure of Sexual Harassment in Higher Education: Some Extensions and Applications to the Theory', Paper presented to the Convention of the Association for Women in Psychology, Denver, Colo. and cited in Koss (1987).

FITZGERALD, L. F. and WEITZMAN, L. M. (1990) *Men Who Harass: Speculation and Data*, in M. Paludi (ed.), *Ivory Tower: Sexual Harassment on Campus*, State University of New York Press, Albany.

FITZGERALD, L. F., SCHULLMAN, S., BAILEY, N. , RICHARDS, M. SWECKER, J., GOLD, Y., ORMEROD, M. and WEITZMAN, L. (1988a) 'The Incidence and Dimensions of Sexual Harassment in Academia and the Workplace', *Journal of Vocational Behaviour*, **32**, 152–175.

FITZGERALD, L. F. WEITZMAN, L., GOLD, Y., and ORMEROD, M. (1988b) 'Academic Harassment: Sex and Denial in Scholarly Garb', *Psychology of Women Quarterly*, **12**, 329–340.

FORD, R. C. and MCLAUGHLAN, F. S. (1988) 'Sexual Harassment at Work', *Business Horizons*, November–December 15–19.

GARRETT-GOODING, J. and SENTER, R. (1987) 'Attitudes and Acts of Sexual Aggression on a University Campus', *Sociological Inquiry*, **57**, 348–371.

GAVEY, N. (1991) 'Sexual Victimization Prevalence Among New Zealand University Students', *Journal of Consulting and Clinical Psychology*, **59**(3), 464–466.

GAVEY, N. (1992) 'Technologies and Effects of Heterosexual Coercion', *Feminism and Psychology*, **2**(3), 325–352.

GERVASIO, A. H. and RUCKDESCHEL, K. (1992) 'College Students' Judgements of Verbal Sexual Harassment', *Journal of Applied Social Psychology*, **22**(3), 190–211.

GLASER, R. D. and THORPE, J. S. (1986) 'Unethical Intimacy: A Survey of Sexual Contact and Advances Between Psychology Educators and Female Graduate Students', *American Psychologist*, **41**, 43–51.

GOFFMAN, E. (1956) 'The Nature of Deference and Demeanour', *American Anthropologist*, **LVIII**, 473–502.

GROTH, A. N. (1979) *Men Who Rape: The Psychology of the Offender*, Plenum, New York.

GUTEK, B. A. (1985) *Sex and the Workplace*, Jossey-Bass, San Francisco.

GUTEK, B. A. (1989) 'Sexuality in the Workplace: Key Issues in Social Research and Organizational Practice', Chapter 4 in J. Hearn, D. L. Sheppard, P. Tancred-Sheriff and G. Burrell (eds), *The Sexuality of Organization*, Sage, London.

GUTEK, B. A. and NAKAMURA, C. Y. (1982) 'Gender Roles and Sexuality in the World of Work', in E. Allgeir and N. McCormick, (eds), *Gender Roles and Sexual Behaviour: Changing Boundaries*, Mayfield, Palo Alto, Calif.

GUTEK, B. A. and MORASCH, B. (1982) 'Sex Ratios, Sex Role Spillover, and Sexual Harassment of Women at Work', *Journal of Social Issues*, **38**(4), 55–74.

GUTEK, B. A., MORASCH, B. and COHEN, A. G. (1983) 'Interpreting Social Sexual Behaviour in a Work Setting', *Journal of Vocational Behaviour*, **22**, 30–48.

HADJIPOTIOU, N. (1983) *Women and Harassment at Work*, Pluto Press, London.

HALSON, J. (1989) 'The Sexual Harassment of Young Women', Chapter 10 in L. Holly (ed.), *Girls and Sexuality*, Open University Press, Milton Keynes.

HALSON, J. (1991) 'Young Women, Sexual Harassment and Heterosexuality: Violence, Power Relations and Mixed-sex Schooling', Chapter 6 in P. Abbot and C. Wallace (eds), *Gender, Power and Sexuality*, Macmillan, Basingstoke.

HASTE, H. (1993) *The Sexual Metaphor*, Harvester Wheatsheaf, Hemel Hempstead.

HATTON, C. (1994) 'To PhD or not to PhD? The Psy-PAG Survey', *The Psychologist*, **7**(5), 212–215.

HEARN, J. and PARKIN, W. (1987) *'Sex' at 'Work': The Power and Paradox of Organizational Sexuality*, Wheatsheaf, Brighton.

HEMMING, H. (1985) 'Women in a Man's World: Sexual Harassment' *Human Relations*, **38**(1), 67–79.

HEY, V. (1986) *Patriarchy and Pub Culture*, Tavistock, London.

HOLROYD, J. C. and BRODSKY, A. M. (1977) 'Psychologists' Attitudes and Pratices Regarding Erotic and Nonerotic Physical Contact with Patients', *American Psychologist*, **32**, 843–849.

HORN, P. AND HORN, J. (1982) *Sex in the Office*, Addison-Wesley, Reading, Mass.

HUGHES, J. O. and SANDLER, B. R. (1987) '"Friends" Raping Friends', Project on the Status and Education of Women, Association of American Colleges, Washington DC.

JAY, T. B. (1980) 'Sex Roles and Dirty Word Usage: A Review of the Literature and a Reply to Haas', *Psychological Bulletin* **38**, 614–621.

JENSEN, I. W. and GUTEK, B. A. (1982) 'Attributions and Assignment of Responsibility in Sexual Harassment', *Journal of Social Issues*, **38**(4), 121–136.

JOHNSON, G. D., PALILEO, G. J. and GRAY, N. B. (1992) '"Date Rape" on a Southern Campus', *Sociology and Social Research* **76**(2), 37–44.

JONES, C. (1985) 'Sexual Tyranny in Mixed Sex Schools: An In-depth Study of Male Violence in G. Weiner (ed.), *Just a Bunch of Girls: Feminist Approaches to Schooling*, Open University Press, Milton Keynes.

KANIN, E. J. (1985) 'Date Rapists: Differential Sexual Socialization and Relative Deprivation', *Archives of Sexual Behavior*, **14**, 219–231.

KELLER, E. A. (1990) 'Consensual Amorous Relationships Between Faculty and Students: The Constitutional Right to Privacy', in E. K. Cole (ed.), *Sexual Harassment on Campus: A Legal*

Compendium, 2nd edn, National Association of College and University Attorneys, Washington, DC.

KENIG, S. and RYAN, J. (1986) 'Sex Differences in Levels of Tolerance and Attribution of Blame for Sexual Harassment on a University Campus', *Sex Roles*, **15**, 535–549.

KINGSMILL, D. (1989) 'What is Sexual Harassment?', *The Sunday Times*, 23rd April.

KITZINGER, C., WILKINSON, S. and PERKINS, R. (1992) 'Theorizing Heterosexuality', *Feminism and Psychology*, **2(3)**, 293–324.

KOSS, M. P. (1981) *Hidden Rape on a University Campus*, National Institute of Mental Health, Rockville, Md.

KOSS, M. P. (1990) 'Changed Lives: The Psychological Impact of Sexual Harassment', Chapter 4 in M. Paludi (ed.), *Ivory Tower: Sexual Harassment on Campus*, State University of New York Press, Albany.

KOSS, M. P., DINERO, T. E. and SEIBEL, C. A. (1988) 'Stranger Acquaintance Rape', *Psychology of Women Quarterly*, **12**, 1–24.

KOSS, M. P., GIDYCZ, C. A. and WISNIEWSKI, N. (1987) 'The Scope of Rape: Incidence and Prevalence of Sexual Aggression and Victimization in a National Sample of Higher Education Students', *Journal of Consulting and Clinical Psychology*, **55**, 162–170.

KREMER, R.J. and CURRY, C. (1986) 'Attitudes Towards Women in Northern Ireland', Equal Opportunities Commission, Belfast.

KREMER, J. M.D. and MARKS, J. (1992) 'Sexual Harassment: The Response of Management and Trade Unions', *Journal of Occupational and Organizational Psychology*, **65**, 5–15.

LABOUR RESEARCH DEPARTMENT (1987) 'Sexual Harassment at Work', Bargaining Report, 4–11 December.

LAKOFF, G. (1987) *Women, Fire and Dangerous Things*, University of Chicago Press, Chicago, Ill.

LAMING, S. (1985) 'Sex in the Suburbs', *News of the World*, 22 December.

LINENBERGER, P. and KEAVENY, T. S. (1981) 'Sexual Harassment in Employment', *Human Resource Management*, **20**(1), 11–17.

LIVINGSTON, J. (1982) 'Responses to Sexual Harassment on the Job: Legal, Organizational, and Individual Actions', *Journal of Social Issues*, **38**(4), 5–22.

LIVINGSTONE, D. W. and LUXTON, M. (1989) 'Gender Consciousness at Work: Modification of the Male Breadwinner Norm Among Steelworkers and their Spouses', *The Canadian Review of Sociology and Anthropology* **26**(2), 240–275.

LOTT, B., REILLY, M. E. and HOWARD, D. (1982) 'Sexual Assault and Harassment: A Campus Community Case Study', *Signs*, **8**, 296–319.

MCCARTHY, T. E. and STONE, R. J. (1986) *Personnel Management in Australia*, Wiley, Brisbane.

MCINTOSH, J. (1982) 'Sexual Harassment: You Tell Us It's Not a Joke', *Cosmopolitan*, October.

MACKINNON, K. (1979) *Sexual Harassment of Working Women: A Case of Sex Discrimination*, Yale University Press, New Haven, Conn..

MAIHOFF, N. and FOREST, L. (1983) 'Sexual Harassment in Higher Education: An Assessment Study', *Journal of the National Association of Women Deans, Administrators and Counsellors*, Winter, 3–15.

MAINIERO, L. A. (1986) 'A Review and Analysis of Power Dynamics in Organizational Romances', *Academy of Management Review*, **11**, 750–762.

MAINIERO, L. A. (1993) 'Dangerous Liaisons? A Review of Current Issues Concerning Male and Female Romantic Relationships in the Workplace', Chapter 6 in E. A. Fagenson (ed.), *Women in Management*, Sage, Newbury Park, Calif.

MAHONEY, P. (1989) 'Sexual Violence and Mixed Schools' Chapter 6 in *Learning Our Lines, Sexuality and Social Control in Education*, Women's Press, London.

MALAMUTH, N. M., HABER, S. and FESHBACH, S. (1980) 'Testing Hypotheses Regarding Rape: Exposure to Sexual Violence, Sex Differences and the "Normality" of Rapists', *Journal of Research in Personality*, **1**(4), 121–137.

MEAD, M. (1980) 'A Proposal: We Need Taboos on Sexuality at Work', in D. A. Neugarten and J. M. Shafritz (eds), *Sexuality in Organizations*, Moore, Oak Park, Ill.

MEYER, M. C., BERCHTOLD, I. M., OESTREICH, J. L. and COLLINS, F. J. (1981) Sexual Harassment, Petrocelli, New York.

MIDDLEBROOK, P. N. (1974) *Social Psychology in Modern Life*, Alfred Knopf, New York.

MILES, R. (1985) 'Sex on the Job', *Cosmopolitan*, July.

MILLS, A. J. (1992) 'Organization, Gender and Culture', Chapter 5 in A. J. Mills and P. Tancred (eds), *Gendering Organizational Analysis*, Sage, London.

MORGAN. G. and KNIGHTS, D. (1991) 'Gendering Jobs: Corporate Strategy, Managerial Control and the Dynamics of Job Segregation', *Work, Employment and Society*, **5**(2), 181–200.

NALGO, Liverpool (1982) Equal Opportunities Working Party, Report on Sexual Harassment.

NATIONAL ON-CAMPUS REPORT, 4 September 1989 (reported in Williams *et al.* 1992).

NATIONAL UNION OF STUDENTS (1985) Survey reported in 'Sexual Harassment at Work', Labour Research Department Bargaining Report, 4–11 December 1987, London.

NEW JERSEY TASK FORCE (1984) Task Force on Women in the Courts, New Jersey Supreme Court, first year report cited in Angel (1991).

PALUDI, M. A. (ed.) (1990) *Ivory Tower: Sexual Harassment on Campus*, State University of New York Press, Albany.

PARRY, G. (1983) 'Equal Rights on the Wedding Night', *Guardian*, 26 July.

PHILLIPS, C. M., STOCKDALE, J. E. and JOEMAN, L. M.(1989) 'The Risks of Going to Work: The Nature of People's Work, the Risks They Encounter, and the Incidence of Sexual Harassment, Physical Attack and Threatening Behaviour', *Suzy Lamplugh Trust*, London.

POPE, K. S. (1988) 'How Clients are Harmed by Sexual Contact with Mental Health Professionals: The Syndrome and its Prevalence' *Journal of Counselling and Development*, **67**, 222–226.

POWELL, G. N. (1983) 'Sexual Harassment: Confronting the Problem of Definition', *Business Horizons*, **26**(4), 24–8.

POWELL, G. N. (1988) *Women and Men in Management*, Sage, London.

PRESTON, K. and STANLEY, K. (1987) 'What's the Worst Thing . . .? Gender-directed Insults, *Sex Roles*, **17**, 209–219.

PRINGLE, R. (1989) 'Bureaucracies, Rationality and Sucality: The Case of Secretaries', in J. Hearn *et al.* (eds), *The Sexuality of Organization*, Sage, London.

PRYOR, J. (1987) 'Sexual Harassment Proclivities in Men', *Sex Roles*, **17**, 269–290.

PRYOR, J. B. and DAY, J. D. (1988) 'Interpretations of Sexual Harassment: An Attributional Analysis', *Sex Roles*, **18**(7/8), 405–417.

QUINA, K. (1990) 'The Victimization of Women', Chapter 5 in M. Paludi (ed.), *Ivory Tower: Sexual Harassment on Campus*, State University of New York Press, Albany.

QUINN, R. E. and LEES, P. L. (1984) 'Attraction and Harassment: Dynamics of Sexual Politics in the Workplace', *Organizational Dynamics*, **13**(2), Autumn, 35–46.

RABINOWITZ, V. C. (1990) 'Coping With Sexual Harassment', Chapter 6 in M. Paludi (ed.), *Ivory Tower: Sexual Harassment on Campus*, State University of New York Press, Albany.

RAMAZANOGLU, C. (1989) *Feminism and the Contradictions of Oppression*, Routledge, London.

RAY, E. L. (1976) *The Washington Fringe Benefit*, Dell, New York.

REDBOOK (1976) Sexual Harassment Survey Results, *Redbook Magazine*, Claire Safran, November.

REILLY, M. E., LOTT, B., CALDWELL, D. and DELUCA, L. (1992) 'Tolerance for Sexual Harassment Related to Self-reported Sexual Victimization', *Gender and Society*, **6**(1), 122–138.

REILLY, T., CARPENTER, S., DULL, V. and BARTLEY, K. (1982) The Factorial Survey: An Approach to Defining Sexual Harassment on Campus, *Journal of Social Issues*, **38**, 99–110.

RICH, A. (1980) 'Compulsory Heterosexuality and Lesbian Existence', *Signs*, **5**(4), 631–660.

ROBERTSON, C., DYER, C. E. and CAMPBELL, D. (1988) 'Campus Harassment: Sexual Harassment: Policies and Procedures at Institutions of Higher Learning', *Signs*, **13**, 792–812.

ROGAN, H. (1981) *Mixed Company: Women in the Modern Army*, G. P. Putman's Sons, New York.

RUBENSTEIN, M. (1988) 'The Dignity of Women at Work: A Report on the Problem of Sexual Harassment in the Member States of the European Communities', European Communities Commission, Brussels.

RUBENSTEIN, M. (1991) 'Devising a Sexual Harassment Policy', *Personnel Management*, **23(2)**, 34–38.

SAAL, F. E. (1992) 'Sexual Harassment in Organizations', Chapter 11 in K. R. Murphy and E. E. Saal (eds), *Psychology in Organizations*, Erlbaum, New York.

SAAL, F. E. JOHNSON, B. and WEBER, N. (1989) 'Friendly or Sexy? It May Depend on Whom you Ask', *Psychology of Women Quarterly*, **13**, 263–276.

SANDLER, B. (1981) 'Sexual Harassment: A Hidden Problem', *Educational Record*, **62**, 52–57.

SANDROFF, R. (1988) 'Sexual Harassment in the Fortune 500', *Working Woman*, December, 69–73.

SAVERY, L. K. and GLEDHILL, A. C. (1988) 'Sexual Harassment of Women in Industry and Commerce by Co-workers: Some Australian Evidence', *Personnel Review*, **17(6)**, 34–37.

SCHWICHTENBERG, C. (ed.) (1993) *The Madonna Connection: Representational Politics and Subcultural Identities and Cultural Theory*, Westview Press, Oxford.

SAFRAN, C. (1976) *Redbook Magazine*, November.

SHEPPARD, D. (1992) 'Women Manager's Perceptions of Gender and Organizational Life', Chapter 8 in A. J. Mills and P. Tancred (eds), *Gendering Organizational Analysis*, Sage, London.

SMITH, D. E. (1987) *The Everyday World as Problematic*, Open University Press, Milton Keynes.

SMITH, E. R., BECKER, M. A., BYRNE, D. and PRZYBYLA, D. P. (1993) 'Sexual Attitudes of Males and Females as Predictors of Interpersonal Attraction and Marital Compatability', *Journal of Applied Social Psychology*, **23(13)**, 1011–1034.

SOUTAR, G. N., SAVERY, L. K. and DUFTY, N. F. (1987) 'Sexual Harassment in the Banking Industry: Some Australian Evidence', *Human Resource Management Australia*, **2(3)**, 82–88.

STATE OF ILLINOIS (1980) Testimony of Barbara Hayler on research conducted by Sangamon State University and the Illinois Task Force on Sexual Harassment in the Workplace, Hearings before the House Judiciary II Committee, 4 March.

STOCKDALE, J. E. (1986) 'Sexual Harassment in a University Setting', paper presented to London Conference of the British Psychological Society, December.

TERPESTRA, D. A. and COOK, S. E. (1985) 'Complainant Characteristics and Reported Behaviours and Consequences Associated with Formal Sexual Harassment Charges', *Personnel Psychology*, **38**, 559–574.

TERPESTRA, D. E. and BAKER, D. D. (1992) 'Outcomes of Federal Court Decisions on Sexual Harassment', *Academy of Management Journal*, **35(1)**, 181–190.

TUCRIC, Leeds (1983) 'Sexual Harassment of Women at Work: A Study from West Yorkshire'.

TYSON, M. (1982) 'The Sexual Harassers', *New Society*, 62.

UCLA SURVEY, The Sexual Harassment Survey Committee (1985) A Survey of Sexual Harassment at UCLA, Administrative Report, February.

US MERIT SYSTEMS PROTECTION BOARD (1981) *Sexual Harassment in the Federal Workplace: Is it a Problem?*, Government Printing Office, Washington, DC.

WARFIELD, A. (1987) 'Coworker Romances: Impact on the Work Group and on Career Oriented Women', *Personnel*, **64(5)**, 22–35.

WEBER-BURDIN, E. and ROSSI, P. H. (1982) 'Defining Sexual Harassment on Campus: A Replication and Extension', *Journal of Social Issues*, **38**, 111–120.

WILLIAMS, E. A., LAM, J. A. and SHIVELY, M. (1992) 'The Impact of a University Policy on the Sexual Harassment of Female Students', *Journal of Higher Education*, **63(1)**, 50–64.

WILLIS, P. (1979) 'The Shop Floor Culture, Masculinity and the Wage Form', in J. Clarke, C. Critcher and R. Johnson (eds), *Working Class Culture*, Hutchinson, London.

WISE, S. and STANLEY, L. (1987) *Georgie Porgie: Sexual Harassment in Everyday Life*, Pandora Press, London.

WITZ, A. and SAVAGE, M. (1992) 'The Gender of Organizations', introduction to A. Witz and M. Savage (eds), *Gender and Bureaucracy*, Blackwell, Oxford.

WORKING WOMEN'S UNITED INSTITUTE (1978) *Sexual Harassment on the Job: Questions and Answers* WWI, New York.

ZALK, S. R. (1990) 'Men in the Academy: A Psychological Profile of Harassment', Chapter 8 in M. Paludi (ed.), *Ivory Tower: Sexual Harassment on Campus*, State University of New York Press, Albany.

ZALK, S. R., PALUDI, M. and DEDERICH, J. (1990) Women Students' Assessment of Consensual Relationships with their Professors: Ivory Tower Reconsidered', in E. K. Cole (ed.) *Sexual Harassment on Campus: A Legal Compendium*, National Association of College and University of Attorneys, Washington DC, USA.

Conclusions

To date, organizational behaviour has been male oriented, focusing on, and directed, in the main, towards the interests and activities of men in a gender-differentiated society. Men and women are in different social situations, and these situations are structurally and ideologically discrepant. The dominant value system assigns greater importance and prestige to the masculine than to the feminine. Further, organizational behaviour has been gender blind. Sexual harassment, though widespread in organizations, has been largely ignored by mainstream texts. Organizational theory has done little to acknowledge research on women. This book has tried to do more than just redress that balance by adding a lacking dimension to the old view; the hope is that subsequent students of organizational behaviour will replace the concept of masculinity that presently dominates the subject with a view that includes women. One question which has been ever present throughout the book is: can you expect the behaviour of men and women in organizations to be essentially different or the same? To answer the question the idea of adopting different lenses may prove useful.

Sandra Bem (1993) asks us to look *at* the lenses that shape how people perceive, conceive, and discuss social reality in organizations, rather than look through those lenses. She identifies three lenses. All the three lenses she describes have one feature in common; they all argue that men and women are different. Firstly there is the lens of androcentrism or male-centredness. This is not just about seeing and believing that men are inherently superior but also defines the male and the male experience as a neutral standard and the norm. Females and female experience are a sex-specific deviation from that norm. Man is human and woman is 'other'.

This view of women as 'other' has been touched on in Chapter 3 and the divide between men and women can be seen as a public/private divide. In the distinction between the public and private sphere, public life is seen as important and as giving authority and value to the roles of men, while domestic life, the other, is of little consequence. The public sphere is rational, universalist, and unemotional, while the private is affective, particularistic, and ruled by the passions. This view probably derives from the disciplinary character of modernity. The private, the

'other', has to be repressed in organizational contexts (Burrell and Hearn, 1989; Brewis and Grey, 1994). The skill of being human requires the repression of the passions and the cultivation of reason but not everyone is considered equally capable of such a task. Women are construed as being inherently passionate, sexual beings who cannot function as well in the rational public sphere as men as they are overly prey to their basic emotions.

Bem's second lens is gender polarization. Men and women are fundamentally different and this perceived difference is an organizing principle for the social life of the culture. Women and men dress differently, have different social roles, and express themselves differently.

The third lens is of biological essentialism which rationalizes and legitimizes the other two lenses by treating them as the natural and inevitable consequences of the biological natures of men and women. The three lenses systematically reproduce male power through discourses and social institutions, which make men and women different and unequal, and through enculturation in which the individual internalizes the cultural lenses and constructs an identity consistent with them. This male power, though not held by all men, disadvantages women, those from ethnic groups, and sexual minorities (homosexuals and lesbians) as well. The oppression of lesbians and gay men directly derives from the androcentric, gender-polarizing, and biologically essentialist definition of what it means to be a man or a woman.

These three lenses help us to see men and women as different. We have learned to be different. We can only think of differentiation and the emergence of self relationally. Differentiation occurs and separation emerges in relationship; they are not givens. But this is not the only way we can discuss the emergence of self or what constitutes strong self. Essential important attitudes towards, and expectations of, mothers emerge in the earliest differentiation of self (Chodorow,1994). We must recognize the ideologies of difference which define us as women or men and the inequality that is produced by this creation of difference.

Modernist-feminism would say that women are defined and construed as different by the operations of a patriarchical power. Some (e.g. Benson and Thomson, 1982) would suggest that women, traditionally devoid of economic power and subject to male domination, have been left powerless and so use their sexuality as if it possessed exchange value. Certain jobs use this sexuality, e.g. waitress and air hostess. Women, then, have a distorted view of themselves. Women's views are distorted by the operation of patriarchy.

Carol Gilligan, as we have seen, rather than argue that these three lenses bring about our seeing women and men as different, or saying we have learned to be different, argues women *are* different. Gilligan argues that women have a 'different voice'. Those who wish to argue that women are different, and have a different voice, have to adopt a lens similar to the lens of androcentrism as it sets men and women apart. The difference lobby would argue that women's physical sexual difference from men results in a different psychology and different moral values. Women construct and value knowledge in ways that are relational, oriented more towards sustaining connection than achieving autonomy, and governed by interests to attend to others' needs (Gilligan, 1982). Others (e.g. Smith, 1987) might argue that women, because of their particular standpoint, have a more holistic view of the world.

Discussion point

The topic of masculinity has arisen frequently in this book; books on masculinity are now common. Is such literature a takeover bid by men, a renewal of hegemony (supremacy) in areas to which women have laid claim? Or is it important that men and women 'problematize' masculinity so that men confront themselves? Are women, then, less likely to be seen as the 'dark continent'?

A spate of articles has addressed this basic question of differences, particularly Gilligan's view of a different moral development of men and women. They have included qualitative, quantitative (meta-analyses), and empirical studies of hypotheses generated by Gilligan's theory (e.g. Friedman *et al.*, 1987; Gibbs *et al.*, 1984; Kerber *et al.*, 1986; Luria, 1986; Thoma, 1986; Walker, 1984). Gilligan, says Faludi (1991), may have left herself wide open to misinterpretation and to a backlash that could have caused real harm to women. Some have tried to defend Gilligan's view (e.g. Tavris, 1992: 80) but conclude that the popularity of the theory does not rest on on its scientific merit.

Many have tried to dampen enthusiasm for the belief in a 'different voice', but it appears to be a symbol for a cluster of widely held social beliefs that argue for women's difference (Mednick, 1989). As we saw, particularly in Chapters 2 and 6, there appears to be a strong belief in sex differences, particularly those congruent with stereotypes. As Friedman (1987) notes, 'gender differences are alive and well at the level of popular perception i.e. both men and women on average, still conceive of women and men as differently moralized' (see also Greeno and Maccoby, 1986). The 'different voice' is resonant with gender stereotypes about the qualities of women and men and fits with social expectations about gender specialization. We know what the disadvantages of holding a view of differences brings, particularly for women. It also raises many unanswered questions. For example, how do we know if men and women are behaving in conformance to the stereotype of how they have been socialized to behave and whether they would behave differently if the stereotype did not exist? If, for example, we challenged the view that men were more aggressive than women, would women be as aggressive, and demonstrate their aggressiveness as men do? Does a difference view, like Gilligan's, which also focuses on what is common for women, produce a view of women as a homogeneous group (see Alvesson and Billing, 1992)? Neither women, images of maleness, nor organizations are homogeneous and unitary.

Adopting this view of men and women being different brings some further difficulties. Those who adopt this view and predict stable sex differences will have trouble accounting for the limited ability of sex to predict behaviour, and for the variability in behaviour which sometimes appears random (Deaux and Major, 1987: 369). But there is a more serious consequence. We are warned that if we intuitively feel that Gilligan must be right, women are trapping themselves, as they have done for generations, by people's willingness to accept their own intuitions about the truth of gender stereotypes.

Maybe the question you should ask when reading about sex differences is who benefits? If people in organizations wish to promote the view that women are less reliable than men because of their hormones and their pregnancies, what are the consequences for equity at work and in law and politics (Tavris, 1992: 289)? If women are relational and attend to others' needs, will they be seen as ideal managers? The status quo of gender politics will be maintained if the view of gender stereotypes is maintained. We have to guard against women being seen as 'the other', as the 'second sex'. To be 'other' is to be outside, to be deviant, and it allows both sexism and racism to construct catergories in which understandings will be clouded.

There is now a postmodernist emphasis on the significance of difference in the construction of organizations and organizational identities (see Hekman, 1994). Difference is seen as a central mechanism whereby domination may be established over subordinate groups. The approach stresses the significance of cultural under-pinnings of organizations and their structures and power within organizations (Crompton and Le Feuvre, 1992; Mills, 1993). The emphasis is on language and discourse. It may be important for women to emphasize their lack of difference in order not to maintain the position of subordinate grouping.

Another view you may choose to adopt could be one in which the differences are acknowledged but without allowing women to be relegated to second sex status. This is the view of, for example, Irigaray (1991). It should be recognized that men and women are different but the full range of human characteristics must be made admissible in the public arena. Both women and men have to be recognized and respected in order for equality and harmony to be established.

We have to acknowledge biological differences. It is only women who become pregnant. Parenthood has different consequences for men and women's lives, transforming most women's lives in a way that it does not transform most men's. We have to acknowledge that it is men who rape and mainly men who harass, so there is at least one major sex difference in behaviour between men and women. There appear to be some sex differences in managerial work motivation but little to acknowledge in leadership, though this topic is very discursive in nature. We also need to acknowledge differences in style and expression. We have each learned to 'do gender', adjusting our behaviour and our perceptions depending on the person we are working, playing, or talking to (West and Zimmerman, 1987). Gender is, in Kessler and McKenna's (1978) term, a practical accomplishment, something accomplished by social practice. The social practices of dress and adornment grossly exaggerate the difference: 'They are part of a continuing effort to sustain the social definition of gender, an effort that is necessary precisely *because the biological logic*, and the inert practice that responds to it, *cannot sustain the gender categories*' (Connell, 1987: 81). The differences in style and expression we saw, e.g. in Chapter 6, must not be confused with differences in male and female nature, or capacity, or personality traits (Tavris, 1992: 87). Men and women are not as different as night and day; men and women are closer to each other than either is to anything else. Far from being an expression of natural differences, exclusive gender identity is the suppression of natural similarities (Rubin, 1975).

Men and women differ in life experiences, resources, power, and reproductive processes. Context repeatedly overwhelms personality in the search for differences between men and women (Deaux and Major, 1987, 1990; Eagly, 1987). Context refers to everything in the environment of a person's life: work, family, class, culture, race, and so on. Individual men and women differ in terms of power. According to Lott (1987) and Hare-Mustin and Maracek (1986), we must not lose sight of the fact that individuals do differ and the dimension on which they differ is on the social hierarchy. If you are high on that hierarchy, then you will be high in power and thus focus on rules and rationality; if you have less power you will emphasize relatedness and compassion. The qualities associated with 'women's voices' prove to be qualities associated with women or men who are powerless (Tavris, 1992: 87).

The context is historical. Women, throughout history, have lacked power and there is little room for optimism as the proportion of women in positions of power have declined this century and the proportion of women in senior management has dropped. The increases in the number of women's jobs are in the part-time sector. Little is being done to remove the obstacles for women workers—childcare arrangements, flexible working, and access to training. Without affirmative or positive action, or action in terms of leave or training, women are not likely to increase their power within organizations.

Male power is, and without major change will remain, a structural dimension of organizations. It is not safe to generalize from the male standard to all women. Men and women are not equal; that lack of equality has not come about because of any feature that women lack. But the myths about women as workers and their lesser competencies remain, and lead to underachievement. Men and women are popularly believed to have contrasting qualities and those female qualities are of less value than the male. The fact is, however, that men and women are distinct from one another but not, on average, very different. Male and female abilities overlap considerably. Where there are differences of behaviour to observe it is because people are playing out gender roles, roles where men have more power. There is an ideology of patriarchy which makes women's subordination seem natural. The primary mechanism which ensures that women will serve their husbands is their exclusion from paid work on the same terms as men (Walby, 1994). This view would not accept stereotyping of men and women but would look to perception, learning, and socialization to help explain where differences come from. It would look to developing a new direction for the social psychology of gender.

We also need to understand and take account of the culture of organizations that has led to their gendered nature, to look at the rules of behaviour that distinguish one social organization or group from another and bring about their cultural identity. Organizational culture is not genderless: 'The notion of organizational structure as an objective, empirical, genderless reality is itself a gendered notion' (Sheppard, 1989: 142). We need to uncover what has not already been 'seen'. We need to look specifically at the gendered nature of organizations and the study of them. We may also need to emphasize different kinds of organizational culture in relation to gender discrimination (Alvesson and Billing, 1992: 76).

We need, then, to look at the conditions people find themselves in to explain the differences, particularly in organizational behaviour and conditions of employment. It would appear to be the conditions of employment, not qualities of the individual, that determine what most people value about their work. Men and women who are in dead-end, low-paying, unstimulating jobs tend to focus on aspects of the job that are the most pleasurable, relationships with others. Men in jobs with little opportunity, like women, will limit their aspirations, seek satisfaction in activities outside work, dream of escape, interrupt their careers, emphasize leisure and consumption, and create sociable peer groups in which interpersonal relationships take precedence (Kanter, 1977: 161).

There is a view which complements this and sees men and women as the same. The sameness lobby would argue that women and men are more or less a blank slate on which gender identity is inscribed in the process of a lifetime of learning experiences (Cockburn, 1991: 9). There is little physical or psychological evidence to justify gender stereotypes as reflecting clear distinctions between the sexes. As Pateman (1988) has argued, if women seek equal rights with men, they seek to become surrogate men. Even remaining childless will not negate the difference.

It is important to emphasize how a broad sociocultural perspective must be adopted in order to understand what is happening and why. Male dominance is built into familial, economic, political, religious, and legal structures of society.

Power structures the relations between men and women and are reflected in all aspects of life, including, for example, their communication patterns. Women's language is the language of the powerless.

The issue of language has been dealt with in some depth. Some (e.g. Haste, 1993) have argued that real changes will only occur when there is a profound change in the underlying metaphors of gender. The metaphors of masculine and feminine need to be challenged; we need to challenge the dualism on which so much of our thinking rests. Women need to claim their own authentic voice and view. We need to perceive the world through women's eyes rather than holding a mirror up to men; to see the self as one experiences it rather than through the eyes of men. Authenticity would mean recognizing the validity of women's experience and women's interpretation. Claiming authenticity requires that the other be a valid alternative, to coexist with the masculine experience rather than be alien to, a threat to, or antithesis of maleness.

> The search for authenticity, and ending Otherness requires a new framework for looking at the female self. This search means deconstruction, demolition, of many of the ways in which women view their selves, and many of the ways in which men view women. (Haste, 1993: 204)

One could argue that gender differences arise from the sex-segregated division of labour. Men's place is primarily seen to be in the public sphere and is associated with, and generates, power and authority. Women's place is in the domestic sphere. The division of labour creates differences in, for example, women's vocabularies and the content of their speech and interests. Women's talk thus centres around relationships and the interpersonal; men's around work and the public sphere.

There is considerable evidence here, and in many other texts, that male and female managers differ in some ways, and at some times, but for the most part they do not differ (Powell, 1988: 165). When men and women are in the same high-prestige jobs, their values are identical and their behaviour is similar (Major, 1987). This should be the response to those who would argue that women are a less sound investment as employees. There is no clear-cut sex difference in managerial commitment or in symptoms of stress experienced. There is no reason to believe either men or women managers as superior in executing, involving themselves in, or coping with the responsibilities of their jobs. The stereotype of the male manager being the better manager does not hold. It may be dangerous to reproduce 'patriarchal stereotypes of men and women—flirting with essentialism, distorting the diverse dimensions of human knowing, and falsifying the historical record of women's manifold uses of reasons in everyday life' (Hawkesworth, 1989: 547).

————————— *Review Question* —————————

Do women have a 'different voice'? Review the research and evidence and reach your own conclusions.

How would you explain the differences that can be observed in men and women's behaviour in organizations?

Are men and women just blank slates on which gender is inscribed or is there more to the argument?

REFERENCES

ALVESSON, M. and BILLING, Y. D. (1992) 'Gender and Organization: Towards a Differentiated Understanding', *Organization Studies*, **13**(1), 73–104.

BENSON, D. J. and THOMSON, G. E. (1982) 'Sexual Harassment on a University Campus: The Congruence of Authority Relations, Sexual Interest and Gender Stratification', *Social Problems*, **2**(9), 236–251.

BEM, S. (1993) *The Lenses of Gender*, Yale University Press, New Haven, Conn.

BREWIS, J. and GREY, C. (1994) 'Re-eroticizing the Organization: An Exegesis and Critique', *Gender, Work and Organization*, **21**(2), 67–82.

BURRELL, G. and HEARN, J. (1989) 'The Sexuality of Organization', in J. Hearn *et al.* (eds) *The Sexuality of Organizations*, Sage, London.

CHODOROW, N. (1994) 'Gender, Relation and Difference in Psycholanalytic Perspective', Chapter 4 in *The Polity Reader in Gender Studies*, Polity Press, Blackwell, Cambridge.

COCKBURN, C. (1991) *In the Way of Women*, Macmillan, Basingstoke.

CONNELL, R. W. (1987) *Gender and Power: Society, the Person and Sexual Politics*, Polity Press, Oxford.

CROMPTON, R. and LE FEUVRE, N. (1992) 'Gender and Bureaucracy', in M. Savage and A. Witz (eds) *Gender and Bureaucracy*, Blackwell, Oxford.

DEAUX, K. and MAJOR, B. (1987) Putting Gender into Context: An Interactive Model of Gender-related Behavior', *Psychological Review*, **94**(3), 369–389.

DEAUX, K. AND MAJOR, B. (1990) 'A Social-psychological Model of Gender', in *Theoretical Perspectives on Sexual Difference*, D. L. Rhode (ed.), Yale University Press, New Haven, Conn.

EAGLY, A. H. (1987) *Sex Differences in Social Behaviour: A Social Role Interpretation*, Erlbaum, Hillsdale, NJ.

FALUDI, S. (1991) *Backlash: The Undeclared War Against American Women*, Crown, New York.

FRIEDMAN, M. (1987) 'Beyond Caring: The De-moralization of Gender' in M. Hanen and K. Neilson (eds), *Science Morality and Feminist Theory, Canadian Journal of Philosophy*, **13**. (Suppl.).

FRIEDMAN, W. J., ROBINSON, A. B. and FRIEDMAN, B. L. (1987) 'Sex Differences in Moral Judgement?', *Psychology of Women Quarterly*, **11**(1), 37–46.

GIBBS, J. C., ARNOLD, K. D. and BURKHART, J. E. (1984) 'Sex Differences in the Expression of Moral Judgment', *Child Development*, **55**, 1040–1043.

GILLIGAN, C. (1982) *In a Different Voice*, Harvard University Press, Cambridge, Mass.

GREENO, C. G. and MACCOBY, E. E. (1986) 'How Different is the "Different Voice"?', *Signs*, **1**, 310–316.

HARE-MUSTIN, R. and MARACEK, J. (1986) 'Autonomy and Gender: Some Questions for Therapists', *Psychotherapy*, **23**, 205–212.

HASTE, H. (1993) *The Sexual Metaphor*, Harvester Wheatsheaf, Hemel Hempstead.

HAWKESWORTH, M. E. (1989) 'Knowers, Knowing, Known: Feminist Theory and Claims of Truth', *Signs*, **14**(3), 533–557.

HEKMAN, S. (1994) The Feminist Critique of Rationality', Chapter 5 in *The Polity Reader in Gender Studies*, Polity Press, Blackwell, Cambridge.

IRIGARAY, L. (1991) in M. Whitford (ed.), *The Irigaray Reader*, Basil Blackwell, Oxford.

KANTER, R. M. (1977) *Men and Women of the Corporation*, Basic Books, New York.

KERBER, L., GREENO, C., MACCOBY, E. LURIA, Z., STACK, C. and GILLIGAN, C. (1986) 'On a Different Voice: An Interdisciplinary Forum', *Signs*, **11**, 304–333.

KESSLER, S. J. and MCKENNA, W. (1978) *Gender: An Ethnomethodological Approach*, Wiley, New York.

LOTT, B. (1987) 'Feminist, Masculine, Androgynous or Human', paper presented at the meeting of the American Psychological Association, New York City, cited in Mednick (1989).

LURIA, Z. (1986) 'A Methodological Critique', *Signs*, **11**, 316–321.

MAJOR, B. (1987) 'Gender, Justice and the Psychology of Entitlement', in P. Shaver and C. Hendrick (eds), *Review of Personality and Social Psychology, Sex and Gender*, **7**, 124–148, Sage, Beverly Hills, Calif.

MEDNICK, M. T. (1989) 'On the Politics of Psychological Constructs', *American Psychologist*, August, 1119–1123.

MILLS, A. J. (1993) 'Organizational Discourse and the Gendering of Identity', Chapter 8 in J. Hassard and M. Parker (eds), *Postmodernism and Organizations*, Sage, London.

PATEMAN, C. (1988) *The Sexual Contract*, Polity Press, Oxford.

POWELL, G.N. (1988) *Women and Men in Management*, Sage, Newbury Park, Calif.

RUBIN, G. (1975) 'The Traffic in Women: Notes on the "Political Economy" of Sex', in R. R. Reiter (ed.), *Towards an Anthropology of Women*, Monthly Review Press, New York.

SHEPPARD, D. L. (1989) 'Organizations, Power and Sexuality: The Image and Self-image of Woman Managers', in J. Hearn, *et al.* (eds), *The Sexuality of Organizations*, Sage, London.

SMITH, D. (1987) *The Everyday World as Problematic: A Feminist Sociology*, Northeastern University Press, Boston, Mass.

TAVRIS, C. (1992) *The Mismeasure of Women*, Simon & Schuster, New York.

THOMA, S. (1986) 'Estimating Gender Differences in the Comprehension of Moral Issues', *Development Review*, **6**, 677–691.

WALBY, S. (1994) 'Towards a Theory of Patriarchy', Chapter 2 in *The Polity Reader in Gender Studies*, Polity Press, Blackwell, Oxford.

WALKER, L. J. (1984) 'Sex Differences in the Development of Moral Reasoning: A Critical Review', *Child Development*, **55**, 677–691.

WEST, C. and ZIMMERMAN, D. H. (1987) 'Doing Gender', *Gender and Society*, **1**, 125–151.

Appendix—Sexual Harassment: Anne's Experience

Anne joined the finance department of a company in her home town in East Asia on graduation. She was eager to learn and excel in her job. In this job she was treated, she said, 'like everyone's little sister'. Six months later she was transferred to the project department. The project manager, Kent, addressed her as 'the little girl'. She did not complain as she had been taught, from a young age, she felt, to please her superiors and not make a fuss. She believed she should work diligently and quietly and avoid confrontation. She was learning a great deal from her job and was given much responsibility.

Anne felt uncomfortable with the way Kent stared at her each time she walked into his office. His eyes would move from her head to her toes but his gaze would always end at her chest. Anne felt he was undressing her. Each time she told herself she should just ignore this.

Kent invited Anne for dinner at his house. He said that his wife had gone back to America. 'You and I could spend a quiet evening together at my place.' Anne declined the invitation. However, invitations to dinner continued. Each time Anne declined with reasons such as 'My parents would not allow me to stay out late in the evening', or 'I have to be back home for dinner.' She says that he acted with annoyance with her replies.

Next he started to touch her. They would be looking at a set of documents together when he would touch her, then produce an excuse like 'Oh, your collar was creased.' He expressed his wish to go on business trips alone with her. Anne continued to ignore Kent's behaviour. She was not sure how she could deal with this situation, but felt that she should pretend everything was going fine. She was unsure if anyone would believe her if she voiced the problem. Kent had been with the company some time and nobody, even those who had worked with him previously, had said there was any problem of harassment. But she had noticed that none of the secretaries or assistants who had worked with Kent before had stayed longer than two months.

However hard she tried to ignore what was happening, she felt she was suffering. She felt victimized; she 'felt raped'. There was a sense of injustice as she had not done anything wrong. She lost her appetite and her weight dropped. She came down with colds more often and no longer looked forward to work. She resolved not to dress as smartly or have her hair done because she did not want him to comment on how 'nice' she looked.

One day during lunchtime when the office was almost empty, Anne found herself talking to a female colleague. Anne told her about Kent's behaviour. The colleague was initially surprised but very concerned. She suggested that Kent was feeling very lonely without his wife and could just be treating Anne like a daughter. She asked what Kent had said to Anne and then suggested how Anne could answer the innuendos and invitations. She added that if the matter persisted or worsened, Anne should let her know.

Anne felt stronger and better able to deal with Kent's unwanted behaviour but during the next few months he became more persistent in his demands. Anne continued to ignore what she could of the sexual remarks and looks. She minimized the frequency of meetings with him. When he turned business talk into private talk, she cut the conversation short and left the room. She tried to be as polite and diplomatic as she could while indicating that she did not welcome the sexual advances.

The frequency of invitation to dinner did not decline; he said he would like to thank Anne for all her help. One day she decided to accept, suggesting that another colleague, who had also helped, could come too. He exploded on hearing this suggestion from Anne. 'Why do you always want to include Sonia whenever I ask you to join me? Why can we not go alone, just the two of us?' Anne assessed that if she went alone with him to dinner that evening he would not dare be 'indecent' in public. She tried to be distant from him during dinner and left very early.

One afternoon she took an incoming fax into Kent's office for further instructions. While she was talking to him, he took a pad of paper and drew the shape of two breasts with the words 'attractive looking' below. He then smiled at Anne and waited for the response. Anne understood but pretended she did not and asked him what he was trying to say. 'You really don't understand?' He stopped smiling and tore up the piece of paper, scrunching it into his pocket. He was staring at her chest. She asked him what he was looking at and he replied 'Oh, just the colour of your jacket'.

Anne was upset and angry. She had had enough but she did not know what to do. She wanted to leave her job and could not sleep at night because the ugly incident kept playing back through her mind.

Again, at lunchtime, Anne found herself alone with the colleague with whom she had confided. She told the colleague about what had happened. The colleague offered to bring the matter to the attention of her boss, one of the chief executives of the company and checked with Anne that she felt comfortable with this. Anne agreed.

Later that day Anne was asked to go to the chief executive's office. She asked Anne to describe what had happened. She told Anne that the matter would be handled fairly and that Anne would be transferred to her own department. Her career would not be jeopardized. She told Anne that if, in future, she was obliged to accept an undesirable dinner invitation she should accept but turn up with a group of friends. Any kind of sexual harassment should be reported without delay.

■ What should Anne have done?
■ What should the chief executive have done?
■ How do you react to how Anne's case was handled?

Author Index

Subject Index